CHRISTIAN COMMUNITY
IN HISTORY

CHRISTIAN COMMUNITY
IN HISTORY

VOLUME I

Historical Ecclesiology

ROGER HAIGHT, S.J.

continuum
NEW YORK • LONDON

To *Edward Schillebeeckx, O.P.*

2004

The Continuum International Publishing Group Inc
15 East 26th Street, New York, NY 10017

The Continuum International Publishing Group Ltd
The Tower Building, 11 York Road, London SE1 7NX

www.continuumbooks.com

Printed in the United States of America

Library of Congress Cataloging-in-Publication Data

Haight, Roger.
    Christian community in history / Roger Haight.
      p. cm.
    Includes bibliographical references and index.
    ISBN 0-8264-1630-6 (v. 1 : hardcover : alk. paper)
    1. Church. 2. Church history. I. Title.
BV600.3.H35 2004
262'.009 – dc22
                        2004004006

Contents

Part III
THE CHURCH IN THE MIDDLE AGES

Preface

This work grew out of a course that I began teaching in the early 1980s and that provided the initial idea and inspiration for the project. But it has grown in scope and in size. I initially intended that this work appear in a single volume. The representation of the whole sweep of the development of the many ecclesiologies that mark the church today cannot fail to communicate a deep sense of historicity, which is one of the main goals of this work. But the work has grown beyond the limits of one readable volume. In addition to that, in volume two, entitled *Comparative Ecclesiology*, I more or less spontaneously introduce a shift in the tactics by which I carry out the strategy of an ecclesiology from below. I will say more of that shift in the introduction to the second volume.

This work pushes forward a kind of theological reflection that was analyzed in *Dynamics of Theology.*[1] *Dynamics* outlines an interpretation of the bases upon which theology builds, the nature of its sources, the quality of its language, and the method by which it unfolds. By nature such works remain somewhat abstract until one takes up the theory and applies it. This I did in *Jesus Symbol of God.*[2] When *Dynamics* was republished in 2001, I wrote an "Afterword" which drew out some of the main features of the theological method outlined there, showed how they were applied in *Jesus Symbol of God*, and projected how they would influence a sustained reflection on the church.[3] I will not repeat that analysis, but I do want simply to note the continuity between these works. They are intended as a kind of trilogy dealing with the nature of Christian theology, Jesus Christ, and the church.

---

1. Roger Haight, *Dynamics of Theology* (Mahwah, N.J.: Paulist Press, 1990; Maryknoll, N.Y.: Orbis Books, 2001).

2. Roger Haight, *Jesus Symbol of God* (Maryknoll, N.Y.: Orbis Books, 1999).

3. Haight, *Dynamics*, 237–56.

The discipline of theology attempts to mediate understanding of the object of the Christian community's faith. As such it engages reflective and thinking people. The audience for theology in the United States has expanded as citizens generally and Christians specifically have become more educated. It is possible that this broad education of people in the West has caused them to lose faith in their churches, if not in God, but it is also possible that theology has become so polemical and introverted that it has failed to offer critical accounts of the faith that respond to people's questions. Catechism alone will not do it. For the critically educated segment of the church and for outsiders who turn to the church for answers to their ultimate concerns one needs a theology that appeals to contemporary experience and responds to probing questions.

For Christians, the theme of critical questioning takes the form of calling into question the received notions of catechism and Sunday school; for outsiders approaching the church it takes the form of looking for meaning in the face of the world as they find it. Both groups drive theology back to its foundations in religious epistemology, the notions of faith and revelation, and how these can yield a framework for coherent hope that can sustain one into the future. Responding to these exigencies, *Dynamics of Theology* established the category of symbol, its dialectical structure, and its twofold form of concrete symbol and conscious symbol as a way of integrating the epistemology of faith and revelation, the kind of language used in theology, and a critical, hermeneutical method for continually interpreting the classical symbols of Christian revelation so that they remain meaningful.

One determines the dialectical structure of a symbol from the way it functions. A symbol makes present and mediates to consciousness something other than itself, usually something that cannot be known or contacted in any other way. It thus expands consciousness and the reach of human knowing beyond the empirical or what can be reasoned to from it. It both is itself and points to something other than itself which it makes present and available. It both is and is not what it symbolizes. When I took up christology in *Jesus Symbol of God* I explained how I presupposed the conceptions of faith and revelation that were laid out in *Dynamics,* and I employed the hermeneutical method of critical correlation to the texts of the tradition concerning Jesus. But the category of symbol names the center of gravity of that work. "Symbol" illumines Jesus Christ best when it is applied to his person. One can understand the dynamics of Jesus' saving activity when he is considered as a conscious symbol, that is, when Jesus is regarded as revealer communicating God to human history. One can also approach the fundamental Christian doctrine of Chalcedon concerning Jesus' humanity and divinity when one considers Jesus as a concrete and ontological symbol with a dialectical structure. On the one hand, Jesus stands at the center of Christian faith as the one who reveals the reality of God; on the other hand, the human being Jesus who mediates for humankind the salvation that can only come from God bears within himself that which he makes present and actualizes. One can see that in the religious realm symbol and sacrament are synonymous terms.

Just as christology is the theology of Jesus of Nazareth, so too ecclesiology is the theology of the Christian community in history. And just as the category of symbol is descriptive of how Jesus is mediator of God, so too is the church often described as the community that continues to represent Jesus Christ in history, thus making it as a community a kind of primal social sacrament. The dialectical tension that obtains in christology finds its correlate in ecclesiology. Just as christology demands a restoration of Jesus of Nazareth to the imagination as he in whom God was incarnate, so too ecclesiology demands a consideration of the concrete, social, and historical community and institution of the church as that in which God acts in grace. As the human person, Jesus of Nazareth, was constituted as an incarnation of God's Word and the one empowered by God's Spirit, so too the church is called by Christians the "body" of Christ and the "temple" of God as Spirit. In christology binding theological conceptions of Christ to the historical figure of Jesus of Nazareth employed the results of the historical retrieval of Jesus of Nazareth; in ecclesiology theological images of the church will have to correlate with historical, social, and political considerations of the genesis and history of the community. Thus the fundamental insight of *Dynamics*, that critical theology must keep theological assertions attached to the historical symbols that mediate the experiences on which they depend, runs consistently through these three works. I will explain more fully in the introduction and in chapter 1 how this conception becomes a methodological strategy and provides a structural outline for each chapter.

I am grateful for a great deal of collegial help in writing this work. Such support is crucial when one wanders into fields other than one's own; they always appear green and enticing in their offerings of new learning; but the uninitiated can frequently step on land mines buried in the battlefield of scholarship. Many have read chapters, substantial parts, or the whole text of the current volume: T. Howland Sanks, S.J., Paul Fitzgerald, S.J., Bradford Hinze, Ghislain Lafont, O.S.B., Christopher Matthews, Peter Phan, Daniel Harrington, S.J., John Coleman, S.J., Francine Cardman, Catherine Mooney, Rahel O'More. I have integrated just about all of their wise counsel into the text. I am indebted to Gerard Jacobitz for comprehensively indexing the book. And, finally, I extend a special word of thanks to the editor, Frank Oveis, who has worked with me and the text with relaxed precision and easy attention to detail.

Introduction

Globalization and an experience of new dimensions in our intellectual culture beyond what is symbolized by the category "modern"
form the background of this work in ecclesiology. Globalization refers
to the growing interdependence of peoples who formerly lived their
lives separate from and ignorant of each other and thus in many ways
were historically independent. Globalization does not, however, imply an automatic homogenization but seems to entail a heightened
sense of the other as different and a new sense of self-appropriated
identity over against the inroads of external norms and standards of
existence. Globalization also quite definitely entails two dimensions
of Christian self-consciousness that are genuinely new. The one consists in a distinct awareness among Christians that Christianity is
one religion among many others that are ancient, venerable and vital,
and provide all-encompassing frameworks for understanding reality.
The Christian church must make its way among them; it will not
overcome them. The other experience may be an implicit corollary of
the first; it consists in a sense that the distance between Christianity and other world religions makes the quarrels among Christian
churches appear parochial and relatively unimportant. On the logic
of a common identity won by contrast with the other, globalization
is enabling the Christian churches to appreciate with new eyes the
enormous common ground that unites them. The heat of differences
among the churches can be turned down as all Christians take up the
dialogue with other faiths.

Christian Community in History is an essay in ecclesiology. It is
quite important that this be stated to distinguish it from a history
of the church. The method of ecclesiology underlying this work will
be discussed at greater length in the first chapter, but I want to draw
the reader into the logic of the work at the very outset. Ecclesiology
cannot be done apart from the history of the church and the world in

1

which it has existed along the way. Therefore this work tries consistently to insert the church at any given time into its context in order implicitly to draw out the influence of the age on the particular forms of the church. Thus while the ultimate focus of this study falls on the structure of the church and its theological self-understanding, it tries to be faithful to the historical reality of the church in each period. But while the ideal of such a work would include an analysis of the historical development of the church that depicted it in some detail and included interpretation of the various reasons and causes of new ecclesial forms, a short work such as this must remain on the surface of history. Many major events in church history have been ignored or left undeveloped because they did not leave significant marks on the structure of the church, on ecclesiology.[1] In some cases I can do no more than report that certain movements occurred and that events took place. In the historical narratives I have sought no contentious theses, but have drawn eclectically from a variety of general works, and I readily yield to historical interpretations that better state or account for the data. The work, then, unfolds in a tension between principle and fact: in principle one cannot adequately understand the church apart from its historical conditioned existence and one must strive to get it right; yet a holistic grasp of the church as a theologically grounded organization cannot be reduced to one particular historical reconstruction rather than another.[2]

This work has more affinity with the history of ecclesiology than church history. But the work also intends to do more than simply lay out the various ecclesiologies that have been generated in the

---

1. A good example is the discovery of the Americas in the late fifteenth century and the subsequent missionary movements that were unleashed in the course of the sixteenth century. This major event in the history of Europe changed the view of the world and world history itself. But it did not substantially alter the ecclesiology of the European church, whereas the Protestant Reformation accomplished precisely that.

2. It may not be improper to register the tension within the systematic or constructive theologian who takes up historical ecclesiology. Scriptural history and exegesis are technical disciplines; the discipline of history operates according to methodological standards as well as assumptions attached to its subdivisions of period and place. One cannot enter these fields without a sense of having to remain on the surface. But it has to be done in order that, in addition to learning the content, the differentiation of the thinking of the systematic or constructive theologian be affected.

course of history. Behind that effort lies a further systematic and constructive intent which manifests itself in reflection on the dynamic process by which various ecclesiologies were generated. Within these processes one can discern axioms and principles that are latent in their formation and which show themselves to be perennial or constant across the history of ecclesiology. Drawing out these principles results not in a metahistory of ecclesiologies, but a more empirically based set of guidelines for reflection on the church at any given time.

When I look for analogies for this work, I realize that the intuition guiding it has been in place for some time, probably since the deepening of historical consciousness in the nineteenth century and the process leading to the formation of the World Council of Churches in the twentieth. Several examples of historically conscious ecclesiological works may be cited as being in some respects similar to what is going on in this work, even though they are not carried forward with exactly the same intentionality. Joseph A. Komonchak, *Foundations in Ecclesiology*,[3] provides the grounds for an anthropological turn in ecclesiology that explains why historical and sociological analysis are intrinsic to the discipline. Ernst Troeltsch's *The Social Teaching of the Christian Churches*,[4] which examines the church in its relation to society, supplies a model for this type of approach. Another such example is the historical account of the genesis and development of various ministries in the church by Bernard Cooke, *Ministry to Word and Sacrament*.[5] Eric G. Jay has provided a very useful history of ecclesiology in his *The Church: Its Changing Image through Twenty Centuries*.[6] Hans Küng's *Structures of the Church*[7] is also roughly analogous to the project imagined here, as is the history of

---

3. Joseph A. Komonchak, *Foundations in Ecclesiology* (Boston: Supplementary Issue of the *Lonergan Workshop Journal*, 11, 1995). I refer to essays by Komonchak that have been gathered into this volume. It also contains four hitherto unpublished lectures that methodically ground the church as a social-historical mediation of God's grace.
4. Ernst Troeltsch, *The Social Teaching of the Christian Churches* (New York: Harper Torchbooks, 1960).
5. Bernard Cooke, *Ministry to Word and Sacrament* (Philadelphia: Fortress, 1980).
6. Eric G. Jay, *The Church: Its Changing Image through Twenty Centuries* (Atlanta: Knox, 1980).
7. Hans Küng, *Structures of the Church* (New York: T. Nelson, 1964).

ordained ministry and ecclesiology presented in two distinct volumes by Edward Schillebeeckx.[8]

In the first chapter on method in ecclesiology I will develop the idea of a historical ecclesiology. I use the phrase "ecclesiology from below" as an alternative way of saying the same thing. This latter phrase appropriately relates ecclesiology to christology from below and draws out the continuity of the methods and content. But just as the idea of christology from below generates more opposition than it really should, so too some may read into the idea of an ecclesiology from below more than is warranted by its use in this work. I therefore want to introduce the idea in the Introduction before the more technical analysis of chapter 1 that distinguishes it from an ecclesiology from above.[9]

The meaning which I intend with the phrase "ecclesiology from below" can be explained in four points that draw out several dimensions of an approach to understanding the church. First and most generally an "ecclesiology from below" refers to a method that is "concrete, existential, and historical." In this work these two phrases are synonymous. "Existential" means attending to the corporate experience that lies within the ecclesiology, whether the ecclesiology be drawn from the formulas of self-description or the structures of human relations. "Concrete" and "historical" together mean to focus attention on the actual church as it exists in history in various times and places. The primary object of ecclesiology is the historical organization that has a historical life; to understand it, one must attend to it. Against the background of an ecclesiology that is abstract, idealist,

---

8. Edward Schillebeeckx, *Ministry: Leadership in the Community of Jesus Christ* (New York: Crossroad, 1981) and *The Church with a Human Face* (New York: Crossroad, 1985).

9. The sources cited in chapter 1 will show that these ideas have been influenced on a methodological level by a whole series of theologians. Prominent among many are Troeltsch, H. R. Niebuhr, Gustafson, Komonchak, Schillebeeckx, Cooke. All share the conviction that social history and theology have to intersect in discussion of the church. I also share an appreciation of a certain use of the construction of types in reflection upon historical, social, and theological data when the subtle logical status and function of types are clearly kept in view. In this work I use types heuristically; they are never an object of study; they provide different ways of appreciating and understanding historical and theological experiences and data.

and a-historical, an ecclesiology from below is concrete, realist, and historically conscious.

Second, "ecclesiology from below" finds further definition in a genetic approach. This is based on the axiom that in order to fully understand any historical organization one needs to understand its origins as well as its journey from them to the present. This translates in this case to going back to Jesus to find the origins of the church, without of course short-circuiting the antecedents of Jesus in his own Jewish tradition.

Third, "ecclesiology from below" refers to a method that considers the social and historical situation within which the church exists as crucial for understanding its full reality. Moreover, historical and social analyses are also employed to analyze the church itself. The correlation of the church as organization with social forces enters intrinsically into this method. In this way the qualities of being concrete, existential, and historical take hold.

Fourth, ecclesiology from below as it is understood here is a theological discipline, and as such it cannot be reduced to conclusions that can be generated by history or sociology alone. But the way theological "perception," insight, and judgment relate to historical or sociological accounts makes all the difference. The principal object of ecclesiology consists in the empirical organization or collectivity or community called church, although it is also more than that as the history of ecclesiology plainly shows. The "more" lies in the fact that this church is experienced religiously or theologically, because in it and through it people recognize the presence and activity of God. Also, and correlatively, when symbols pointing and referring to God are used to illumine the full reality of what is going on in the existence of church, a theological imagination and judgment are at work. For example, the insight and conviction that God as Spirit is present and active in the church, and that Christ is the principal agent in the preaching of the Word or the operation of the sacraments, are theological judgments.[10] But these insights and convictions in their

---

10. I use the phrase "God as Spirit" randomly as a synonym for "the Spirit," the "Holy Spirit," "the Spirit of God" in order to protect the doctrine of the trinity from tri-theism and to verbalize the axiom from trinitarian theology that the fullness of God

specificity ultimately cannot be abstracted from the church organization, the sermons, and the sacraments in question.[11] In terms of the religious knowledge involved in theology, ecclesiology from below means that theological statements about the church that do not in some way refer to the concrete, existential, and historical church fail in characterizing the object of the discipline; and statements about that church which do not illumine the historical institution with the light of God's presence and activity relative to it are in that measure not theological and thus not ecclesiological. The distinguishing marks of an ecclesiology from below are together its point of departure and its mediation of the imagination into transcendence.

In the first chapter on method I contrast an ecclesiology from below with an ecclesiology from above not out of polemical motives but in the interest of definition and clarity. In fact I see no reasons why an ecclesiology from below should be resisted. It is not the case that an ecclesiology from below renders theological interpretation dependent upon some particular social reconstruction. It is rather the case that just as God's Word was incarnate in Jesus, so that to encounter God there one must turn to that history, so too God's activity in forming the church occurred in history, so that to understand God's action in forming the church one must attend to that history. These origins will be historically reconstructed in a variety of ways by different historians and will be debated on the evidence; but if historical origins are not considered explicitly, they will be implicitly imagined and affirmed in a naive way. One can hardly avoid some imaginative contextual construal of how the church came to be. In the end the only way to critically recognize and understand God's activity in the genesis of the church and in the contextual life of the community in specific times and places entails analysis of its unfolding historically.

The goal of the work is to display a historical and developing church with multiple ecclesiologies. This will lead to assembling a set of common characteristics of the church manifested in the life of the

---

is always involved in God acting *ad extra* so that reference to a person of the trinity relative to such action is by accommodation.

11. The point that is being made here is grounded in the fundamental theological insight that all knowledge of God is mediated or channeled through finite or this-worldly symbols or analogies that deliver its content. For a general treatment of these issues see Roger Haight, *Dynamics of Theology* (Maryknoll, N.Y.: Obis Books, 2001).

whole church as displayed in the various churches, and to developing a set of principles and axioms culled from the history of ecclesiology that will be useful in a constructive ecclesiology at any given time. Several of the points in this broad agenda deserve comment.

One is that this work intends to provide a sweeping view of the church as a developmental and pluralistic movement. Most people can repeat the cliché that the church exists in history and thus is developmental; not so many study the history of the church with a critical eye toward its twists and turns. Everyone possesses some measure of historical consciousness, but few deeply realize the contingent character or dimension of every single church institution. This has to be mediated by the study of history, and this is best introduced by a panoramic view of the whole, however schematic it is forced to be. Historians by and large have a strong sense of the relativity of historical institutions as they develop, whereas systematic theologians may implicitly impose a teleological premise that sees historical development as headed toward turning out in a specific way in a particular church.

This work is also intended to communicate a sense of the logic of change, the reason why change and continual adaptation to its environment constitute an essential dimension of the church as a historical community. By the logic of change, therefore, I do not mean a projected sense of teleological development or any specific metahistorical or metaphysical plan, but on the contrary the seeming lack of strictly rational logic that marks historicity. Historical ecclesiology shows a church tied to history, so that constant historical movement and change characterize the church radically or in its very roots. The church in history never settles down; change is constantly being negotiated; there is no "established" church apart from the eschaton.

Also, the point of this work includes providing a sense of continuity and, by historical analogy, sameness of intrinsic identity that are preserved across the developing paths of the church. Recognition of this requires a dialectical imagination that can balance sameness and difference, and which is in its turn a cliché unless the perception is schooled in what happened. One can locate and affirm the constant identity of the Christian community in history, but this can only be realistically affirmed amid the sharp changes that history produces across time. This lesson in diachronic pluralism, or unity amid difference, should be helpful in enabling us to deal more constructively with synchronic pluralism than we have done up to now.

Connected with discovering continuity, another goal of this work consists in drawing out of the history of the Christian community principles for a constructive ecclesiology. In order to make the unity within difference in the church across history applicable to an understanding of the church today, I try in this work to formulate into principles constant patterns that recur amid the plurality and diversity. Historical, sociological, and theological principles that seem to operate continuously may be brought forward and used in a systematic and constructive ecclesiology for our time that is simultaneously historically sensitive.

The significance of this work has to be seen against the background of systematic ecclesiology. It is meant to open up the foundations for a historically conscious constructive ecclesiology for our time. A judgment regarding the import of such a work will probably depend on the degree to which one estimates the intelligibility and adequacy of ecclesiologies that are in place today. For the most part ecclesiologies tend to reflect the particular church or communion of the author. By contrast this work will provide a significantly different imaginative framework for understanding the church. Ecclesiology from below begins with a critical historical account of the protracted genesis of the church, analyzes the sociological dynamics of its original formation and constant change, and integrates the theological understanding of the church gathered from the historical witnesses into the historical and sociological understandings. From the outset the assumption of a method "from below" sets the imaginative framework for understanding in the context of a world of many religions; it considers the emergence and development of the Christian religion and opens up the possibility of a multidenominational analysis of the church by positing as the object of study the whole Christian movement and not a particular church.

I intend this work to be read by all Christians; its projected audience is not limited to one particular church or Christian denomination. I am in fact a Roman Catholic, and this membership surely manifests itself in a variety of ways.[12] But we live in a pluralistic church in a pluralistic world. Thus I do not write confessionally as a Catholic but try to represent an evenhanded approach to the many ecclesiologies that have developed in the course of history and thus speak to all Christians. I suppose that this work could be called ecumenical, but its goal is not ecumenical in the sense that some form of Christian unity constitutes the limit toward which it strives. Rather the work presupposes Christian unity, a Christian unity made more apparent by the pluralism of religions in the middle of which all of us now exist. Surely this unity could be better represented by institution and practice. But the goal of such ecumenical activity should be to preserve integral traditions, while at the same time consolidating common Christian identity, in order to provide an open Christian voice in a global, human, interreligious conversation.

Ideally the best entry into an ecclesiology from below would be a social history of the church. While this volume in no way approaches that ideal, it tries to be attentive to the variety of factors that form part of church life. It attends to the reality of the church that is referred to by the name: house church, small group of families, marginal congregation, small visible minority with a firm self-identity, church in a medieval rural village, eschatological church of the saved in heaven, small group of the graced within the larger organization, city church with a prominent bishop, town church with mission stations, regional metropolitan church with obedient bishops, a whole communion of churches, European church united under Charlemagne, Western church united under the papacy, Eastern church with partnered responsibilities of patriarch and emperor. It describes the offices of ministry and what people do in them; it looks at the sacramental life, devotional life, the ideals and practice of religious in monasteries, and of laity in the world. It takes up along the way ethics, spirituality, and theories of the Christian life. It considers church law, church authority, church administration. It considers the relation of the church to the world, that is, to society and its

---

12. It will be evident most clearly, for example, in the next chapter where I use a pre–Vatican II Roman Catholic manual of theology as a source for constructing a "typical" ecclesiology from above. Other examples could be drawn from other church traditions.

goings-on and to government or ruler, both in terms of activity and of the understanding of the relation between the spheres of church and world. The theology of the church lies embedded in all this corporate practice but it comes to expression in various texts that describe these practices or define the relationships.

The principle sources of the work consist in historical studies, that is, histories of the church and various institutions of the church and the works of major historical figures in the church that are relevant to ecclesiology along with secondary sources analyzing their works. The analysis is informed by certain fundamental works in sociology and the sociology of religion, with special attention to the sociology of organizations, and general works in ecclesiology that deal with the development of the church's organization and ministries. These help to keep the understanding of the church close to history. For example, I have borrowed from the sociology of organizations a certain grid for understanding and comparing groups and institutions. This is employed somewhat loosely, but it offers specific guidelines for reflection that correlates with other historical institutions.[13]

Because the work is historical, the outline of the work follows the history of the church. In each period the development will roughly consist in four logical moments. First, each chapter schematically tells the story of the church during the historical period in question as a way of indicating its situation, context, particularity, distinctiveness. Second, I then turn to a contextual analysis of key texts of major figures of the period who were significant for the development of the church. I have called this a social and theological analysis because the texts often do not differentiate these perspectives and thus provide data for both kinds of study. It will be noted that sociological categories are most helpful in describing the earliest church when it consisted in small communities. As the church gets larger and the perspective more inclusive of a massive movement, sociological categories are gradually supplanted by political

---

13. For example, the sociological framework has a considerably different function when one uses it to analyze a small house church in the first century, or the local church in Carthage under Cyprian, or the whole Western church under Gregory VII. The sociological framework becomes less and less descriptive and more and more formal as the object-referent of "church" becomes more massive.

considerations of authority, law, and government.[14] Third, I then attempt a description of the church using the categories that provide a
holistic perspective on an organization. This description transcends
the sociological by integrating the theological self-understanding and
mission of the church while retaining a sociological structure. The
theological self-understanding of the church defines its nature, and
in theological language mission is its goal or purpose. But as the
object of the description becomes more massive, sociological categories become more heuristic. Yet I try to attend to examples of
life in the church on the ground.[15] Finally, in a fourth section of
each chapter I formulate a set of principles or axioms or distinctions
that further illumine the theological and corporate human dynamics at work in the particular developments of the church. I draw
them from the development of the church during the period in question. These are depicted as ecclesiological constants that illumine
the church across history. The constructive intention is to gather a
certain number of formal theological and ecclesiological principles
that will be useful for understanding the church at any given time
and place.

It will become evident in the reading that the contribution of this
work does not arise out of an examination of new sources or the
representation of a new theory of history or a new interpretation
of any particular period of history. Whatever contribution it makes
lies in bringing together kinds of analyses readily available in other
sources into a focus of a multidenominational and interdisciplinary
analysis of the church. The work combines in a distinctive way historical and sociological perspectives, analysis of some of the major
texts which have influenced the development of the church and its
self-understanding, a recognition of the value of all the churches in

---

14. In the second chapter analyzing the genesis of the church, I differentiate more
clearly the historical, sociological, and theological dimensions of the church, because
social analysis has a good deal of purchase on this material. I do not however present
a description of the New Testament church because it is still in formation and quite
pluralistic.

15. This third descriptive section entails a good deal of repetition of material drawn
from the history and analysis of texts. I minimize this somewhat by schematization,
but it seems unavoidable. The synthetic description is crucial for building contextual
models of the church, a feature of the method that I shall discuss at length in chapter 1.

the tradition of the large community, and a theological appreciation of the value of pluralism in one church, one Christian movement.

In embarking on such a project, one quickly becomes aware that such a study of the church can only be undertaken within limits. One such limit lies in the choice of texts and their relation to the wider history of the developing church. Why are these texts chosen rather than others? And does not the analysis of texts by definition run counter to an ecclesiology from below that seeks to allow the abundant life of the church on the ground assume its role in historical process? These questions point to problems that are at best resolved in dialectical tensions if at all. The constant tendency of a work such as this is to move too quickly to the abstract level of synthetic understanding. In a desire to assume some control over the subject matter one relies on specific texts which serve as witnesses to what is transpiring within particular communities. But every time a text is chosen as representative of a particular community, it also fails to represent other churches which have their own character. By what stretch of the imagination can one choose the church of Carthage in the mid-third century to represent the whole church? The assumption cannot be that the church in Asia Minor is no different. And even in the case of Carthage, Cyprian's texts reveal the church as seen through a bishop's eyes. But at the same time, Cyprian's church existed in the period prior to the Constantinian shift, and not afterward, so that it represents in some detail a particular church, which is part of the whole church, at that particular time. One needs a sense of analogy to even embark on this project. The chapters try to keep the texts in dialogue with the narrative of events. One also has to accept the tension between the sheer multiplicity of historical data and a striving for interpretive integration that texts promote by their abstracting and schematizing the issues for discussion. For a work in *ecclesiology*, does it contain too much history so that the reader gets bogged down in the analysis of the reasoning of historical figures or too much concern for details? Or, for a work in *historical* ecclesiology, does it move so selectively over texts that key insights remain behind and so rapidly that developments are essentially misconstrued? I know of no formula to adjudicate this balance in what essentially remains a short work relative to the subject matter. But the chapters have the merit of clear divisions, despite their porous quality. Those who want only a synthetic portrait of the church at a given time can skim the evidence; to those who require more and better historical analysis I can only apologize.

Another limitation of the work is its inability to live up to the ideal of evenhandedness. The development here does not represent the various lines of ecclesial development in an equal way. The work veers toward the West and Europe early in the development and almost exclusively in the medieval period. Even a fuller treatment of the Greek Church centered in Constantinople would not do justice to other Eastern traditions. Can the goal of this work be achieved with so many sheer lacunae in the development? From this example, and there are many examples of churches left unattended, traditions unrecounted, data not reviewed, one can discern another methodological ploy used in this work. This work unfolds on a level that bears some resemblance to a method of typology but with major differences. A type is a construct that is intended to transcend the data; it is a purely heuristic structure that does not intend to describe reality but to provide a series of norms and questions for comparative analysis of the real. By contrast the description of the church in each period and the ecclesiological principles and axioms developed in this historical ecclesiology are generated by the data. But the fact that they are broad descriptive characterizations and general axioms or formal principles gives them features that bear analogies to types. These characterizations are therefore more historical than typical, but their abstract quality makes them useful for comparison and contrast between the churches in different times and places.

In sum, *Christian Community in History* is an essay in ecclesiology. *Historical Ecclesiology* is the first part of a two-part ecclesiology from below which I hope will be followed by a more systematic and constructive essay. Ecclesiology from below begins with a critical historical account of the church, analyzes the sociological dynamics of its original formation and constant change, and integrates the theological understanding of the church gathered from the historical witnesses into the historical and sociological understandings.

The outline of the work is historical: it follows the history of the church with a focus on the multiple ecclesiologies that describe its self-understanding at any given time and successively in the course of its entry into new historical situations. It aims at establishing the suppositions for a constructive analysis of the church in a theological language closely aligned to historical experience and thus more comprehensible to both insiders and outsiders.

Part I

THE QUESTION OF METHOD

Chapter 1

Historical Ecclesiology

The phrase "historical ecclesiology" contains a paradox, or at least an inner tension, and a brief consideration of it may serve as an introduction to the aim of this chapter. Ecclesiology is the study of the church in an effort to understand its nature and mission. The quest to define the "logos" of the church suggests that, like other realities, the church has a distinctive nature or even essence that can be determined by systematic investigation. However, historical realities, especially social realities, communities or institutions that have an ongoing historical life, continually develop and change. What is historical is usually considered mutable and relative precisely because of its historicity. One has a variety of ecclesiologies across the church's history as well as a pluralism of ecclesiologies at any given time because different historical conditions and contexts determine different viewpoints, premises, basic values, and methods of approach to the church. As a result, every study of the church must give an account of the perspective and method that governs its unfolding.

The point of this chapter is to give such an account of the method of this work. It will focus on the factors that force an engagement with history in the study of the church, some of the formal characteristics of an understanding of the church within the framework of a turn to history, and, more concretely, some of the principles that flow from and govern historical appreciation of the church. Broadly speaking, then, the goal of this chapter is to open up the logic or method of a historically conscious study of the church.

In order to accomplish this with a certain amount of clarity, I have adopted the framework of a broad contrast between what may be called "an ecclesiology from above" and "an ecclesiology from below." But these categories can function effectively only when their heuristic character remains fully in view. These categories are a device, a way of presenting things in a clear way by contrast. This is done by constructing types, where a type by definition does not exist, and does not describe any particular existent, but rather portrays an ideal, a constructed idea against which to measure and contrast existing realities.[1] When types are reified, in the sense of, in this case, being predicated of particular ecclesiologies or authors, this objectification begins to render the categories or the types dysfunctional; they begin to caricature reality. But at the same time, if the types bear some ideal relation to reality, they remain useful in their ideality; to some more or less ostensible degree they reflect actual churches and the ecclesiology of particular theologians.

The first part of this chapter consists in a schematic outline of the construct, "ecclesiology from above."[2] The second part follows the outline of the first and develops by contrast factors that have moved ecclesiological thinking away from the logic represented in an ecclesiology from above. The third concluding section is a summary sketch of the contrasting suppositions and method of an ecclesiology from below.

ECCLESIOLOGY FROM ABOVE

The abstract portrait of ecclesiology from above can be described in six points. These characterize not the content or subject matter which is the church, but a method or approach to understand it. Many of these variables overlap, but together they add up to a loose

---

1. Max Weber's account of his use of types shows that an ideal type is like a pure essence: clear, understandable, and without ambiguity. The more sharply and precisely a type is designed, the more unrealistic it is in its lack of ambiguity, and the better it serves to reveal reality by contrast and thus perform its methodological function of clarifying, classifying, and attempting explanations. Max Weber, *The Theory of Social and Economic Organization* (New York: Free Press, 1964), 92, 111.

2. A specific ecclesiology which in several respects exemplified this ideal construct is Ludwig Ott, "The Church," in *Fundamentals of Catholic Dogma* (St. Louis: B. Herder Book Co., 1964), 270–324. This Roman Catholic ecclesiology was written prior to the Second Vatican Council and has in many respects been superceded by the ecclesiology of that council. This makes it a good contrasting background for describing ecclesiological method today, for it represents an ecclesiological method that is no longer operative, and this allows for a nonpolemical representation.

phenomenology of a typical way of thinking theologically about the church.

A-historical Context

This ecclesiological method aims at defining the essential nature and structure of the church that transcends any given context. The actual church, of course, has always existed in history: it has a long history, has existed in many different cultures and epochs, and subsists today in different societies and nations. But the goal of this ecclesiology is not to survey the accidental differences among the cultural forms of the church, but to characterize the invariant and invariable essence, nature, or substance of the church. The essence of the church according to this a-historical point of view is determined by those constitutive elements that transcend its particular instantiations, and these can be grasped precisely by abstracting from those individualizing particulars which characterize the church wherever it is, but are precisely not of its defining substance. The substance of the church is precisely that which has a history. The thrust of this method tends to be exclusive in the sense that defining the church means setting forth the limits or frontiers beyond which is nonchurch or a defective embodiment of it. One could characterize this method as pre-critical because it reflects a kind of classical consciousness untroubled by a sense of historical conditioning that tends to relativize thought on the basis of so large a variety of different limiting perspectives.

Specific Church as Object or Principle of Interpretation

It is typical that each church develops its own ecclesiology from above. According to the structure of thought developed thus far, it is natural that one would appeal to one's own tradition to understand one's own ecclesial community or communion. Thus one has a plurality of ecclesiologies across the confessional spectrum. For the most part in what follows I have in mind a Roman Catholic ecclesiology from above.

The practice of understanding the church in terms of one's own tradition correlates with an imagination that construes the whole church in terms of one's own church. In the case of a Roman Catholic ecclesiology from above, the universal church is the Roman Catholic Church writ large. No one fails to see that a pluralism of Christian churches prevails in the world today, a variety of churches whose ecclesiologies or self-understandings are significantly different. But for an ecclesiology from above, the church is doctrinally one, and its correct form is displayed in the church generating the ecclesiology. If that were not the case, it would change. But it will always appear that the ecclesiologist's own church provides the norm for the church because the circle of interpretation is closed and one spontaneously appeals to one's own tradition. An ecclesiology from above contains the following dialectic: on the one hand, a particular tradition that stands over against the others controls the imagination of the theologian and those for whom he or she writes. For example, the identity of the Roman Catholic Church stands out by contrast with the other churches. On the other hand, this imagination reaches out toward the one universal church but imagines it in terms of itself. It is the one true church, so that in describing itself, it describes the way the whole church should be.

Foundation in Authority

Another characteristic of an ecclesiology from above resides in the basis or foundation of its thinking. One might call this its point of departure, or the presuppositions which implicitly support the reasoning and to which it makes appeal. In Christian theology generally the scriptures are taken as a norm. In Roman Catholic theology, the councils and other traditional teachings are part of the magisterium which bears authority. An ecclesiology from above is one that makes appeal to the authority of these sources as something unquestioned and shared in common. Its fundamental principles either consist in or include doctrines about the church which are part of the tradition. And, more generally, it presupposes and readily uses doctrinal language as a common medium of self-understanding. In sharp, bold terms, it presupposes the intelligibility of the doctrinal language about the church, and it appeals to its normative character.

An extreme form of such an ecclesiology from above may carry the theme of the church standing over against the world and human culture; the world becomes conceptualized as that which is outside the church. In contrast to the world in its secularity, the church defines the sphere of the sacred. In Roman Catholic ecclesiology in the past, this polarity took the form of the supernatural over against the "merely" natural, or the "fallen" and sinful; the supernatural was considered as elevating and transforming the natural order. Implicitly, the church represented a social reality that was in some measure set apart from the world, usually in some sense "above" it. This self-contained church had its own language generated by its own distinct tradition, by which it understood itself. This language was given it by revelation and received by faith and was often viewed as distinct from, if not in contrast with, the language of the world. An ecclesiology from above can be measured by the degree to which it is based on and mediates an understanding, of the church in a distinctive, revealed, supernatural, and doctrinal language that in some measure sets the church apart from the secular world.

Origin of the Church Understood in Doctrinal Terms

The church is a historical movement, and the various churches are themselves historical institutions or societies with a wide variety of organizational forms. Because the church is a historical institution with a historical origin, ecclesiology invariably contains some account of how it came to be. This constant provides another axis for distinguishing an ecclesiology from above and an ecclesiology from below. In an ecclesiology from above, the development of the church is understood in terms of doctrines about the historical origins of the church as distinct from critical history. Ecclesiology is a distinct subdiscipline of theology, and in this pattern of theology the authority of doctrinal or theological interpretations of the origins of the church governs the theological imagination. God's providence in history led to the church; God more or less "directly" founds the church in the work of Jesus Christ; and God as Spirit animates and directs the development of the church from its beginnings at Pentecost.

Thus in an ecclesiology from above, one can make a direct appeal to the New Testament in understanding the church. And by extension, the whole history of the church's doctrinal self-definitions constitute an authoritative tradition. At one extreme, an ecclesiology from above may simply cite scriptural and traditional sources as proof-texts that reflect divine authority in representing the character of the church. Or it may also appeal to these sources with a concern for their historical and contextual meaning. But in both cases, an ecclesiology from above distinctively appeals to authority in understanding the development of the church.

This aspect of an ecclesiology from above, that is, the understanding of historical origins in terms of the authority of revealed doctrine, can be generalized: historical consciousness is controlled by doctrinal understanding. The church since its beginning has never ceased to develop in the course of history. But that development has always unfolded according to God's eternal plan. On the one hand, Jesus Christ established the basic forms or structures of the church. On the other hand, the internal principle of God as Spirit within the church has kept it within the boundaries of providence. What appeared late in the church was present in an embryonic form in the beginning. Generally speaking, a confidence in God's providence guiding the church keeps at bay the radical historical consciousness that is more typical of postmodernity.

Christocentrism

Insofar as an ecclesiology implies other doctrines, one should expect that there will be a certain coherence between an ecclesiology from above and a christology from above. Jesus Christ is the eternal Son, incarnate as Jesus of Nazareth, and now the risen Christ and head of the church. Jesus Christ functions both as Jesus of Nazareth, the one who lived back then, and as the eternal and risen Son who is always present sacramentally to the church. As a historical figure Jesus plays the important role of being the founder of the church. In less critical appreciations Jesus may be depicted as having set up, in embryonic form, the organizational structure of the church which then took time to become fully institutionalized. But perhaps more importantly Jesus Christ defines the church in the present. Myriad forms and structures reflect the presence of Christ to the church: Christ is found in the church's institutions, its scripture, in the pope, in the bishop, in the pastor of the congregation, in the sacraments, in the disciplinary ideals of Christian life, in the presence of Jesus Christ to each member of the church through prayer. The descent of Christ in a descending ecclesiology is not restricted to the single event of the incarnation; it is the continuing immanent presence of the risen Christ to the church in a mystical way. In this way, the image of the church as the Body of Christ can appeal to all sorts of reinforcing experiences and conceptions that make such an image not only plausible but also real and compelling in terms of religious experience. The risen Christ is located at the center of an ecclesiology from above. And God as Spirit is subordinated in a variety of ways to Christ in this christocentric form of understanding the church.

One can measure christocentrism in ecclesiology by examining the topic of the relation of the church to the salvation of all people. This central and diagnostic topic in christology today has profound ecclesiological implications. Generally speaking, the mainline Christian churches have transcended the view that the availability of salvation is limited to their own members or more generally to Christians. But many churches retain the idea that the event of Jesus Christ causes the salvation of all, so that the whole range of God's saving activity is more than christomorphic; it is intrinsically constituted as the very grace of Christ. This means that the church, even when it is not considered constitutive of the salvation of all, is the summit of all religious forms, and the single, normative religion that is superior to all others because the church is constituted by Christ as its center. In short, in an ecclesiology from above christocentrism has a tendency to become an ecclesiocentrism.[3]

Structures and New Ministries

Consistent with a doctrinal understanding of the church and a christocentric form of understanding, the structure of the church reflects a hierarchical grounding of church organization and its forms of ministry. I use the term "hierarchy" in a nontechnical and descriptive way to point to a layered or tiered organization of the church, perhaps in a pyramidal form. The levels of power and authority have their foundation in God, and they descend. In the medieval Roman Church the descent took this form: God, Christ, Spirit, Peter, pope,

---

3. See J. Peter Schineller, "Christ and Church: A Spectrum of Views," *Theological Studies* 37 (1976): 545–66 for a typology of correlated views on christology, salvation, and the role of the church in the economy of salvation.

bishop, priest, laity. This structure in some measure reflects or corresponds to the monarchical structure of the universe, or reality itself, insofar as God is creator, Jesus Christ is savior and founder of the church, the Spirit of Christ is the animating principle within the church. It corresponds with a structure of revelation and of authority. Because it stems from the one God as source of all, however this is understood, it carries in this respect and to this degree a sacred character.

A hierarchical structure such as this is concomitant with a hierarchical imagination. In other words, this generalized framework may vary in its details, but it is always present and at work structuring understanding. The church as institution is willed by God, informed by God in Christ and as Spirit, so that the church is holy in its institutional forms. The institutions of the church enjoy a certain sacrality: scripture is holy, sacraments are holy, but so too are the bishops and priests who administer them. The word of God is holy, but so too is the sacred authority with which the leaders of the church speak. One objective state or way of life may be considered holier than another. A good example of the hierarchical character of the church can be seen in some perceptions of the priest in the Roman Catholic Church. The office of the priest has its pattern in Jesus Christ: the priest is an *alter Christus,* especially in celebrating the eucharist, announcing the good news, and in forgiving sin. This entails an implicit transfer of qualities of authority related to Christ to the person who holds the office of priest.

One familiar with the history of the church over almost two millennia knows that the church has undergone considerable change as it adapted to new situations. Sometimes these changes were slow and gradual; sometimes events demanded more rapid adjustment. In the course of these changes the structure of ministry was altered in a more or less substantial way. By ministries I mean offices or positions within the church through which people work for or in the name of the church in some public way. The category of "new ministries" suggests shifts in the structure of ministry that more or less significantly or substantially change the way ministers serve the community. To be sure, "substantiality" will not be understood by all in the same way; it may be precisely what is at issue, and thus cannot be presumed to be a clear category. However, the goal here is not to address any particular question, but to introduce an axis of interpretation along which there will be considerable difference between an ecclesiology from above and an ecclesiology from below. How do each of these types of ecclesiology understand the ability of the church to adjust to new situations, or to change, in history?

Consistent with what has been said thus far, an ecclesiology from above tends to view its structure of ministries as corresponding to the will of God. Within this framework there will inevitably be considerable nuance and distinction between basic structures and the precise details with which they are deployed. For example, a very common belief among the churches is that the scriptures and baptism are divine institutions. In Roman Catholic ecclesiology it has been commonly taught that the threefold structure of pope, bishop, and priest are a divinely established structure of the church. Luther for his part could only find two sacraments clearly attested to in the New Testament. Such conclusions are drawn from an appeal to the scriptures or to a tradition of doctrine or practice or to both. The magisterium, or teaching authority of the Roman Catholic Church, draws its authority both from this past and from its own charismatic ability to discern the truth at any given time. Other churches do roughly the same thing. How deeply or extensively the various provisions of these ministerial structures can all claim divine prescription will usually be a debated question. But what characterizes an ecclesiology from above is the conviction that one can rely on these divine authoritative sources of theology and the corresponding method of appealing to them to establish a supernatural or divine or revealed structure of the church and its ministry. This structure will allow for adjustments within itself to meet the exigencies of ministry, the needs of the church. But the basic structure itself will not be changed, for in an ecclesiology from above it has been established by or according to the will of God. In sum, new ministries are absorbed into traditional structures or patterns.

These six characteristics could be expanded at greater length. This presentation, however, represents a clear outline that points to a recognizable type of ecclesiology.

TOWARD AN ECCLESIOLOGY FROM BELOW

Given this type of ecclesiology which I have called ecclesiology from above, I now want to begin to build a contrasting type of ecclesiological thinking which will then be further illustrated in the chapters that follow. This can be done by indicating with reference to each of the six elements of an ecclesiology from above various historical and cultural forces which point toward and even demand a different way of thinking. I begin with elements of historical life today that make contextual thinking unavoidable.

The Historical Context of Ecclesiology

More will be said about the method of ecclesiology further on. At this point it may be presumed that the context, situation, and standpoint of the one trying to understand will enter into the understanding itself. This ancient principle of Thomas Aquinas, that whatever is known is known according to the situation of the knower,[4] is taken over into theology as a method of correlation. A method of correlation means that theological understanding arises out of the conjunction of theological data or sources with the context or situation of a particular culture in order to bear meaning and relevance for that culture. In other words, our present situation enters into our understanding whether we are aware of it or not. A coherent theological method begins by making explicit the context in which we live so that it can come to bear on our understanding self-consciously and critically.

How would one characterize the context for theology today insofar as this impacts ecclesiology? Innumerable different factors determine the situation of theology today, and they can never be completely summed up.[5] But one can typify the situation by describing the problems or dilemmas which the church must face today. The following developments help define the context for understanding the church today. While few people are ignorant of these factors, piling them up

---

4. *Summa Theologiae*, II-II, 1, 2.

5. T. Howland Sanks, in the first chapter of his *Salt, Leaven, and Light: The Self-Understanding of the Christian Community* (New York: Crossroad, 1992), provides a thorough and lucid characterization of the North American cultural context for understanding the church.

by enumeration suggests the serious character of the new demands on ecclesiological reflection.

Historical consciousness. Historical consciousness can be described from a variety of points of view; several features can be singled out as defining characteristics. Historical consciousness recognizes the particularity, individuality, and unrepeatability of every event, a certain desacralization and deprovidentialization of history, discontinuity in history because freedom can reverse itself, the novelty of the present, the relativization of every understanding of the past because of the particularity of all standpoints: the changing past as history is always open to new reinterpretations into the future.[6]

In some degree one may presuppose that all ecclesiology today operates within the framework of a historical consciousness. But the notion remains ambiguous in its abstraction. For as a form of consciousness that reflects our historical condition, historical consciousness is experiential and, like the notion of freedom, the precise conception of it and the significance it bears can vary considerably. There are degrees of historical consciousness; each person and in some measure discrete groups maintain a threshold of limits to the change, relativity, lack of stability, and pluralism that historicity implies. Historicity, too, carries negative and positive valences: in freeing us from the past it causes insecurity; in binding us to the past it provides identity but may stymie communication with other traditions. Historical consciousness involves one in a dialectic across temporal distance. The church is bound to the past and freed from its particularity: but one must study the data of the historical church to become free within it for its future.

The ecumenical movement in the Protestant churches and the Second Vatican Council in the Roman Catholic Church were very influential in bringing this historical consciousness to bear on theology and in mediating it to their constituencies. The ecumenical movement explicitly recognized pluralism, and Vatican II opened the church up to dialogue with the modern world and its various histories and cultures. This historical consciousness, in turn, has considerable

---

6. John W. O'Malley, "Reform, Historical Consciousness, and Vatican II's Aggiornamento," *Tradition and Transition: Historical Perspectives on Vatican II* (Wilmington, Del.: Michael Glazier, 1989), 73–77.

bearing on how we are to understand the church. For in a historically conscious framework it becomes apparent that the church, in all of its developments through history, took on the social forms and ideas of the age in which it existed. But if this is the case, what form should the church assume today? Can a God-given and divinely willed hierarchical constitution of the church make sense in a historically conscious age? If the structure of the church can be completely explained by historical development, and if, as a product of history, it is always changing, it becomes a task to make sense of any divine claims for particular ecclesial structures.

Globalization and pluralism. Globalization has created a new cultural context for theology.[7] All are aware of the historical mechanisms of planetary unification which became so effective after the Second World War and picked up more energy with the fall of the Soviet Union. This global process has set up sometimes dramatic examples of tensions between closed local cultures or worlds of meaning and an invading world culture, alien ways of thought and doing things, foreign norms and patterns of standardization. This can be deeply threatening to groups even as it can be liberating for individuals within them. As more and more people are moving faster and farther in a world that is smaller and smaller, so, too, local ideas and local identities and local ways of doing things become disrupted. But, it seems too, the more the race becomes unified, the more it resists homogenization: the universal and the local and particular seem to be in constant tension. It is reasonable to think that globalization is largely responsible for a new intellectual culture which is being called postmodern and which presents a challenge to an ecclesiology from above.

Globalization has helped a sense of pluralism become more generalized and deeper than it has ever been before. Because of travel, migration, and the media of communication, more and more people can actually experience the cultural differences that have always separated peoples. Today these differences are often lived out within a community as different peoples come together in the large cities of the world and as people do business together across territorial and

---

7. Robert Schreiter, *The New Catholicity* (Maryknoll, N.Y.: Orbis Books, 1997).

cultural boundaries. There seems to be a greater need for tolerance today because there is a deeper sense that the differences between cultural values and ways of life are unbridgeable. A sense of pluralism so marks the consciousness of the young people in developed nations that the very idea of universally normative values or ideas seems quaint or utterly strange.

Other churches. Another factor that defines our situation is the positive appreciation of the other churches. This positive recognition has been acted upon to form the ecumenical movement. The ecumenical movement, which depends upon historical consciousness, could only have occurred in the modern period. Since the Second Vatican Council the majority of the mainline churches are committed to some form of ecumenical work or understanding.

But commitment to the ecumenical movement involves some suppositions that have a major impact on ecclesiology. For example, churches based on creeds and churches based on an evangelical reading of the scriptures come together in the World Council of Churches. As another example of a more ecumenical position, Vatican II refused to identify, in the simple terms that had been used before, the "true church" with the Roman Catholic Church.[8] Vatican II also recognized other churches as genuine churches, and it promised that the Roman Catholic Church would work toward unity. These commitments officially recognize the part-whole tension, a tension that opens up fundamental problems for ecclesiology. For example, how is it to be decided whether a particular church institution is theologically sound or acceptable? Relative to the institutions of ministry and church organization, each church tends to appeal to its own tradition for legitimation. But if each church appeals to its own, unique tradition on basic issues, by definition unity seems to be methodologically excluded. In other words, the commitment to the ecumenical movement means that the appeal to one's own tradition as a criterion of theology has to be modified. Particular traditions cannot be viewed

---

8. See Edward Schillebeeckx, *Church: The Human Story of God* (New York: Crossroad, 1990), 189–98, for a rehearsal of the history and significance of the famous phrase *"subsistit in"* in *Lumen Gentium* against neo-conservative efforts to trim its significance.

as absolute or exclusive norms; appreciation of every particular tradition must be set in a context of pluralism and possible coexistence with other institutions. The question of whether institutions can be conceived of as being willed by God and what such language can mean will have to be looked at more carefully. These are not easy tasks for churches that define themselves as traditional.

Other religions and "the world." For an ecclesiology from above, the world's religious pluralism represents a challenging situation. The problem transcends the mere existence of other religions; one must reckon with a new appreciation of these religions. Due to historical consciousness or, inversely, as a partial cause of our historical consciousness, educated Christians today tend to view the various religions of the world positively. That there are many religions is not a negative fact; it is expected and is a value, for one particular religion could never unfold the richness of the mystery of God and of God's dealings with human beings. One must say, therefore, that "there is more religious truth in all the religions together than in one particular religion," and therefore "the multiplicity of religions is not an evil which needs to be removed, but rather a wealth which is to be welcomed and enjoyed by all."[9] Vatican II also stimulated this positive appreciation of other religions with its doctrine of the universal availability of God's grace. If God's grace is offered to every single person, and if this grace always comes to people in and through their concrete historical situation, one must also appreciate the religions as the actual mediators of God's grace. As Karl Rahner pointed out, for these reasons, one must look upon the other religions as willed by God.[10]

These views put particular strain on the long held doctrine and maxim that there is no salvation outside the church. In fact that doctrine does not represent the majority of churches in the World Council of Churches, and in its obvious sense it was rejected by Vatican II. Moreover that doctrine is now being turned on its head

---

9. Schillebeeckx, *Church*, 166–67.

10. See the development of these ideas in Catholic theology by Karl Rahner, "Christianity and the Non-Christian Religions," *Theological Investigations* V (Baltimore: Helicon Press, 1966), 115–34. This essay represents the state of the question at the time of Vatican II. The discussion has advanced considerably in all the churches during the last third of the twentieth century.

by many theologians. If grace abounds outside the church, and if one thinks, as one must, that God's grace is effective, then one must also say with Schillebeeckx that the world and not the church is the ordinary place of salvation and that "there is no salvation outside the world."[11]

What has happened here is that the appreciation of God's grace working in other religions is extended generally to the whole sphere of human life in the world. This in turn entails a new understanding of the role of the church as an instrument of God's salvific presence to human history. Many see God's presence to the world transcending the church. The sphere of God's presence is frequently called the kingdom of God, that is, the sphere of the influence and reign of God's grace. The recognition of the universality of God's grace undermines an "ecclesiocentrism" that tended to identify the church with that kingdom of God. In this way the church becomes decentralized in history. To understand the church today one will have to interpret how it relates to the wider sphere of God's effective saving activity in history at large.

While these ideas have become commonplace in ecclesiology, their significance has yet to be felt in the discipline as a whole. What is described here adds up to a fundamental change in the understanding of the mission of the church. During the first part of the twentieth century, the Doctrine and Life movement strove to keep the mission of the church to society at the forefront of the ecumenical movement. It became a leading impulse for the formation of the WCC. Analogously, the single most significant contribution of the Second Vatican Council to the understanding of the church consists in the new definition of the church in its relation to the world. This occurred most notably in its concluding document, *Gaudium et Spes,* but, perhaps, more profoundly in its decree on the missionary character of the church, *Ad Gentes.* In both the church was presented in terms of its relation to the world and human history. The church is an open institution that looks out upon the world and understands itself in service to the world because it mediates something of value for the world. The church is not an enclave within the world closed

---

11. Schillebeeckx, *Church,* 5–15.

in upon itself but is essentially missionary, that is, sent to the world. In our age of statements of mission and goals, it is hard to decipher why the understanding of the nature of the church has not undergone a change when its mission and goals appear to be transformed. One finds very serious problems of coherence in ecclesiology around this juncture between the mission and nature of the church, a topic that from a certain perspective governs all the rest.

Human suffering on a social scale. What about the world to which the church is sent? The world today displays a degree of suffering structured socially, politically, and economically that in terms of sheer magnitude appears unprecedented in human history. This massive poverty, hunger, sickness, dehumanization, and social oppression are the concern not only of its victims but also of every thinking human person. As to the general trend, the quotient of suffering in terms of poverty and disease increases both in absolute numbers and in proportionate percentage. The question for the church is this: what does the church have to say or do about this common situation of humankind? That which the church claims to "possess" or "contain" it calls God's salvation as this is mediated through Jesus Christ. But what this has to do with the common condition of the human race today, that is, concretely in its actual history, must be continuously asked anew. The church, Vatican II said, is a sign to the nations of God's salvific presence to human beings in their history. The church's response to the social injustice that keeps so many people in bondage today is a very basic key to its credibility before the nations. It is impossible today to understand the church in any credible way without formulating this self-understanding so that it is directly responsive to global social injustice, poverty, and dehumanization.[12]

The experience and situation of women. Very few people in North America are unaware of the feminist movement or, in some respects, revolution that has occurred over the past two decades.

---

12. The issues of the relationship of the church to other religions, to the world generally, and to the major problems of poverty and oppression are connected. Their interrelation is shown very clearly by Paul Knitter, "Toward a Liberation Theology of Religions," *The Myth of Christian Uniqueness,* ed. P. Knitter and J. Hick (Maryknoll, N.Y.: Orbis Books, 1987), 178–200.

Whatever one's judgment may be regarding various aspects of this movement, for it is highly differentiated, one cannot fail to be impressed by the witness of women to their own experiences of various forms of oppression. But listening and attending to this witness forces one to examine the objective situation of women in our society today and in societies and cultures throughout the world. It may be taken as a matter of fact that women throughout the world have been and are consistently the victims of discrimination. From a perspective that expects that relationships between all people should be governed by social institutions that are just, evenhanded, and nondiscriminatory, one has to say that, throughout the world and our past history generally, women are and have been the victims of injustice and, in many areas, violence. This consciousness which is well developed in Western culture can only continue to grow worldwide. The bearing of the experience of women on ecclesiology is direct. One expects the church to be structured by a justice inspired by Jesus' values of the kingdom of God. Lacking that, the church will have little prophetic leverage in preaching God's word.[13]

Secularization and individualism: decreasing church participation. The term "secularization" is particularly hard to apply consistently to North American culture.[14] For example, in comparison with some other Western societies the United States still exhibits a pious and religious environment. But it is also clear that this culture includes a large separation between the lives of the churches and the running of our secular institutions of society, industry, and government. This can be verified by a comparison between our society and, for example, that of Europe during the Middle Ages or some Islamic nations today. The secular sphere has been separated off from

---

13. See Serene Jones, *Feminist Theory and Christian Theology* (Minneapolis: Fortress Press, 2000), 79–93 where she sums up women's experience of socially structured oppression under the five headings of exploitation, marginalization, powerlessness, the prevalence of masculine cultural norms, and violence. On the relevance of feminist theology to ecclesiology, see Anne Carr, "Ordination for Women and Christian Thought: History, Theology, Ethics," *Transforming Grace* (San Francisco: Harper & Row, 1988), 134–53.

14. For the sociological ambiguity of this concept see John A. Coleman, "The Situation of Modern Faith," *Theological Studies* 39 (1978): 601–32.

the religious and remains quite autonomous, even if not in every respect. As for the life of the churches themselves, one cannot say that
society has become less religious, for the rise of fundamentalism and
the electronic churches has demonstrated the opposite. But members
have become more individualistic, and especially educated people do
not participate actively in the mainline churches in the way they did
formerly. In fact, church participation has become a voluntary activity. People no longer experience any public, social constraint to be
active members of a church. The church, even the Roman Catholic Church, has ceased to be conceived as a necessary institution
for one's salvation but has become itself a voluntary association to
which one belongs only when one so chooses. This phenomenon is
usually expressed this way: in Western secular societies, which share
in some degree a historical consciousness and the experience of pluralism, the church and even being a Christian no longer have social
support. Being a member of the church has become more and more
a matter of personal commitment.[15]

This social phenomenon and the change that it has wrought in or
on the church in terms of the people who make up the church have
rather dramatic effects for the notion of the authority of the church,
both the way it can be understood and the way it can be exercised. For
example, if the church is a voluntary organization, will not church
authority have to involve dialogue and consent as in a congregational
or free church polity?[16] The most far reaching example of a change
in this regard in the American Catholic Church was found in the
general reaction to its teaching on sexual morality. In the case of
Humanae Vitae the doctrine on birth control was simply rejected, or
in more technical terms not "received," by a majority of the members of the Catholic Church in North America. This case is in some
measure paradigmatic. The Roman Catholic Church today is filled
with "pick and choose" Catholics, that is, members who adhere to

---

15. See Karl Rahner, *The Shape of the Church to Come* (London: SPCK, 1974),
57–58, and earlier in *The Christian Commitment: Essays in Pastoral Theology* (New
York: Sheed and Ward, 1963), 3–37.

16. James Gustafson, "Authority and Consent in the Voluntary Church," *The
Church as Moral Decision Maker* (Philadelphia: Pilgrim, 1970), 126–32.

some doctrines but not all. A former ecclesiological doctrine of comprehensive authority which said that not to accept all the doctrines taught by authority was to reject the authority itself, has simply broken down; it no longer functions. This raises anew the question of the authority of the church: what does, or better, what *can*, the authority of the church mean today in a secular and individualistic culture? Is there such a thing as an authority which at the same time is subject to interpretation, dissent, and nonobedience, all of which seem to be the ways in which many Christians now respond to church authority?

These features and the problems and questions to which they give rise characterize the situation or context for ecclesiology in a particular place and culture. The point is not to try to describe a worldwide matrix of the whole church. Yet some such historical analysis and contextual appreciation must enter into any and every ecclesiology because such contextual issues are always actually at work. An a-historical ecclesiology no longer makes sense in a historically conscious and critical culture.

The Object of Ecclesiology

The empirical church. The primary object of the study of ecclesiology is the empirical church. To phrase the same thing somewhat differently, the subject matter of ecclesiology is the concrete community that exists in history, although not without hope in its eschatological fulfillment. Ecclesiology is a discipline that deals with or is about this historical community.

Having said this, it follows that "ecclesiology cannot be restricted to the interpretation of statements about the church, whether these be biblical, traditional, liturgical, magisterial, theological, or other."[17] Scriptural and traditional statements about the church are certainly part of the object of ecclesiology; they have been or are expressed by the church and thus become internalized as part of the self-definition of what the empirical church is. Indeed, that about which such theological and authoritative statements on the church speak "is that

---

17. Joseph A. Komonchak, "Ecclesiology and Social Theory: A Methodological Essay," *The Thomist* 45 (1981): 273.

which occurs in the mutually related conscious operations and acts that make a group of people what is called 'the church.' "[18] These statements themselves, as ecclesiological statements, are directed in their first moment to the empirical church and are thus part of the data concerning the concrete, historical church.

A human reality. A historical approach to the study of the church correlates with the assumption that this empirical church is a human reality. This premise will almost inevitably meet with the objection by some that the unequivocal statement that the church is a human reality undermines or compromises the transcendent and divine character of the church. This is a recurring theme involved in the use of a historical and sociological method. But such a reduction does not necessarily follow and must be consciously avoided. Moreover the risk of such a reduction in no way undermines the human reality of the church. The following observation definitively lays this objection to rest: "Whatever Christian faith may say about the divine origin, center, and goal of the church, it never pretends that the church does not stand on this side of the distinction between Creator and creature. The church is not God; it is not Jesus Christ; it is not the Holy Spirit. If the church is the People of God, the Body of Christ, the Temple of the Holy Spirit, it is all of these as a human reality, that is, because certain events occur within the mutually related consciousness of a group of human beings."[19]

In short, the statement that the church is a human community need not be taken in an exclusive sense that denies a certain specific relationship to God, indeed, a constitutive relationship to God.

---

18. Ibid., 274–75. In another place Komonchak states that "the biblical, traditional, dogmatic, and theological language always refers to a concrete social reality constructed around the transformed intersubjectivity of concrete persons in the world." Thus the object of ecclesiology is the concrete process of self-constitution "by which the church comes to be in Christian men and women." Joseph A. Komonchak, "Lonergan and the Tasks of Ecclesiology," *Creativity and Method: Essays in Honor of Bernard Lonergan, S.J.,* ed. Matthew L. Lamb (Milwaukee: Marquette University Press, 1981), 273. In sum, the primary subject matter or object of ecclesiology is the visible or empirical church.

19. Komonchak, "Ecclesiology and Social Theory," 269. See also Joseph A. Komonchak, "History and Social Theory in Ecclesiology," *Lonergan Workshop* II, ed. Fred Lawrence (Chico, Calif.: Scholars Press, 1981), 1–53.

Rather it defines a premise for the discipline of ecclesiology: this empirical, human church is the starting point for the study of the church and the basic referent for the word "church."

Theological reductionism. The church is not only an empirical and human reality, it is also a historical reality. The church is a phenomenon of and in history. As such it should not and really cannot be conceived of as being constituted by some essence or constitutive platonic idea that subsists above and out of history.[20] The nature of the church is not to be conceived of as determined by a revelation that is itself not historically conditioned in its being received by the community itself. As a historical reality the church had a beginning in time, indeed at a definite and discernable point in time. One can determine with relative clarity the origin of the church. This church has been and is the subject of historical development and this development must be expected to continue into the future. This historical development has been charted and studied, and while there will always be more work to be done, one can point to a great deal of consensus on the basic turning points of this history. As an empirical and human community the church cannot be imagined as immune from the "laws" and vicissitudes of historical existence; and the study of the church cannot prescind from these and claim to understand the church as it really is. In other words ecclesiology in its first moment must expect continuity between the developmental, historical existence of the church and that of other human communities and organizations. This does not mean that the church does not have either its own specific self-constituting historical existence or its theologically defined transcendent dimension. Rather it simply implies that the first movement of an inquiry that strives for an adequate understanding of the church should not be governed by a private language taken exclusively from theological sources. The church is a historical community.

These three rather basic observations, namely, that the church is an empirical, human, and historical community, are interdependent;

---

20. Joseph A. Komonchak, "The Church," *The Desires of the Human Heart: An Introduction to the Theology of Bernard Lonergan,* ed. Vernon Gregson (New York: Paulist Press, 1988), 232–33.

they imply each other. The point of insisting upon them may be summarized as an effort to avoid "theological reductionism." This phrase is taken from James Gustafson who defines it as follows: "By theological reductionism we mean the exclusive use of Biblical and doctrinal language in the interpretation of the church."[21] "A doctrinal reductionism refuses to take seriously the human elements in the church's life, or if it acknowledges them it does not explore or explicate them except in doctrinal language."[22] Theological reductionism, Gustafson claims, is a methodological fallacy. It presumes that the church is an absolutely unique historico-social reality in every respect. It thus implies that the church has no commonality with the ordinary laws of historical human communities. The result is a language and understanding that bears no relationship with the rest of common human experience of communities. These thus become unintelligible both to those outside the church and to those inside the church to the extent that they appreciate the mechanisms of historical life and common secular existence. Such language then can be at best inadequate to the full reality of the church; at worst, it falsifies or distorts a proper understanding of the church insofar as it does not correspond to its full reality.

A simultaneously historical and theological reality. The church is simultaneously a human, historical, social reality on the one hand and a theological reality on the other hand. These two dimensions of the church are quite distinct, but it is crucial that the discipline of ecclesiology not focus its attention on either dimension to the exclusion of the other.

The distinction and relation between these two aspects of the church can be understood and explained by conceiving the church as constituted by a simultaneous twofold relationship, a relation to God and a relation to the world.[23] The church is related to God through its

---

21. James M. Gustafson, *Treasure in Earthen Vessels: The Church as a Human Community* (New York: Harper & Brothers, 1961; Chicago: University of Chicago Press, 1976), 100. Many of the ideas that govern the methodology presented here are also clearly set forth in this book of Gustafson.

22. Ibid., 105.

23. Ernst Troeltsch finds this double relationship of the church to God and to human society and history as being entailed by the core of Christian revelation itself. What is revealed in and through Jesus Christ is an anthropology that revolves around

faith and its self-understanding as having come into existence by the grace of God. The church is always to be understood theologically as being more than a voluntary association, that is, a group that comes together on the basis of no more than human initiative. According to the understanding of its members, the church has a deep grounding in the will, initiative, and active presence of God. The real and dynamic relationship to God constitutes the reality of what the church is. But this church is also constituted by its horizontal or historical relation to the world and history. It takes its place among and alongside of other social groups and entities. In principle, the inner workings of the church, although they may be distinctive because of the community's perception of its relationship to God, are not discontinuous with the mechanisms of other social entities. One should understand the church according to the dynamics revealed by social sciences; one should recognize that its self-understanding follows the principles of the sociology of knowledge. The church is continually changed and even reconstituted by the ongoing interactions with the world and the other institutions of history.

Edward Schillebeeckx expresses this insight by saying that the church is one single reality in history, but one that must be understood in two irreducible languages.[24] Theological language describes the church in its relation to God; critical, historical, sociological language accounts for the church insofar as it is continuous with other historical institutions. But the point here is that these are two dimensions of one reality; there are not two churches. We need a theological method that respects these two dimensions of the one church, that does not hold them in balance over against each other but integrates them in a single understanding. For the same people who make up

---

human beings being simultaneously related to God and their fellow human beings. These two relationships at all times mutually impact each other. Troeltsch uses the dialectical interaction between the two poles of this double relationship as an axis or a formal framework in which to measure changes in the church as it moves through history. It is thus both a material and formal underpinning of the whole of *The Social Teachings of the Christian Churches* (New York: Macmillan, 1931).

24. Schillebeeckx, *Church*, 210–13. Lonergan defined these two languages by their use of "general categories" and "special categories." General categories refer to objects that are studied by other disciplines than theology. Special categories refer to objects proper to theology and thus strictly transcendent, not knowable by "reason" but by revelation grasped in faith. Komonchak, "Church," 227.

the church participate in the organizations of society, and they know how these work.

The universal church. Once the church is recognized as the social reality that had a beginning in a point of time and has a lengthy historical career, it becomes necessary, at least at the outset, to affirm that the object of the discipline of ecclesiology is the whole or universal church.

The church was one in its source or beginning; it stems from the Jesus event and began with the banding together of disciples of Jesus. Although single in its origins and inspiration, this historical movement in fact fragmented into many churches. The great or whole church today is divided into many churches. As churches became differentiated from each other in institution and self-understanding, the discipline of ecclesiology became as multiple as the churches in which it was pursued. Thus the actual object of ecclesiology is often not the universal church but only a segment of it, as in the type of an ecclesiology from above.

Against this disciplinary fragmentation, historical consciousness forces one to view the object of ecclesiology as the whole Christian movement. Historical consciousness exposes the degree to which the reasons that caused the divisions in the church were contingent and historically relative. Historical consciousness allows an acceptance and positive appreciation of pluralism and an insight into how people can share a common faith which allows for differences in interpretation and expression. A global historical consciousness and a positive appreciation of pluralism allow members of the Christian church to transcend many intra-Christian struggles and to envisage the whole church vis-à-vis other religions which are vast, well established, and very different than Christianity. A world-historical context functions as a great relativizer; it allows the theologian to minimize the differences among Christians by casting them against a horizon of far wider proportions. Viewed from the perspective of other religions, within the context of world history, Christianity appears as a distinctive and in that measure unified movement. From within such a consciousness, the Christian theologian can see that to limit the Christian church to one's own confessional group makes little sense. The rise of historical consciousness was the presupposition for the ecumenical movement, and participation in the ecumenical movement has produced a consciousness of "we" among educated Christians that prevents the equation of the term "church" with one's own particular church.

The part-whole dialectic. Historical consciousness is multifaceted. It includes the recognition that all thinkers and their thought are historically situated, contextualized, and partially determined by their particular point of view. The ability abstractly to project and in this sense envision the universal context of history, and the inability to escape one's own particular situation in the world with all that this entails, thus define a dialectical situation which in turn qualifies the discipline of ecclesiology. An individual envisions the whole church always from the point of view of some particular local church. No ecclesiologist directly belongs to the world-church, but shares, as it were, a dual membership and loyalty to his or her own confession and, through the former, to the church as a whole. But the question goes well beyond matters of motives and loyalty. The point is that ecclesiologists cannot escape entirely from the church or confession in which they reside.

This historical exigency reflects the common theological appreciation which says that the whole church exists in any part of the church. That is to say, the local church cannot be reduced to being simply a part or fragment of a universal entity called the church. Rather, the whole of what it means to be church comes to realization in a local church, or in "a part" of the whole Christian movement.[25] But being an essentially integral realization of church does not mean that any given church can be isolated from the larger church. The local church is still a part of the whole.

This part-whole interplay is genuinely dialectical. The church as a whole and the church in each of its instantiations give rise to two

---

25. Hans Küng, *The Church* (New York: Sheed and Ward, 1967), 169–71, 227–34. This part-whole dialectic is discussed by Joseph Komonchak in "The Church Universal as the Communion of Local Churches," *Where Does the Church Stand? Concilium*, 146, by G. Alberigo and G. Gutiérrez (New York: Seabury, 1981), 30–35. The discussion, however, is conducted within the framework of the Roman Catholic Church. It would be profitable to study how the significance of the terms "local" and "universal" change, sometimes almost assuming opposite values, when the framework is the whole Christian church.

distinct perspectives on the church which always mutually interact and influence each other. One can define further the logic of this dialectical interaction as follows: On the one hand, while the object of the study of the church in systematic ecclesiology must remain the universal church and not merely a local or confessional part of the church, still this universal church will always be seen through the lens of a particular church, at least when the ecclesiology is developed by a single theologian.[26] This applies to both the theological and the sociological languages one uses of the church. The theological tradition of a particular communion and, less consciously, the "social sources of denominationalism" will always be a determinant of any understanding of the church.[27] Thus it appears that every ecclesiology tends to reflect the church of a single confession. On the other hand, this particular ecclesiology should always be presented against the background of the whole church. In the measure that a systematic ecclesiology is conscious of the whole, it will tend to determine what it takes to be normatively Christian in more general and comprehensive terms than those of a particular confession.[28]

In sum, when the object of ecclesiology is recognized to be the whole or universal church, the following dialectical principle emerges: Every conception of the whole church will be filtered through the lens of a particular church; each particular ecclesiology should be relativized by being presented within the horizon of the wider Christian movement.

---

26. It is at this point that many ecclesiologies fail today. Even when they accept the principle that the church is larger than one particular confession and propose to study the whole church "in the light of" a particular tradition, in fact they simply portray a particular church. In that measure such an ecclesiology is systematically deficient, even though it may be useful as a denominational study.

27. H. Richard Niebuhr, *The Social Sources of Denominationalism* (New York: World Publishing, A Meridian Book, 1957). In this work, as the title implies, Niebuhr shows how nondoctrinal factors such as class, race, nation, ethnic affiliation, ethical custom, region, and so on are major factors that cause and sustain distinctiveness and division within the wider Christian world.

28. This explains why some of the most satisfactory ecclesiology is being done today in situations of dialogue. On the one hand, ecumenical ecclesiology helps to break open the particularisms of churches. On the other hand, however, this ecumenical theology itself must unfold within the context of dialogue with the world, lest it become narrowly introverted. It may be, as Fahey suggests, that more and more an integral and comprehensive systematic ecclesiology will have to be done collaboratively, across confessions and across multiple subdisciplines. Michael Fahey, "Church," *Systematic Theology*, II, ed. F. S. Fiorenza and J. P. Galvin (Minneapolis: Fortress Press, 1991), 16.

How has this been played out in Western ecclesiology since the sixteenth century? Protestant churches had their genesis in efforts at reform over against the Roman Church. In that respect they represent partial or particular ecclesiologies. The movement to redress the ensuing division among the churches began in earnest with the missionary movement of the nineteenth century which gradually opened up to the ecumenical movement in the twentieth. Roman Catholic ecclesiology from the sixteenth century up to the Second Vatican Council was also implicitly polemic and had the Roman Catholic Church as its ecclesiological paradigm. The universal church was identified with the Roman Catholic Church as the object of the discipline. One of the revolutionary aspects of Vatican II was the official recognition of other ecclesial bodies as churches.[29] The twentieth century, therefore, was a watershed; from the perspectives generated during the course of the ecumenical movement everything looks different. Within the context of the whole church one can transcend one's own church, project a broader vision, think more inclusively, and begin to recognize elements within the doctrine of one's own church that justify a positive appreciation of the other churches. For example, Vatican II taught that virtually the whole Christian movement shares the same Christ, baptism, and faith, and is animated by the same God as Spirit. Nothing compares in importance. But this in turn relativizes without dismissing particular juridical understandings of individual churches. One cannot presume without comparison and argument that they are in any measure universally normative. The particular provisions are by no means done away with or minimized, but they are put in their logical place as provisions of a particular segment of the church. They thus appear as particular, historical, and changeable institutions.[30]

---

29. Francis A. Sullivan, *The Church We Believe In: One, Holy, Catholic and Apostolic* (New York and Ramsey, N.J.: Paulist Press, 1988), 23–65, documents this with the appropriate nuance in the texts of Vatican II.

30. The logic that is being described here appears very clearly in the common statements that are produced in bilateral ecumenical dialogues. It also appears in theological essays that are devoted to generating an ecumenical consensus on any particular matter. One could say that all this amounts to is simply that all ecclesiology should be ecumenical. But one could also say that a common method for ecclesiology will absorb the ecumenical problematic into itself; ecumenism will cease to be a topic of ecclesiology. For, in the context of historicity, no church can even understand itself except

Pluralism of ecclesiologies. The historical character of the object of ecclesiology and the part-whole dialectic that this imposes on the discipline reveal a first limitation or restriction of the very meaning of ecclesiology. There will never be a single ecclesiology. Materially speaking, no ecclesiology will be able to encompass the whole church. For not only is the whole church constantly changing so that nothing in it, including any one of its parts, remains quite the same, but also, at any given time, the whole church always bursts the boundaries of the particular point of view that every ecclesiology imposes on its subject matter. Presently ecclesiology as a discipline, therefore, does not share a single common body of truths. Whatever unity it may possess might be gained on the level of method. But one has to expect different ecclesiologies based on different shared suppositions and premises that are dictated by the different situations of the churches. Even if one could agree on certain features of a common method in ecclesiology, the differences of perspective in and on the world-church will necessarily generate different understandings of the whole. This in no way voids the discipline. If ecclesiologists generated a set of presuppositions, axioms, and principles that were shared in common, ecclesiology would then be able to become eclectic; as in some ecumenical dialogues, ecclesiology becomes constructive on the basis of critical or dialectical conversation between segments or parts of the one church.

The Method of Ecclesiology

Various considerations of the method of ecclesiology run counter to an ecclesiology founded on authority alone. The method of ecclesiology should not differ substantially from the method of theology generally. Unlike other theological disciplines, however, the direct object of ecclesiology is a finite reality, a social movement and institution that understands itself in faith as responding to God's grace. What kind of reasoning, or what pattern of thought underlies, guides, and determines the assertions that are made about the church? Method in this sense is not a formula for producing the

---

as part of a historically, and not simply eschatologically, more universal church and, therefore, as relative to and a part of that whole church.

same results by all theologians; theology is not a hard science, and a similar method in ecclesiology can yield a variety of understandings of the church. The following characteristics of ecclesiology and the criteria of theology described in a later section suggest a method definite enough to be distinctive and open enough to admit a good deal of variety.

Historical. Because the visible church is a this-worldly, historical, and social entity or movement, the method that studies it must be historical. The first step in answering any substantial question about the church consists in going back to the history of the movement. The church is a historical tradition. In order to understand what it is, or any element within it, one must begin by tracing its origin and practice in history.[31] The historical and sociological character of ecclesiology protects it against the "theological reductionism" described earlier. An exclusively theological and doctrinal language will easily drift away from the concrete historical reality that the church actually is and present it in idealist terms that are scarcely credible to the critical observer. There will always be a fruitful tension between the ideal and the real in ecclesiology. As a normative discipline ecclesiology seeks to change the church by proposing theological ideals. But these ideals still have to keep close to actualities and real possibilities.

Sociological. Another level of analysis characteristic of the ecclesiology from below employed here involves a social-anthropological imagination.[32] The deliberate vagueness of the term "imagination" is meant to allow space for the disciplines of cultural anthropology, the sociology of knowledge, a social anthropology, and more purely sociological analysis of human groups, movements, organizations, and communities. Some authors in these disciplines are not far from

---

31. One can say that the church is constituted by an objective element and a subjective appropriation of it by the community. "The objective moment involves reference to the founding and perennially constitutive means that center around the life, teachings, death and resurrection of Jesus Christ." Komonchak, "Church," 232.

32. C. Wright Mills defines the sociological imagination as that which "enables us to grasp history and biography and the relations between the two within society." *The Sociological Imagination* (New York: Oxford University Press, 1959), 6. For the role of sociology in ecclesiology see Sanks, *Salt, Leaven, and Light,* 27–30, and Komonchak, "Ecclesiology and Social Theory," *passim.*

offering a socially conscious philosophical anthropology. In any case, the sociological imagination that explicitly understands the human as socially constituted, so that every person is a social individual, provides another level in the analysis of the original self-constitution or formation of the church. On the one hand, these analyses permit one to perceive common patterns in the way the church developed. On the other hand, the customs and social habits thus formed can be related to fundamental human needs that transcend the contingency of these circumstances. Social analyses from these various perspectives give the historical data roots that extend below the surface of temporal and local immediacy. They thus broaden and expand the meaning and consequence of what otherwise might appear as sheer contingency.

Theological. This historical social institution is also related to God. It is a gathering together of people on the basis of a common faith in God; it is this common faith that most deeply unites the church. As a result, the church is constituted by its relationship to God. This can be understood on two levels. The self-understanding of the membership that makes up the community construes it objectively as the gift of God. And, more existentially, this faith experiences God as Spirit actively present to the church and, as it were, holding it together. An illicit sociohistorical reductionism would fail to take into account this element which makes the church distinctively different from other social bodies. An exclusively historical and sociological language will easily leave behind the effects of God's grace operative within the church. This dimension of the church requires the theological language that appeals to transcendence and faith.[33]

It was said earlier that these two languages are about one reality. One can formulate an axiom for holding them together so that neither one drifts away from the other as follows: the church's relationship to God can only be understood integrally as mediated in and through its relationship to the world, history, and society; and

---

33. In parallel with Gustafson's definition of *theological* reductionism cited earlier, social-historical reductionism refers to an exclusive use of social and historical language in the interpretation of the church. See also Komonchak, "Church," 226.

the church's relationship to the world can only be understood adequately on the basis of its relationship to God.[34] This axiom joins the two languages about the church together and provides a criterion for the adequacy of any specific characterization of the church or any element in it. Theological explanations of the church cannot bypass human, finite, historical intelligibility. Social explanations of the church must account for the common faith of its members.

Apologetic. The term "apologetic" describes a general characteristic that theology should bear in our current situation. It does not mean a theology that proves or demonstrates the data or conclusions of faith, for this cannot be done. Rather it signifies a critically conscious method that seeks to explain, or render intelligible, or make understandable and comprehensible the beliefs of the community.

Traditionally, apologetics was addressed to the outsider, as in the theology of the apologists of the second century who sought to explain Christianity to the Roman empire and Hellenistic culture. Today, the function of addressing the outsider may be transposed in terms of using a public language and appealing to common human experience. This appeal to common human experience and use of a public language can be seen to be required from several points of view. In our pluralistic world, one cannot simply use or appeal to the "private" language of one's own group if one wishes to communicate to society at large. And since the common language and experience of a culture is found also *within the church,* one must use this common experience and language in order that the church will make sense to its own members. If one does not, then the internal language of the church becomes cut off from everyday experience and life in broader society.

Finally, this apologetic language also has the function of defending the language of faith and belief against interpretations of reality that either systematically ignore it or are hostile to it.[35] It does this by rendering the language of faith not only intelligible but credible in opposition to visions that seem to negate it. Thus the critical quality

---

34. Roger Haight, "Historical Ecclesiology," *Science et Esprit* 39 (1987): 356–57.
35. See Johann Baptist Metz, *Faith in History and Society: Toward a Practical Fundamental Theology* (New York: Seabury, 1980), 3–13.

of an apologetic ecclesiology applies both to the church itself and to views that are hostile to the church.

Hermeneutical. If theology generally speaking is a hermeneutical discipline, so too is ecclesiology. But theology is such a discipline. Therefore, as far as ecclesiology is concerned, it always consists in going back to the history of the church and bringing forward its self-understanding by interpretation and appropriation. This must be done in such a way that that understanding is relevant to the world or situation in which the church exists at any given time. Such interpretation always involves, however implicitly, some form of a method of correlation.[36] And this entails bringing into conjunction the data about the church from tradition and the present-day context or situation within which current understanding must unfold. It is not my intention here to develop the elements of a method of correlation, which are well known.

The Sources of Ecclesiology

That which is to be interpreted in ecclesiology is the church, for this is the subject matter. This church of the past exists today primarily as a lived tradition. Certainly the church today is constituted by its past, but the church of the past is also represented to the present objectively through textual witnesses. Those written records provide the sources of ecclesiology in scripture, church history, the confessional doctrines of the churches, and common human experience.

Scripture. The primary source and norm for Christian theology is scripture; this is recognized by virtually all theologians. Scripture is the norm which is not itself normed by any other norm. The reason for this is that the scriptures are the constitution of the church.[37] Scripture is such a constitution because it is the first record of the founding, revelational experience of Christians which the church decided early on to make its canon or rule of faith.[38] Another reason for the primary normativity of scripture in an ecumenical context

---

36. Haight, *Dynamics of Theology*, 189–95.

37. See Karl Rahner, *Inspiration in the Bible* (New York: Herder and Herder, 1961), 47–50.

38. See James Barr, *The Bible in the Modern World* (London: SCM Press, 1973), 114–18.

is that it is the one norm which all churches agree on and share in common.[39]

All of this does not imply that the meaning of scripture is obvious for our time; the scriptures have to be and always are interpreted. Nor is it true that one authentic, genuine, or true interpretation of scripture rules the day. The New Testament itself presents a pluralistic interpretation of Jesus and the church, one which not only lies open to diverse interpretations but also normatively prescribes pluralism. And, finally, there is no single method for interpreting scripture. Reliance on scripture, then, is only one source among others for the theology of the church. It provides a necessary norm, but by itself hardly a sufficient one.

Church history. An axiom of historical consciousness would affirm that the human is historically and socially constituted, and that all particular understandings of the human phenomenon are intrinsically limited. Therefore, to understand the human one must chart its history. Understanding of a particular phenomenon of history always begins with origins. The only way to understand a historical institution or movement is to comprehend its origins and subsequent history. Thus the history of the church provides another source for understanding the church. One part of this historical reconstruction consists in the history of the doctrine of the church and of theologies about the church. For history includes the experience, the interpretation, the receiving, and the assertion of the tradition within ever new situations. These testimonies to the nature and mission of the church provide cumulative data for an understanding of the church.

But it is important to note that the meaning of "history" here transcends the history of doctrine to include as well and perhaps more importantly the concrete praxis of the church in history. Expanding what was said earlier on the empirical church, the institutional history of the church and the history of the praxis of the church often reveal more about the nature of the church than what the church says about itself, both positively and negatively. An actual pastoral practice may contradict or subvert an explicit doctrine. The praxis of

---

39. Küng, *The Church*, 292.

the church may be used as a hermeneutical principle for understanding what the doctrines mean. Corporate praxis may be the source of a particular doctrine. In general, focusing on the concrete life of the church gives one a way of opening up the meaning of the history of doctrine contained in both the scriptures and the history of doctrine. This praxis of the church, moreover, is susceptible to many different kinds of analysis. One may use sociological, cultural anthropological, political, or economic categories to get a fuller theological understanding of the religious praxis of the church that lies beneath its doctrinal witness.

Confessional doctrines. Another source of data for understanding the church is the confessional doctrines or teachings of the particular churches. At this point, given the first part of this discussion, one must presume that the subject matter of ecclesiology is the whole church. But this is inevitably approached by each theologian from the perspective of his or her own particular church and its doctrines. In fact the church is divided, and for all practical purposes every Christian who actively participates in the church does so within a particular confession, communion, and tradition, that is, a particular church with its distinctive doctrines and polity. Thus the doctrines and way of life of this particular church, insofar as these are internalized, constitute a framework for understanding the church or the focal point through which the church is interpreted. This raises the question for ecclesiology of the normative value of the doctrines of one's own church for understanding the universal church.

Several things can be said on this delicate question. First of all, these doctrines cannot presumptively be taken to be normative for the whole church. They provide a view on the whole church. And insofar as they refer to the whole church, which is in fact pluralistic, their universal applicability must be the fruit of critical dialogue and not a priori assertion.

Second, it cannot even be maintained that these doctrines as they are stated and without remainder are normative for the particular church in question. These doctrines are data for interpretation; they cannot not be interpreted; and merely to assert them is to interpret them. Therefore, in terms of ecclesiological method, these doctrines are authoritative data to be interpreted. All structures and all doctrines are changeable because in fact, willy-nilly, their meanings and functions do change. One has to work at retrieving continuity and sameness in their meaning and function. Thus even for a particular church the doctrines that define its ecclesiology are subject to reinterpretation.

Third, the doctrines of the particular churches should always be understood against the horizon of the great or whole church. When they are thus situated, one can easily recognize that their particular truth and value may not be exclusive. That is, they can be true at the same time that other doctrines, which are different and on the surface contrary, may also be true and valid.

Historical experience. Another source for ecclesiological reflection is actual historical experience. The term "experience" is an ambiguous category. Sometimes it seems to point to a level of human consciousness that is below or prior to reflective conceptual awareness. Sometimes it refers to what passes for immediate or direct perception. But the term is used here with as general a scope as possible simply to refer to the sum total of present-day common knowledge that defines our perception of reality. Experience, therefore, exceeds a narrow theological framework. The insistence on experience as a source of data for ecclesiology may seem from one point of view redundant, for all human knowing unfolds within the framework of experience. But at the same time it makes the point that common human experience at any particular time enters intrinsically into every understanding of the church. Common experience provides a source for ecclesiology because appreciation of the other data can never prescind from the broader framework of current meanings and values shared by "all" people.

Because this experience should be appropriated critically and self-consciously, it is referred to as common human experience. This stands in opposition to merely individual or private experience which, in the same measure, may be eccentric and idiosyncratic. Such common human experience can be found in objective and public form within or by means of the human sciences. This common human experience is the ever-present and changing catalyst that continually calls into question accepted interpretations of the other data for ecclesiology and thus drives the discipline forward with new questions.

These four sources, scripture, church history, present-day Christian beliefs, and common human experience, supply data about the church that are rich and diverse. Ecclesiology is not a simple discipline; its complexity calls upon a variety of disciplines and kinds of expertise. I move now to another dimension of ecclesiology, namely, its theological grounding in the presence and activity of God as Spirit.

The Role of God as Spirit in Ecclesiology

The symbol "Spirit" in the Jewish and Christian scriptures represents God as immanently present and active in the world: in creation, in prophets, in charismatic leaders. God as Spirit is one of the symbols expressing the experience of God at work within the parameters of space and time: in world events, in the nation, in the community, and within the self. The renewed activity or "pouring out" of the Spirit during and especially in the wake of Jesus' ministry was a sign that God acted and is acting decisively in Jesus of Nazareth: in his life, death, and especially his resurrection. Luke forcefully and dramatically portrays the role of the Spirit in the church in Acts in the events of Pentecost: divine presence and action, in the name of Jesus, toward a mission to extend Jesus' ministry of the kingdom of God in history. The church is the community of God as Spirit unleashed into world history in the name of Jesus.

The main sources that we have for tracing and understanding the beginnings of the church are the New Testament along with some other noncanonical texts. Directly or indirectly the whole New Testament is a witness to the development of the early church. A critical theological appropriation of these many different kinds of texts requires distinctions among the various symbols used to express the way God was and is at work in the formation of the church. For example, Jesus of Nazareth is portrayed in various ways as of and from God, and the church as movement emerged out of his person and ministry. God as Spirit symbolizes the animating and driving divine force all along the process of the gradual formation of the church: this is portrayed dramatically in the life of Jesus and in the disciples after Jesus' departure. The risen Christ presents himself to the gathered community, especially in the eucharistic meal. Sometimes the risen Christ and God as Spirit appear interchangeable, so that the presence and activity of the risen Christ in the church is synonymous with the presence and work of God as Spirit in the name of Jesus. To make these distinctions, however, does not mean that the usage across the New Testament is consistent or can be rationalized. This symbolic religious language does not intend tight or exclusive definitions; the New Testament is a collection of different works by different authors in different contexts; it opens up experiences and meanings that remain untidy, overlapping, unsystematic, and pluralistic.

A historical appreciation of a developing early church forbids the idea of Jesus setting up a structured Christian church during his lifetime. It also suggests that the distinction between Jesus during his lifetime and the latter interpretation of him as the Christ be maintained in understanding and speaking about the genesis of the church. Moreover, several factors suggest that the symbol God as Spirit better portrays the presence and activity of God to the process of how the church came to be than does the symbol "Christ." The language of God as Spirit at work in the Jesus movement allows full range to human freedom in the development of the church as an organization. God as Spirit implies divine presence, power, energy, inspiration, and enthusiasm. "Spirit" language, however, should not be understood as opposed to or exclusive of "risen Christ" language; God as Spirit in the emerging Christian community was intimately bound to the person of Jesus.[40] The Spirit keeps alive the prophetic meaning of Jesus; the Spirit sustains the church as an indwelling

---

40. The designations "christocentric ecclesiology" as opposed to "pneumatocentric ecclesiology" have to be used cautiously. The distinction tends falsely to dichotomize because a circle can only have one center. In the New Testament, the Spirit of God generally is associated with Jesus, and Jesus is the one empowered by God's Spirit. This intimate linkage accounts for the development of the doctrine of the trinity. Therefore all Christian language about the church is implicitly trinitarian in its source. Some ecclesiologies will give more weight to the role of God mediated through Jesus or the Risen Christ in the church; and others will place more emphasis on the role of God as Spirit; but neither Spirit-language nor Christ-language can dispense with the other. This issue is more appropriate to systematic ecclesiology; one can see displayed in this work ecclesiologies that give more attention to Christ and others to the Spirit. But to call them christocentric or pneumatocentric risks raising a false problem unless the distinction is recognized as a matter of emphasis. But this does not mean that

guide and impelling source of power within the life of the community, binding, as it were, absolute past and absolute future. In all of this, Spirit language suggests more the work of God from within the community, less an external power operating on the community. God as Spirit is the reason why the emerging church community itself is one reality in two languages, a human social-historical reality but one with theological depth and height.

The Historicity of the Church

The turn to history in the study of the church has accented a historical consciousness and a "sense of historicity" with reference to the church. As was said in the opening paragraph of the chapter, nothing, absolutely nothing in history does not develop and change; existence in history is synonymous with movement: life and death, novelty and entropy, even in the material order. In the sphere of human existence in freedom, the experience of change today is dramatic and overwhelming. When this cognitive background is brought to a focus on the church, the perennial question of sameness and change itself changes as it receives a new formulation. The question presents itself no longer as "Can or does the church change?" The question is rather "Can there be any permanence and stability in the church's structures, values, beliefs?" A formal structure may remain in place, but its meaning and function shift. Values and ideals of one age and culture are never the same in others, even when the words remain the same. The language of belief, doctrine itself, takes on new meanings in new situations. How is the church to measure its identity and continuity with its past in history?

The response to the question of sameness and difference across history must be given in historical terms: no sameness without accompanying difference, analogous sameness amid difference, continuity and analogy across differences of time and place. The subject matter of this book in large measure consists precisely in a charting of the changes and continuities that mark Christian history. Within this history of change one will find the development of institutions

---

the different emphases do not entail trajectories and consequences; they can make a difference.

that have lasted over time, stable values that take on new relevant meanings in new situations, and a set of beliefs that in their changing forms expressed constant self-defining Christian perceptions of reality.

Ecclesiological criteria. The further normative question of how one adjudicates between changing structures, values, and beliefs, however, raises the issue of the criteria of ecclesiology as a discipline. These follow the general criteria of theology itself transposed to the narrower subdiscipline that deals with the church. The three criteria are fidelity to the past, intelligibility and coherence today, and empowerment into the future. To these may be added communion with the church as a whole.

First, ecclesiology deals with the church which is a historical tradition. This means that the church is its history. One cannot sit down and design a church out of whole cloth. The only church that exists and can exist is the particular one that has come to be out of its past. The identity of the living church is bound to its past history, and this past history defines this church as distinctively itself. In terms of theological method, and for theological reasons, this correlates with the normativity of scripture. One criterion of ecclesiology is its faithful correspondence with scripture and its continuity with at least the self-defining landmarks in the history of the church.

Second, and in dialectical tension with the last point, one's interpretation of the church at any given time cannot be completely limited to its past, but must transcend it. For not only is the church constantly changing by virtue of its historical existence, but also present-day understanding of the church must be intentionally geared to this change. Ecclesiology seeks to affirm the truth about the church, and such truth can only be affirmed within the context of what is intelligible within a contemporary context or horizon of understanding. The exigency of truth, then, means that one must affirm what the church is or can be today and not what it was in the past. Ordinarily this is done under the pressure of the critical questions about the church that have arisen at any given time. The second criterion of ecclesiology, then, is intelligibility and coherence. What is said about the church must be intelligible to people of any given culture and coherent both with other doctrines and with other things that are known about the world through common human experience. This will be displayed in changing structures of the church and shifting doctrines about the church and about the world.

Third, ecclesiological interpretation must not only be traditional, coherent, and intelligible, it must also be empowering. It was said earlier that the corporate praxis of the church constitutes it in the present. This sets up a reciprocal and mutually conditioning relationship between the self-understanding of the church and the praxis that constitutes it. But this means that understanding of the church bears upon the praxis of the church, the lives lived by its members. Ecclesiological understanding is drawn from the church's past praxis and is essentially oriented toward praxis into the future. If ecclesiological positions do not empower any praxis at all, it is fairly safe to say that they are irrelevant and negligible. Positively, like all understanding, ecclesiology contains an intrinsic orientation to human living. This category of empowerment, then, introduces ethical reasoning and moral norms into criteriological thinking about the church.

Finally, the whole-part dialectic of the church implicitly contains the criterion of communion. It is difficult to imagine an authentic Christian church that cuts all ties to other churches. An exclusive Christianity mirrored in an isolated church would negate the very message of Jesus upon which the church should be founded.

These dimensions of a hermeneutical method of correlation and these criteria for theological adequacy entail some other practical axioms that become operative in the study of different specific topics within ecclesiology. But at this point I want to conclude with a summary statement of an ecclesiology from below that runs parallel to and in contrast with an ecclesiology from above.

ECCLESIOLOGY FROM BELOW

The factors considered in the last section make up forces that together have pushed ecclesiology toward the adoption of new suppositions and descriptors. These six categories describing an ecclesiology from below are designed in counterpoint to an ecclesiology from above to enable a comparison and to heighten the contrast. I do not have to repeat the limitations of this kind of exercise and the cautions with which such a sketch is to be understood.

Postmodernity

All theology is bound to some culture and historical situation; no theology can prescind from it; every theology should explicitly identify its place in a context and the problematic that drives it. For a theology to pretend to be above culture or to claim that it can speak adequately for all cultures invites appraisal as either naive or intellectually dishonest.

I have referred to the culture addressed by this book as postmodernity, a term which too requires further specification by each one who uses it. In this work postmodernity remains a context out of which the work is written; it is not explicitly addressed. The category does not refer to a set of doctrines, nor to the specific positions assumed by individual authors who are often called postmodern. The word, instead, points toward an ill-defined and diffuse set of experiences that are shared by many educated people around the world, and which feed into what can loosely be called a "culture." This culture is defined precisely by this set of experiences, ideas, values, and symbols that are relatively new and go beyond what is usually referred to as modern.[41] Such experiences include: a historical consciousness that is deeper and more radical than that of modernity; an appreciation of pluralism that is suspicious of all absolute or universal claims; a consciousness of the social construction of the self that has completely undermined the transcendental ego of modernity and, ironically, encouraged a grasping individualism; a sense of the size, age, complexity, and mystery of reality that modern science never even suspected. One can participate more or less in this postmodernity; the experiences that characterize it may be weakly or strongly shared; one can remain modern and still be affected by postmodernity and seek to address it appreciatively. But whatever one thinks of the category of postmodernity, one cannot prescind from the historical context in which one lives, and this deliberately

---

41. T. Howland Sanks, "Postmodernism and the Church," *New Theology Review* 11 (1998): 51–59.

vague characterization of today's intellectual culture at least allows this strong affirmation: things are different today than they were, and one cannot avoid being affected by the new things that are happening in our world.

The Whole Christian Movement as Object

Whereas an ecclesiology from above ordinarily fixes on a particular denomination as its object, an ecclesiology from below takes as its object the whole Christian movement. It is true that every ecclesiology will ordinarily be conceived and written from a particular ecclesial perspective, since a particular ecclesiologist will belong to a tradition which will be reflected in the work. But the appeal to experience and a critical, historical differentiation of the imagination invite an effort to transcend the particularity of one confession or denomination. When the outsider looks at the Christian church, he or she does not immediately see the divisions among Christians. And when Christians regard the differences among themselves and other religions, the differences among themselves are minimized. The critical perspective that is being gained more and more in the wake of an astonishing globalization is having an impact that is consciously being internalized into ecclesiology. It is reinforced in a new way by the theological conviction that Christians really are united in their one basic faith, one baptism, and one Spirit, and that most of their differences need not be dividing. Pluralism is not only tolerable, it is a value. The ecumenical movement, including the whole rationale behind it, is another reason for positing the whole Christian movement as the explicit object of ecclesiology. If one designs an ecclesiology from the narrow perspective of one's own community without explicitly trying to transcend its boundaries, one effectively negates the ecumenical spirit and intentionality. Speaking of the church and referring to one's own communion is precisely what ecumenism seeks to overcome.

It is not easy to achieve the ideal here because of the actual divisions within the great church and the deep sensitivity to differences held by each particular communion. Moreover, it is impossible to achieve a neutral or a universalist perspective. A way of conceiving the perspective of an ecclesiology from below, however, might be expressed in the dialectical terms of a tension between the whole and a part. Every Christian church tradition, every communion, is part of the greater whole and the whole Christian movement is the object of ecclesiology. But the whole is always approached from the historically conditioned perspective of a particular tradition. Explicit consciousness of this dialectical situation will lead to a style of thinking that is consistently aware of the "other" and the particular and limited character of one's own perspective; it will also encourage an effort to imagine ecclesial forms that are open to and accommodate other perspectives on the church.

Foundation in Experience and Praxis

An ecclesiology from below in one way or another will make its appeal to experience. Such an ecclesiology forms part of a theology that has made a certain "turn to the subject" as the basis of its theological reasoning. For Christian theology the experience to which it appeals belongs to the Christian community, not an individual or particular group. This experience includes the praxis of the community; and this corporate praxis constitutes the main carrier of the tradition. The fundamental dynamics of this ecclesiology call for an analysis of Christian self-understanding in the past, especially in the formative period represented in the New Testament, through history to the present time. Its fundamental principles can be explained in terms that appeal to Christian experience past and present.

An ecclesiology from below will have an apologetic structure. By that I mean that it does not take its suppositions and premises for granted, but explains them in a critical or self-reflective way. A supposition in an ecclesiology from below is that the church exists not apart from the world, but as a part of the world, and in such a way that the world is not outside it, but inside it. Therefore, the categories and thought patterns of secular culture and everyday life become part of the experience, vocabulary, and self-understanding of the Christian community. Whereas an apologetic structure often means explaining oneself to others, since the world is inside the church, an apologetic structure means that self-understanding has to pass through cultural forms. More concretely, this will mean that an ecclesiology from below will use the various human sciences or disciplines in order critically to appreciate its own experience. The disciplines of critical history, sociology, social psychology, anthropology, and disciplines concerned with human management are not foreign to an understanding of the church.

A way of expressing this integration of the theological discipline of ecclesiology with other secular disciplines in understanding the church is proposed by Edward Schillebeeckx in his idea of one reality in two languages discussed earlier, or the simultaneous relevance of general and special categories.[42] The symbiotic relationship between the church and the world, or history, or human culture, means that the one reality which is the church must be understood in two distinct languages, the one secular, the other theological. But the crucial element in this construct flows from the one reality of the church which implies that the two languages cannot be separated. One language without the other distorts the reality of the church, for the two dimensions must continually be held together. The balance between these two dimensions will be echoed in the other characteristics of an ecclesiology from below.

Origin Understood in Historical Terms

Perhaps the characteristic of an ecclesiology from below which best describes its method is the employment of a critical historical method in understanding how the church developed. This move results from the shift in the suppositions and the basic framework of thinking that was outlined in the first point. An ecclesiology from below *begins with* a critical reconstruction of the origin of the church. The church is a historical phenomenon, and to understand any historical phenomenon requires an understanding of the events that caused it to emerge. This desire to know the historical and social mechanisms which brought the church into being penetrates deeply into the structure of the imagination that governs an ecclesiology from below.[43]

---

42. Schillebeeckx, *Church*, 211; Komonchak, "Church," 227.

43. The phrase "begins with" is stressed in the text in order to emphasize that this does not imply "ends with." But one should note that a historical-sociological reconstruction of the genesis of the church exerts an influence on one's theological understanding of it, because every theological construal of origins tacitly carries or implies an imaginative conception of how the church emerged in the first century. In

When this imaginative framework is in place, the New Testament will provide not only a theological source for understanding the church; it will also serve as a major resource for a historical reconstruction of the genesis of the church. Because it is one reality in two languages, the church will be understood theologically through its historical and sociological development. There is no reduction implied in an ecclesiology from below when it insists that the church is a product of historical and sociological development. On the contrary, this historical understanding provides a window for understanding how God works to form the church through Jesus Christ and through his disciples. Moreover, a historically conscious ecclesiology from below, precisely on the theological grounds that dictate the New Testament account as normative for Christian self-understanding, will find in the logic of the church's early development a paradigmatic fluidity and a responsiveness to rapidly changing conditions. The adjustment, change, development, expansion, pluralism, and authority that are all reflected in the development of the early church characterize the very structure of a living institutional community in history. It thus becomes clear that a genetic analysis of the self-constitution of the church for the first time also reveals the self-constituting character of the church at any given time. The structure of church-formation itself is opened up by the critical historical-theological analyses of the emerging early church.

An ecclesiology from below is open to the historical consciousness that has developed in late modernity and has been radicalized in postmodernity. In an ecclesiology from above, change is problematic and has to be explained. In an ecclesiology from below, change is a given; it is the condition of historical existence. Constant structures are problematic, because they are continually losing their relevance, and must be explained and adjusted. Ecclesiology from below is sensitive to the freedom and arbitrariness with which the church has moved through history. God as Spirit is recognized as the animating principle of the church, but God as Spirit cannot be grasped in objective terms of content and cannot be appealed to as a justification for

---

other words, ecclesiology from above also implies some historical-sociological account of how the church came to be. The problem arises when this is not explicitly laid out.

the various historical decisions or routes the church has chosen. God as Spirit accompanies faith and human freedom; God as Spirit may urge different decisions in different communities; the Spirit works through historical conditions and sociological patterns of behavior in the self-constitution and organization of the church. An ecclesiology from below is open to the categories of genuine novelty, of continuity by analogy, of fidelity to the past by means of historical adjustment.

Pneumatocentrism

The two theological foundations of ecclesiology are Jesus Christ and the Spirit of God; neither can be absent in an ecclesiology. "The Christian church is the community that results from the outer communication of Christ's message and from the inner gift of God's love."[44] But whereas an ecclesiology from above will tend toward christocentrism, the logic of an ecclesiology from below calls for a pneumatocentrism. Jesus is still the risen Christ, and the mediator of God to the Christian community. But the structure of an ecclesiology from below places more emphasis on Jesus as the historical source or head of the tradition, the Jesus movement, out of which the church emerged. God's experienced presence in the community is more spontaneously expressed by the symbol God as Spirit. Beginning with the story of Pentecost, the history of the community is a narrative of the way God as Spirit, sometimes identified with the risen Christ, accompanies and animates the growing and spreading body of Jesus' disciples.

It is important that this Spirit-centered understanding of the church not cut the experience of God as Spirit off from Jesus Christ. The Christian imagination measures its experience of God as Spirit by Jesus of Nazareth who is the Christ.[45] All experience of God has a historical mediation which identifies its content in some distinct way. And Jesus remains the norm for identifying what constitutes authentic experience of the Spirit within the Christian tradition.

---

44. Bernard Lonergan, *Method in Theology* (London: Darton, Longman & Todd, 1972), 361; also 360, 363.

45. I mean to define Christian experience here. The proposition does not exclude the experience of God as Spirit outside the Christian community, something that the Christian rather expects.

Christian experience of God as Spirit, then, is christomorphic; the memory of Jesus guides the language of the Spirit. Or, more positively, the memory of Jesus continually challenges Christian experience as it moves along the paths of history in a way that corresponds to Jesus' revelation of the rule of God. This allows for the significant variety of experiences of God as Spirit that one finds in the communities reflected in the New Testament. A pneumatocentric church adhering to Jesus Christ as its norm opens up to a good deal of pluralism.

Structures and New Ministries

An ecclesiology from below finds the theological grounding and source for ministry in God as Spirit, normed by Jesus Christ, and found present and at work within the community. Because the church is one reality with both theological and social-historical dimensions, an ecclesiology from below does not hesitate to find the sources of ministry in the actuality of the community at any given time. The sources of ministry do not lie exclusively in the past, but in a continuing present time, as God as Spirit is experienced in the community as it moves through history, and as an appreciation of these ministries has a broad, expansive norm in the memory of Jesus that is preserved in the New Testament and in the living tradition. The authority to evaluate and judge the prudent exercise of ministry and the establishment of ministerial forms or institutional organs of service does not lie above or outside the church, but precisely within the charism of the church as the community of the Spirit.

The communitarian grounding of ministries can be expressed sociologically and theologically by the principle of functionality. By functionality I mean the manner in which something gains its value from its relation and service to something else on which it is dependent. The dynamics of functionality are analogous to the interrelationship between means and ends: measures taken lead to certain results; and goals or projected results determine the means to be employed. The principle of functionality in ecclesiology refers to the way ministries were adopted in the church to meet the needs of the community. The institutionalization of the church proceeded according to sociological patterns of routinizing the charismatic ministry that addressed the needs of the community as they arose. The goal is always the well-being of the community and the exercise of its mission to continue the ministry of Jesus Christ in history. Whatever is needed to accomplish its mission, wherever there is a need to be met by a certain ministry, that ministry is provided spontaneously by the community in its self-constitution in and through God as Spirit.

An ecclesiology from below also understands the ministries of the church to be willed by and grounded in the will of God. But the connection with God is understood in a more historically conscious way. The principle of functionality, which from one point of view describes how the ministerial structures of the church emerged, also provides a principle or a criterion for the creation of new ministries. When there is a need or an exigency in the community, ordinarily it is met by an impulse to address it. Charisms in the church may be understood in a broad way as addressing such needs; and the routinization or the institutionalization of such charisms to guarantee their presence for the well-being of the community and its mission entails the creation of an office of ministry. In short, the criteria for new ministries are the needs of the community and the requirements for carrying its mission forward. These are held in an organic tension with origins and tradition, that is, the past of the church which accounts for its being in the present.

The theological grounding for this understanding lies in the presence of God as Spirit to the community. But it is important to understand this theological principle in terms of a critical epistemology of religious experience and in a historically conscious way. God as Spirit is not an object that can be directly known; no one has purchase on God as Spirit as something that can be objectively possessed. Negatively, when there is conflict, opposite sides make a claim on the Spirit. Positively, the quest for the enlightenment of God as Spirit is always in terms of discernment, which is at best a vague concept or process. Perhaps it is best to think about the process of establishing new ministries in terms of critical reflection by the whole community upon its own needs in the hope that, in trying to decide what is best for the community and its mission, God's providence and God's active presence to the community as Spirit will be at work in the whole process. This does not necessarily describe concretely the process of how such decisions are finally made. Ordinarily the churches have a variety of ways in which the ministry of oversight and administrative decision are accomplished. But the whole community supports this process as its ground and source. And God as Spirit symbolizes the divine correlate of the basic faith and hope of the whole Christian community as it continues to constitute itself anew in its movement through history.

On this understanding, the church can never be without the ministries it needs to pursue its mission. Ministry is not something that is added on to the community in history. The church *is* its ministry; the church is ministry in act. The ministerial functioning of the church constitutes the church at any given time in history to be the kind and quality of church that it is. A church with a defective ministerial structure is a defective church in the measure in which it fails to meet the exigencies of its mission. But, more positively, on this understanding the church never lacks the resources for actualizing those ministries it needs. One of the signs of the presence of God as Spirit in the church is precisely those movements in the church which strive toward the recognition of those ministries which respond to the demands of its mission.

•

This brief outline of method in ecclesiology with a focus on historical ecclesiology provides a number of the presuppositions that guide the analyses which follow. The chapters of this book are arranged chronologically. In each phase of the developing church that is blocked out for commentary I will characterize the historical context, the developments that occurred within the church, and aspects of the ecclesiological self-constitution and self-understanding of the period. The point of the inquiry and examination is to arrive at an appreciation of the developing and changing character of the church in the course of its history. This can be detailed in several discrete objectives. I want to show the extent to which the church changes and why. I want to capture as well the continuities of the church as found in the patterns of behavior which remain constant and the institutions that last. I want to discern and try to articulate the principles and axioms that one can detect constantly at work within the dynamics of its history, for these will help to understand the church at any given time and thus in the present period. And, finally, I hope to document certain permanent tensions, or dynamic interacting polarities, that drive the church forward in time. All of these insights will provide resources for a constructive and systematic appreciation of the church that will follow this historical ecclesiology.

Part II

THE FORMATION OF THE CHURCH

Chapter 2

Genesis of the Church

One of the keys that opens up an understanding of a social organization is familiarity with the story of its genesis. This explains why historians and theologians continually return to the origins of Christianity. The Christian church emerged in history as a product of historical development. It did not spring into existence all at once but over a protracted period of time. Opinions will vary on when the basic structure of the church was in place. The year 100 seems too early, since its organizational structure and foundational documents were still in a process of formation; some date within the course of the second century would appear more accurate, and an estimate would depend on what one considered constitutive of the essential nature of the church. The sources for grasping these beginnings yield the story only grudgingly to patient inquiry and not without debate.

This chapter discusses the genesis of the church through the first and into the second century with a fourfold analysis. The first traces the historical progress of the church's development. This narrative does not break new ground, but it provides a framework for the analyses which follow it. The second part of the chapter introduces a sociological and anthropological level of analysis. It tries to get at the socially defined human dynamics of the church's formation. The third part of the chapter offers a theological account of the foundation and development of the church. One should, of course, presuppose the influence of faith in Jesus and the Spirit's presence within the development toward an autonomous Christian church. A theological account of the church is not added on to the historical, but is discerned as implied within the historical development itself. The fourth, concluding section draws out of the data some principles and axioms for understanding the church.

Although this description of the earliest church is schematic and limited, the multidimensional analysis of the emerging character advances the point of this work: to contribute to an ecclesiology within the framework of critical reflection upon its life in history. The chapter does not provide an account of the contextual environment into which the church spread and grew but rather presupposes it.[1] One should read the sociological reflections as eclectic and not in terms of a unified, theoretical perspective.[2] The theological analysis selectively describes ways early Christians expressed faith in the presence of God to the dimensions of the church that was being formed. To these three levels of analysis, historical, social-anthropological, and theological, is added a fourth consisting of reflection on general, formal principles implicit in the data. Together these stages make up a genetic method for understanding church origins, that is, an application of the historical, social, and theological method developed in the last chapter. The analyses focus on how the elements that ultimately constituted the church came into being during the first 100 to 150 years. Two aspects in this development bear special significance for understanding the church. The first is the process of development itself, as distinct from but not excluding attention to the objective institutions that actually developed. What are the principles or dynamic processes that govern the development of the institutional forms of the church? Second, attention to the processes of the church's coming to be illumines its constitutional structure. Appreciation of the dynamics of the genesis or development of the church "for the first time" enables one to discern some general principles for understanding the church "at any given time." The chapter, therefore, aims at a first, open, heuristic understanding of the church in history. By directing attention primarily on the dynamic sociological principles manifested in the early historical development of the church, this method preserves the New Testament and earliest church history as a normative guide for understanding the church,

---

1. As in, for example, Gerd Theissen: *Sociology of Early Palestinian Christianity* (Philadelphia: Fortress Press, 1978) and *The Social Setting of Pauline Christianity* (Philadelphia: Fortress Press, 1982).

2. John A. Coleman assesses the use of sociology in the study of the New Testament in "The Bible and Sociology," *Sociology of Religion* 60 (1999): 125–48.

and at the same time postulates or anticipates new developments to meet new historical conditions.

EMERGING CHURCH:
A HISTORICAL NARRATIVE

The historian possesses few direct historical sources for the constitutive events of Christianity during the first and second centuries, but the confessional documents of the New Testament have been exploited to this end with remarkable ingenuity. The goal here is simply to give an account of some of the key turning points in the development rather than a detailed reconstruction. The perspective is one that attempts to look forward from beginnings in order to grasp the serendipitous character of the development, and not one that looks back from points reached by the development as though it were teleological. The six stages used to mark the development are somewhat arbitrary.

From Jesus to the Jerusalem Community

The origin of the Christian church goes back to Jesus of Nazareth. This does not mean that Jesus himself had no tradition or social formation; indeed, the Christian church is a breakaway movement from Judaism. But in many respects that will become clear, Jesus lies at the origin and center of the Christian movement. During his ministry Jesus gathered disciples; he taught them; it is likely that he sent them out to preach the kingdom of God that he preached. This is, as it were, point zero of Christianity: "Jesus has the disciples whom he has called participating in his 'messianic task,' which itself must be described essentially as a 'mission.' Here we are confronted with the real starting point of the primitive Christian mission: it lies in the conduct of Jesus himself."[3]

Jesus' personal mission culminated in his arrest, crucifixion, and death. Evidence suggests that this event left the disciples in disarray;

---

3. Martin Hengel, *Between Jesus and Paul: Studies in the Earliest History of Christianity* (Philadelphia: Fortress Press, 1983), 62. This view appears in an essay entitled "The Origins of the Christian Mission" whose point is to explain the expansive missionary character of Christianity.

many think they scattered in their confusion. And yet some time later, whether or not the traditional timing of two days is historically exact, the followers of Jesus gathered in Jerusalem confidently preaching that he is alive, exalted by God, raised from death. Between these two historical points one must postulate some kind of Easter experience, a sudden or protracted event that is reconstructed in various ways by theologians, but which accounts for their conversion or change of heart: he is truly risen.

Those who try to reconstruct the character of the Easter experience commonly refer to its "missionary" character. The disciples who affirmed that Jesus is alive by the power of God recognized this as God's validation of Jesus' career, ministry, or mission. The experience impelled disciples to affirm that Jesus' mission was God's mission and must go forward. This experience, whatever its exact character was, bore an intrinsic relation to Jesus' own activity during his ministry. Those who proclaimed Jesus alive-with-God after his death were his former disciples; Jesus remembered is the object of their experience; and the preaching they took up was Jesus' preaching. But with a difference: these disciples integrated the person of Jesus into his message. In their new confession of faith they announced not simply the kingdom of God but also Jesus as its mediator.[4]

Thus the religious movement begun by Jesus survived his death; it was established in Jerusalem in some respects on the same terms as during Jesus' lifetime, a movement within Israel, one of several different kinds of Jewish faith, hardly yet a sect, but bearing a distinctive allegiance. How did participants in the Jesus movement relate to other Jews? Did they separate to nurture their difference and new identity? Acts says that the first disciples attended the Temple together and broke bread in their homes (Acts 2:46). Was this in eucharistic memory of Jesus? Important here is the fact that this was not the only distinct movement within the Judaism of this time.

---

4. Joachim Wach believes that this accords to a pattern in the development of a new religious movement with the death of its charismatic leader. The original leader becomes a founder because the message that goes forward was his in the sense that it made its appearance in and through him. This is not a change in the message but part of the logic of its continuation in history. See Joachim Wach, *Sociology of Religion* (Chicago: University of Chicago Press, 1944), 138. I will come back to Wach's view later in the chapter.

From Jerusalem to Antioch: Tensive Relationship with Judaism

During this period, from the time of Jesus' death to around the year 50, the Jesus movement spread out of Jerusalem into Palestine, to the costal towns, and to other cities through travelers and missionaries, until significant events occurred in Antioch that brought about accommodations for Gentile Christians. Acts is a main source for these events, sketchy as it is, and what follows is Martin Hengel's reconstruction of this history.[5] But the distinction and inseparability of history and theology posited in the first chapter requires a commentary on this phase of the historical narrative which deals pointedly with Christian origins.

Practically speaking Luke provides the main source of information concerning the spread of the Jesus movement; he alone recounts the specific events beginning in Jerusalem and culminating in Antioch around the year 50. But rather than the church originating solely in Jerusalem, it seems more plausible that a variety of Jesus movements already begun in Galilee would have continued after Jesus' death. In fact the earliest Christian literature we possess shows a pluralism of communities with quite different relationships to Jesus.[6] Text by text the historicity of the early accounts of Acts can be called into question.[7] The basis of the problem is that Luke provides the sole source of the standard historical account of the emergence of the church through Jerusalem and in the writing of Acts operates on a constructive theological basis.[8]

---

5. Martin Hengel, *Acts and the History of Earliest Christianity* (Philadelphia: Fortress Press, 1980) and Hengel, *Between Jesus and Paul.*

6. "The pluriformity of the Jesus groups, together with the variety of mythologies they produced, is a very important recognition in recent scholarship. It is no longer possible to posit a monolinear trajectory of development, true to a single, original impulse from which these many different groups must be thought of as divergent." Ron Cameron and Merrill P. Miller, "Introduction: Ancient Myths and Modern Theories of Christian Origins," *Redescribing Christian Origins*, ed. Cameron and Miller (Atlanta: Society of Biblical Literature, 2004), 20.

7. Christopher R. Matthews, "Acts and the History of the Earliest Jerusalem Church," in *Redescribing Christian Origins*, 159–75.

8. See Burton L. Mack, "On Redescribing Christian Origins," *The Christian Myth: Origins, Logic, and Legacy* (New York/London: Continuum, 2001), 59–80. For example, on the existence of Hellenists in the Jerusalem church: "Luke invents the Hellenists because he and his community are Hellenists, who reckon their lineage back through Paul,

But the source of the problem also suggests a working strategy if not a solution. Because Luke provides the only historical narrative relative to these earliest years, his removal as source leaves a blank space. Those who discredit the historicity of Acts do not offer an alternative historical narrative but reconstruction on more theoretical grounds.[9] Because something happened between Jesus' death and Paul's ministry, and because Acts is the only account of it, we turn to it without making a case for the historical authenticity of any particular detail.[10]

Speaking broadly Luke depicts two cultural-linguistic groups in Jerusalem: Palestinian Aramaic-speaking Jews and Greek-speaking Jews more acclimated to Hellenic culture. Correspondingly, the Jesus movement contained Palestinian Jews and those whom Acts refers to as Hellenists who were attracted to Jesus. Thus both Hebrew and Hellenist Jews made up the Jesus movement (Acts 6:1), and the Hellenists themselves spread out along a spectrum of self-understanding from conservative Jewish to more deeply Hellenist. A serious dispute flared up among these Greek-speaking followers of Jesus polarized by Stephen. On the reckoning that Jesus was executed around the

---

who is understood after his conversion to have emerged as the principal spokesman for the Hellenist position." Christopher R. Matthews, "Luke the Hellenist," *Early Christian Voices: In Texts, Traditions, and Symbols. Essays in Honor of François Bovon*, ed. David H. Warren et al. (Leiden: Brill, 2003), 107.

9. It solves the problem by abandoning a historical reconstruction. Instead of tracing the history from Jesus to communities who profess him their founder, it shifts attention to the earliest communities themselves for which we have representative texts, understands the texts in terms of the social self-constitution of religious communities, and thus offers an understanding of Christian origins in terms of the self-constitution of groups by the activities of "*social formation* and *mythmaking.*" Cameron and Miller, *Redescribing Christian Origins*, 21.

10. Much of the criticism of the use of Acts in recreating the origins of the church is focused on using particular historical events to generate theological conclusions. No theological conclusions are drawn here from the historicity of the particular events narrated in Acts other than the fact of development itself. Luke's interpretive narrative is part of the history of this development. Luke's story is treated here much like the miracle stories in the synoptic gospels: the criteria of historicity point to the fact that Jesus actually performed wondrous deeds even though what he actually did cannot be reconstructed with historical accuracy. Analogously, it is historically certain that there was a community of the followers of Jesus in Jerusalem sometime after Jesus' death, and I see no reason why the existence of such a community stands in the way of other "original" communities, or plural interpretations of Jesus, or plural church organizations thereafter.

year 30, Hengel dates this Hellenist controversy between 32 and 34. The issue was an interpretation of Jesus that pitted him over against Temple and Law: "This man [Stephen] never ceases to speak words against this holy place and the law" (Acts 6:13). Stephen's preaching so aroused the conservative element among Hellenistic Jews (including Hellenistic Jewish followers of Jesus) that Stephen was summarily lynched and a more general persecution of the Jesus community broke out, forcing the leaders of Stephen's Hellenist wing to flee the city. "Now those who were scattered went about preaching the word" (Acts 8:4), indicating that these Hellenists, not "the apostles" (Acts 8:1), became the first missionaries to Samaria, the whole of Judea, Gaza, and cities to the north.

The scattering of the Hellenists bore momentous consequences for the Jesus movement of which Hengel underscores three. First, they translated Jesus' message into Greek and thus gave it a universal form and a worldwide relevance. Second, they preached in Greek to non-Jews and thus began the disconnection between Jesus' message and Jewish law. And third, by moving to other cities, they began the shift of a rural religious movement to an urban context. The Hellenistic community in Jerusalem "was the 'needle's eye' through which the earliest Christian kerygma and the message of Jesus, which was still indissolubly connected with it, found a way into the Graeco-Roman world."[11]

What about Peter and Paul during this period? Hengel dates Paul's conversion not long after the destruction of the group of left-wing Hellenists. He himself was a Hellenist at the orthodox Jewish end of the spectrum and converted to the type of interpretation of Jesus that he opposed. Little is known of Paul's work during the years after his conversion. "Paul's almost fourteen years of activity [after his conversion] in the then double province of 'Syria and Cilicia' (Gal 1:21; 2:1) form one of the great unknown areas in a history of Christianity. Virtually all that is certain is that it was in the milieu of the self-confident and active community in Antioch, that Paul's later program for the missionary conquest of the then known world was

---

11. Hengel, *Between Jesus and Paul*, 27, echoing Luke's theological construction.

gradually prepared and brought to maturity."[12] Peter, however, left
Jerusalem in the early 40s and became associated with Jewish Christians and Gentiles outside of Jerusalem. "When in about A.D. 43 or
44 King Herod Agrippa I, a friend of the Sadducees, had James the
son of Zebedee beheaded (Acts 12:2), arrested other members of the
community (12:1), and compelled Peter temporarily to leave Jerusalem or, more probably, the area of Palestine under the kings's control
(Acts 12:17), the more conservative James, the Lord's brother, with
his stricter attitude towards the law, took Peter's place in the earliest Jewish community."[13] Hengel depicts James as convinced that
the Jesus or "Christian" community could only survive within the
embrace of Judaism; Peter by contrast was more open to Gentile converts, as the story of Cornelius's conversion and baptism indicates
(Acts 10), and thus leaned in the direction of the Hellenists.

Around the year 48 in Antioch, where followers of Jesus were called
"Christian," the issue of whether Gentiles could be full-scale members without circumcision and thus bypass that aspect of ritual law
came to a head. A delegation was sent to the Christian-Jewish community in Jerusalem; this in itself indicates a certain dependence on
the part of Antioch and concern on the part of Jerusalem. Generally
speaking, this was not an entirely new issue, since Jewish synagogues
had been dealing with the same problem of a core of Jews and an
attached group of "godfearers" who were both part of the congregation and not, insofar as they were not circumcised. Such people
were tolerated in Jewish synagogues. In parallel fashion, Christians
in Jerusalem defended strict observance of Jewish law and rejected
entrance into the Christian community without circumcision. Nonetheless, the results of the consultation were positive for Antioch.
This was clearly a watershed decision, opening up the church to
the Roman empire in a new way. "Despite the inner tensions and
considerable suspicions, at the 'apostolic council' the Jerusalem community, which was by no means at one on this issue, in principle
gave the green light to a universal mission to the Gentiles which did

---

12. Hengel, *Acts and the History of Earliest Christianity,* 103. Hengel may overstate
Paul's intentions; at least Paul sought to establish Gentile communities throughout the
world.

13. Ibid., 95.

not call for obedience to the law."[14] Acts suggests that the Jerusalem church took responsibility for the mission to the Jews, and the
church at Antioch assumed responsibility for the mission to Gentiles. This would have given Antioch a large responsibility, raised the
community up to a significance alongside the mother community
in Jerusalem, and made it the staging area for the mission to the
whole Roman empire. But this accommodation still involved some
conditions and did not mean the complete separation of "Christians"
and "Jews."

The Pauline Churches: Communities Distinct
from the Synagogue

After the decisions at Antioch, Paul's missionary career flourished.
Besides founding Christian communities, he corresponded with a
number of churches he founded and thus provided future generations with a direct witness to certain aspects of these communities.
Paul's travels followed the trade routes of the empire and brought him
to urban centers: Ephesus, Philippi, Thessalonica, Corinth. Paul's
missionary career was eventful: he returned to Jerusalem; was im-
prisoned there but appealed to Rome as a citizen; suffered shipwreck
on his captive journey to Rome and, according to a second century
testimony, died in Nero's persecution between 64 and 68.

How did Paul go about preaching and establishing Christian communities? Did he go first to the synagogues as Acts 13–14 describes
his earlier missionary endeavors with Barnabas? Who else would
know what he was talking about? But why would the apostle to the
Gentiles go first to the Jews?[15] In Meeks's view, though he does not
rule out the Jewish connection, the neighborhood and especially trade
and work connections in the *polis* provided a link for meeting individuals and patrons who put their houses at the service of the apostle
and the movement. Who were the most likely converts to Christianity? A good hypothesis focuses on Jews and Gentiles interested in

---

14. Ibid., 122.
15. Wayne A. Meeks, *The First Urban Christians: The Social World of the Apostle
Paul* (New Haven: Yale University Press, 1983), 26.

Judaism who were at the same time thoroughly at home in Greek urban culture.[16]

The Pauline churches possess a distinctive character when contrasted to the community at Jerusalem.[17] These gatherings and communities-in-formation were urban; the environment was cosmopolitan and religiously pluralistic; all sorts of religious cults could be found. The Jews were Diaspora Jews who, while retaining their Jewishness as a minority in a polytheistic environment, remained culturally Greek and at home in their world. According to Meeks and others, the key to the Pauline church is the household. "Below the level of the ethnic quarter and the neighborhood of similar trades came the individual household. Our sources give us good reason to think that it was the basic unit in the establishment of Christianity in the city, as it was, indeed, the basic unit of the city itself."[18] Households of the relatively wealthy had stratified populations: immediate families, servants, employees, slaves, and wider kinship bonds. The household also served as the meeting place for clubs or associations. It thus fitted the needs of Christian assemblies. One has the sense that the Pauline churches did not split off from the synagogues but were communities that began in their own households, and thus enjoyed more autonomy relative to Judaism than assemblies in either Jerusalem or Antioch.

Authority in the Pauline Christian communities was also somewhat distinctive. Meeks breaks down the lines of authority into three large categories. The highest authority belonged to the apostle, who possessed it less in virtue of an office than as the function of being the missionary who founded or supported the community from the outside. Paul was the chief apostle for the Pauline churches, but there were many different apostles (as distinct from "the twelve"), and Paul had rival apostles in some of his churches. A second level of authority lay with "fellow-workers" of the apostle, a fluid category referring to emissaries, delegates, quasi-autonomous agents who could come

---

16. Rodney Stark, *The Rise of Christianity* (San Francisco: HarperCollins, 1997), 57–63.

17. They are also, in a lesser degree, distinct from the community at Antioch which is larger, older, and more closely connected with Jerusalem.

18. Meeks, *First Urban Christians*, 29.

and go or settle in. If they settled in, they became local leaders. A third level of authority, then, would be such local leaders, "those who labor among you and are over you in the Lord and admonish you," as Paul wrote (1 Thes 5:12). These were not three offices, but functions of various kinds of people who worked in various capacities including exercise of governing authority. It may be assumed that the patron of a house church would have had some governing authority. But other forms of "laboring" in the community obtained: there were prophets, teachers, miracle workers, healers, speakers in tongues, interpreters, discerners of spirits. The grounds for this authority consisted in an appeal to the Spirit as the source of these charismatic gifts.[19]

The Jesus movement reached Rome before Paul began founding churches, probably by the early 40s, through the travel connections between Palestine and Rome. The source was thus probably Jerusalem, so that the Roman church retained a certain Jewish character through the first century. Raymond Brown thinks that "Christians" probably met in Jewish synagogues in the 40s, but by the 50s would have moved to the houses of wealthier members with no overall or citywide superstructure. Brown characterizes this church in the 50s as consisting of both Jews and Gentiles with moderately conservative Jewish sympathies, to which Paul seems to have accommodated himself in his letter to this church.[20]

Subapostolic Churches: Breaking with Judaism

We possess little direct evidence about particular churches during the time after Peter and Paul, the second generation, roughly between 65–95. What is said here summarizes the analysis of those New Testament writings that fit in this period (Mark, Luke-Acts, 1 Peter, Matthew, Colossians-Ephesians, and John's gospel) and inferences about the church that can be drawn from them. The conclusions remain quite general and abstract.

---

19. Ibid., 131–36. I shall develop this in terms of theology on pp. 121–123 below.
20. Raymond E. Brown, in Brown and John P. Meier, *Antioch and Rome: New Testament Cradles of Catholic Christianity* (New York: Paulist Press, 1983), 92–127.

Raymond Brown believed it impossible to reconstruct a profile of the community addressed by Mark.[21] Yet using literary analysis one can characterize the self-understanding of the community represented there. Assuming the community is a small group, how does it understand itself in relation to the wider world? On the one hand, the gospel manifests an open, voluntaristic community, whose mission is to communicate the eschatological message of Jesus. Membership does not rest on hereditary qualifications, but on decision and conversion. On the other hand, it stands over against the world with its own "esoteric instructions, intended for those who are committed to Jesus and his words."[22] Life in this eschatological community unfolds within the understanding that fulfillment lies ahead when Christ comes again, when God who raised Jesus from the dead will also vindicate the community.[23] This understanding of the community as God's new covenant people, a new eschatological family, people, flock, vineyard, building, and so on, entails a certain ethic, the elements of which can be discerned in the portrayal of Jesus' teaching.

Luke's gospel, too, may not represent a particular community: it may reflect many communities, Hellenic in character, probably, like the Pauline churches, separated off from Judaism, who need a sense of historical connection with their origins.[24] This is an ecclesiology in narrative form. Together with Acts it tells the story of the continuity of God as Spirit working in the world for salvation from the time of Israel, through Jesus, and after his death in the church, in Peter for half of Acts, in Paul in the second half, to the center of the earth: Rome.[25] Analogously, one can characterize the church in Asia Minor addressed by 1 Peter as also needing confirmation of its identity as it exists as a minority group, partly Gentile, partly Jewish, perhaps

---

21. Raymond E. Brown, *The Churches the Apostles Left Behind* (New York: Paulist Press, 1984), 28.

22. Howard Clark Kee, *Community of the New Age: Studies in Mark's Gospel* (Philadelphia: Westminster Press, 1977), 165.

23. Ibid., 175.

24. Eugene A. LaVerdiere, in LaVerdiere and William G. Thompson, "New Testament Communities in Transition: A Study of Matthew and Luke," *Why the Church?* ed. Thompson and Walter J. Burghardt (New York: Paulist Press, 1978), 39.

25. Brown, *The Churches the Apostles Left Behind*, 61–74.

feeling cut off, in a religiously pluralistic world. In contrast to their perceived status in society as strangers, aliens, uprooted transients, and dangerous nonconformists, the letter describes the people in the household church as living within the religious tradition of Israel in continuity with the people of God from the distant past, i.e., part of a long tradition with an identity now defined by Jesus Christ as God's people. The church is also united with people all over the empire who share the same condition and a common experience. Along with this solidarity in a common identity comes a corresponding ethic, one typical of a household of God. Analogous to the Pauline communities, the idea of household provides a metaphor responding to basic needs: identity, unity, and ethics leading to a future with God.[26]

Exegetes are more confident about the setting and problem of the community reflected in Matthew's gospel. The gospel was written around 85 and portrays a community, or more loosely a group of house churches, in the area around Palestine and Syria, probably Antioch, which is in critical tension with the synagogue. Some say Matthew's community has broken away; others maintain it is a deviant community still within the Jewish fold; in either case it bristles with tension between itself and Jewish authority.

The identity of the community can be summarized in three aspects of its institutional base, the household.[27] First, the community's group relations were described with kinship language: God as Father and the familial mutual relations of brothers and sisters in God's family. This was the primary bond which, in the broader scope of the kingdom of God, was also cosmic. Second, Jesus was depicted as teacher, not a teacher, but the authoritative teacher. Members of the community became disciples, the ones taught, and the community or church was where they were taught. The author thus created a social identity vis-à-vis Jewish authority for this group by use of

---

26. John H. Elliot, *A Home for the Homeless: A Sociological Exegesis of 1 Peter, Its Situation and Strategy* (Philadelphia: Fortress Press, 1981), 220–33.

27. I am following Anthony J. Saldarini here: "In order to find the setting of Matthew's group and expose its inner fabric, we turn first to kinship terminology and the master-disciple relationships, then to the household, which was the seat of education and governance of life, and finally to the assemblies which met in the household." *Matthew's Christian-Jewish Community* (Chicago: University of Chicago Press, 1994), 91.

kinship and school language. And, third, these Christian *Jews*, in Saldarini's view, met in distinct households and employed the term *ekklesia* to designate themselves. Among its several resonances, this word connected these assemblies with assemblies of Israelites. The organization of the Matthean groups at this time bore the marks of the Jewish synagogue, but with an egalitarianism typical of some new religious movements. The deep structure of authority stipulated that only God was Father, and only Jesus was teacher and master.[28]

The church in Colossians and Ephesians is the body of Christ in a theological sense of Christ being the head of a corporation and people being called together into a mystical corporate union with him. The kingdom of Christ becomes objectified in a group, the object of special divine love, and a holy, sanctified people. "Holiness is a very important characteristic of the church as the body of Christ."[29] Christ died so that the church might be holy and without blemish. The divinity of Christ dwells within the church as Christ's body. This mystical and cosmic vision proposes a reconciliation of all reality, a church bridging the angels and humankind (Col 1:20; Eph 1:10). I will consider the theology behind this image later on.

The fourth gospel represents a community so distinct that it appears to some as "sectarian" relative to other Christian groups.[30] But one can imagine that every early Christian community had its own distinct and perhaps dramatic history. The ecclesiology of this community, however, cannot be separated from its distinctive high christology. Jesus is presented as one who preexisted; one with the Father, he enjoyed a life before being on earth. The church provides the environment in which each believer is united with God in Jesus Christ. This does not spell individualism: by inhering in Jesus one becomes part of the community. Christ is the vine; Christ is the shepherd; life depends on attachment to Jesus. The church appears as less the place of finding Christ than the result of finding

---

28. Ibid., 84–123.

29. Brown, *The Churches the Apostles Left Behind,* 51.

30. See the reconstruction of this community by Raymond E. Brown, *The Community of the Beloved Disciple* (New York: Paulist Press, 1979), who proposes reasons for not so estimating it.

Christetc.[31] One also finds in the Johannine community a highly developed sense of the sacraments, baptism and eucharist, that unite one to Christ, and a strong sense of discipleship, egalitarianism, and stress on mutual love.[32]

Theissen sums up first century Christianity by distinguishing four basic currents: Pauline Christianity represented by his letters; Jewish Christianity represented canonically by the Letter of James, Matthew, and Hebrews; synoptic Christianity represented by these gospels as combining both Jewish and Gentile dimensions; and Johannine Christianity with its distinctive prehistory and christology. Four currents with two tributaries, the one flowing from Judaism and the other from the Gentile world.[33]

Early Catholicism

As we will see in chapter 3, Rodney Stark has estimated that there were around 7,530 Christians in the year 100. They were spread throughout cities around the Mediterranean, from Alexandria to Rome and perhaps further west. One would expect that most Christians lived in larger cities, twenty-two of which are mentioned in the New Testament.[34] The narrative of this period is drawn from *1 Clement*, written from the church at Rome to the church at Corinth, the Pastoral Epistles, representing the Pauline churches a generation or two after Paul, the *Didache*, probably put together in the second century with materials from the first century and often thought to represent the church in Syria, and the letters of Ignatius of Antioch written to churches in Asia probably in the first decade of the second century.

A major concern among all the churches at this time was unity. The churches were becoming ever more distant from their origins in space and time. They were growing and with growth came new or false teachings, the sources of controversy and division. One response to the problem of unity, both within each community and among the

---

31. Brown, *The Churches the Apostles Left Behind*, 87.
32. Ibid., 84–101.
33. Gerd Theissen, *The Religion of the Earliest Churches: Creating a Symbolic World* (Minneapolis: Fortress Press, 1999), 254–56.
34. Stark, *The Rise of Christianity*, 7.

communities in different cities, was found in organization. "Early Catholicism" represents tighter and more standardized structures of ministry.

The organizational structures represented in these texts differ. *First Clement* addresses a situation in Corinth in which duly appointed presbyters have been put out of office by others causing division in the community. It urges the reinstatement of legitimately appointed leaders in the community.[35] The aim of the Pastoral Letters, written in the name of Paul, is to "ensure that competent and honorable officials protect the household of God against false teachers."[36] They also lay down criteria for those who would be fitted for such offices.[37] The *Didache* does not respond to a particular crisis, but as a manual of discipline represents an ordering of the community, a regularizing of organization, ritual, prayer, and moral expectations. Ignatius of Antioch responds to division and false teaching by urging a tri-partite order of community organization and ministry: the bishop, a clergy of elders who were assistants and perhaps a council, and deacons. "You cannot have a church without these."[38]

That seems a sudden and arbitrary claim at the beginning of the second century. Where did these organizational structures originate? No clear response to this question has been formulated, not for lack of information, but because so many different influences converge in their making. "There is no conclusive evidence that the early Christian communities were exclusively dependent for their pattern of organization on any one of the institutions which we have considered — Graeco-Roman cities, Roman colonies and cities, voluntary

---

35. Francis A. Sullivan, *From Apostles to Bishops: The Development of the Episcopacy in the Early Church* (New York and Mahwah, N.J.: Newman Press, 2003), 91–101 analyses this text for its relevance to structures of governance.

36. Margaret Y. MacDonald, *The Pauline Churches: A Socio-historical Study of Institutionalization in the Pauline and Deutero-Pauline Writings* (Cambridge: Cambridge University Press, 1988), 203.

37. James D. G. Dunn, *The First and Second Letters to Timothy and the Letter to Titus, The New Interpreter's Bible,* XI (Nashville: Abingdon Press, 2000), 867. *The New Interpreter's Bible* is cited hereafter as NIB. This work of Dunn will be cited as *Pastorals.*

38. Ignatius, "Letter to the Trallians," 3.2, *Early Christian Fathers,* ed. Cyril C. Richardson (Philadelphia: Westminster Press, 1953), 99.

associations, the family, or the Jewish synagogue."[39] More important
for our purposes, however, is a recognition that this historical question is not crucial for the normativity of the early church relative to
later institutional developments.[40] This development, then, was not
recorded in what became canonical literature and yet was historically
significant because Ignatius promoted this organizational structure
in the Asian churches and in the course of the second century it
became universal.

The first decades of the second century are important for another
reason: one can discern the beginnings of a major shift in the context
of the church's self-understanding from its status vis-à-vis Judaism
to its relationship to the Roman empire. This should not be over-
stated, for *1 Clement,* and thus the Roman church, and the *Didache*
are Jewish in character. And a case has been made that Jews continued to be the main source of converts to Christianity into the third
century.[41] Moreover, the break with Judaism was a gradual process

---

39. Andrew D. Clarke, *Serve the Community of the Church: Christians as Leaders and Ministers* (Grand Rapids, Mich.: Eerdmans, 1999), 169. J. T. Burtchaell, *From
Synagogue to Church: Public Services and Offices in the Earliest Christian Communities* (Cambridge: Cambridge University Press, 1992) makes the case of influence of
the synagogue's structure on the Christian church, which all admit in some degree.
Harrington reads in the Pastorals a process merging two forms of polity, one from the
East where the Jewish influence of elders predominated, the other the Pauline or Gentile tradition of bishops and deacons. At the time of the Pastorals these two distinct
church orders "were in the process of fusion. The *presbyteral* model found in Acts and
1 Timothy 5:17–20 (see also James 5:14; 1 Peter 5:5; 2 John 1; 3 John 1) was based
on the organizational model of the Jewish synagogue. The 'bishop and deacon' pattern
as it is mentioned in Philippians 1:1 and 1 Timothy 3:1–13 was founded more on the
structures of voluntary associations in the Greco-Roman world. It appears that in the
Pastorals, as in Titus 1:5–9, these two models were in the process of being put together." Daniel J. Harrington, *The Church according to the New Testament: What the
Wisdom and Witness of Early Christianity Teach Us Today* (Chicago: Sheed & Ward,
2001), 162.

40. This question will be taken up further on. But it makes little sense to argue that
monoepiscopacy is an absolute requirement today on the basis of the canonical Pastoral
Epistles which do not unambiguously affirm such a structure. In fact, the author of the
Pastorals "does not seem to be especially interested in promoting a particular type of
ecclesiastical organization in the way that Ignatius of Antioch, for example, seems to
be." MacDonald, *The Pauline Churches,* 219.

41. Stark proposes the thesis "that not only was it the Jews of the diaspora who
provided the initial basis for church growth during the first and early second centuries,
but that Jews continued as a significant source of Christian converts until at least as
late as the fourth century and that Jewish Christianity was still significant in the fifth
century." *The Rise of Christianity,* 49.

through various phases, and it transpired in different scenarios and timetables in different churches. But the principal point of separation lay in the conception of the person of Jesus Christ and the role he played in Christian spirituality. The gradual acceptance of Johannine christological language in the church seemed to compromise Jewish monotheism, and this sealed the breach.[42] Justin Martyr's *Dialogue with Trypho* indicates that this conversation was still going on in the middle of the second century. But as the church became more uniformly and stably organized, it also sought to define its own autonomous place in world history.

Theissen proposes a three-stage analysis of the break from Judaism and the formation of the church as an autonomous religion, one that correlates with the first three generations.[43] The first stage consisted in renouncing certain rituals that defined Jewish identity, most importantly circumcision. This reached a decisive point in the events at Antioch and Jerusalem in the years 48–50, and the significance was played out in the Pauline churches. The next step was taken in the generation after the destruction of the Jewish Temple and consisted in the writing of the synoptic gospels. The gospels contained an implicit canonical claim, and they provided Christians with their own narrative. By their portraying Jesus as a divine figure, they ratified the communities' sense of autonomy and distinction from Judaism. The final stage occurred in the third generation as represented in Johannine Christianity. In John "primitive Christianity not only made itself *de facto* independent of Judaism but also became aware of its inner autonomy."[44] John's gospel shows that the community gave Jesus an absolute status, so much so that Christians appeared to Jews to be abandoning strict monotheism. The reflective appropriation of Jesus' absolute and universally relevant status confirmed the break.

---

42. James D. G. Dunn, in *The Partings of the Ways: Between Christianity and Judaism and their Significance for the Character of Christianity* (Philadelphia: Trinity Press International, 1991), charts this development in terms of four pillars of Judaism: Monotheism, Election, Torah, and Temple.

43. Theissen, *The Religion of the Earliest Churches*, 161–206.

44. Ibid., 164.

The Church and the Empire

A chronicle of the development of the church in the second century would be out of place here, for this is the subject of the next chapter. But it is important to see in it a certain closure to the process of ecclesiogenesis of the first century. The church, as a movement of loosely affiliated communities, continued to expand territorially and grow numerically. Despite local persecutions, the main problems included internal threats from prophetism and gnosticism. These problems stimulated internal developments that enabled the early church to ensure its pristine identity in institutional forms. This can be indicated briefly by reference to two figures, Justin Martyr who flourished in Rome during the 150s and Irenaeus, bishop of Lyons in the last decades of the century. Justin's apologetic theology represents the church engaging the empire; Irenaeus represents a number of syntheses that came together in the course of the century.

The genre of an apology, of which Justin provides an exemplary form, signals an attempt to engage the world.[45] Insofar as the world is the state, Christians are loyal subjects; but they have a higher allegiance to God under whom the emperor himself serves. Relative to Roman culture and society, Christians too participated in everyday life. But insofar as social practices were idolatrous or ruled by demons, the ethical code of Christians kept them apart. This open confession or self-explanation went so far as a description of the most esoteric of Christian acts, the weekly eucharistic assembly. Justin describes in plain narrative language what Christians do at liturgy and how they pray. Christians thus related to the world in a real but nuanced and ambivalent way. Being a member of the church clearly involved a double loyalty, but one of the two was higher.

Irenaeus's work *Against Heresies* satirizes and pillories the wide variety of bizarre teachings proffering the secrets of salvation.[46] External threat to a community unites; internal threats cause fear and division; gnosticism appeared as an enemy within. The problem to

---

45. "The First Apology of Justin, the Martyr," *Early Christian Fathers*, 242–89.
46. Irenaeus, *Against Heresies*, in Robert M. Grant, trans., *Irenaeus of Lyons* (London and New York: Routledge, 1997).

which this text responds is widespread diffusion of speculative interpretations of Christianity within the communities themselves. The question is, how does one determine what are true and authentic beliefs? The one-word answer is apostolicity: what came from and goes back to the source is authentic. But how does one know what is apostolic? The classic response of the early church consists in the institutions that preserve and guarantee it. They are: first, the writings which were being formed into a canon; second, a succession of bishops who handed things down; third, a universal short formula of belief, the creed. Two other norms are also implied: the importance of a church in Rome, in which both Peter and Paul had resided, as a clearing house and a standard for the whole movement, and the universality of beliefs and practices held in common among the old churches.[47] But the great achievement of the second century is the development of a canon of scriptures, one that is pluralist, so that it preserves the tension between multiple strains of belief. Yet within the differences the foundational faith is preserved: monotheistic faith in God and in God's salvation mediated in Jesus. As the church moves forward in history it will reflect back on primitive Christianity as contained in these scriptures.[48]

The other synthesis reflected in Irenaeus lies in the large imaginative framework or metanarrative that provides a cosmic identity to the Christian community. It is seen in the catechetical work in which Irenaeus gives a short summary of the Christian faith in terms of salvation history.[49] History is meaningful in its coherence; it has a beginning, a middle, and an end; and Jesus Christ, the centerpiece, was operative in the beginning as creative Word and will act in the end as Judge. This large worldview, together with an organized church constituted in its beliefs by its scriptures, finally separates the

---

47. See the text from *Against Heresies*, 3.1–5 in *Early Christian Fathers*, 369–77.

48. Theissen, *The Religion of the Early Churches*, 249–74. "A" canon rather than "the canon" because the process did not reach closure until a later time.

49. Irenaeus, *Proof of the Apostolic Preaching*, ed. Joseph P. Smith (Westminster, Md.: Newman Press, 1952). Wayne Meeks highlights the importance of the breadth of Irenaeus's vision in his *The Moral World of the First Christians* (Philadelphia: Westminster Press, 1986), 160 and *The Origins of Christian Morality: The First Two Centuries* (New Haven and London: Yale University Press, 1993), 191.

church from Judaism and forms a clean boundary separating it from paganism. Christians are the third race.

A SOCIAL-ANTHROPOLOGICAL ACCOUNT

The historian is not completely limited to recounting positive data. At various levels the historian tries to make sense of the data, to construe it in a meaningful way. Often this involves instinctive, imaginative reconstruction. For example, if Caesar recounts that he is in one town at a certain date, and in another a few days later, the historian must imagine that he traveled from the one to the other. And knowledge of how armies moved in the first century BCE is helpful in the reconstruction. Analogously, insights from sociology, especially the sociology of organizations, will be helpful in understanding from a socially dynamic and anthropological perspective the gradual formation of the Christian community. These reflections, however, do not purport to establish a sociological portrait of the early church. They rather open a perspective on the formation and development of the early church from below. They introduce a social-anthropological language or set of categories and apply them to the church in order to introduce a level of understanding beneath or within the historical chronicle. Thus the following section remains intentionally schematic and amounts to an outline of how a sociological imagination must be integrated into an account of the early church. Recognition of the social construction of human response to reality is a good place to begin.

A Sociological Imagination

The sociology of knowledge. Contemporary intellectual culture, postmodernity, is acutely aware of the degree to which human organizations and evaluative human perception and knowledge are conditioned by historical place, time, and circumstance. Since the nineteenth century, and especially following the insights of Marx, sociologists and philosophers have analyzed the ways in which the deepest perceptions of reality are socially constructed, that is, influenced by a whole myriad of the social conditions that form the very framework within which experience unfolds. While this binds all knowledge to society, it does not entail relativism, because relative knowledge is still real knowledge. "Relativism does not imply subjectivism and scepticism. It is not evident that the man who is forced to confess that his view of things is conditioned by the standpoint he occupies must doubt the reality of what he sees."[50] More deeply, socially constructed customs and habits can be related to fundamental human needs that transcend the contingency of particular circumstances. Social analyses can thus give historical data roots that extend below the surface of temporal and local immediacy. They expand and deepen the meaning and import of what otherwise might appear as sheer contingency.

A particularly useful schematization of the dynamics of the social construction of knowledge is offered by Peter Berger and Thomas Luckmann.[51] They analyze three "stages" in the formation of the habitual knowledge of a group: a generalized social or group experience, the objectification of that experience in language to become the presuppositions of common sense, and the internalization of that "objective" knowledge to shape the patterns of experience and understanding of the group. This model, however, describes less a temporal process, more a theory of how these three dimensions or aspects of common knowledge have roots in social existence and are the result of a dynamic process of social interaction. The chronological aspect of this model, however, helps to clarify what is going on in this chapter. The analysis of the formation of the church defines not merely the genesis of an institution or an organizational structure but also of a way of life and a way of perceiving reality.

The study of the sociology of knowledge helps to engender what may be called a sociological imagination.[52] This phrase calls

---

50. H. Richard Niebuhr, *The Meaning of Revelation* (New York: Macmillan, 1962), 18. Karl Mannheim makes the same point: "Knowledge arising out of our experience in actual life situations, though not absolute, is knowledge none the less." *Ideology and Utopia: An Introduction to the Sociology of Knowledge* (New York: Harcourt Brace, A Harvest Book, 1985), 86.

51. Peter Berger and Thomas Luckmann, *The Social Construction of Reality* (Garden City, N.Y.: Doubleday Anchor, 1967), and Peter Berger, "Religion and World Construction," *The Sacred Canopy* (New York: Doubleday, 1967), 3–27.

52. Generalizing from C. Wright Mills, *The Sociological Imagination* (New York: Oxford University Press, 1959) where he develops the basic insight into the interconnectedness of the individual and society. See above, pp. 45–46.

attention to a certain way of appreciating human realities. Some elements of a sociological imagination are the following: a recognition of dialectical tensions in knowledge between objective statement and subjective experience, and between the objective statement of an individual or group and the community to which he or she belongs or the segment of the society that is being represented. Dialectical tension exists between an individual's experience and a socially mediated experience so that, for example, meaning does not simply lie "on the surface" of texts, and an author does not communicate directly with his or her reader. A sociological imagination recognizes the changeability of all social institutions because they are historical, dynamic units of multiple relationships and forces. The durable and constant elements of the human, of anthropology, must be discovered within this interrelational social matrix. Social structures themselves are historical, functional, pluralistic, contextual. For those who share in some degree in a postmodern culture, religious authority must be distinguished from mere power to coerce; it possesses no purely a-historical basis but can only exist as an appeal to freedom within a social structure of plausibility. Such factors as these move the discussion of the formation of the church to a deeper anthropological level.

With a sociological imagination serving as a horizon, two quite generalized sociological theories represent how the church was formed. One comes from sociology as applied to the formation of religious organizations, the other from the history of religions. These are not raised up as standards, but as examples that focus a sociological imagination into a more structured framework of analysis.[53]

Weber: routinization of charisma. Weber describes the origin of religious communities in the following way: "Primarily, a religious community arises in connection with a prophetic movement as a result of routinization, i.e., as a result of the process whereby either the prophet himself or his disciples secure the permanence of his

---

53. In other words, with the choice of Weber and Wach on the origin of religious organizations I am not making a commitment to other positions of these authors on sociological method or general theory. My choice finds its rationale in the descriptive quality of these views, and their broad applicability. Their analyses are so generalized that it is difficult to imagine space outside them. Yet they provide a clear structure for a more detailed or nuanced map.

preaching and the congregation's distribution of grace, hence insuring the economic existence of the enterprise and those who man it, and thereby monopolizing as well the privileges reserved for those charged with religious functions."[54] Without some form of permanent organization one has only a disparate movement. Those who want to regularize the cult or assembly "endeavor to create a congregation whereby the personal following of the cult will assume the form of a permanent organization and become a community with fixed rights and duties. Such a transformation of a personal following into a permanent congregation is the normal process by which the doctrine of the prophets enters into everyday life, as the function of a permanent institution. The disciples or apostles of the prophets thereupon become mystagogues, teachers, priests or pastors (or a combination of them all), serving an organization dedicated to exclusively religious purposes, namely a congregation of laymen."[55]

In Weber's conception, then, religious communities begin with a charismatic leader. The charismatic leader possesses authority grounded in personal or individual qualities or powers of an extraordinary kind. Routinization consists in a gradual transfer of authority from the person of the prophet to the community formed by a set of stable relationships. The *telos* of the organization is to preserve the message and ideals of the charismatic leader in the structures of the organization itself.[56] On this theory, one can read the first 150 years of the church as a gradual routinization of the charisma of Jesus.

Wach: the history of religions. Wach's theory of the founding of a religious community shares much of the Weberian analysis. But he adds a schematization of three stages in the process of routinization.[57] It so closely fits the formation of the Christian church that one must suspect that Christian beginnings were the implicit referent. The circle of disciples makes up the first stage. The image of the circle points to the centrality of the prophet. "The circle is

---

54. Max Weber, *The Sociology of Religion* (Boston: Beacon Press, 1963), 60–61. He has a more expanded description of the routinization of charisma in Max Weber, *The Theory of Economic and Social Organization* (New York: The Free Press, 1964), 358–92.

55. Weber, *Sociology of Religion*, 62.

56. Weber, *Theory of Economic and Social Organization*, 358–70.

57. Wach, *Sociology of Religion*, 130–45.

not strictly organized, but the variety of individualities and the differences in age are harbingers of future differentiation of function among the members."[58]

The second stage Wach calls the brotherhood, and it is distinguished neatly from the earlier stage by the death of the prophet. The crucial question at this stage concerns the future of the group, and to ensure its identity a shift in belief occurs, one that makes the person of the founder central to the definition of the group. A gradual growth in elementary forms of religious assembly and ritual, organization and structure also mark this stage. "The cultus, more than its doctrinal expression, unites and integrates the brotherhood."[59] The third stage arises out of a transition to an ecclesiastical body or church. This requires a differentiated organization, a passage from informal ministry to professional or formal positions of leadership. It also involves developing a public face directed to the outside world.

These models provide a general, descriptive, and almost commonsensical pattern of behavior. They are useful because they open up a heuristic for appreciating at a socially dynamic level the formation of the Christian church. I move now to an organizational analysis of the early church.

Organizational Analysis

An organizational analysis of the church will show how, within a common pattern of community organization, the Christian movement defined for itself a distinctive manner of being a church. Five categories correlate with each other to form the basic elements of a social organism: the participants or members, the goals, the activities, the structures, and the environment in and with which the organization interacts.[60] These categories in themselves do not represent a diachronic or developmental account, but some attention will be paid to that dimension so that the analysis characterizes sociologically some elements of the self-constitution of the church.

---

58. Ibid., 136.
59. Ibid, 140.
60. See W. Richard Scott, *Organizations: Rational, Natural, and Open Systems* (Englewood Cliffs, N.J.: Prentice-Hall, 1981), 13–19.

Members. Organizations, like individuals, are all distinctive, and so varied that one needs a typology of the very typologies that try to control them.[61] One such typology differentiates organizations according to authority structure and compliance. Coercive organizations like prisons use coercive power commanding obedience; utilitarian organizations like industries use remunerative stimuli that appeal to a calculative reason; normative organizations like religions use symbolic normative authority that appeals to moral commitment.[62] Whether or not there is a common genus called "religion," the Christian church is a religious organization because its members are bound together primarily by their religious faith focused in Jesus of Nazareth. The church came into being as a voluntary association based on conversion and free commitment. Its distinctive character will come from its most basic faith mediated through Jesus.

The members of the early church were Jews and Gentiles, and the first two centuries saw a gradual but overall reversal in the balance of these backgrounds. At the beginning the church was not a church but a part of Judaism; it was a Jewish movement. By the end of the second century, while still heavily Jewish in its constitution, it was thoroughly distinct from institutional Judaism.

Multiple and changing goals (mission). A second basic element of an organization consists in its goals. Considering the mission of the church in a loose analogous correlation with organizational goals opens up a series of analytical questions about the formation of the early church. For example, organizational theory distinguishes a variety of basic models for an organization: a rational model in which the goal controls all aspects of its functioning in a teleological way as in a tight bureaucracy; or a natural model where goals are multiple and ways of achieving them are more fluid; or an open system which recognizes that historicity and interaction with the environment will occasion adjustments or changes in the goals themselves; or a combination of elements of all of these conceptions.[63] Which is best suited to an analysis of the emerging church? Organizational theory

---

61. Ibid., 27–54.
62. Amatai Etzioni, *A Comparative Analysis of Complex Organizations* (New York: Free Press, 1975).
63. Scott, *Organizations*, 57–132.

also discusses changing goals, especially due to an interaction with the environment, a multiplicity of goals, formal and informal goals, organizational and individual members' goals. "Thus, to ascribe the single, specific goal of an organization is to say very little about it. Actual goals are discovered only when the public or official goal is factored into operational goals — those for which specific operations can be discovered."[64] These distinctions invite many propositions about the formation of the early church. Three reflections on the goals of the church merit attention.

One is that the church that was formed in the first two centuries had a predominant, centering mission, namely, to extend forward in history the ministry and message of Jesus, to keep his memory and mission alive. It is nowhere formulated in these words. Rather this formula is a distillation of many different ways of expressing this mission, a mission that could surely be expressed in still other ways as well.

This mission remained a constant in the developing church while at the same time it underwent several changes as the movement and then church interacted with its environment. For example, consider the contrast between the objectives of the Jesus movement during his lifetime and the Christian groups founded by Paul. Jesus' group was preparing the conditions for the advent of the kingdom of God. Paul's Christian groups were preparing people for cosmic salvation. The one had a more social aim, the other was more geared to the individuals within the group.[65] Frequently, interaction with the world in which it existed generated incremental change. Around the years 48–49 the change that occurred regarding membership affected the fundamental mission or goal of the Christian movement; the change can be considered radical as the community began to be formally reconceived in terms extending beyond Judaism into the Gentile world and the Roman empire. This enormous change in the concrete or imaginative framework for understanding the goals of the church shifted everything, because everything had to be reappropriated in a

---

64. Charles Perrow, *Complex Organizations: A Critical Essay* (Glenview, Ill.: Scott, Foresman, 1972), 160.

65. Bruce J. Malina, "Early Christian Groups," *Modeling Early Christianity*, ed. Philip E. Esler (London: Routledge, 1995), 96–113.

new context. The basic mission of the church, while remaining the same in terms of Christ, had changed fundamentally in terms of its intended constituency.[66]

The sketch of the history of the formation of the church during this period offered earlier is enough to show that the church was a very open, flexible organization with multiple goals. The apostle and the prophet were interested in the expansive missionary character of the church; the writings at the end of the first century were dominated by the goals of survival, consolidation of the teachings, and guarding unity. The energy of the church was distributed between mission and maintenance,[67] between realizing the formal goals of the church *ad extra*, and guaranteeing the survival of the church by internally accommodating the goals of individual constituents. The church has multiple goals, then, and they vary in their relative prominence within the process of the genesis of the church according to different environments, conditions, and constituents. The fact that this fluidity and openness were written into the scriptures which are the church's canonical or normative documents should have major importance for its self-understanding in the future.

Activities. The activities in which any organization becomes engaged significantly define its nature. Acts 2:42 summed up the internal life of the earliest movement in four activities: "And they devoted themselves to the apostles' teaching and fellowship, to the breaking of bread and the prayers." "Like the parent Christian community at Jerusalem, a Christian community can and should be identified as one which devotes itself to the teaching of the apostles, to *koinonia*, that is, fellowship, brotherhood, common life and sensitivity, to sharing in the breaking of bread and to the prayers characteristic of the community."[68] The salient religious activities

---

66. Another significant event, the destruction of the Temple in the year 70, amounted to a watershed that radically changed the framework of the thinking of Jew and Christian alike.

67. See Gregory Baum, "Contradictions in the Catholic Church," *Theology and Society* (New York: Paulist Press, 1987), 230–46 for a development and application of this distinction.

68. LaVerdiere, "New Testament Communities in Transition," 46. Luke could, of course, be retrojecting the activities of his own community back into the originating community.

of the later but still nascent church include the assemblies, the rituals, the ministry, the ethics that governed moral life within and outside the community. An analysis of these activities is important for any deep understanding of the church-in-formation.

Assemblies. In many ways, for the sociologist, assembly is the rock-bottom constitutive dimension of the church. The church is constituted in the coming together of people, as the name for the church, *ekklesia,* indicates. The gathering of people into household meeting places was the church in act. This is the reason why the household as an institution was so formative of the church. Assemblies were made up of many different activities: prayer, singing the psalms, celebrating the Lord's Supper, scripture reading and interpretation, exhortation. The size of these assemblies was undoubtedly uneven, but it is generally assumed that they were small.

Rituals. Ritual activity is of the essence of religion, according to Durkheim. "However complex the outward manifestations of religious life may be, its inner essence is simple, and one and the same. Everywhere it fulfills the same need and derives from the same state of mind. In all its forms, its object is to lift man above himself and to make him live a higher life than he would if he obeyed only his individual impulses. The beliefs express this life in terms of representations; the rites organize and regulate its functioning."[69]

The two most important rites of early Christianity are baptism and the eucharist. Jewish precedents for the development of baptism as the rite of initiation into the Christian community can be found in ritual washings generally, more specifically the purification rites of Qumran and still more pointedly the baptism of John.[70] It is debated whether Jesus himself baptized. The case of Paul provides evidence that baptism was practiced by the followers of Jesus soon after his death and resurrection, and an early formula of baptism in

---

69. Emile Durkheim, *The Elementary Forms of Religious Life* (New York: The Free Press, 1995), 417. I describe baptism and eucharist in this section sociologically. Later I will consider the theological language of the New Testament.

70. Daniel J. Harrington, "Baptism in Scripture," *The New Dictionary of Sacramental Worship,* ed. Peter E. Fink (Collegeville, Minn.: Liturgical Press, 1990), 83–84. Christian baptism shared the following characteristics with the baptism of John: it was a water ritual, administered by another, once-for-all, requiring a conversion, and oriented toward the eschatological kingdom of God. Ibid., 84.

the name of Jesus is mentioned in Acts in connection with Pentecost: "Repent, and be baptized every one of you in the name of Jesus Christ for the forgiveness of your sins; and you shall receive the gift of the Holy Spirit" (Acts 2:38). Some think that this early form of the rite was thoroughly Jewish, though baptism developed gradually into a boundary that actually separated Christians from Jews.[71] By the time of Paul's letters baptism had taken on rich and complex meanings: immersion into water and being lifted out is associated with the death and resurrection of the Lord; buried with Jesus, one then rises to new life and walks in the Spirit toward one's eschatological home.[72] Teaching or instruction was associated with preparation for baptism, and by the beginning of the third century, as witnessed by Hippolytus's *The Apostolic Tradition,* the normal preparation was three years.

The second central and centering ritual of the early church was the eucharist or Lord's Supper. One can chart the background of the eucharist in the religious significance of meals in the Jewish tradition and the blessings built into them. The earliest written testimony to the eucharist is in Paul who probably learned the tradition in Antioch,[73] and who makes it clear that the ritual consisted in a real meal that was commemorative of the death and resurrection of Jesus and associated with the last meal that Jesus had with his disciples before he died.[74] By the time Mark writes a narrative account of the Last Supper and other eucharistic stories such as the feedings of the crowds, there was a 40 year tradition of common meals among disciples to draw from.[75] The practice of common meals of the disciples carried a link with the time before Jesus' death. In Luke, an appearance of Jesus, and thus revelation of his resurrection, is associated

---

71. This is the opinion of Rudolf Bultmann as cited by G. R. Beasley-Murray in *Baptism in the New Testament* (Grand Rapids, Mich.: Eerdmans, 1973), 99.

72. Oscar Cullmann, *Baptism in the New Testament* (Philadelphia: Westminster Press, 1950), 14.

73. Jerome Kodell, *The Eucharist in the New Testament* (Wilmington: Michael Glazier, 1988), 57.

74. Meeks, *First Urban Christians,* 157–62.

75. Eugene LaVerdiere, *The Eucharist in the New Testament and the Early Church* (Collegeville, Minn.: Liturgical Press, 1996), 47. In other words, practice and interpretation, ritual and myth, are so deeply intertwined in the development of the eucharist that there is no agreed upon history of its development.

with a meal with Jesus (Lk 24:13–35). Thus gathering for this commemorative meal has to be considered a constitutive factor in the formation of the early church.

Theissen proposes a two-stage theory of the origin of the Christian sacraments. The first stage is the adoption by the community of symbolic actions of John and Jesus, the baptism of the forgiveness of sins and the meals of Jesus with his disciples. In a second stage, evidenced in Paul, both of these ritual actions were then related to the death of Jesus and became sacraments of the sacrificial death of Jesus for human salvation.[76] In the first stage these actions have a historical referent or starting point in the ministry of John and of Jesus. They were symbolic actions to convey a prophetic message. Both have a liminal character of mediating a crossing of a threshold into the transcendent world of God: in baptism, the new world of eschatological judgment; in Jesus' meals, the eschatological feast of the kingdom of God. In the first stage the ritual symbolism is iconic, simple actions in which water signifies cleaning and meal signifies the eschatological joy of the final banquet. In the second stage, however, these symbolic actions are transformed into sacraments. The symbolic actions are reinterpreted in terms of the sacrificial death of Jesus. The iconic relationship between performed symbolic action and its religious significance is broken: they are no longer simple cleaning or eschatological meal, but participation in the sacrificial death of Jesus. One is baptized into the death and resurrection of Jesus, and one shares the meal of Jesus, recalling his last meal with his disciples before his death and resurrection.[77]

From a theological point of view, these rituals are part of the fundamental goal of the church. They also have a social function. They impose self-discipline and foster virtues needed for social life. They have a cohesive function of binding people together, helping to

---

76. "Baptism and eucharist stand out by virtue of a common semantic reference: both are (at a secondary stage) interpreted in terms of the death of Christ. Baptism originally took place for the forgiveness of sins in the face of the imminent judgment. After Romans 6 it becomes baptism into the death of Christ. The eucharist came into being from the meals that Jesus held. In remembrance of the last supper it is related to the death of Jesus. And this death of Jesus in turn takes the place of the ancient sacrifices." Theissen, *The Religion of the Earliest Churches*, 124.

77. Ibid., 121–38.

provide identity and stimulating solidarity. Rituals and sacraments revitalize the tradition out of which people live, the inherited past which defines who a group is. And they engender a generally positive conception of life itself and nurture it in periods of crisis and negativity.[78] These multiple facets explain why baptism and eucharist were a primary way of defining the boundaries and identity of the new Christian community.

Ministries. Ministries may be considered as public service in behalf of the organization or community. Paul provides several lists of various ministries in the community. Generally people in these positions were self-designated on the basis of talent or charisma. Others, it seems, were appointed by the community on the basis of a need as, for example, those who were "to serve" in Acts or the overseers in the *Didache.* Generally speaking, the routinization of charisma explains the development toward offices of ministries which in an earlier stage and a Pauline context were regarded as Spirit-inspired.

A sociological perspective on ministries reveals among others four salient aspects. First, communities generally have within themselves all the resources they need for their own survival or to meet the goals they were designed to attain. This means that ministries arise from within the organization itself. Second, ministries respond to needs; they actualize the community assuming responsibility for interacting with its environment, the needs of its members, and the goals for which it was founded. When a need arises, as in the case of the Hellenic community in Jerusalem, people are either appointed, as were those who were to serve, or assume responsibility to meet the crisis. Third, very often ministries or structures for ministry are borrowed from those at hand, from what is familiar because operative in other communities. Thus a great deal of analysis has gone into reconstructing in what measure Christian ministries come from Judaism, or other organizations in the Greek *polis,* or some mixture of both in a hybrid.[79] Fourth, these ministries can be understood functionally,

---

78. Harry Alpert, "Durkheim's Functional Theory of Ritual," in *Emile Durkheim,* ed. Robert A. Nisbet (Englewood Cliffs, N.J.: Prentice-Hall, 1965), 137–41. See also Durkheim, *Elementary Forms,* 321, 375, 379, 392–93, 400–401, 415–16.

79. Relative to the Pauline churches, Richard S. Ascough's *What are They Saying about the Formation of the Pauline Churches* (New York and Mahwah, N.J.: Paulist Press, 1998) surveys the recent literature dealing with these issues.

that is, as part of a social system or subsystem of behaviors that are designed to meet a need and are integrated into the organization on the basis of their fulfilling this function.[80]

Ethics. Ethics in a broad sense, or more accurately morality in the sense of the basic attitudes and responses of Christians to the world, their social milieux, and themselves are deeply constitutive of the community itself. Thus to describe moral formation is to describe from another perspective the identity of the church.[81] This moral identity of the early church was a synthesis of many social and cultural influences that evolved over the first two centuries. It included the Jewish tradition of wisdom and law, the Hellenic tradition of Greek philosophy, the social world of the Greek *polis* in the Roman empire, and the close immediate influence of the household which was the first and most influential school of morality. But deep down and determinative of the content of Christian morality in the course of its evolution is the basic belief in Jesus as the Christ.

Meeks sees two large stages in the development of Christian morality that parallel the stages in the formation of the community described earlier in the language of Weber and Wach. The first stage extends from Jesus' preaching the kingdom to the development of a Jewish messianic sect, with apocalyptical dimensions of asceticism and expectations of a new and better world. Sectarian identity was established very soon on the basis of allegiance to Jesus as Messiah, the adoption of baptism as an initiation rite, and the practice of the Lord's supper. Negatively, the nonacceptance of certain Jewish rituals, Sabbath observance, circumcision, and others, also contributed.[82] By the turn of the century, however, the autonomous identity and structure of a church facing the empire appeared: "Something new was emerging in the private homes where believers in 'Jesus the Christ' gathered, in the town-wide gatherings for the Lord's Supper that a

---

80. See Talcott Parsons's analysis of social systems in functional terms in *Societies: Evolutionary and Comparative Perspectives* (Englewood Cliffs, N.J.: Prentice-Hall, 1966), 5–29. There is no doubt that to understand ministry or ritual or prayer in merely functional terms would be an unsatisfactory reduction of what they claim to be. Durkheim, for example, is such a reductionist. But neither does the risk of reductionism prevent such a sociological analysis from shedding more light on such ministries.

81. Meeks, *The Origins of Christian Morality*, 3–8.

82. Meeks, *The Moral World of the First Christians*, 99.

wealthier householder sometimes made possible, in the small circles of catechumens taking instruction from a Christian 'philosopher.' The new thing was what we call 'the church.' "[83]

The church in this period is constituting itself with all its common practices, so that one can perceive in this development the intrinsic connection between ritual and moral attitude. Baptism is the sacrament that is most often related to moral exhortation, paraenesis; baptism initiates members into a community of holiness and an expected holiness on the part of the individual. Paul proposes an explicit life-death-life pattern of being baptized into the death of Jesus to be a new, holy, moral person. Eucharist becomes the sacrament of community providing integration that overcomes in some measure and at a deeper level the social segregation on the basis of various stratifications and thus helps unify the community. This appears by contrast, for example, in the dispute over the eucharist in 1 Cor 11:17–34.[84] Other rituals, songs, prayer, and fasting foster a moral life in less dramatic ways. And other practices of the community indirectly foster moral attitudes: admonitions and sanctions to protect the unity and holiness of the community, e.g., shunning sinners; the practice of hospitality; the practice of giving and helping the poor, widows, orphans, and other communities.

Structures. A fourth element of an organization consists in the variety of structures that hold the group together and coordinate the activities of the participants toward their goal. Some of the axioms that arise from the sociological analysis of structures bear relevance for understanding the genesis of the church. One is the principle of contingency which says that there is no single best way to design the structure of an organization. The best structure is contingent upon the work, the goals, and the environmental demands or conditions that confront the organization.[85] Another is the general rule that ordinarily greater complexity of activities will demand greater complexity of structures. This rule, however, admits an exception,

---

83. Ibid., 119–20.
84. Wayne A. Meeks, *The Origins of Christian Morality*, 92–98; Gerd Theissen, "Social Integration and Sacramental Activity: An Analysis of 1 Cor 11:17–34," *The Social Setting of Pauline Christianity*, 145–74.
85. Scott, *Organizations*, 207–8.

when complex tasks are met "with more highly qualified and flexible performers — with professionals."[86] This occurred in the early church, when the earlier and more informal diversity of ministries was consolidated into the hands of a more professional clergy.[87] Finally, another axiom charts the positive correlation between the size of an organization and its structural differentiation. Larger size often means greater diversity of activities and thus increased structuration to coordinate them.[88] This too describes the evolution of the church, but along a path not followed here. Rather the analysis turns to consider some of the major structures of the church and the functions they perform. These are the scripture and canon, the creeds, law, governance, and bonds of intercommunication.

Scripture and canon. It could be argued that in writing its scriptures and establishing a canon the early church generated its single most important structure.[89] The reasons for such a claim lie in the many quite basic functions the canon of scripture serves. It stabilizes the foundational faith experience of the community; it provides its classical expression; it objectivizes this faith and creates a distance that allows it to reach across space and time to be normative into the future; it opens it up for future reflection and provides the possibility for it to be interpreted relevantly in other situations; it thus serves as the main instrument of organizational continuity. In sum, the writings serve as a basic constitution of the church and provide the objectified source for both stability and flexibility and innovation.[90]

Creeds. Creeds are short forms of the beliefs of the community, summaries of what is more elaborately contained in Christian

---

86. Ibid., 222.

87. See Edward Schillebeeckx, *The Church with a Human Face: A New Expanded Theology of Ministry* (New York: Crossroad, 1987), 69–72. I considered the development of ministries under "activities" to show how the offices of ministry evolved from ministerial activities. They could also be regarded as emerging offices of ministry and thus "structures" in the social-political organization of the community. In the chapters which follow they will be regarded as structures of the community for ministry.

88. Scott, *Organizations*, 237.

89. This is suggested but not said so boldly by Theissen, *The Religion of the Earliest Churches*, 270–71.

90. Parsons, *Societies*, 26–27; Paul Ricoeur, *Interpretation Theory: Discourse and the Surplus of Meaning* (Fort Worth: Texas Christian University Press, 1976), 25–44; James Barr, *The Bible in the Modern World* (London: SCM Press, 1973), 114–118.

writings. By defining belief, they play multiple functions in instruction and initiation; they provide norms in time of conflict. Creeds developed; they were generated out of continual reflection on the faith-experience of the community directed toward the person and message of Jesus. Thus creeds have a history within the community and move from embryonic forms to more standardized language. Like the Christian scriptures, they are centered on Jesus as the Christ and express a faith centered in God mediated through him.

This simple historical and sociological account of creeds does not communicate the depth of the role they play, their foundational function in a religious organization on a par with ritual and moral conduct. A creed crystallizes the worldview, or mythos, or sacred canopy that situates the church on a cosmic level. The role of a basic christological belief is well illustrated by Paul's most fundamental appreciation of Jesus Christ, the one by which and to which he was converted. In Paul the pattern of life through death to resurrection becomes a basic structure of human reality and existence. He exemplified this in the Philippians hymn with the second Adam motif. It controls how he thinks about basic moral values: "Have this mind among yourselves" (Phil 2:5). This pattern also mirrors the pattern of conversion: Adam and Christ, darkness and light. By contrast, it marks outsider — insider, one's old life and the new. Or more concretely: Christ was rich, but became poor; therefore, share wealth with the poor. Christians should model their lives — and their deaths — on the example of Christ. This provides the grounds for a spirituality of combat, and the martyrs were the heroes because they played out this Christic life-death-life pattern in their lives most fully and dramatically.[91]

Law. The formation of an organization and routinization are in some measure synonymous. Organization signifies patterned behavior, behavior according to rules. In varying degrees of "solidity" these patterns become normative, unwritten or written laws. Thus even the freedom of Gentile Christians in Antioch around the year 50 from

---

91. Meeks, *The Origins of Christian Morality,* 86–88. "Paul's most profound bequest to subsequent Christian discourse was his transformation of the reported crucifixion and resurrection of Jesus Christ into a multipurpose metaphor with vast generative and transformative power — not least for moral perceptions." Ibid., 196.

some aspects of Jewish law entails other boundary-defining rules or conditions. In the *Didache* one has an early example of what would become a genre of Christian writing, a manual of community laws.

Law entails authority, and authority entails some kind of power in the community. Weber describes routinization as a passage from charismatic authority to rational or legal authority, that is, the grounds for authority pass from residing in personal qualities to social contract or legally established patterns.[92] Scott distinguishes two broad types of authority in organizations: endorsed authority is accepted and in that measure constituted by the participants; authorized authority is more objective; it is set and regulated by a superior power. The two kinds can exist separately or in combination.[93]

Using these categories, how could one characterize very broadly from a sociological perspective the emergence of church law and authority? First of all, the very model of routinization to describe the formation of the church entails the growth of law from within the organization; it is the condition of its sustained existence. Second, as a small nascent group the church depends on converts and thus is constituted as a voluntary association. In that measure, the authority of the early church should be classified as "endorsed"; it is socially constituted as a function of the social freedom of the members; it is not coercive authority. Third, however, as religious authority it receives divine sanction and a theological rationale.[94] It finds support or reinforcement in the creeds. But, finally, from a sociological perspective the grounds for authority lie in the credibility and authenticity of the church itself. The church sustained the obedience of its members by providing a coherent and integrated way of life for its members and an identity vis-à-vis the outside world.[95]

Governance. The governmental structure of the church provides an enormous topic in ecclesiology, and its importance matches its complexity. One cannot expect a few paragraphs to loosen its many

---

92. Weber, *The Theory of Economic and Social Organization*, 324–423.

93. Scott, *Organizations*, 383.

94. Divine authorization is strongly affirmed in the letters of Ignatius of Antioch. A further discussion of the theological dimension of the church is reserved for the following section of the essay.

95. See David J. Stagaman on the "Authoritative" in his *Authority in the Church* (Collegeville, Minn.: Liturgical Press, 1999), 55–57.

knotty problems. But the confluence of a historical and a sociological perspective does throw some light into dark corners. The three theses proposed here need further research and argument.

First, the early church's governmental structure was a product of development, a development that extended throughout the first and second centuries. It developed along several distinct axes, that is, in a variety of its aspects or dimensions. One of them moved from a more charismatically grounded authority structure, where ministries were assumed on the basis of inspired ability, toward a more rationalized system of offices of ministry. This development is historically demonstrable, and it coheres with the broad sociological models of Weber and Wach.

Second, according to the sociological principle of contingency, the dynamics of the development of governmental structures can be understood within the framework of an encounter with the environment. The particular communities met their needs by borrowing from structures that were at hand, that were known. These structures had their sources in or were influenced by the Jewish synagogue, by the household in a Greek *polis*, by other voluntary associations that carried on analogous activities. This development can be called natural and spontaneous, not in the sense that it was unreflective or unconsidered, but in the sense that it conformed with no fixed blueprint from or at the beginning. This spontaneous character can be argued on the basis of the silence of the New Testament on systems of governance, as if there were no interest at all in defending a particular governmental order.[96] The very difficulty that New Testament scholars have in determining any common pattern in church governance shows that few if any of the authors of the New Testament taught or argued for a particular order.

Third, the New Testament displays a plurality of church orders or governmental structures. Insofar as the New Testament is a canonical or normative document, it teaches pluralism in church polity. It does not uniquely endorse an episcopal system, as Orthodox, Catho-

---

96. The point here is not that the communities reflected in the New Testament were uninterested in church unity and order; they surely were, but they did not unanimously or uniformly defend any particular system of governance to insure it.

lic, and Anglican theologians have habitually found, nor a presbyteral system, as Calvin and reformed churches have found, nor a complete absence of a divinely authorized system in favor of freedom of structure to mediate word and sacrament, which fits a Lutheran conception of things. This means that while one can find aspects of early church polity which fit all of these systems, it would be wrongheaded historically and sociologically and theologically to try to justify a single system against others on the basis of the early church as reflected in the New Testament. Generally, but here quite plainly, the pluralism of the New Testament rules out proof-texting as a theological method.

Communication. Christianity began with missionaries from Jerusalem and probably other groups in Galilee. It spread through trade, travel, and communication. The apostle (Paul) was itinerant; also some prophets. Messengers were sent; letters written; visits made. A sense of solidarity marked the movement as a whole, and some sense of mutual responsibility. Jerusalem was concerned about the church at Antioch; Paul made a collection from the Gentile churches for the church in Jerusalem; Rome was worried about the church in the Roman colony of Corinth. From the beginning of the movement frequent communications between local churches make it difficult to say whether this is one movement with many outposts or many churches forming a unity of churches. However one decides that relative to the first century, as the church faced the empire in the second century it moved toward becoming more solidified into a single, large corporate entity.

The dialectical interaction and interpenetration between the larger Christian community as a whole and local primary communities reinforced the church in the second century. Borrowing from the sociology of organizations one can see how "the norms (and their enforcement apparatus), ideals, and history of the [large] community form a part of a culture of smaller groups, overriding particular interests, limiting power and dependency within smaller groups to those consistent with community norms. Penetration of primary groups gives larger groups the capacity to socialize loyalty to themselves into deeper levels of the personality. Rewards of primary group life and loyalties to other members of primary groups become resources at the disposal of the larger group."[97] Most importantly from a cultural anthropological perspective, the large community supplied a long common tradition and a wide context of belonging that solidified personal identity and strengthened local churches.

Environment and boundaries. A fifth dimension of organizations concerns boundaries and identity within an environment. Normally organizations in history cannot be conceived as closed, rationalized systems mechanically oriented toward their goals. Consistent reference has been made to the open and interactive relationship with environment that makes identity questions, in terms of differentiation from others, a constant and shifting problem at a variety of levels: self-definition, organizational boundaries, ritual, ethics. On the hypothesis that during the first century the Christian movement was preoccupied with its relationship to Judaism, and during the second the emphasis shifted toward its relationship with the empire, a word about each of these environments is necessary.[98]

The church and Judaism. The Christian movement began its existence as a sect within Judaism. The term sect has a variety of meanings; I use it here in the tradition of Weber and Troeltsch as involving a tension between the group and the established religious social milieu and the world. A sect exists both within a larger whole and over against it. Jesus and the Jesus movement that sprang from him began as a part of and totally within its parent cultural system, Judaism. At the same time, allegiance to Jesus gradually set the Christian movement at odds with Judaism. This means that one can understand the beginnings and origin of Christianity as a distinct religion in terms of the sociology of deviance, understood as a socially constructed process of distinction and separation. This process can be schematized in a series of moves toward separation: "these stages include (1) being publicly identified as a rule breaker, (2) being excluded from participation in nondeviant activities, (3) coming to

---

97. Arthur L. Stinchcombe, "Social Structure and Organizations," in James G. March, ed., *Handbook of Organizations* (Chicago: Rand & McNally, 1965), 186.

98. The shift from preoccupation with the relation to Judaism to that with the Roman empire is one of emphasis, a matter of a certain center of gravity, because both relationships engaged the church during both centuries.

define oneself as deviant, and (4) managing one's deviant identity."[99] This process should be understood as one that engages a community over a period of time and fits within the stages of a socially constructed conviction. As such it roughly describes the dynamics between Judaism and the early Christian community, whether pointedly as in the case of Matthew's community, or more generally as in the case of the whole Christian movement.

This process established a basic ambiguity in the relation of the Christian community to Judaism. The relation was such that, even after complete organizational separation, there could not have been complete distinction or separation. Jesus was a Jew; Christianity was unintelligible without Judaism; its main recruits through the second century were Jews; its tradition was Jewish; its scriptures, including parts of the New Testament, were Jewish writings. This symbiotic relationship to Judaism, across the boundaries already considered in organization, ritual, and creed, was also paradoxical. As Judaism moved in the course of the second century away from priesthood and sacrifice, Christianity adopted that very language as its own.[100]

The church and the empire. The church appears in relation to the empire as a sect. Here the term "sect" conveys the sense of the religious organization's reaction to the world. "Men seek salvation in a world in which they feel the need for supernatural help. Sectarians necessarily seek that salvation in some other way than by acceptance of the secular culture and the institutional facilities that it provides for men to attain social and cultural goals. Clearly, by definition, they also reject the orthodox or dominant religious tradition in respects important enough for them to separate from it,

---

99. Erdwin H. Pfuhl and Stuart Henry, *The Deviance Process* (New York: Aldine de Gruyter, 1993), 121.

100. Speaking of the second century, Dunn writes: "At that period, priesthood and sacrifice were constitutive of a religion or cult; a religion or cult, indeed, was scarcely imaginable without priesthood and sacrifice. Rabbinic Judaism did not succumb to that pressure: the loss of its own Temple and the focus on Torah enabled it to resist the attraction of the social norm. In contrast, Christianity found itself unable to resist the pressure: the centrality of Christ was insufficient to withstand the pressure towards social conformity, whereby the typological use of Old Testament cultic ideas and terms naturally tended to give way more and more to a literal transposition." Dunn, *The Parting of the Ways*, 257.

at least in worship, and usually also in other ways."[101] The relationship of the church to imperial culture was truly ambiguous: it was in it but not of it. It dialogued with the empire; it adopted Greek philosophical categories in its self-understanding; its ethics were influenced by Greek philosophical traditions; its members were Roman citizens with dual loyalties for they prayed for the emperor; they moved toward a language of priesthood and sacrifice. But Christians built firm boundaries between themselves and paganism and its demon-dominated institutions. They were "atheists" relative to the pagan gods, strict monotheists, members of an exclusive religion, who sought salvation from a strictly transcendent source, and lived in the expectation of a final home in eternity.

To sum up here, these five organizational loci provide a heuristic field or framework that raises a variety of questions about what was going on in the historical development of the church. The historical sources, of course, do not always respond with clear answers. Nevertheless, the categories provide a deeper purchase on the historical developments.

A THEOLOGICAL ACCOUNT

A third level of understanding the early church is theological. I presuppose the intimate and nonreductive relation between the historical-sociological data and theological construal of these same realities. The development of the church is related to God because God is active in it. Given these presuppositions, I take up the discussion of the theological character of the church as this is perceived in and by faith and proposed in theological language. I enter the discussion from two points of view, the first relating to what may be called the theological foundations of the church in Jesus and God as Spirit, and the second addressing the theological understandings that attach to the various elements that make up the church as an organized faith community.

---

101. Bryan R. Wilson, "Sociological Analysis and the Search for Salvation," *Magic and the Millennium: A Sociological Study of Religious Movements of Protest Among Tribal and Third-World Peoples* (New York: Harper & Row, 1973), 19.

Theological Foundations of the Church

Jesus as the foundation of the church. Jesus is the foundation of the Christian church theologically from two perspectives: historically he stands at the origin of the church as the source of the movement that became the church; and theologically he continues to function as the theological foundation of the church into the future, that is, at any given time.

We have already considered the historical development of the church. In this development the person of Jesus provided the principle of unity. The unity of the whole church and each church in it, as testified to by the New Testament, placed Jesus at the center: the whole New Testament is directly or indirectly about Jesus. And Jesus was most fundamentally at the basis of the separation between the Christian movement and Judaism. The main reason for this split at bottom was theological, namely, the interpretation by Christians that Jesus was Messiah and that he represented salvation from God in a decisive and definitive way, and was thus a universally relevant figure for the salvation of all, not just Jews.[102]

Thus the deepest reason why Jesus is the foundation of the church is theological and not merely historical. This foundation lies in the experience of Jesus as bringer of salvation. This very recognition of Jesus as salvation from God, which occurred fully only after his death in the Easter experience, constitutes the foundation of the church. In terms used by Francis Schüssler Fiorenza, the theological foundation of the church consists in the interpretation of Jesus as a mediator of salvation from God.[103] The interpretation that Jesus is savior from God continued to develop, but it remained an interpretation of Jesus himself, the earthly figure now risen. This marks the continuity in

---

102. An adequate analysis of Jesus as the foundation of the church should include an account of the development of the belief in Jesus' divinity and the implications of this for the status of the church. A version of this discussion, which is too complex for inclusion here, may be found in Roger Haight, *Jesus Symbol of God* (Maryknoll, N.Y.: Orbis Books, 1999). On the pointed issue of the separation of Christians from Jews, see Dunn, *The Partings of the Ways,* 244–47 for a theological analysis of reasons related to christology.

103. Francis Schüssler Fiorenza, "The Church and the Task of Foundational Theology," *Foundational Theology: Jesus and the Church* (New York: Crossroad, 1985), 155–73.

this development. But exactly how the early communities understood Jesus to be the theological foundation of the church varied historically according to different interpretations of Jesus. They all agreed that Jesus was their salvation and as such the foundation of their new communities. But because there was a pluralism of understandings of Jesus, so too a variety of aspects or ways in which Jesus came to bear on different communities defined his being foundation. In other words, the New Testament shows that the way Jesus is foundational of the church is pluriform.[104]

Besides being the historical foundation of the church theologically in the past, so to speak, Jesus is also foundational for the church into the future and at any given time. With his death and exaltation Jesus as a historical figure became absent from history. Thus it became historically necessary, if Jesus was not to disappear from memory or become completely distorted by time, that a record of Jesus be preserved in writing. And so it happened: the emerging church captured its experience of Jesus in writing and ritual, the very experience upon which the church was built. It is the gospels which principally portray Jesus and the church's appreciation of him. But the whole New Testament relates back to the significance of Jesus insofar as it is Christian scripture.

Jesus continues to be the foundation and norm for the church, then, by being at the heart and center of the New Testament and, for the Christian, the whole bible. Jesus is the foundation because the New Testament is the codified memory and experience of Jesus as precisely the foundation of the church. This Jesus is made present in the church through the various forms of reading, listening to, and interpreting the scriptures as well as ritual activity.

It should be noted, once again, that this foundational presence of Jesus to the church through its scriptures will always be appreciated pluralistically. Not only is the document itself pluralistic, but it is constantly being received in ever new situations and hence pluralistically. In other words, just as the way Jesus is the foundation of the church is pluralistically portrayed in the New Testament, so too will appreciation of how he is foundational today be pluralistic

---

104. See Haight, *Jesus Symbol of God*, 152–84.

for the same reasons. Although the logic of how Jesus functions as theological foundation of the church leads through interpretation and reception, Jesus remains normative for the church: he is the critic and judge of every exercise of ministry and authority within the church.

God as Spirit as foundation of the church. The church is not only founded on Jesus. In the common language of the church, the church is the temple of the Spirit of God. Acts represents the church as beginning at Pentecost with the pouring forth of the Spirit. It will be helpful briefly to reflect on what the Spirit as foundation of the church means and to begin by recalling the meaning of the symbol "Spirit."

The word "symbol" in this case refers to a conscious symbol as distinct from a concrete or material symbol. The category "symbol" indicates that concepts applied to God are not applied in the same way as in knowledge of this world. God is transcendent, and a conceptual symbol points beyond itself to the reality that transcends or goes beyond its this-worldly meaning. The symbol, "the Spirit of God," refers to God as active in the world; it designates the power of God in the world as the source of dynamism, life, exalted human energy, and inspiration. The Spirit designates God present and active invisibly, like the wind, in the world and in human beings. As indicated earlier, I use the phrase "God as Spirit" to make clear that the Spirit is God and not other than God. In its primordial sense it is not a person of the trinity but simply God, God as operative in the world.

The meaning of the symbol God as Spirit today does not substantially differ in theology and ordinary Christian language. Theologically, God as Spirit may be interpreted as God's presence to God's creation; to human beings it is God's "personal being present to," or God's self-communication.[105] God may be experienced as totally other, as transcendent and absolutely holy mystery. But insofar as God is experienced at all, God has become present to and in a certain sense within a person.

It is this God as presence, God as Spirit present "outside of God's self" in the effects of God's action, so to speak, that is the foundation of the church. The pages of the New Testament amply display

---

105. See Karl Rahner, *Foundations of Christian Faith: An Introduction to the Idea of Christianity* (New York: Crossroad, 1994), 117–33, 136–37.

this experience. The pouring out of the Spirit symbolizes that Jesus is the eschatological or decisive event of salvation. The Spirit worked within Jesus, and now that Spirit has been released into the Jesus movement. The church is the community of the Spirit, and the Spirit is the presence of God to the church. The Spirit is the cause, basis, and foundation of the church, the energy within its ministries, the impelling force empowering its mission. Thus, as the New Testament says, one could not even recognize Jesus as Lord without the prior presence and power of the Spirit, even as Jesus is the norm for discerning the Spirit (1 Cor 12:3; 1 John 4:1–3).

But what does it mean to say that one experiences or knows the Spirit? One may accept as a principle that God, and hence God as Spirit, cannot be known immediately; all knowledge of God is historically mediated. Therefore, whoever encounters God as Spirit does so within or through a finite experience of this world as a transcendent horizon or theme that exceeds immediacy. The content of knowledge of God as Spirit, that is, the way God is encountered and understood, must be mediated through or by some contact with the finite world.

In Christianity knowledge of God is mediated by Jesus. In a way this could stand as a definition of what Christianity is, namely, the religion in which one's contact, conception, and construal of God is given through the event of Jesus. For Christians, Jesus mediates what God is like. Therefore, in the New Testament the Spirit active in the church is not simply God at work, but God as God is made know in the ministry and person of Jesus. The Holy Spirit is defined as the "power of Christ made manifest in the present."[106] The symbols "Spirit," "Spirit of God," "Holy Spirit," have become associated with Jesus Christ and all refer to "the abiding presence of God and Christ in Christians" and thus in the church.[107] The New testament abounds in Spirit language relative to the church, and it bears this double reference: to Jesus of Nazareth as bearer and revealer of God's Spirit, and to the abiding presence and power of the risen Jesus or Christ within the community at any given time. In the

---

106. Harrington, *Church*, 58.
107. Ibid., 59.

following section I will take up some of the images that expand upon this conviction.

Finally, the predominance of Spirit language describing God's presence and activity in the community leads to the thesis that the Spirit is the foundation of the church. But this thesis has to be appreciated in a historically and sociologically nuanced way. The relation of God as Spirit to actual historical institutions should not be uncritically mystified. God or God as Spirit becomes manifest in and through historical media, and cannot be known apart from historical media. Thus one experiences God as Spirit in Jesus Christ and in and through the church and its various institutions. Early Christians did not know the Spirit outside and independently of these institutions in a way that such knowledge became an objective criterion. They could not say the following: "We know God as Spirit, and on the basis of this objective knowledge of God as Spirit we know that God justifies and supports or wills this institution in the church but not that institution in the church." One cannot appeal to an independently known Spirit or will of God and argue deductively from it to the validity of a specific historical institution in the church. Rather the Spirit as it were presides over by being present to and mediated by a pluralism of church institutions in the church represented in the New Testament, and a pluralism of developing institutions in the course of history.

In sum, one should not think of Jesus Christ and the Spirit as two separable theological foundations of the church. They are rather two aspects or dimensions of a divine grounding that operate as one. In the formation of the church God as Spirit is mediated by Jesus of Nazareth who is the Christ. And Jesus can be recognized as the Christ only through the presence and influence of God as Spirit. Together these symbols designate the manner in which God is the single theological foundation of the church.

The Theology of Ecclesial Organization

The first two parts of this chapter outline the historical and sociological development of the church. This social analysis of the church must be complemented by a theological account of the divine height and depth of the religious experience of what was so generated. Jesus and God as Spirit provide the foundations of that experience. But it remains to point out how theologal experience underlay the formation of the organizational structures themselves and thus formed a part of their constitution. In what follows I will analyze key New Testament passages which illustrate how every feature of the organizational structure that was taking shape was construed in theological language that indicated its relationship to God.[108]

Members: chosen in the Spirit to be the body of Christ. I turn to Paul for the first and fullest theological account of the members of the church and nature of the church.[109] In the beginning, becoming a member of the church required conversion and faith. We have several accounts of such conversions of Gentiles and Jews, but Paul's own is the most famous. He characterizes his conversion in terms of revelation: God "called me through his grace" and "was pleased to reveal his Son to me" (Gal 1:15–16). "Gift" and "grace" provide the premise and theme of revelation, and revelation communicates a sense of being chosen: "For those whom he foreknew he also predestined to be conformed to the image of his Son, in order that he might be the firstborn within a large family. And those whom he predestined he also called" (Rom 8:29–30). Paul inculcated in the members of his churches a sense of being singled out by God.

God as Spirit, revealed in Jesus and thus the Spirit of Christ, designates the way God calls each member to the church. God as Spirit dwells in each member of the church who is a true follower of Jesus Christ (Rom 8:9). Each member becomes united with Christ by participation effected by the Spirit's indwelling. This results in the whole community of the local church being collectively filled with, animated by, constituted in, and led by the Spirit of Christ.[110]

This theology of membership leads to the rather concrete consequence of recognizing the effects of the Spirit as the charism of each

---

108. This analysis of the theological dimension of the church draws extensively from Harrington, *The Church.*

109. The relevant texts here are Rom 8; Rom 12:1–8; 1 Cor 12–14. See Harrington, *Church,* 57–68.

110. The Spirit bestows life over against sin and death. The Spirit dwells in each Christian and the community as Wisdom or Shekinah dwelled in the tabernacle and then the Temple. The church is thus the new exodus community. N. T. Wright, *The Letter to the Romans,* NIB, X (2002), 555–56.

individual in the church. A church filled with the Spirit is a charismatic community. Each member is gifted by the Spirit in a manner exceeding his or her natural talents. Yet all the charisms are meant for the service in harmony of the one church. "Now there are varieties of gifts, but the same Spirit; and there are varieties of services, but the same Lord; and there are varieties of activities, but it is the same God who activates all of them in everyone. To each is given the manifestation of the Spirit for the common good" (1 Cor 12:4–7). Paul provides several lists of what he means by these charisms: for example, to speak wisely, to speak knowingly, to heal, to work miracles, to prophecy, to discern spirits, to speak ecstatically in tongues, to interpret such speech (1 Cor 12:8–10). The theological point, however, is divine empowerment and authorization.[111]

Paul formulates the content of the theology of the charismatic community into the striking metaphor of the body of Christ. The image has many veins, each with a rich yield. Referring to the local community he writes: "For as in one body we have many members, and not all the members have the same function, so we, who are many, are one body in Christ, and individually we are members one of another" (Rom 12:4–5). This emphasizes how the many talents cooperate to make the church a complex organic unity. But another statement of the same images suggests that the subject of the body is Christ so that the members make up his body (1 Cor 12:12). The Spirit of God who is the Spirit of Christ is the lifeblood of this identification, thus suggesting active participation in God and giving the metaphor a mystical realism. The image pointedly celebrates the pluralism and diversity of gifts, and simultaneously insists that they constitute the unity of the one body and have to be exercised toward that end. It provides a criterion for their use. It also bears more than a hint of egalitarianism: the different gifts correlate with different functions, some more important than others; but all are members of the same body, so that "If one member suffers, all suffer together

---

111. Paul gives another list in Rom 12:6–8 and still another in 1 Cor 12:28 which reads as follows: "God has appointed in the church first apostles, second prophets, third teachers; then deeds of power, then gifts of healing, forms of assistance, forms of leadership, various kinds of tongues." In this text one sees that while charisms and offices are not identical, they correlate with each other, and offices should be filled with people possessing appropriate charismatic gifts. See Harrington, *Church*, 61, 63–64.

with it; if one member is honored, all rejoice together with it" (1 Cor 12:26).[112]

In sum, Paul's theology of the church community brings together the two theological foundations of Jesus Christ and the Spirit in coherent integrated terms that are both mystical and at the same time descriptive of what the community is called to be.

Divine mission in history. Although it is not its primary intention, no text in the New Testament expresses the mission of the church better than the two volume work of Luke. He proposes a straightforward thesis that can be stated in a proposition: the mission of the church is to extend forward in history the saving mission and ministry of Jesus of Nazareth. His mode of explanation provides a good example of ecclesiology from below in its intimate combination of the historical narrative and theological interpretation. Luke's work first depicts the saving work of Jesus of Nazareth and then moves on to describe how that work continued in the band of his disciples whom he commissioned at his ascension: "you will be my witnesses in Jerusalem, in all Judea and Samaria, and to the ends of the earth" (Acts 1:8).[113] This mission is laid out in narrative form, first through the leadership of Peter and then the leadership of Paul. This historical account, however, carries theological depth: the thread of continuity in the whole drama from beginning to end is God as Spirit. God as Spirit, the power of the Most High, was operative in Jesus' conception and birth, empowered him in his ministry, took hold of the band of disciples after his exaltation at Pentecost, and supplied the energy and charismatic dynamism for the expansion of the Jesus movement. Luke provides the churches, especially churches whose constituency is mainly Greek, with a historical sense of identity: he connects them

---

112. The egalitarianism does not suggest that any member can do any ministry, for diversity of roles is highlighted. The church is genuinely pluralistic. But the problem was divisiveness, and Paul insists that all charisms are for the common good so that, as members of the whole Christ, "all individuals have equal standing and importance." J. Paul Sampley, *The First Letter to the Corinthians*, NIB, X, 940.

113. Also the missionary mandates of Mt 28:16–20; Mark 16:14–18; John 20:21. These texts condense what the narrative of Acts shows took time to recognize, that the church was to be a community inclusive of all nations. This insight is portrayed theologically as a bestowal of authority on the disciples by the risen Christ. M. Eugene Boring, *The Gospel of Matthew*, NIB, VIII (1995), 501–5.

with their Jewish origins and the ministry of Jesus; he presents them as a prophetic fulfillment of the universal mission of salvation of God as Spirit realized in Jesus.[114] In Luke's view the very reason for the church is its mission to extend into history the ministry of salvation of Jesus.[115]

The mission in the sense of the very purpose of the church finds theological expression in terms analogous to Luke in other New Testament writings as well. 1 Peter calls the church community "a chosen race, a royal priesthood, a holy nation, God's own people, in order that you may proclaim the mighty acts of him who called you out of darkness into his marvelous light" (1 Peter 2:9). Another statement of the inner purpose of the church comes in the later voice of Paul in Ephesians. It situates the church in the great plan of God: "Although I am the very least of all the saints, this grace has been given to me to bring to the Gentiles the news of the boundless riches of Christ, and to make everyone see what is the plan of the mystery hidden for ages in God who created all things; so that through the church the wisdom of God in its rich variety might now be made known to the rulers and authorities in the heavenly places" (Eph 3:8–10). Well before the end of the first century, therefore, the mission and purpose of the church was understood in the context of the whole world.

Activities that unite people to God and one another. Earlier I introduced Theissen's theory of the development of baptism and the Lord's Supper in which a second stage consisted in Paul's theological interpretation of the religious rituals. Romans 6:1–11 provides a concise summary of Paul's theology of baptism. Through the rite of baptism the new Christian becomes united with Christ in his

---

114. LaVerdiere, "New Testament Communities in Transition," 45.

115. Ibid., 48. See Harrington, *Church*, 89–93 for a summary of the contributions of the Acts of the Apostles to ecclesiology. It may be useful to note the connection between "apostles" and the "mission" of the church in the sense of its "being sent." Harrington indicates how "Luke is most responsible for bringing together the terms *twelve* and *apostles*." The key sentence is Luke 6:13: "he called his disciples and chose twelve of them, whom he also named apostles" (*Church*, 110). This idea supports the broader notion that the twelve apostles are the foundation of the church. But a deeper historical logic of the possibility of the corruption of a historical revelation over time is also responsible for raising "apostolicity" to the prominent level of being a criterion for ecclesial authenticity.

death in order to share with him his resurrection. "For if we have been united with him in a death like his, we will certainly be united with him in a resurrection like his" (Rom 6:5). One should understand this in the light of the Last Adam soteriology and christology developed immediately prior to his treatment of baptism (Rom 5:12–21). There Jesus is presented as the new paradigmatic head of a new human race. His life of obedience, faithful death, and resurrection become the new pattern of humankind. The passage on baptism has a moral dimension: freed from the death of sin, one should live a new Christian life of righteousness. But the metaphysical level surpasses morality. The new Adam initiates a new humanity. By being united with Jesus Christ, the new head of the human race, the Christian becomes a new being.[116]

The death and resurrection of Jesus, and the deeper pattern of life-death-life that it revealed, is central in Paul's theological imagination. His theological interpretation of the eucharist is also drawn into this framework, and 1 Corinthians 11:17–34 represents a concise statement of it. Paul begins with a reprimand of the Corinthians for division and lack of concern for poorer members of the community. He then recalls the tradition of Jesus' final meal with his disciples, and proposes the true meaning and conditions for this signature Christian practice. It binds the Christian to Jesus Christ's death: "for as often as you eat this bread and drink the cup, you proclaim the Lord's death until he comes" (1 Cor 11:26). But it can only be celebrated worthily in the spirit of love and concern for all in the community: "For all who eat and drink without discerning the [members of the] body, eat and drink judgment against themselves" (1 Cor 11:29).[117] In sum, theologically the eucharist nourishes Christian life on a personal and social level: it unites the Christian to Jesus Christ

---

116. Christians are lifted out of solidarity with sin to live in a new sphere of grace and righteousness. "The transfer is effected by dying and rising with the Messiah. And the event in which this dying and rising is accomplished is baptism" (Wright, *Romans*, 533). By joining the messianic community, one identifies with the Messiah; what happened to him, resurrection, happens to the Christian. Ibid., 535.

117. Jerome Murphy-O'Connor, "The First Letter to the Corinthians," *The New Jerome Biblical Commentary* (Englewood Cliffs, N.J.: Prentice Hall, 1990), 810. Cited hereafter as NJBC.

and it solidifies the community with bonds of love empowered by God as Spirit through Jesus.[118]

Regarding a theology of ministries, I noted earlier that in some degree Paul's lists of charisms correlate with ministries. This means that in Paul's mind the power to be a minister ideally lay in the corresponding personal gift of the Spirit. More generally, since the church was a community filled and led by God as Spirit, the whole community provided the medium wherein such charisms were nurtured and recognized. But Harrington shows that for Paul the ministries of the word of God enjoyed a certain priority. Whereas the New Testament shows little concern with clearly identifying who exercises administrative oversight over the community or who baptizes, or with determining who presides at the Lord's Supper, one notices a definite bias toward various ministries of the word: preaching, teaching, prophesying. In some measure the mission to extend Jesus' ministry into history comes to a focus in preaching and witnessing to the gospel, the good news of Jesus Christ, the revealing word of God.[119]

Divine authorization of governance. How did the early church understand theologically the basis of the authority of those who led the community? This question which becomes so important in later ecclesiology does not have the clear answer in the canonical literature that one might desire. In fact the development that one can discern in the New Testament comes to a significant conclusion in the early first century and is reflected outside the canonical literature in the writing of Ignatius of Antioch. I shall deal with it in the next chapter. But the New Testament data suggests a broad theological conclusion which can be explained in the following steps.

First, we have seen how Paul tends to relate ministries to charisms in the church community formed and led by God as Spirit who is

---

118. Harrington sums up Paul's eucharistic theology concisely by drawing together all the allusions contained in 1 Cor 11:23–26 as follows: "It is a meal shared with Jesus' friends. It is a meal hosted by Jesus for sinners and marginal people (since at it Jesus prophesies that his disciples will betray him). It involves participation in Jesus' suffering and death. It is at once a Passover celebration, a covenant meal, a sacrifice, a memorial, and Wisdom's banquet. And it looks forward to the banquet to be shared in the fullness of God's kingdom and at the glorious return of Jesus." Harrington, *Church*, 48.

119. Harrington, *Church*, 153–56.

Christ's Spirit. The divine source of authority is the Spirit within the community. But leadership or administration is one of these ministries (1 Cor 12:28; Rom 12:8). This charism and position of leadership does not have as high a profile in Paul's churches as it will assume later.

Second, as the church settles in and grows, one would expect the structure of the Pauline churches to develop, and the Pastorals reflect this. First Timothy 3:1–13 contains a description of the qualities of the bishop and the deacon, ministries not inconsistent with Pauline churches; 1 Timothy 5:17 and Titus 1:5–9 refer to elders which are not typical in the Pauline churches.[120]

Third, 1 Timothy urges Timothy to remain faithful to his charism for ministry as a bishop, but in this case it is a charism that was given him through the laying on of hands: "Do not neglect the gift that is in you, which was given to you through prophecy with the laying on of hands by the council of elders" (1 Tim 4:14).[121] These loosely defined stages reflect the transition to the more professionalized ministry in the late first century indicated in the sociological account of development.

Fourth and finally, moving to the theological level, it appears that throughout the transition in the organizational structures, God as Spirit, who is Christ's Spirit, provides the consistent and continuous source of the authority of the minister, in this case the governor or overseer or administrator or leader of the church. Manifestation of this Spirit appears to have been more spontaneous in the Pauline communities since there is little talk of formal structures in the sense of objective laws or criteria to regulate it. In the Pastorals, however,

---

120. See n. 34. The qualities recommended for bishops, deacons, and presbyters resemble each other (Dunn, *Pastorals*, 864). These are married men with children, of solid virtue and able to govern their own household. This provided a clue to their ability to manage a house church or the household of God (Robert Wild, *The Pastoral Letters*, NJBC, 894, 896–97). Dunn sees a natural slide from the church meeting in private households to modeling itself on the household, and finally understanding itself as the "household of God" (Dunn, *Pastorals*, 806–7). This illustrates well the interactions between history, sociology, and theology.

121. "The description envisions a public ratification of Timothy's charism 'through prophecy,' the laying on of hands as both calling down God's blessing upon him and handing on spiritual power to him, and the presence of the board of 'elders' (senior either in age or in Christian faith)." Harrington, *Church*, 96.

the same Spirit is channeled through a process of public ratification, the laying on of hands by the elders, and a set of criteria contained in a profile of an ideal bishop or elder or deacon. The institutional development lies in the Spirit's being channeled through a public process of laying on of hands that became ordination; theologically the element of continuity lies in the source of authority as the Spirit of God within the community.

Divine identity vis-à-vis the world. I move finally to the question of the theological understanding of the boundaries that define the church by setting it in relation to various entities that make up its environment. Some control over such a vast terrain can be gained by a division into relationships with Judaism, the Roman empire, and the world in the sense of the whole of reality. But each one of these areas is complex, and the New Testament does not yield a single view on any of them. Rather different communities at different times in different contexts reflect different views for different reasons. With that caution, some broad considerations are still possible.

The church in relation to Judaism. Some general statements concerning the relationship of the developing church vis-à-vis Judaism can be gleaned from 1 Peter, Galatians, and Romans.[122] First Peter appropriates for the Christian community the designation of "God's own people" (1 Pet 2:9), using the exact language used in Exodus by which God designated Israel its chosen and covenanted people, "a priestly kingdom and a holy nation" (Exodus 19:1–7). The key to the theological logic in this move consists in looking beyond Jesus Christ as the boundary dividing Jews and Christians and recognizing him as the link that unites them. Jesus the Jew is the link of continuity between the Israel of the promises and the mixed Christian communities of Gentiles and Jews. Paul makes this point in a sustained exegetical argument in Galatians 3:6–29 which concludes: "if you belong to Christ, then you are Abraham's offspring, heirs according to the promise" (Gal 3:29). The mixed Christian communities, in which there is "no longer Jew or Greek" (Gal 3:28), are in continuity with the people of God's promise (see Eph 2:11–22).

---

122. I am closely following Harrington's construction on the basis of these texts in *Church*, 69–81.

What then is the relation between a growing and increasingly autonomous Christian church and the Israel that did not accept Jesus? Paul's extensive response to this question in Romans 9–11 is characteristically open ended. On the one hand, Israel's election is permanently valid, and it sustains Christianity as the root upon which the churches have been grafted (Rom 11:18). On the other hand, if it is the case that "a hardening has come upon part of Israel, until the full number of the Gentiles has come in," nevertheless, another part of Israel lives on within the Christian church, and in the end "all Israel will be saved" (Rom 11:25–26).

The church in relation to the empire. Christian attitudes toward the Roman empire and subordinate offices of civil authority range from conformist to subversive on theological grounds. Moving from right to left, Paul counsels obedience to Roman authority because it comes from God: "Let every person be subject to the governing authorities; for there is no authority except from God, and those authorities that exist have been instituted by God" (Rom 13:1). Later in the first century Christians are urged to honor, obey, and pray for the emperor and all who hold authority (1 Tim 2:1–2; 1 Pet 2:13–17). In the period after Paul, Jesus' response to the trap of recommending obedience to competing authorities in the synoptics became a classic Christian text: "Give to the emperor the things that are the emperor's, and to God the things that are God's" (Mark 12:17). This represents a hierarchy of values and implies the supreme level of authority that is God's. Moving further to the left, reflecting a context of a persecution of the Christian church by the emperor, the book of Revelation holds out endurance, resistance, and martyrdom as signs of salvation (Rev 13:8).[123]

The church in God's scheme of things. These horizontal relationships of the church appear diminished in comparison with the vision of the church in Ephesians. Here the horizon opens up to the cosmic plan of God in Christ from all eternity. The metaphor of the body of Christ reaches beyond the local community to embrace the

---

123. "So there are several attitudes displayed toward the Roman empire in various New Testament texts: the cautious ambiguity manifested by Jesus, the apparent acceptance of and cooperation with the empire promoted by Paul and his followers, and the nonviolent resistance proposed by John the prophet." Harrington, *Church,* 132.

whole Christian movement and the whole of reality. The author presupposes and builds upon the exalted conception of Christ found in Colossians: "He is the image of the invisible God, the firstborn of all creation; for in him all things in heaven and on earth were created, things visible and invisible.... He is the head of the body, the church" (Col 1:15–16, 18). This cosmic Christ was incarnate as Jesus. In him God's plan for the fullness of time was revealed: "to gather up all things in him, things in heaven and things on earth" (Eph 1:10). God effected that plan in raising Christ from the dead and establishing him "far above all rule and authority and power and dominion, and above every name that is named, not only in this age but also in the age to come. And he has put all things under his feet and has made him the head over all things for the church, which is his body, the fullness of him who fills all in all" (Eph 1:21–23). The church becomes "the place in which the reign of the Risen and exalted Christ over all creation is made actual and manifest."[124] Here the ecclesiological imagery matches the christological heights of John's prologue. It situates the Christian not only in history but in the cosmos.[125]

PRINCIPLES FOR
A HISTORICAL ECCLESIOLOGY

After examining the genesis of the church on three distinct but inseparable levels, I now turn to the task of thinking constructively. Can one cull principles and general formulas relative to the church, especially from the process of its genesis, that will be instructive for understanding the church as it moves through history? Another question relates to the normative function of the original church: how can the earliest community in its historicity be considered normative for the future history of the church?

---

124. Harrington, *Church*, 87.
125. "The risen Christ is exalted above all the powers in the universe. Combining that insight with the Pauline metaphor of the church as the 'body of Christ,' originally an image of local churches, produces the striking new image of Ephesians 1:22–23, Christ is head of a body that fills the entire cosmos." Pheme Perkins, *The Letter to the Ephesians*, NIB, XI (2000), 386.

Multiple Tensions in the Original Self-Constitution of the Church

The analysis thus far has exhibited the plurality that characterized the organizational form and the theological self-understanding of the early Christian communities. At this point the analysis moves in a new direction of trying to establish constants in the church other than the crucial and basic theological constants of belief. These are found in certain tensive relationships that pertain to the intrinsic nature of the church because they characterize the internal dynamism of the historical life of any organization. As organizational constants they will show themselves throughout the course of the church's historical existence as that is described in subsequent chapters. At this point, however, the intrinsic, constitutive role they play in the formation of the earliest church is highlighted.

Charisma and office. The large model marking the self-constitution of the church drawn from the sociology of Max Weber proposes a passage from a group or movement, less structured because based in the charisma of Jesus, to a more structured organization with more objective, rationalized, and defined roles. But the two terms of this transition are not absolute and exclusive, as if one form could exist without the other; they are rather mutually related tensive qualities of any group or organization. They exist at opposite ends of a spectrum, as it were, in a polar relationship of more and less. Thus Weber writes: "Revolutions under a charismatic leader, directed against hereditary charismatic powers or the powers of office, are to be found in all types of corporate groups, from states to trade unions."[126] Loosely, because at times the inverse can also be true, charisma represents progressive forces in a community, and offices, especially of oversight or governance, represent conservative forces, for this was the *telos* of routinization. Offices account for the continuity of the direction of charismatic energy. What is said here of charisma and office correlates with two types of authority in the community, one resting in charisma, the other in legitimate office. Each can be genuine authority, even when they are in tension with each other. When this is recognized, the tension can elicit creative movement instead of stalemate. This seems to have

---

126. Weber, *The Theory of Economic and Social Organizations*, 370.

been illustrated in the momentous debate in the years 48–50 around the ritual Jewish law of circumcision and initiation into the Christian community.

Analogous to office and charisma are the two categories of "structure" and "communitas" developed by anthropologist Victor Turner: they are strictly reciprocal and mutually interdependent, and thus always present and in tension with each other. Structures are "the patterned arrangements of role sets, status sets, and status sequences consciously recognized and regularly operative in a given society and closely bound up with legal and practical norms and sanctions."[127] By contrast, community does not mean a close, small, unified group opposed to a large, impersonal society. Rather Turner defined it as "a relational quality of full unmediated communication, even communion, between definite and determinate identities, which arises spontaneously in all kinds of groups, situations and circumstances." "It (communitas) is the *fons et origo* of all structures and at the same time their critique."[128] Unmediated "community" thus transcends the structured order of life; it threatens ordered life, yet it is the life of the community, and structure structures it. What one sees here is a dynamic tension that characterizes a social unit or entity in its life in history. No society can function without the dialectic between these two tensive forces, the mediacy of structure and the immediacy of communitas. The tensive balance is precisely the energy-giving and creative force of a society, as opposed to resolution at either end, which would cause a reaction.[129]

Change and continuity. The tension between change and continuity is related to the tension between charisma and office, and communitas and structure, because these latter are often the agents of change and stability. Bourdieu's notion of a social *habitus* broadens this dialectic and brings it into connection with the tension which follows. He defines this category in this way: "The *habitus* — embodied history, internalized as a second nature and so forgotten as history —

---

127. Carl F. Starkloff, "Church as Structure and Communitas: Victor Turner and Ecclesiology," *Theological Studies* 58 (1997), 649, quoting Victor and Edith Turner, *Image and Pilgrimage in Christian Culture: Anthropological Perspectives* (New York: Columbia University, 1978), 252.
128. Ibid., 649, citing Turner, ibid., 250.
129. Ibid., 652.

is the active presence of the whole past of which it is the product. As such, it is what gives practices their relative autonomy with respect to external determinations of the immediate present. This autonomy is that of the past, enacted and acting, which, functioning as accumulated capital [i.e., cultural capital], produces history on the basis of history and so ensures the permanence in change that makes the individual agent a world within the world. The *habitus* is a spontaneity without consciousness or will [i.e., thematic will, for indeed it is a subjective or human disposition], opposed as much to the mechanical necessity of things without history in mechanistic theories as it is to the reflexive freedom of subjects 'without inertia' in rationalist theories."[130]

One way of understanding Bourdieu's *habitus* is to compare it with Aristotle's notion of habit. An Aristotelian habit is a quality, an inner disposition, or a propensity that so structures the person that he or she performs certain actions easily and routinely. One normally builds up such an internalized tendency by repeated actions as in an athlete's practice. Like a second nature a habit orients the person toward certain actions. Analogously, and on a social level, corporate practice and routine experience become the internal objective dispositions of a group that are at the same time subjective and acted out. A social *habitus* thus combines structure and agency, objective patterns and corporate freedom and action. In the comparison with Aristotle, a social *habitus* might be called a third nature, a socially

---

130. Pierre Bourdieu, *The Logic of Practice* (Stanford, Calif.: Stanford University Press, 1990), 56. *Habitus* (plural) are existential dispositions, structured on the basis of socialization, that in turn structure response to reality. "In reality, the dispositions durably inculcated by the possibilities and impossibilities, freedoms and necessities, opportunities and prohibitions inscribed in the objective conditions (which science apprehends through statistical regularities such as the probabilities objectively attached to a group or class) generate dispositions objectively compatible with these conditions and in a sense pre-adapted to their demands" (54). These *habitus* are like superactual value responses [Dietrich von Hildebrand, *Christian Ethics* (New York: David McKay Company, 1953), 241–43], internalized dispositions to act in a certain way. They are built up on the basis of past experience. These dispositions constitute the framework of basic cognitive and valuational responses to reality: the experiences of one's group or class build up a system which becomes the heuristic lens upon life itself: "the structures characterizing a determinate class of conditions of existence produce the structures of the *habitus*, which in their turn are the basis of the perception and appreciation of all subsequent experiences" (54).

constructed habit of a group that orients the behavior of the individuals in it. The dynamic unity of both "objectivity" and "subjectivity" or freedom is what makes this category both subtle and useful. It unites structure and community. It holds together social custom and actual behavior, the stable or constant with response to new exigencies, socially constructed patterns of knowing and valuing with the dynamic life of a group and its engagement with the real, concrete dilemmas of existence.

What one witnesses in the development of the early church is a confluence of a variety of *habitus* to form a community with its own set of conditioned and conditioning responses. Although this is codified in the New Testament, the reality far exceeds what can be inscribed. One can see in this codification both these *habitus* and their dialectical mediation of change as the community faces historical newness. The category has major relevance for the theological idea of tradition.

Organization and environment. This third polar tension too is closely related to the first and the second because the constant encounter of the organization with its environment provides one of the main engines of change. The process by which the early Christian church was constituted contains one of the most dramatic instances of such change, namely, the shift away from Palestine to an interface with the Roman world and Greek culture. Ordinarily histories of the church and its doctrine emphasize the smooth character of the development that occurred across this transition, and rightly so, because of the dominant Christian *habitus*. But one can also dwell on the radicality of the changes that occurred in the course of this transition. Because "Hellenization" became a pejorative term in church history, one can perhaps view this process more neutrally when it is called inculturation: adjustment to Greek culture is the classical instance of inculturation because it encompassed the early church and the New Testament itself. The church will always be pluralistic because it must interact with its environment, and this will mean constant shifting and adjusting of boundaries.[131]

---

131. The idea of inculturation is anything but simple. Today this category has as its context the historic shift of the center of gravity of Christianity from European to other centers and cultures throughout the world. The debates entailed in this process are

Closely enough related to this tension, so that it need not be separated from it, is the dialectical relation between mission and maintenance in the church mentioned earlier.[132] The mission of the church is to engage the world, and concretely this means the environment in which it finds itself. The church as mission is an outwardly oriented organization in dialogue with the secular or non-Christian world. At the same time it must preserve its self-identity. Thus both energy and structure must be devoted to this immediate goal. This tension promises dynamism and creativity on the condition of balance and dialectical interaction. Too heavy an emphasis on either side of the tension can compromise the identity of the church in a flurry of activity or strangle its dynamic life. Measuring the proper balance will always be a matter of debate. But the sociology of organizations makes it clear that frequently enough organizations veer from their specific foundational purpose in the effort to preserve a form of identity more suited to the past.

Still another distinction fits within this tensive relationship with environment, one between those activities which are "missionary" in the sense of reaching outward to engage the variety of different aspects of the world "outside," and those activities meant to build up the inner life of the community. Ideally these two kinds of activities will not coexist in a competitive zero-sum relationship but will reinforce each other. The controversy with the Judaizers in Paul and the generally ambivalent relationship of the early church with Greek culture exemplify and illumine this intrinsic tension in the constitution of the church and how it may be generative.

Ideals and actuality. Do not dialogue with the world and every manner of inculturation by definition entail compromise of the primitive ideals of the church or at least a watering of them down? The

---

connoted by the positive meaning of the term: the process by which the Christian faith and message become actualized within a specific culture. This process may include all sorts of negative associations when it is viewed from different perspectives. For example, does inculturation alter traditional faith? Does it presuppose that Christianity has one "proper" cultural form that gets translated into other languages and behavioral patterns? Today's sense of historicity and cultural pluralism makes inculturation less a clear concept and more a topic of conversation or intricate worldwide discussion concerning the process and its optimal results.

132. Baum, "Contradictions in the Catholic Church," *Theology and Society*, 230–46.

goal and mission of the church relate to the utopic but always approaching kingdom of God preached by Jesus; the actuality always falls far short, increasingly so as the church grows and develops. When these ideals are understood in terms of ethics and "holiness" or moral uprightness of the church in its members, these observations appear obvious. They rest on social dynamics that have to be taken into account in any understanding of the church. Two such dialectical tensions appear in the early church. The first is a realism that recognizes multiple ideals: no organization is fully defined by its stated ideals; all organizations contain a host of "operational" and perhaps conflicting ideals, internalized by the members, and which do not measure up to its explicit ideals.[133] But, second, the distinction between sect and church proffered by Ernst Troeltsch, as broad as it is, still teaches that ideals and expectations themselves can sharply diverge.[134] This results in polities and the premises for Christian morality that have become definably differentiated. One does not quite see a distinction between sects and churches in the first two centuries of the church, even though the small community is moving in the direction of becoming a "church." But one can already see sharp differences in the ideals of the Christian life and spirituality in the communities of James and Paul.

Practice, institutional form, and theology. The church is self-constituting; it arises out of practice. The elements of the church's organization, including its reflective forms of self-understanding such as scripture and theology, are generated by practice. The history of the development of the church as a whole portrays this, and any given event may be taken as illustrative. For example, the story of Cornelius shows that Gentile desire for baptism led to the realization that the Spirit was not restricted within the Jewish Jesus movement, and the response to this led to far-reaching shifts in the direction of the movement.

---

133. The point was made earlier in terms of goals and seems transferable to the question of ideals. See Perrow, *Complex Organizations*, 160–61.

134. Troeltsch distinguishes a "sect" type of church organization and self-understanding from a "church" type. The one is usually smaller in size and stands over against society; the other tends toward becoming coterminous with society. Each type has a set of attendant qualities. Ernst Troeltsch, *The Social Teaching of the Christian Churches* (New York: Harper Torchbooks, 1960), 331–43.

Bourdieu is helpful in sorting out how institution and reflective thought emerge out of the logic of practice.[135] Among others he proposes two theses, one negative, the other positive. Negatively, with the phrase "the logic of practice" he wishes to distinguish the lived reality from its theoretical mappings or interpretations. Logical models give an account of observed data in the most coherent and economical way; but they become "dangerous as soon as they are treated as the real principles of practices, which amounts to simultaneously overestimating the logic of practices and losing sight of what constitutes their real principle."[136] The logic of practice cannot be reduced to a theoretical or discursive portrayal of it; one should not confuse the perspective of the actor with that of the spectator. Positively, however, practices "have as their principle not a set of conscious, constant rules, but practical schemes, opaque to their possessors, varying according to the logic of the situation, the almost invariable partial viewpoint which it imposes, etc."[137] This practical, pragmatic logic relies on internalized guidance, and flows quasi-instinctively out of the *habitus* (plural) that constitute the community as it confronts new situations.[138] These distinctions help to clarify how both church organization and its theology, which is a part of this superstructure, were generated from below. The principle of contingency in historical development does not mean sheer randomness; response to the variations of environment is guided by the deep *habitus* provided by faith, traditions, and the memory of Jesus.

Unity and plurality. The tension between unity and plurality in the early church is obvious and intense. Two distinct issues latent in the tension will throw light on the church in history.

The first is the fact of pluralism. Pluralism means not simply diversity, but unity and diversity together, or differences held together within a common field of reference. The early church is a pluralistic organization. On the one hand, the value of unity suffused the

---

135. See in particular Bourdieu, *The Logic of Practice*, 80–97. Bourdieu speaks of practice, and not praxis, because he is interested in maintaining a firm distinction between practice and reflection (as distinct from an idea of praxis as reflective behavior) in order to show how these two distinct dimensions relate to each other.

136. Ibid., 11.

137. Ibid., 12.

138. Ibid., 95–97.

community wherever it existed and according to all of its historical witnesses. The metaphors for the unity of the church abound. On the other hand, it is hard to exaggerate the differences among the Christian communities that made up the early church. The earliest Christian church is a pluralistic movement, group, collection of groups, and finally organization.

The second issue, perhaps more important, are the mechanisms by which the church managed this pluralism. How was the emerging church able to control and organize its pluralism? Perhaps the single most important institution here is the scriptural canon which is a collection of different communitarian witnesses to the church. This made the very norm for the unity of the church a pluralistic constitution. The other mechanisms for holding the movement across the empire together and giving it a broad sense of identity were also loose and developing: the various methods of communication and the fundamental character of its creeds and basic structure.

Interpenetration of large community and small community. Closely related to the unity-diversity tension is the relationship between the whole and its parts. So closely do the whole movement and the distinct communities interrelate with each other during the period of formation that it is difficult to draw clear axioms from this period that would be relevant to the wrenching problems that arose in later history. Two things, however, do seem clear. One is that a dialectical relation obtains here, and that neither the isolation of individual churches nor the view that the church is a single organization is satisfactory. The relationship must be tensive. The other is that the principle of subsidiarity in some measure characterizes the early church. This says that the whole church should not assume responsibility for that which can be accomplished on a "lower" or more local level. The principle preserves an integral whole church as a union of churches.

To sum up here, these seven areas of tension within the church are not meant to be exhaustive. They are highlighted to show that they are intrinsic to the constitution of the early church. In fact, they are perennial qualities of the church. The interaction of the opposite extremes of these thematic polarities function in the manner of types, providing heuristic devices for the analysis of dynamism, movement, and life of the church in history. It is important to recognize that actual tension along these lines is not anomalous but intrinsic to the nature of the church.

The Normativity of the Early Church

The view that Jesus intentionally founded the church as the autonomous institution it came to be is no longer common among exegetes and historians. Historical research displays the developmental and pluralistic character of the early church. But this seems to call into question its normativity for future generations: can the early church retain its normative character and how is this to be envisioned? The following proposal responds to these questions by offering, first, a broad definition and description of the early church and, second, a consideration of how this church might be considered normative for all churches in the Christian movement into the future. This will be done in the schematic form of an outline in keeping with its heuristic status.

Characterization of the church in the first and second centuries. I begin by offering two working definitions of the Christian church, two in order to indicate that many such definitions are possible. Both are spare but able to be expanded into the multiple dimensions that are constitutive of the church. One definition of the church says that the church is the institutionalization of the community of people who, animated by the Spirit of God, live in the faith that Jesus is the Christ of God.[139] An alternative definition makes explicit the goal or mission of the church: the church is the historical community of the disciples of Jesus animated by God as Spirit whose goal is to continue and expand Jesus' message in history. Both of these definitions are quite simple. They combine the historical-social aspects with the theological; apart from the phrase "animated by God as Spirit," the definitions are empirical and descriptive. The following qualities sum up the church as it has appeared in the previous analyses.[140]

---

139. Haight, "Historical Ecclesiology," 36.

140. Theissen sums up his anthropological portrayal of the formation of early Christianity as a religion, i.e., a semiotic system of religious meaning and value, with a characterization of its essence in two foundational axioms (monotheism and redemption through Jesus) and eleven basic motifs (general principles of belief, ritual, and

Jesus the generative principle. Although Jesus probably did not intend to found a new religion, he is the generative principle behind the church that arose. He is its dynamic foundation, dynamic in the sense that he continued to inspire disciples, even when the prophetic charisma became channeled into more objective social forms. The Spirit of God which accounts for the divine energy and life of the church cannot be separated from Jesus Christ.

Developmental. The church is developmental in the sense that it is the product of development over two centuries and beyond. It thus takes on an "historical" character in the sense that it is constituted over time and by increment, as distinct from being made all at once according to a set of blueprints. The church is the old house described by Bourdieu thus: "old houses, with their successive annexes and all the objects, partially discordant but fundamentally in harmony with them, that have accumulated in them in the course of time, [stand in contrast] to apartments designed from end to end in accordance with an aesthetic concept imposed all at once and from outside by an interior designer."[141] The whole house possesses harmony, pattern, shape, unity, coherence, and integrity, but these are qualities that people continually got used to as it grew by addition out of practice schooled in the memory of Jesus.

Pluralistic. The church is pluralistic. Difference marks just about everything that exists in its explicit and objective forms: beliefs, most centrally christologies, ministries and ministerial structures, ethnic backgrounds, governmental structures. The canon of its normative writings is a disparate collection that mirrors these differences.

One: churches in communion. Despite the development in different situations and the differences that accumulated, all the churches held up the unity of the whole movement as a value. There were grounds for this: one body, one Spirit, one Lord, one faith, one baptism, one God (Eph 4:4–6). These theological grounds were supported by various organizational forms of communication and intercommunion to make the unity historically real or actual.

---

ethics). His summary instructively expands the narrower and more schematic analysis offered here.

141. Bourdieu, *The Logic of Practice*, 13.

Jesus-centered and Spirit-filled. From beginning to end, therefore, the early church remained Jesus-centered and Spirit-filled. As a religious organization, one must assign a priority to this deep dimension of the church in any consideration of its essential nature.

How this church can be normative. The question, however, is whether such a church can function as a norm for future churches. The places where normativity seems to be undermined lie in the seeming loss of a divine intention for the church that followed the loss of a clear sense that Jesus intended to set up any church, let alone this particular church. Moreover, the developmental character of the early church and the fact that it is continually developing in new directions in different situations negate a fixed or rigid sense of normativity that previously prevailed. The idea of replicating the past, or of appealing to the past with proof-texts, is virtually eliminated. Change is intrinsic to history; static identity is impossible. This requires a dynamic concept or logic of normativity.

The normativity of the past in any organization has to do with identity. A natural tendency aims at preserving the identity of a group as that was constituted in its origin or genesis. This natural tendency is enhanced in the religious organization that was formed around Jesus the Christ in whom was encountered a self-revelation of God and salvation. This was apparent in the deep logic of apostolicity that drove the community to fashion organizational mechanisms that would ensure the original identity of the group against alien and corrupting influences. The principal institution here was scripture itself, and even those Christian communities which have rejected some of the other institutions, such as episcopacy, still cling to scripture as a norm of authentic Christian revelation and practice. We have seen in the human technology of writing how, after the classical form of faith is codified in scripture, reflection thereafter bends back on it as on the constitutional ground of Christian identity. But just as historical consciousness prevents the normativity of scripture from being understood in terms of proof-texting, so too the normativity of the early church generally must transcend literal imitation. It is better understood in terms of a social anthropology, the continuity in existence of communities, and hermeneutical habits of interpreting the past and applying it to the present.

Human beings are social, and human knowledge is socially constructed. Plato conceived of the a prioris that are revealed in human discovery, insight, and knowing according to a theory of recollection; one had to possess an original set of ideas simply to construe present finite reality. In a historically conscious social theory of knowledge, it appears that these a priori ideas are provided by memory: corporate memory and socialization into the language and culture of a community.[142] At the core of the Christian language and culture of the church is the *memoria vitae, passionis, mortis et resurrectionis Jesu Christi.*[143] This memory, and the whole constellation of insight, response, and openness to the future that accompany it, are contained in the community of disciples who encountered the God of salvation in Jesus. Indeed, this memory constituted the origin and genesis of the movement that actively and developmentally, under the influence of the Spirit, constructed the Christian church. What was thus self-constituted in and by this community was the corporate *habitus* of Christianity, of Christian identity. This is an existential and pluralistic ground of practice that cannot in the end be fully captured, not in scripture and not in the Christian church. But neither would nor could the Christian *habitus* survive without institutionalization on the one hand and an actual set of followers on the other. The early church is normative because it represents the original, classical reception of and response to the saving revelation of God in Jesus Christ which constitutes the church.[144]

---

142. This analysis does not rule out all transcendental a priori contributions to knowing on the part of the human subject. But all such dynamisms operate dialectically in a socially mediated knowledge. Typically human structures of knowing, anthropological constants, always operate in a historically and socially constructed way.

143. Borrowing from and expanding upon the phrase of Johann Baptist Metz on the dangerous memory of the freedom and suffering of Jesus Christ, that basic "contrast experience" which releases freedom, benefits all who suffer, and is dangerous for all who benefit from the suffering of others. See J. B. Metz, *Faith in History and Society: Toward a Practical Fundamental Theology* (New York: Crossroad, 1980), 89–94 and *passim.*

144. I take it that the scriptures and more broadly the early church are both normative for the historical church in analogous ways. Scriptures are a more focused and clearly defined norm. But the early church, let us say somewhat arbitrarily the church of the first two centuries, also has a normative function insofar as the church was not fully developed, even in its most basic forms, by the end of the first century or with the writing of the last of the canonical scriptures. Also, it was the church of the second century which decided the canon and thus set the scriptural norm.

Although the memory and *habitus* of a community explain how origins can be normative, these categories do not measure fidelity to the classical ideal or reduce conflict in the interpretation and implementation of its normative character. The constitution of an organization and the whole course of its history lie open to interpretation and appropriation by different factions in relation to different concerns and interests. Fidelity to a community's norms and mission are possible but not easy, and never free from a pluralism that involves some level of conflict. Such conflict, perhaps bitter at times, has to be expected as a "normal" dimension of the church.

How then can this normativity be accessed in a credible way? The following principles describe in a very general way a hermeneutic that correlates with the character of the early church as outlined in the previous sections of this chapter.

Focus on the generative principle. First of all, a hermeneutic that draws forward the early church as normative for life in the church into the future must focus on the generative principle of the church itself, namely, the message, ministry, and person of Jesus of Nazareth. This appreciation finds its core in the vision of the Paschal or "redeemed" character of human existence that is revealed in and through God at work in Jesus: life-death-life.

Developmental. Such a hermeneutic must be attentive to the developmental character of the early church. One cannot consider one phase of that development normative and another phase not. It is rather the developmental character itself that is normative. This means that interpretation must negotiate across the developments in beliefs, rituals, ministries, governmental structures, and ethics to find the logic of the practice that generated them. Normativity does not and cannot function by literal appropriation, but must be found in the spirit or "communitas" within the forms, the primitive logic of experience that generated the structures in the first place.

Across differences. Similarly, a historical, existential hermeneutic reaches across the differences between the various institutional forms that obtained in the early church. This means that one cannot take one institutional form from the early church and make it exclusive of other early church forms. It is rather the point or the deeper *telos* of the function that has to be appreciated and drawn forward in yet another new form for a new context. Beliefs, rituals, ministries, organizational structures, and ethical norms can vary and at the same time all preserve a common inner purpose. An analogical imagination that appreciates continuities amid differences is crucial to the very possibility of accepting normativity within history.

Communion, interdependence, interaction, mutuality. In correspondence with the oneness and intercommunion among the early churches, appropriations of the early church must remain open to other communities and be so understood that they encourage interdependence, interaction, mutuality. This is not a recommendation for separated churches to talk to one another. It is rather a recognition of the deeper unity of the whole that does not concede separation without the gravest reasons or, perhaps, ever. A recognition of the pluralism and unity of the early church as normative should go a long way toward showing the measure in which the present situation is anomalous.

Jesus centered and Spirit filled. Finally, the hermeneutical appropriation of the early church as normative should attend to the motion of God as Spirit. The discernment of the Spirit is always a precarious thing, but with the ministry of Jesus as a historical indicator the risk has to be assumed.

•

These principles, along with the tensions that were described as intrinsic to the social life of the church, will be found recurring in the life of the church across its two millennia of historical existence. The next chapter will describe the pre-Constantinian church as it makes its way in the Roman empire during the second and third centuries.

Chapter 3

The Pre-Constantinian Church

The last chapter represented various dimensions of the genesis of the church as this can be constructed principally through the sources provided by the New Testament. The development reached a certain "closure" in the course of the second century. This chapter interprets the pre-Constantinian church, essentially the church of the second and third centuries. To do this I will reach back into the second century again and knit together some of the data from that period with developments in the third century to form a rough outline of the church up to the Constantinian settlement. Only the broad goals of this presentation can legitimate a sweep of such a mass of data in so short a space. I wish to show the developmental character of the church in this period, illustrate the changes and resultant diversity this movement incurs as it interacts with society and empire, and as a succession of new leaders respond to new problems. Only with a sense of the expanding size and breadth of the Christian movement, and the complexity of the many kinds of interactions with the world that defined it, can one begin to appreciate the essential dimensions of its self-identity and the developing organizational institutions that held it together. The focus thus has a somewhat formal cast: unity in diversity, continuing substance within changing forms, the integrity of the whole maintained though changing situations.

The analysis which follows falls into a pattern roughly analogous to that of the last chapter. The first part sets the context of the Roman empire during the second and third centuries. It contains a short account of some of the major events of the church's historical development and introduces certain authors who represent the church during this period. Second, a social-theological account of the church is constructed from the texts of these Greek and Latin figures:

Ignatius, Justin, Irenaeus, Hippolytus, the author of the *Didascalia Apostolorum*, Tertullian, and Cyprian. The reading of selected texts of these authors has been guided by the structural dimensions of organizations highlighted in the last chapter: their members, activities, goals, structures, and environment. All of these texts do not respond to all of these aspects of the church, and they do not yield successive, integral, synchronic portraits of the churches they portray across these two hundred years. But they communicate a forceful impression of various aspects of a given church as it interacts with historical events and society. The third section of the chapter then attempts a description of a pre-Constantinian church with special reference to the church of Cyprian in North Africa. The last section contains some broad principles, simultaneously historical, sociological, and theological, that may be learned from this distinctive period of the church and serve a perennial function.

HISTORICAL DEVELOPMENT

The major transition of Christianity from a Palestinian Jewish setting to the Roman imperial world and Greek culture began immediately. It received a major stimulus at mid-century with Paul's missionary activity. It took off in the second century and thereafter. The new church cannot be understood apart from this context. This section points to this world that shaped the emerging church and introduces the Christian witnesses to the church that I shall consult.[1]

---

1. The following sources have been helpful in this account: Peter Brown, *The Rise of Western Christendom: Triumph and Diversity, AD 200–1000* (Oxford: Blackwell, 1996, 2003), *The Body and Society: Man, Woman and Sexual Renunciation in Early Christianity* (New York: Columbia University Press, 1988), *Late Antiquity* (Cambridge, Mass.: Harvard University Press, 1998); Henry Chadwick, *The Early Church* (New York: Penguin Books, 1967), *The Church in Ancient Society: From Galilee to Gregory the Great* (Oxford: University Press, 2001); W. C. H. Frend, *The Rise of Christianity* (Philadelphia: Fortress Press, 1984), *The Early Church* (Philadelphia: Fortress Press, 1982); Bernard Cooke, *Ministry to Word and Sacraments: History and Theology* (Philadelphia: Fortress Press, 1976); Jean Daniélou, *Gospel Message and Hellenistic Culture* (Philadelphia: Westminster Press, 1973); Jean Daniélou and Henri Marrou, *The First Six Hundred Years* (New York: McGraw-Hill, 1964); Eric G. Jay, *The Church: Its Changing Image through Twenty Centuries* (Atlanta: John Knox Press, 1980); Rodney Stark, *The Rise of Christianity* (Princeton: Princeton University Press, 1996); Walter H. Wagner, *After the Apostles: Christianity in the Second Century* (Minneapolis: Fortress Press, 1994).

The Imperial Context

The church of the early second century would have to be called Jewish in character: its basic beliefs, rituals, and ethics were born out of Judaism. But this Jewish Christianity in its turn toward the empire rapidly assumed Hellenistic and Roman forms. The tension between substance and form allows the ambiguous maxim that Christianity drew its substance from Judaism and its form from Greco-Roman culture.[2] Any close examination of the pre-Constantinian church would require an analysis of how the culture, society, politics, and events that constituted the Roman empire shaped the new religion. The intent here and throughout the book is considerably more humble. The narrative underscores that the situations of empire in antiquity, feudalism and monarchy in the Middle Ages, emerging nationhood in western Europe in the early modern period, and growing world solidarity of our recent past have all given the church a distinctively different existence. The historical account raises up elements in the context of the church during the second and third centuries that, if not taken into account, would render the further development of the church unintelligible. These elements can be sorted according to their depth as cultural, social-political-economic, and discrete persons and events.[3]

Culture. "Culture" refers to the system of meanings, ideas, sets of values, and a comprehensive vision that lies deep enough within a people that it can remain more or less constant amidst observable social and political changes. Culture in this sense exists in alignment with language and traditional public symbols: persons, places, events. The last chapter noted how the earliest Jewish Hellenist followers of Jesus, in translating his gospel message into Greek, opened Christianity to a "universal" and "universalizing" culture. This helped

---

2. The topic of Hellenization is contentious. The ambiguity stems from an inability neatly to distinguish form and content, because cultural form always contributes to religious substance. The point is that the inculturation of the church into the Roman empire involved both real continuity and real change.

3. See the distinctions in historical change, drawn by Fernand Braudel, as noted by Peter Burke, *History and Sociology* (London: George Allen & Unwin, 1980), 94. Historical change occurs at different speeds: the history of events is most rapid; conjunctural history of social systems is less rapid; structural history of human cultural relations to environment is slowest. Edward Schillebeeckx employs the distinction in *Jesus: An Experiment in Christology* (New York: Seabury, 1979), 577ff.

Christianity to spread with a rapidity proportionate to the prevalence of this culture and language; it provided a medium of elementary comprehensibility and transferability. No matter what one's assessment of "Hellenization" might be, one has to recognize the profound impact of this linguistic and cultural "translation."

Part of this inculturation involved the appropriation of the message of Christianity within the framework of Greek intellectual tradition and the specific languages of a highly nuanced philosophical culture. Philo exemplifies an analogous process in the Judaism of the diaspora. Right from the beginning, even within the New Testament, one can discern the influence of the reflective, critical-mindedness of Greek philosophy. As philosophically astute Greeks appropriated the Christian message and interpreted it to their own culture, they proposed new interpretations and expressions of the original message. The importance of pagan philosophical critique and Christian response, as in the genre of "apology" or defense, generated genuinely new self-understanding. It would be hard to over-estimate the significance of the transition of Jesus' message from the cultural context of Palestine to those represented by the symbols of Rome and Alexandria.

One aspect of this shift, one way of measuring its importance, consists simply in reflecting on the emergence of doctrine and the importance that doctrines assumed during these centuries in terms of truth and error. Preserving the truth, justifying it against error, preserving the church within the boundaries of truth as opposed to error: these themes came to be central to Christianity as a religion during these centuries. It has become customary within Christian theology to see the development of doctrine as a "smooth" process of continuity; development preserves original meaning, augments it, expands it, explains it. But one can also note "sharp" transitions and even breaks or significant changes of meaning as church teaching moves from its Jewish context to the more formal structures of Greek and Latin doctrine.

Religious beliefs lie near the heart of a culture. The polytheism of the Roman empire, together with its relative tolerance of myriad assorted local cults or broader religious traditions centering on a specific god, deeply conditioned the self-appropriation of Christians. On the one hand, Christianity firmly asserted its monotheism and an exclusivism as the only true religion over against Graeco-Roman religion while it benefited from the relative tolerance that a culture of religious pluralism afforded. On the other hand, Christianity shared with its culture the belief in a whole world of "goblins and evil spirits."[4] The lesser gods and demons were omnipresent and constantly at work in the world, so that superstitious practices, by one standard or another, were a way of life. In terms of basic ideas, values, and vision of reality as a whole, Graeco-Roman culture entered into Christian self-understanding and the church's self-constitution by both opposition and positive sympathetic resonance.

Society. The term "society" refers to the social, political, and economic arrangements that are far less stable than culture, but which shift more or less rapidly over periods of time and under the pressure of accumulating events. So, for example, Christianity was born into the period of the *pax romana* which provided a center of peace within extensive and often violent frontiers. At the very center was the Mediterranean which provided water lanes of commerce, travel, and mobility. The actual communications among local cultures provided a social network for exchanging or appreciating or developing deeper cultural presuppositions. It was pointed out in the last chapter that the spread of Christianity followed the routes of trade between cities, by sea lanes and Roman roads.

The dominant part of Christianity that spread westward into the Mediterranean basin became an urban religion, as distinct from a rural or peasant religion. Ninety percent of the people in the empire lived in rural areas. The church established its beachhead in the cities and only gradually spread to the towns. Its life in the city meant that it had to cope with religious pluralism. Christians lived and worked with pagans, in a pagan society, along with people who shared a wide variety of different religious beliefs. A sociological contrast between

---

4. Frend, *Rise of Christianity,* 168. "The Christians attacked the gods, not by denying their existence: they existed; but they were all equally evil. . . . The Demons, faceless invisible powers, past-masters of the art of illusion, merely used the traditional rites, myths and images of polytheism as so many masks, with which to draw the human race even further away from the worship of the one true God." Brown, *Rise of Western Christendom,* 27. In the year 251, one third of the clergy in the Roman church were exorcists. Ibid., 32.

urban and pastoral settings would further illumine the character of the church's development.

In the political order of things, more and more Christians would be Roman citizens. But at the same time they claimed a higher citizenship. The emperor was their emperor, but he ruled by the providence of God. From the other point of view, the state tolerated Christians and accepted them as citizens, while at the same time they were on occasion accused as being enemies of the state. The church as church existed within the empire and thus was part of it. Some aspects of its government had imperial structure as its model. At the same time, in many respects the Christian was taught to understand the church as being apart from the world.

In terms of social relationships, Roman society was hierarchically ordered from the household to the structure of the empire itself. At various levels this rigidly ordered classification of people had to conflict with a religion whose written ideals said there were no more Gentiles and Jews, freed and enslaved, male and female. Whether or not those ideals were ever realized, one has to appreciate every moral and social stance on Jews, slaves, and women as existing in some tension or compromise with social values, as taking a stand against or going along with existing practices.

Events. Events in the end supply the engine of social and political change. A number of kinds of events and personalities had significant impact on the growth of the church. In effect, the chapter will be devoted to some of these persons. From the side of the empire, however, it was common enough to fault Christians for hard times. According to the apologists, Christians were scapegoated for economic failure, defeats in battles, scarcity and famine. Tertullian complained about the tendency to punish Christians to placate the gods.[5] Whether his motives were to punish Christians or simply to placate the gods, Decius (249–251) sent tremors through the communities of Christians with his general order to acknowledge the gods or face severe punishment. In general, the Christian community in various degrees at various times developed under a threat of

---

5. Tertullian, *Apology,* 40 in *Tertullian: Apologetical Works and Minucius Felix: Octavius, The Fathers of the Church* (New York: Fathers of the Church, 1950), 102.

either local or occasionally general persecution. This strengthened boundaries, identity, and unity.

Developments of the Church

The pre-Constantinian church presented here encompasses the second and third centuries as represented in part by Eusebius and other authors writing from different particular churches. The period is marked by an ever-increasing growth in absolute numbers and an expansion of the church over a wider territory. If Tertullian was not exaggerating, members were being converted from all walks of life. By the end of the second century, Christian communities contained long-time-member families and enjoyed a constant influx of new members. By the end of the third century the church was no longer tiny groups huddling in large cities. Individual local churches had become more complex, ordered, and routinized. Churches were being built.[6] Certain institutions held the whole Christian community together in a loose federated unity. For example, regional churches met in synods. Approximately ninety bishops met in synod at Carthage during the time of Cyprian in the mid-third century. A steady rate of growth from the beginning would include a fuller geometric expansion in the second part of the third century and again in the early fourth century. Rodney Stark, figuring that "Christianity grew at the rate of *40 percent per decade,* [calculates] there would have been 7,530 Christians in the year 100, followed by 217,795 Christians in the year 200 and by 6,299,832 Christians in the year 300."[7] This large growth during the second half of the third century seems to correspond to historical testimony. During Cyprian's tenure (248–58), the first generalized and systematic persecution of Christians under Decius was particularly severe and took a toll on the church. But afterward, emperor Galienus issued an edict tolerating Christianity and restoring church property. The church's becoming a public,

---

6. "Christian churches of the third century may have been relatively humble affairs, assembly-rooms created within existing structures of houses. The church at Dura Europos, on the Euphrates, had been constructed, in this manner, in the 230s, to house a congregation of barely more than seventy." Brown, *Rise of Western Christendom,* 24.

7. Stark, *The Rise of Christianity,* 6. Stark's work elicited a good deal of reaction. See three critical reviews and a response by Stark in *Journal of Early Christian Studies* 6 (1998): 161–267.

visible institution, usually associated with the fourth century, was already beginning in the third.[8] In the second century churches were to be found from the banks of the Euphrates to Lyon on the Rhône, a distance of 80 days travel. "Each betrayed the silent presence of a distinctive religious and social landscape."[9] By the year 300 Christians lived throughout the Roman empire. To represent briefly the course of the development of the church in this period I will look to some of the key informants on the church in various places during these two centuries.

Representative witnesses. The writings of Ignatius of Antioch, Justin Martyr, and Irenaeus in the second century represent the development of several elements of the church. A heightened sense of the value of unity and the structure to ensure it on the local level is reflected in the Pastorals but dominates the letters of Ignatius. Justin represents the opening up of dialogue with the empire, a process that included all at once self-explanation, defense, and self-appropriation vis-à-vis the massive empire which now enveloped the church. Justin also provides a short but detailed account of worship in the church around the year 150. Finally, as indicated in the last chapter, a certain closure of a phase of development is represented in Irenaeus's writings. As Frend puts it: "By 175 and the end of the century, Christians attained a self-identity based on their sacred literature, the New Testament, their distinctive liturgy, their rule of faith, and their wide-ranging organization."[10]

The organization of the local church, which took a leap forward with the office of the monarchical bishop, continued to develop. *The Apostolic Tradition* attributed to Hippolytus gives a good indication of church order in the churches within the sphere of Rome's influence between the late second century and the early fourth. It provides a picture of church life, at least in formal terms without thick description. Hippolytus, the scholarly and conservative leader who broke with Callistus, bishop of Rome, in the second decade of the third century represents the tradition of the Roman church going back into the second century: this church seems to consist in a handful of

---

8. Daniélou and Marrou, *The First Six Hundred Years*, 223–30.
9. Brown, *The Body and Society*, 64.
10. Frend, *The Rise of Christianity*, 162.

saints standing against the world. Callistus by contrast represents an expanding institutional church adapting to its size and accommodating with society. Daniélou analyzed these two figures symbolically in terms resembling the distinction between "sect" and "church."[11]

The church in Alexandria at the end of the second century begins to appear in Eusebius's account of Clement and Origen. These Alexandrians reflect the church reaching out to Greek intellectual culture and developing a Christian theology that shares the stress on revealed knowledge found in gnosticism. In Clement the church appears as a house of faith-knowledge and a school of formation into the way of salvation. More than any other patristic figure, Origen communicated to the church an interpretation of its faith expressed in intellectually inculturated, philosophically mediated, and holistic terms. The impulse for preserving the historically given truth of revelation receives a deep philosophical and dialectical grounding. A fuller analysis of the church in this period than is possible here would examine the inculturated self-understanding proposed by the Alexandrian church.[12]

The *Didascalia Apostolorum* possibly represents the church in Syria during the first half of the third century and thus within the sphere of influence of Antioch. It is interesting to compare the church order of the East with that of Rome in the first part of the third century.

The first Latin speaking bishop of Rome was Victor (189–99).[13] By mid-century under the episcopacy of Cornelius the church had grown significantly: it "had a staff of 155 clergy and supported some fifteen hundred widows and poor. Such a group, quite apart from the regular congregation, was as large as the city's largest trade association. It was an enormous assemblage in a city where the average cult-group

---

11. Daniélou and Marrou, *The First Six Hundred Years*, 144–51. Jay finds the same antithesis: see *The Church*, 56.

12. For example, in many respects Clement of Alexandria understood the church as the school of salvation in which members received ordered formation in the culture that leads to final salvation. Wagner, *After the Apostles*, 179–82, 238. See as well Daniélou, *Gospel Message and Hellenistic Culture*, 303–22, 364–86; Daniélou and Marrou, *The First Six Hundred Years*, 127–36, 181–86; and on the contribution of Origen, Hans von Campenhausen, *The Fathers of the Greek Church* (New York: Pantheon Books, 1959), 40–56.

13. Frend, *The Early Church*, 74.

or burial club could be numbered in scores, not in hundreds."[14] Reflection on the Latin church begins with Tertullian in Carthage and continues with Cyprian in the middle of the century. The one clearly displays the ambivalent relationship of the church to the empire at the turn of the third century, while in the writings of the other one can see the effects of persecution on the church and new internal problems as the church grew more at home in and acclimated with society.

The century came to an end with the long and systematic persecution of Christians by Diocletian begun in 302. Imperial society was still deeply polytheistic. "It was assumed, as a matter of common sense, that there were many gods, and that these gods demanded worship through concrete, publicly visible gestures of reverence and gratitude."[15] This persecution brought these two centuries of development to a horrendous climax. It provides one of the clearest historical frontiers marking the end of one era of the church and the beginning of a new one in the social and political context of peace with the empire offered by Constantine.

The problems facing the church. Formulating the historical problems or crises that the church faced is a way of interpreting the developments of the church as responses to them. Somewhat arbitrarily, for they overlap, the problems facing the church at this time can be arranged along two fronts, the one concerned with its internal life, the other with its outer relationships.

The internal problems revolve around unity and self-definition. Against the background of its growth and expansion, several aspects of the church's coherent self-identity were threatened. First of all, the church had to guarantee unity in belief when teachers proposed novel doctrines. What was the church to do in the face of a multiplicity of what were judged to be distorting interpretations of the originating message of Jesus and the first witness to that message? How were internal divisions within the communities to be managed? Although these questions were present from the very beginning in the earliest

---

14. Brown, *Late Antiquity*, 34.
15. Brown, *Rise of Western Christendom*, 20.

churches, they were particularly pressing as the church negotiated the shift into a new cultural world.

Second, the community had to maintain unity in the face of moral relapse of the members and even denial of their faith. The church preached a high moral ideal; what of those members who professed Christianity but did not live according to Christian standards? This became a pressing issue in the time of persecution when some Christians faced the choice of apostasy or torture and possibly death. More generally it accompanied the expansion of the church and its acclimatization with society.

Third, how did the church handle the increasing complexity of community life and the gradual growth in members? How was the church to retain the clearly defined self-identity of a small community and the quality of its religious life when it began to grow into larger groups of people?

Fourth, the issue of the unity among churches in different places also posed a problem. From the very beginning churches developed different traditions in different places. For example, Eusebius tells of the serious dispute between Eastern and Western churches over the calendar date for celebrating Easter in the late second century.[16] How was the church to maintain itself as a unified movement if its many churches were spread all over the Mediterranean world, growing more autonomous, and professing different traditions?[17] This problem was aggravated by the inroads of all sorts of bizarre teachers and teachings. In the earliest period communications between churches through letters, itinerant teachers, and emissaries helped to preserve essential common doctrine and practice. In the second and third centuries itinerant teachers were causing the problem. In sum, the problem of unity was multifaceted and concerned the very identity of the church and hence its survival.

---

16. Paul L. Maier, *Eusebius — The Church History: A New Translation with Commentary*, 5. 23–25 (Grand Rapids, Mich.: Kregel, 1999), 197–200.

17. One can question whether the way the question is stated, with a distinction and tension between the church as a whole movement and the churches that constitute it, corresponds to the pre-Constantinian situation. To what extend does the church as a whole movement have a unity and identity in this period that transcends churches-in-communion?

The second problematic area concerned the relation of the church to the world. At least two aspects to the complex question of how the church should define itself in relation to the world of the Roman empire present themselves. First, the world can be considered as a sphere of existence; the world may be understood as the general culture and overall values and lifestyle that make up a society. How should the church view itself in relation to Graeco-Roman society? How should it define its ethics, values, and way of life in relation to Roman culture? A second aspect of this concerns the world understood as the empire or local government and its structure of authority. How should Christians relate to the authority of the empire? The third section of chapter 3 will take up some of the answers to these questions that arose in the course of these two centuries. I now turn to the witnesses.

SOCIAL AND THEOLOGICAL ANALYSIS

Despite the significance and importance of the development of the church across the second and third centuries, there exists relatively little descriptive information about the church's life. Little is known of the church in Alexandria during the second century. Eusebius's history of the church over this period is sketchy at best. For example, he possessed few sources on the church in Carthage. But we have windows into the church at various key places and times in the writings of several figures. This social-theological account is based on some of these authors; their texts are read with the heuristic guide of the basic elements of social organizations: their members, structures, activities, goals or mission, and interactive relationship to their environment. Since all of these authors or texts do not deal with all of these aspects of the church, the method will not yield a descriptive account of any local church, or even an adequate theological analysis of the "whole" church, but only a schematic, generalized portrait of a developing church put together in a composite fashion from pieces drawn from temporally and geographically dispersed witnesses.

Ignatius of Antioch

The letters of Ignatius of Antioch, addressed for the most part to churches in Asia Minor, provide direct evidence of church life at the beginning of the second century.[18] One should keep in mind that the churches in these cities may have been modest if not tiny communities; in terms of size, a bishop of a church would at best be the equivalent of a pastor in a very small parish today.

Unity of the church. The theme of unity dominates the letters of Ignatius. The church communities were threatened with schism by two forms of false teaching, docetism and judaizing. Ignatius says people should avoid those in schismatic groups; they will not inherit the kingdom of God. This amounts to an early form of the church as an exclusive haven of salvation: no salvation outside the unity of the church. The single bishop represents the central focus of this unity; the one bishop provides the basis of the unity of the community. This unity cannot be reduced to a unity of spirit, but consists in a unity of organization, government, and institution (Mag 13). One belongs to God if one is united with the single bishop (Phil 8).[19]

According to Ignatius, there are three offices: the bishop, a clergy of presbyters or elders, not priests, who were assistants and perhaps a council, and the deacons. The deacons performed works of service and handled temporal affairs (Mag, 2, 6). "Without these three orders no church has any right to the name" (Trall 3). There are other orders as well, for example, widows and virgins.

The role of the bishop is pronounced. Ignatius, it seems, cannot say too much about the position and authority of the bishop. The bishop has a comprehensive authority. The bishop is appointed not by other persons but by God (Phil 1). Look on the bishop as on God, he says; what the bishop sanctions is the will of God; one who honors the bishop is accepted by God. The bishop's role includes three major responsibilities: (1) The bishop has a liturgical function; he presides at and has authority over the eucharist, although this can be delegated.[20] This probably indicates that the one local church is

---

18. References to the letters of Ignatius are to the text of Cyril C. Richardson, ed. and trans., *Early Christian Fathers* (New York: Macmillan, 1970). References in the text are to paragraphs of the letter.

19. "What the saint [Ignatius] is always at pains to stress is the harmony and unity of the Church, that is founded upon obedience to the ecclesiastical authorities, far more than any metaphysical nexus between God and believer." Cyril Charles Richardson, *The Christianity of Ignatius of Antioch* (New York: Columbia University Press, 1935), 33.

20. Great stress is laid on the connection between eucharist and unity in the church. "In each of the three important passages on the subject, this idea of the *henōsis* of the

subdivided into several smaller communities. (2) The bishop has a doctrinal function; he is the official or recognized teacher in opposition to false teaching. (3) The bishop has governing authority; what the bishop prescribes is God's will. All these functions guarantee the unity of the community in worship, doctrine, and polity. But it remains unclear whether Ignatius was describing an order that was in place in the communities he addressed or whether he was promoting a program that would sweep the churches in the course of the century.

Relation to society. Many authors perceive a kind of double relationship of the Christian communities to society, and with different accents this will obtain over the course of the two centuries. On the one hand, the Christian is not at home in the world; martyrdom is a return to one's true home. The community has an attachment to a transcendent world, and ideas of an early parousia still linger. Also, it is a minority group, hated or ridiculed or persecuted. On the other hand, temporal authority is real God-given authority. Christians should obey rulers and pray for them; slaves are to obey masters as if they were in the place of God. God provided the structures of society, and Christians participate in them. The double relationship, then, can be characterized on the one hand as being attached to God, otherworldly, and countercultural, and on the other hand as being located in history, a part of society, and law-abiding. Christians are good citizens who pray to God for the emperor.

One cannot miss the stress on ethics in Ignatius's letters. A real faith is reflected in behavior, especially in lack of dissension. There is hardly a hint of an outwardly aimed social ethics, of Christian participation in the world or society; one finds no ambition to change society. Most of the ethical exhortation concerns personal behavior within the community, an ethic of unity, of getting along, with an especially strong emphasis on love of fellow Christians. Much of the ethical exhortation repeats Jewish ideals in communities which have ties relating back to Jerusalem. It is a strict ethic, and countercultural insofar as it rejects infanticide, abortion, eating of meat offered to

---

Church is uppermost in his mind." Richardson, *The Christianity of Ignatius of Antioch*, 56.

idols. Avoidance of people with false doctrine suggests a small closely-knit community turned in on itself, persecuted, under siege.

A final theme is martyrdom. Martyrdom represents the highest of all Christian ethical achievements.[21] It reflects not only total dedication to Christ and imitation of him, but also a longing for immortality and glory in another world. As a reaction against persecution of the church when it occurred, glorifying martyrdom relativizes the world and suggests a certain otherworldliness or higher horizon of existence. Ignatius writes that one should think of future life and God, not of things of this earth (Eph 9). The eucharist is the medicine of immortality, energy for struggle with the world, and a remedy to escape final death (Eph 20). The world is a symbol for evil (Mag 5).

Ignatius's ecclesiology transcended the practical and rhetorical orders and reached metaphysical depth. In his view church order reflected and was grounded in heavenly models. His parallelism between the hierarchy of the cosmos and church orders lines up in the following way: HEAVENS (OR COSMOS) = God, Christ, councilor angels, serving spirits, humans; EKKLESIA (OR CONGREGATION) = Christ, bishop, presbyter, deacons, members. As the second order was patterned on the first, Christians were urged to relate to the various office holders with a reverence fitting its transcendent counterpart. The metaphysical hierarchy translated into religious obedience and thus structured and solidified unity. The vision bestowed upon the church as congregation entailed participation in a historical and cosmic mission.[22]

Justin

The apologies of Justin and his *Dialogue with Trypho* contain a good deal of data that with analysis would contribute to a reconstruction

---

21. See "The Martyrdom of St. Polycarp," *Early Christian Fathers*, 149–58. The early church did not get used to martyrdom; it never became an everyday occurrence. Martyrdom inspired horror and awe. The few who died embodied the power of their God. It was not simply a question of personal courage, but of the power of God trumping the power of whatever gods were being protected by the persecution. Brown, *Rise of Western Christendom*, 66.

22. Wagner, *After the Apostles*, 151–52.

of the self-understanding of Christians at Rome in the middle of the second century. But two aspects of the church, the one its relation to the empire as that is reflected in the genre of an apology, and the other its activity of worship, especially at eucharist, are especially pertinent.

Church-world relationship and ethic. The letters of Ignatius address the churches and concern their inner lives; apology addresses an outside audience and engages three tasks at the same time: self-explanation, self-defense, and self-appropriation in relation to that other. Much can be said about this church simply on the basis of this kind of literature. It shows a certain self-confidence and maturity to be able publicly to address the empire. It takes the empire seriously; it does not dismiss or ignore Rome and its culture but wants to be understood by it. One can see in this writing a formal or self-conscious step toward inculturation to the extent that to be understood by outsiders one must adopt language that can be understood by them. But this affects the self-understanding of the writer and the community. In the case of Justin, a Palestinian Greek philosopher who converted to Christianity, one sees the language of the church's understanding of itself being shifted into Greek cultural terms.

Daniélou calls this apologetics the missionary literature of the second century addressed to the pagan world of the empire. It deals with fundamentals; it looks for parallels between Christianity and pagan culture, for continuities between the tradition behind Christianity and the tradition of Greek intellectual culture; and it thus performs a catechetical function.[23] Apologists like Justin were seeking to convert pagan philosophers and leaders to the church. The importance of this lies much more in the fundamental ethical and religious stance toward the world displayed in this literature than in the particular, historically conditioned content.

Assembly: liturgy and sacrament. At the end of his *First Apology* Justin gave a brief description of what Christians did when they assembled for the baptism of new members and for the eucharist on

---

23. Daniélou, *Gospel Message and Hellenistic Culture*, 11.

Sunday mornings.[24] When one sets his account in a line between earlier references to the eucharist, for example, in the *Didache* and *1 Clement,* and the later account of liturgy in the Roman church as found in Hippolytus's *The Apostolic Tradition,* one can get some sense of a continuous development.

In *1 Clement,* which represents the church at Rome around the year 95, one finds a long prayer that may be associated with the eucharist and which is striking for its Jewish character.[25] The *Didache,* which may represent a church in the ambit of Antioch at the end of the first century, contains a brief instruction on the ministration of both baptism and the eucharist. Baptism is to be preceded by public instruction. The one baptized, the one baptizing, and, where possible, all involved in the action should fast. The eucharist in the *Didache* is essentially a prayer of thanksgiving, a *berakah,* over the wine and the bread, followed by a meal, at the end of which follows another blessing of God the Father, through Jesus, his child (*Did,* 9–10). It prescribes that "you must not let anyone eat or drink of your eucharist except those baptized in the Lord's name" (*Did,* 9.5), but there is no reference to the body and blood of Christ. "On every Lord's day — his special day — come together and break bread and give thanks, first confessing your sins so that your sacrifice may be pure" (*Did,* 14.1).

Moving to Justin's account of the ceremony of baptism, it too involves prior instruction and fasting. It unfolds in a place where there is water, and is understood as a ritual of repentance and forgiveness. The ceremony effects a rebirth out of ignorance and sin into illumination and freedom.[26] After the baptism, those baptized are brought into the community assembled, where common prayers for all are offered and, at their conclusion, all greet each other with a kiss. Then

---

24. A brief analysis of Justin's teachings on church and sacraments can be found in L. W. Barnard, *Justin Martyr: His Life and Thought* (Cambridge: Cambridge University Press, 1967), 126–50.

25. *1 Clem,* 59–61. Reference to *1 Clement* and the *Didache* are to paragraph numbers in the texts in the edition of Richardson, *Early Christian Fathers.*

26. Justin Martyr, *First Apology,* 61, in Thomas B. Falls, ed., *Writings of Saint Justin Martyr, The Fathers of the Church* (New York: Christian Heritage, 1948). References in the text are to the paragraphs as found in this edition.

the bread and a cup of water and mixed wine are brought to the president (bishop) of the community who offers the formal eucharistic prayer to which all respond "amen." After the communion service the deacons carry "eucharistic food" to those who are absent (1 Apol, 65).[27] Baptism is thus an elaborate ceremony and ritual; entering this community is a momentous life-decision.

Justin explains the belief that "the food consecrated by the word of prayer which comes from him [Jesus Christ], from which our flesh and blood are nourished by transformation, is the flesh and blood of that incarnate Jesus" (1 Apol, 66). One thus has realistic language reminiscent of John's gospel, chapter 6. In his *Dialogue with Trypho* Justin associates the eucharist with Jesus' passion and death and refers to it as a "sacrifice" commemorating Jesus' death.[28] This was significant in the gradual development of the eventual view that the one who officiated at a "sacrifice," the bishop, was a "priest," and still later that his delegates, the presbyters, were priests.

Justin describes the weekly Sunday gathering as having the following order: assembly, reading of the "memoirs of the apostles" or the prophets, an exhortation by the president, standing for prayers, the bringing forth of the bread, wine, and water over which the president offers prayers of thanksgiving "to the best of his ability" and to which the congregation assents "amen," the distribution and reception of the prayed-over elements by each one, and the dispatching of them to the absent through the deacons. This is followed by a collection for the needy (1 Apol, 67). Throughout, Justin links the celebration of the eucharist with ethics. In Justin, then, we find that the eucharist is celebrated as an autonomous rite independent of a meal, with a president who is probably the bishop or his delegate, and a set order

---

27. Barnard explains the reasons why Justin's "president" is probably the "bishop." *Justin Martyr*, 131–33. He also notes that this is the earliest reference to the practice of deacons taking a portion of the eucharistic elements to those who were absent. Ibid., 148.

28. Justin, "The Dialogue with Trypho," 117 in *The Writings of Justin Martyr*. "This conception of the Eucharist as a sacrifice and a memorial of the Passion, which is based on the Pauline words of institution, is peculiar to Justin among second-century writers...." Barnard, *Justin Martyr*, 148.

that probably reflects a practice that transcends the community at Rome.[29]

Irenaeus

In the last chapter I held up Irenaeus as reflecting some form of closure in the earliest formation of the church, with a special emphasis on the development of the canon of scriptures. I wish to briefly reiterate this here by underlining how Irenaeus symbolizes the unity of a universal church. In other words, the value of unity that so dominates Ignatius is transposed in Irenaeus to encompass the whole Christian movement or the many churches. In his reaction against the ominous threat of false teachings infecting the church from within, Irenaeus argued for institutions that were able to encompass in some form of unity the many different churches scattered so broadly around the Roman empire.[30] Basically those institutions consisted in the one "basic" teaching of all the churches, succession of bishops in a teaching office, and a canon of scriptures.

> This is true Gnosis: the teaching of the apostles, and the ancient institution of the church, spread throughout the entire world, and the distinctive mark of the body of Christ in accordance with the successions of bishops, to whom the apostles entrusted each local church, and the unfeigned preservation, coming down to us, of the scriptures, with a complete collection allowing for neither addition nor subtraction; a reading without falsification and, in conformity with the scriptures, an interpretation that is legitimate, careful, without danger or blasphemy.[31]

---

29. See Lloyd G. Patterson, "Eucharist, History of, in Early Church," *The New Dictionary of Sacramental Worship*, ed. Peter E. Fink (Collegeville, Minn.: Liturgical Press, 1990), 398–410.

30. The analogical parallel of this problem in our time is not the unity of one international communion of churches, but the ecumenical unity of all the churches.

31. Irenaeus, *Against Heresies*, 4.33.8, in Robert M. Grant, trans., *Irenaeus of Lyons* (London and New York: Routledge, 1997), 161. References in the text as AH are to this translation. The succession referred to by Irenaeus did not consist in the laying on of hands by successive bishops, but in the legitimate occupying of the office of teaching. In other words, it was social and functional. See Jay, *The Church*, 45–46.

Irenaeus reported the content of this one basic faith, received from the apostles, in brief trinitarian formulas (e.g., AH, 1.10.1, pp. 70–71).[32] In his view, all the authentic churches share this one set of beliefs; it forms the one heart and soul of all Christians scattered throughout the world; all lived in the one house provided by this metaphysical vision. "For if the languages in the world are dissimilar, the power of the tradition is one and the same" (AH, 1.10.2, p. 71). In Irenaeus this unity was held fast by organizational and institutional forms, but it far transcended these. "All humanity has its first head in Adam and its second in Christ. This ontological unity of the church is expressed in the identity of its beliefs about God and God's saving purpose, and it was the polemical utility of the concept of doctrinal unity that made Irenaeus one of the earliest theologians to celebrate the unity of the universal church."[33] Granted that Irenaeus was an influential Greek-speaker who had also served in Rome; it is still remarkable that a bishop in the provinces, in a Roman outpost city in Gaul, testified to the worldwide unity of the church.

Hippolytus

The Apostolic Tradition attributed to Hippolytus is a manual of church order responding to the need to retain the "ancient" way of doing things against change or forgetfulness.[34] Today many regard it as a compilation of material dating from the second to the early

---

32. A similar formulation, though somewhat longer, of the basic rule of faith of the church is found in Origen, *Origen On First Principles*, ed. G. W. Butterworth (Gloucester, Mass.: Peter Smith, 1973), Preface, 4–10, pp. 2–6. Thus apostolicity, succession, and tradition are all of a piece. "The Logos entrusted the treasure of truth to the apostles, who deposited it in the church, ... making God's salvation available to everyone who was willing to be disciplined by the church and the apostles' successors. Irenaeus's handling of the apostolic deposit of truth became central to his struggle with heretics, his ecclesiology, and his lasting influence." Wagner, *After the Apostles*, 217.

33. Denis Minns, *Irenaeus* (Washington, D.C.: Georgetown University Press, 1994), 117. Irenaeus represents a common unified truth spread geographically across the churches in different regions. This unity itself was a sign of truth; novelty, error, heresy, divisiveness, and schism entailed each other. "Irenaeus understood the church to be part of God's cosmic, historical, and geographical plan to recapitulate humanity and the world." Wagner, *After the Apostles*, 219.

34. Hippolytus, *The Apostolic Tradition of Hippolytus*, ed. and trans. Burton Scott Easton (Cambridge: Archon Books, Cambridge University Press, 1962) and *The Treatise on the Apostolic Tradition of St Hippolytus of Rome*, ed. Gregory Dix (London: SPCK, 1968). The work is referred to in the text as AT by paragraph numbers.

fourth century.[35] It is brief yet quite comprehensive as it covers the procedures of initiation, the ordination of ministers and their functions, eucharistic celebration, the agape meal, and a regime of prayer. But is it descriptive of the church or a set of desired norms? Whatever the answer to that question, the document yields some idea of the church in Rome during this period at three points.

Members. New members underwent a three-year initiation period or catechumenate as hearers of the word taught by teachers. Prior to this, candidates were briefly screened on their general condition of life and profession and examined again before being actually admitted to baptism. A whole list of professions conflicted with being a Christian. One can say that all parties concerned deemed becoming a Christian a serious life-decision (AT, 16–20).

Institutional structure or polity. The church order lays down the rites of ordination or installation of the various ministers of the church. From these one can discern the relative place in the community and the responsibilities or expectations of bishops, presbyters, deacons, widows, readers, virgins, and subdeacons. Bishops were chosen by all the people, and at their ordination bishops from the area laid hands upon them.[36] From the prayers of the ordination rite we learn that a bishop is consecrated to feed people with eucharistic bread and to serve as God's high priest. He is to minister to people day and night. He has the authority to forgive sins that was given to the apostles. While the theme of priesthood does not dominate, it is clearly stated (AT, 3).[37] Among other tasks of oversight the bishop is encouraged to visit the sick, indicating the context of a still rather small community. The bishop in the larger cities at this time is still comparable to the pastor of an extended parish today.

---

35. Paul Bradshaw, *Early Christian Worship: A Basic Introduction to Ideas and Practice* (Collegeville, Minn.: Liturgical Press, 1996), 15.

36. "There seems to be a fairly universal pattern of the election of *episkopoi* by the end of the second century," and this lasts until well into the Middle Ages. Cooke, *Ministry*, 418.

37. Tertullian was the first in Christian literature to associate bishops and presbyters with priests, something which thus arose during the second century. Easton, *The Apostolic Tradition of Hippolytus*, 64; David Rankin, *Tertullian and the Church* (Cambridge: Cambridge University Press, 1995), 163.

Presbyters were ordained with a laying on of hands of the bishop including a gesture from their fellow presbyters, and deacons were ordained by the bishop "to serve the bishop and to carry out the bishop's commands" (AT, 9). The presbyter was ordained into the presbyterate, whose function was to govern the people in the church. They were filled with God's Spirit as were the presbyters chosen by Moses. By contrast, the deacon was not ordained to the priesthood, but received the Spirit to be a counselor of the bishop and clergy, caretaker of property and gifts, and general executor of the bishop's will (AT, 9). The impression of a relatively small community is strengthened with the indication that each day presbyters and deacons met with members of the community for instruction and prayer prior to assuming their duties (AT, 33).

Assembly: liturgy and sacraments. The major activities of the church consisted in daily prayer, instruction, eucharistic liturgy, the agape meal, and baptisms. Several paragraphs describe how prayer is to be said seven times a day (AT, 35–36). The evening agape meal, which was separated off from the morning eucharistic celebration by the time of Justin in the second century, is regulated by Hippolytus's church order (AT, 26).[38] Hippolytus's description of the ritual of baptism contains two distinct steps: the first involves immersion in water and anointing, the second a laying on of hands by the bishop.[39] The whole ceremony contains a number of exorcisms of evil spirits that appear striking today (AT, 21–23). In sum, Hippolytus's community was probably still relatively small, perhaps because it was only a segment of the whole. But it was highly differentiated and regulated with clearly defined offices of ministry and patterns of life.

Using the texts of Tertullian and a critical reading of the *Apostolic Tradition*, Bradshaw represents the basic structure of the rites of baptism and eucharist in the West at the turn of the third century. Baptisms occurred preferably at Easter according to the following order: preparation by fasting and prolonged instruction, prayer over

---

38. According to Tertullian, the agape meal was a means used by the community to offer relief for those in need, the poor. *Apology*, 39, p. 101.

39. This distinction of phases of the ceremony is important for understanding the Roman side in the baptismal controversy between Cyprian of Carthage and Stephen of Rome in the mid-third century.

the baptismal water, a renunciation of evil, a triple profession of faith and immersion in water, a post-baptismal anointing, the sign of the cross over the one baptized for protection, an imposition of hands accompanied by prayer, and a welcome into the community's eucharistic celebration. The theology underlying the ritual appeals to a soteriological understanding of Jesus' death and resurrection; the one baptized dies to sin in the water and rises to new life in the Spirit destined for resurrection.[40]

The sacrament of the eucharist at the turn of the century is in a process of development. Already in Justin the sacrament was separated from the context of a meal; the blessing of the bread and the cup were brought together in a Sunday morning ritual. The most basic structure consisted in a remembering of Jesus and an invocation of the Spirit. Earlier the eucharistic prayer focused on God the creator; at this time the emphasis shifts toward redemption and an understanding of the eucharist as a sacrifice. In the *Apostolic Tradition* the eucharistic prayer remembers Jesus' death as a sacrifice and his resurrection. This results in the rite itself becoming a memorial sacrifice. In Cyprian, the bishop-priest imitates Christ in offering the true and perfect sacrifice to God in the church.[41]

Didascalia Apostolorum

The *Didascalia* or *Teaching of the Apostles* probably represents a small church in the region of Syria during the first half of the third century.[42] Although it is part of the line reaching back to the *Didache* and the *Apostolic Tradition*, this work presents a much longer, effusive, and inspirational view of the church: it instructs and preaches; it collects laws and urges the advantages of obeying them. The treatise purports to be a consensus of the Apostles compiled in a meeting in Jerusalem around the year 50,[43] and this gives it a universal outlook:

---

40. Bradshaw, *Early Christian Worship*, 16–21.
41. Ibid., 45–57.
42. R. Hugh Connolly, ed., *Didascalia Apostolorum* (Oxford: Clarendon Press, 1929), lxxxix–xci.
43. "When therefore the whole Church was in peril of falling into heresy, all we the twelve Apostles came together to Jerusalem and took thought what should be done.... And when we had ordained and affirmed and set down [these things] together with one accord, we set forth to go each one to his former province, confirming the

the writing may be local, but it projects one unified, great church. The many topics it considers fall mainly within the confines of the offices of ministry, those who hold them, and the ethical comportment of members of the community. It thus gives a revealing impression of a typical Eastern church community.

Structures and ministries. Space does not allow a creative, imaginative reproduction of life in this community that this source makes possible, but certain details can be highlighted. The bishop is presented as completely in charge of the community, his authority absolute. His ideal character and his responsibilities are described in detail. In language reminiscent of Ignatius of Antioch the author writes: "He is minister of the word and mediator, but to you a teacher, and your father after God, who begot you through the water. This is your chief and your leader, and he is your mighty king. He rules in place of the Almighty" (DA, 9, p. 86). He is also High Priest.

Second in power and effective authority in the church seems to be the deacon who is the appointed right-hand of the bishop. There were to be as many of them as required by the size of the community. And unlike the church in Rome, this church had an order and ministry of deaconesses who attended to women in the community in situations that would have been awkward for men (DA, 16, pp. 146–48). If the people were to relate to the bishop as the Father, they were to consider the Deacon as Christ and the Deaconess as the Holy Spirit (DA, 9, p. 88).[44] From this perspective the role and position of presbyters relative to deacons appear less fully developed. They were the counselors of the bishop who were "to be honored as the Apostles" (DA,

---

Churches." *Didascalia*, 24, pp. 204, 214. Citations in the text are by chapter and page number to this edition.

44. From one point of view feminist sensibilities today would hardly be comforted by the *Didascalia's* teaching on women: women were not allowed to baptize in principle, and widows are described in stereotypes. But from the perspective of patriarchy and moving toward the left, the deaconess is a genuine office in the church with a recognized ministry commanding religious respect. Even widows were not simply regarded as receivers of episcopal concern but as also exercising the ministry of visiting the sick, praying with them, and imposing hands on them (DA, 15, pp. 138–40). On the question of women in the early church see Francine Cardman, "Women, Ministry, and Church Order in Early Christianity," in R. S. Kraemer and M. R. D'Angelo, eds., *Women and Christian Origins* (New York: Oxford University Press, 1999), 300–29.

9, p. 90). It is possible that in a small church where the bishop dominated the public life of the whole community the presbyters had an authority inferior to the deacons who were an extension of episcopal authority.[45]

Community life and ethics. Instruction on ordinary life and religious virtue occupies a great deal of this treatise, so that it gives the impression of an intentional community. It offers moral exhortation for men, for women in general, and for widows. It instructs on how to raise children. It urges every member of the community to be present at the eucharistic assembly on Sunday mornings, lest any single absentee "cause the body of Christ to be short of a member" (DA, 13, p. 124). An important theme in all of this moralistic exhortation concerns mercy and the power of the bishop to forgive. The church in the West during the second and early third century had to wrestle with the possibility of second repentance for sin after baptism, especially the question of whether someone guilty of murder or adultery could be readmitted to the church after a period of penitence. This community recommends mercy: "It behooves you then, O bishops, to judge according to the scriptures those who sin, with gentleness and with mercy" (DA, 6, pp. 50–52).[46] This is a clear marker on the road of developing attitudes on the moral life of the community as a whole. It may also suggest an experience of overbearing and harsh bishops.

Tertullian

The written tradition of the Latin church begins in Carthage in the late second century with Tertullian and is carried forward in the middle of the third century by Cyprian. The church in Carthage, which seems to have been an offspring of the church of Rome, only comes into some clear focus in the writings of Tertullian. No one can report on Tertullian satisfactorily in a short space because of his ardor, irony, complexity, and evolution. For example, his earlier writings defend the monarchical ministry of the bishop; his later writings complain bitterly of an overreaching episcopacy that was

---

45. Connolly, DA, xl–xli.
46. "But if thou [bishop] receive not him who repents, because thou art without mercy, thou shalt sin against the Lord God." DA, 7, p. 76.

compromising the essential holiness of the church. Tertullian offers no comprehensive or systematic understanding of the church. But in his many writings one can discern a distinctive view of the nature of the church that had considerable influence on Cyprian.[47]

In the line of Irenaeus, Tertullian defended the monoepiscopacy, apostolicity, and the criterion of succession for the determination of authentic teaching. In his *Apology* Tertullian gives a short descriptive account of the church. It consists in a religious body of people who come together on Sunday mornings to pray, read scripture, encourage and correct each other. Certain elders, approved on the basis of their good character, preside over the association. They collect money voluntarily given according to the ability of each, and it is used for good works and help of the needy. The members share in common, as at the love feast, which is conducted with prayerful decorum, and where those who are hungry are fed.[48] Tertullian recognized the threefold ministry of bishop, presbyter, and deacon, but also bears witness to other orders of ministry within the church at Carthage: there were widows, virgins, doctors or teachers, lectors, prophets, and martyrs.[49]

One of the most significant developments in the church during the second and third centuries was "the creation of a strict division between clergy and laity in the Christian church."[50] In Tertullian's conception of the church the clergy held a position of authority and dignity superior to the laity. The distinction rested on function and was pragmatic: the laity represented a flock in need of shepherding. In Tertullian's view they were largely ignorant, ill informed, and in need of guidance. The clergy then were leaders of the community. They occupied an office of ministry, a formally constituted and recognized position that carried authority by virtue of the office. But the bishop was so dominant a figure that the other clergy, the presbyters

---

47. See David Rankin, *Tertullian and the Church* (Cambridge: Cambridge University Press, 1995), for a synthetic reconstruction of Tertullian's formal ecclesiology.

48. Tertullian, *Apology*, 39, in *Tertullian: Apologetical Works and Minucius Felix: Octavius*, 98–102. References in the text are to chapter and page in this edition.

49. Rankin, *Tertullian and the Church*, 119. Virgins were women who lived continent lives. They transcended sexuality and did not wear the veil which symbolized the shame of sexuality itself. This was more than self-discipline. To be a virgin, to "stand unveiled among the believers was to declare the fullness of the redemption brought by Christ." Brown, *Body and Society*, 80.

50. Brown, *Body and Society*, 142.

and deacons, had their identities in relation to him. Like shepherds, the clergy protected the members of the church, furnished the services of worship, and functioned as leaders, pastors, nurturers, and providers for those in need. As the central figure the bishop oversaw discipline, presided at liturgical rituals of baptism, eucharist, and Christian burial; he regulated admissions to the church and to orders; he determined the conduct of fasting, public penance, and readmission to the church assembly.[51]

The churches of Tertullian and Hippolytus in the early third century, therefore, were well-ordered communities, and Tertullian's church at Carthage possessed a developed, differentiated character. But particularly two themes in Tertullian's views on the church, its holiness and its relation to the world, reflect the period.

The holiness of the church. "A less than holy church is, for Tertullian, not logically possible. Anything less than holy cannot authentically be the church."[52] In his tribute to the martyrs Tertullian wrote of the Christian: "It does not matter what part of the world you are in, you who are apart from the world."[53] In his view Christians lived in a sphere that transcended everyday mundane life. With baptism, one repented of sin and sin was forgiven. At one point he seemed convinced that one who resumed sinning thereafter was headed for the fire.[54] In his *Apology,* Tertullian judged that serious public sinners were by their sin, as it were, automatically cut off from the community of Christians. Or they could be excommunicated by the community at one of its assemblies (Apol. 39, 44, 46, pp. 98, 109, 114). Tertullian admitted a second repentance and second hope that required an overt and public penitence.[55] Yet he seemed to admit

---

51. Rankin, *Tertullian and the Church,* 115, 142, 190–91.

52. Ibid., 114.

53. Tertullian, "To the Martyrs," 2, in *Tertullian: Disciplinary, Moral and Ascetical Works, The Fathers of the Church* (New York: The Fathers of the Church, 1959), 20.

54. Tertullian, "On Baptism," 8 in *Tertullian's Homily on Baptism,* ed. and commentary by Ernest Evans (London: SPCK, 1964), 19.

55. "Therefore it must not be performed solely within one's conscience but it must also be shown forth in some external act." Tertullian, "On Penitence," 8–9, in *Tertullian: Treatises on Penance: On Penitence and On Purity,* trans. and annotated by W. P. Le Saint (Westminster, Md.: Newman Press, 1959), 31–32. He goes on to describe the public display in sackcloth and the fasting. But eternity is at stake: "Will the sinner knowingly spurn exomologesis, which has been instituted by God for his restoration?"

second repentance begrudgingly, fearing that it could encourage sin. And he reacted strongly when a bishop assumed the power to admit adulterers and fornicators back into church communion. In the end he changed his mind on second repentance; there are sins irremissible by the church, and sex outside of marriage is one of them.[56] Tertullian appears to have moved more and more toward a conception of a church so imbued by the power of the Spirit that the holiness of the community was the collection of the holiness of its individual members. "In Tertullian Law and Spirit are together seen as supporting and requiring the strict eschatological purity of all persons in the Church."[57] The holiness of its members becomes the boundary between church and world.

The relation of the church to the world. Tertullian's view of how the church relates to the world in his *Apology* brims with tensions. On the one hand God created all out of nothing and ordered it according to reason and remains its sovereign ruler (Apol. 17, 52). On the other hand, Tertullian like Justin conflates his extensive belief in demons, whose "business is to corrupt humankind" (Apol. 22, 69), with the Romans' belief in their myriad gods, large and small (Apol. 23, 71). The result is a whole society whose practices are idolatrous because shot through with interlaced religious connections. Correspondingly, on one side Christians become the model citizens (Apol. 36, 94) who are loyal to the emperor, pray for him (Apol. 30, 85), support the whole empire with their prayer (Apol. 30, 86),[58] and blend in and fully participate in all the basic institutions of daily life (Apol. 42, 106–7). Christians are not only an integral part of society, but the linchpin holding the empire in place against the coming of the end of the world (Apol. 39, 98; 32, 88). But on the other side, the

---

(ibid., 12, p. 36) Presumably this second repentance is for the most serious sins. But it is not clear whether the term of the penitence was full reinstatement into the church community.

56. Tertullian, "On Purity [or Modesty]," 1–4, Ibid., 53–62.

57. Robert F. Evans, *One and Holy: The Church in Latin Patristic Thought* (London: SPCK, 1972), 34.

58. "For, in our case, we pray for the welfare of the emperors to the eternal God, the true God, the living God. . . . We ask for them long life, undisturbed power, security at home, brave armies, a faithful Senate, an upright people, a peaceful world, and everything for which a man as a Caesar prays." Apol. 30, 86.

emperor is not God, the Roman gods simply do not exist (Apol. 10, 35), and Christians have a higher allegiance to one eternal and all powerful God (Apol. 33, 88–89). Christian morality forbids church members from participating in the many overtly immoral or idolatrous public activities of society (Apol. 38, 97). In Tertullian the double relationship that defines the existence of the church, its simultaneous relation to society and to God, comes to expression in its purest tensive form. The double relationship takes on a dialectical character in which each of the terms is radical, contrary to the other, and yet in a direct dependence on the other.[59]

This account only brushes the surface of Tertullian and his church. He requires careful analysis because the tensions and nuances of his writing correspond with the dilemmas and contrary forces that pulled this emerging church in different directions. He is also significant for his influence on Cyprian.

Cyprian

Cyprian was well read in Tertullian, and he reflects the African church, specifically the church in Carthage, in the middle of the third century. Social unrest affected the empire. Its boundaries were being attacked by barbarian forces in the north and the east; inflation, plague, and rebellion in the army were taking their toll. The new emperor, Decius, undertook the job of restoring the empire according to the axiom "the peace of the empire depends on the peace of the gods." In 249, then, he published the edict that all citizens must perform a public act acknowledging the gods of the empire. For Christians this amounted to persecution; Cornelius, the bishop of Rome, lost his life; Cyprian, a convert to Christianity as a mature man, baptized in 246, ordained presbyter in 248, and elected bishop of Carthage late in the same year, went into hiding. He died a martyr, however, in 258. In that span of years he became an enormously influential

---

59. For example, Tertullian's language describing the Christian's relationship to God is radical enough to suggest separation from society as this occurred in the monastic movement. But such behavior is never suggested by Tertullian in the *Apology*; the community of Christians is simultaneously participatory in society and never apart from nor a part of society's idolatrous character.

authority within the church of the West through his letters, treatises, and reputation for wise action.[60]

Cyprian's ten years as bishop of Carthage were marked by a series of crises or issues of which three bore lasting significance: the first concerned the conflict of authority within his own church; the second concerned those who lapsed or reneged on their Christian faith during the persecution; the third concerned the way to deal with the baptism administered in schismatic churches, the so-called "baptismal controversy" with the Roman church which handled the situation differently.

Institutional structure or polity. "The Unity of the Church" may date from when Cyprian was still in hiding during the first persecution in Carthage in 250, and a schism in his own church forms its background.[61] In his absence a group of martyr-confessors and presbyters took it upon themselves to advocate the readmission of the lapsed into the church. The text, then, responds to the problem of factions within the church, or of rival churches within one city. It drives home the basis and value of unity in the church at a time when persecution unleashed forces that severely threatened it.

The church is one in its *source*. Appealing to apostolicity, to traditions from the origins, Cyprian refers back to the source for the unity of the church. The unity of the church rests in the unity of its foundation and ultimately in its one source, God. God did not intend multiple churches. Unity was established in history by the founding of the church on one man, Peter. The referent, however, is the local or particular church, and the local bishop is compared to Peter, not the bishop of Rome. "The empowering of Peter and the other apostles first served as a basis for the authority of individual bishops in their local churches, and Cyprian continued to support the autonomy of the local bishop."[62] Other images of the unity of the church in its

---

60. Jay provides a brief synthetic account of Cyprian's ecclesiology in *The Church*, 65–74. For a biographical account of Cyprian's thought see Peter Hinchliff, *Cyprian of Carthage and the Unity of the Christian Church* (London: Geoffrey Chapman, 1974).

61. Cyprian, "The Unity of the Catholic Church," in *Cyprian: De Lapsis and De Ecclesiae Catholicae Unitate*, text and trans. Maurice Bévenot (Oxford: Clarendon Press, 1971). Cited in the text as Unity by chapter.

62. J. Patout Burns, *Cyprian the Bishop* (London and New York: Routledge, 2002), 157. Two versions of Unity, 4 appear in the manuscript tradition, one seeming to

source by succession are the sun, a tree, and a spring. The churches are like rays, branches, and streams coming from the pristine source that is one in essence and cannot be divided. The church is not just a gathering of people in the name of Christ. A church must be united with its source as it spreads out from it through succession (Unity, 5).

The second basis of unity then is its *episcopal structure.* As in Ignatius and Hippolytus the monarchical bishop constitutes the church, and one would not have a lawful church if there were no bishop lawfully ordained in succession. This stands in contrast to rival, schismatic bishops. Over and above this, Cyprian depicts the universal unity of the church as being held together by the communion of bishops with one another (Unity, 5). One can notice a development beyond the ground of universal unity found in Irenaeus, that is, the common religious vision formulated in scripture and its substance formulated in a rule of faith. In Irenaeus succession mediated a unity of faith. In Cyprian and thereafter the principle of unity becomes the episcopate itself. The unity of the office guarantees the unity of the religious vision.[63] Relative to the Christian life, Cyprian insists on the correlative virtues of humility and obedience to bishops.

The third source of unity lies within as *charity and love* (Unity, 14). One cannot accuse Cyprian of thinking only institutionally. The inner Spirit of God is the source of love. The church could never be reduced to an institutional unity; it subsists in one faith, one baptism, the one Spirit of God. And correspondingly the Christian life reflects the correlative virtues of love, peace, concord, and unanimity. Cyprian also consistently urged concern and care of the poor. Love was to show itself in action.

---

endorse some form of papal primacy, the other not doing so. Bévenot has resolved this problem with the theory that Cyprian revised his first version of Unity at this point a few years later in the context of a controversy over baptism with the bishop of Rome. This generally accepted view explains Cyprian's earlier language relative to Peter in a way that is consistent with his nonacceptance of a juridical primacy of Rome. See Bévenot, *Cyprian*, xi–xv.

63. Jay, *The Church*, 67. Another way of stating this subtle development might be in terms of a shift of weight or focus within the functionality of institutions: the shift is from emphasis on the charisma preserved by the office to more emphasis on the office that preserves the charisma. But the tensive relationship still obtains, as the next point makes clear.

As an affront to this unity, schism perpetrates one of the worst crimes against the church and against God. As serious as heresy, it attacks the essence of the church, namely, its unity from its source, as sustained by God's Spirit of love and organized by church structure. Schismatics are worse than the lapsed who deny the faith and are repentant. Confessors who faced martyrdom and even martyrs for the faith will not be saved if they witness outside of the unity of the church (Unity, 14).[64] Good people *cannot* break with the church (Unity, 9), because anyone who does is evil. In short, there is no salvation outside the one church whose institutional boundaries are set by communion with the one bishop of any city and communion among bishops. Cyprian is not thinking of non-Christians at this point, but of those who break from the church. He speaks of the church as mother; the church as institution and communion gives birth to and nurtures grace and salvation.[65] One does not have God as a father unless the church is one's mother (Unity, 6). In schismatic churches one finds no baptism, no eucharist, no salvation.

Cyprian along with his fellow bishops considered the case of unworthy bishops in Spain who were deposed, but who got themselves reinstated by appealing to the bishop of Rome.[66] Two things are noteworthy in his judgment: first, Cyprian described the process of an election of bishops. It was to be done with other bishops of the province in attendance, and approved by and in the presence of the faithful. The people could also legitimately depose a bishop. Second,

---

64. The force of this point can only be grasped over against a martyrdom which was recognized as the highest manifestation of Christian commitment that fully wiped out sin and introduced the dying person directly into glory. This is the view of Tertullian, the *Didascalia,* and Cyprian himself. See Cooke, *Ministry,* 60, 69 n. 21, 235.

65. Cooke interprets this image as an indication that the church is beginning to be conceived as an objective reality distinct from its members, a "living abstraction with an identity and essence and destiny of its own," "apart from and beyond the people who make it up." *Ministry,* 66. Cyprian's view of the church as mother comes from Tertullian, who takes it from the New Testament. Tertullian too used the image decisively to establish "the Church as possessing a personalized identity separate from her members." Rankin, *Tertullian and the Church,* 112. Metaphors have a natural tendency to move through usage toward objectification.

66. Cyprian, Letter 67.1–9, in Cyprian, *The Letters of St. Cyprian of Carthage,* vol. 4, *Ancient Christian Writers,* nos. 43, 44, 46, 47, trans. and annotated by G. W. Clarke (New York and Ramsey, N.J.: Newman Press, 1984–89). References in the text are to this edition by letter number and paragraph.

the bishop should be holy. God does not hear the prayers of sinners. If a bishop were a public or serious sinner, the church and all the people would be contaminated by his sin and share in his guilt. Nor should the rest of the churches remain in communion with such bishops. The holiness of the church thus resided in a special way in the episcopal class. This theology together with his ecclesiological theology of the sacraments helped provide a basis for the Donatist schism.

The members of the church. Many Christians lapsed or apostatized during the persecution of Decius.[67] How was Cyprian to deal with this on a large scale? The situation was complicated by the fact that the martyrs/confessors, on the basis of their recognized charismatic authority, allowed some of the lapsed back into communion or peace with the church. Cyprian's treatise, "The Lapsed," describes how he handled the problem of apostasy, and it contains several points of interest. First of all, it provides a description of how the church behaved in the face of this persecution and Cyprian's analysis of it (Lapsed, 4–14). It is not a heroic picture. He notes all sorts of degrees of infidelity and willingness to renounce the faith, from those who lined up to offer sacrifice before being asked, to those who succumbed only under torture. Evidently the numbers were large, and Cyprian was shocked. His analysis depicts something of a "middle class" church whose faith appears shallow and untried; people were too attached to possessions and real estate.[68] A mere forty years after Tertullian, this description of the church seems to foreshadow a church domesticated by the empire at the end of the fourth century.

Just as important was the system that Cyprian sets up to handle the situation. First of all, no lapsed Catholic could be admitted back

---

67. Cyprian, "The Lapsed," in the edition of Bévenot. Cited in the text as Lapsed by chapter. Burns believes that a majority of church members lapsed in one way or another and thus had to be reconciled with the church. Burns, *Cyprian*, 20, 35, 68.

68. These judgments may be somewhat harsh. Under a threat of execution, much of the behavior witnessed to weakness or compromise rather than willed apostasy. Grant characterizes typical members of the church who owned property as "middle class," while at the same time including those at either extreme of the economic spectrum. Church teaching did not disparage private property. Rather it warned of the moral dangers of wealth, encouraged both hard work and an ascetic ideal, and strongly urged support of the poor. Robert M. Grant, *Early Christianity and Society: Seven Studies* (San Francisco: Harper & Row, 1977), 79–123.

into the church without the authority of the bishop. Initially Cyprian admitted them only to the state of penitents, not communicants. This involved confession of guilt, of penance that does satisfaction to God for the sin, and finally remission of sin and acceptance by God. The martyrs, the prayers of the church, and works of charity all help make satisfaction before God. At one point, perhaps rhetorically, Cyprian encourages enough works to put God in our debt (Lapsed, 35). If penance is done and satisfaction made, one will merit not only the pardon of God but a crown (Lapsed, 36). At first Cyprian was not willing to admit the more seriously lapsed back into communion; he wanted a North African consensus on that. But surely penance, satisfaction, and good works would win final forgiveness by God in the end.

In his letter to Cornelius, Bishop of Rome, written with other bishops in synod a year later, one notes a clear shift in Cyprian's response to new historical conditions, namely, the fear of another wave of persecution (Letter 57). The bishops wrote that the eucharist gives strength, and that therefore they were willing to accept the lapsed back into full communion with the church. It is better to err on the side of mercy and recognize the difference between the lapsed who leave the church altogether and those who wish to remain in the church. Therefore they would examine the case of each one and admit them to the eucharist. Rarely will one find a clearer case of development in practice and theology in response to a concrete situation.[69]

The baptismal controversy. The so-called baptismal controversy concerned both Cyprian's sacramental theology and his relationship with the bishop of Rome.[70] Briefly the situation was this: Novatian, a Roman presbyter, split from the elected bishop of Rome, Cornelius,

---

69. This issue goes back to the second century and the question of second repentance, from which time bishops were involved in the reconciliation of sinners. See Hippolytus, *The Apostolic Tradition*, 3. The bishop "decided what penance was commensurate with the sin involved, and it was he who officially reconciled the penitent at the end of the process" (Cooke, *Ministry*, 417, 63). The details of the process, however, are not known, and in the case of apostasy, adultery, and murder the ability of the bishop to reconcile the penitent into communion with the church was contested. Tertullian, for example, reacted vehemently against it. Cyprian at this point moves beyond the legacy of Tertullian and the tradition of the Carthaginian church.

70. The essential lines of the debate can be retrieved in Letters 69 to 74.

and set up a rival church. After studying the matter, Cyprian decided that Novatian was a schismatic, not validly elected, and he sided with Cornelius. A few years later, with a new bishop of Rome in place, Stephen, the question arose of what to do when those Christians who were first received into the church of Novatian or any other schismatic church wished to pass over to the catholic church. Should a person moving from a schismatic church to the church with a lawfully elected and valid bishop be baptized again? The Roman policy, which Stephen maintained was confirmed by tradition, did not prescribe another baptism but merely a laying on of hands, a gesture of conferring the Spirit and forgiving sins.[71] Baptism outside the true church was still baptism in the name of Jesus Christ. This view naturally facilitated the movement back into the lawful church, and this doctrine would prevail in the end, especially with the help of the theology of Augustine.

But Cyprian proposed a counter doctrine and practice. First of all, his view on baptism followed logically from his view of the church. The argument was utterly simple and the same in all of its variations: without the Spirit there could be no baptism. But the Spirit was contained in the one and unified church, and was found nowhere outside of this church, the one church measured by valid bishops ordained in succession. One was either inside the church or outside the church; and a given church either had the Spirit or did not. In short, a schismatic church could not give what it did not possess. Therefore it was not a question of rebaptism at all, but of real baptism for the first time. "[A]ll who come from adversaries and antichrists to the church of Christ must, indeed, be baptized in the baptism of the church" (Letter 69.11).

In another letter to Stephen, Cyprian simply informed him of his practice which reflected the truth of the matter. But although they disagreed on basic points of theology and discipline, matters one might have considered regulated by divine law, he would not break communion with Stephen. Ultimately the universal unity of the church was based on the communion of bishops; each bishop was

---

71. Recall that baptism in Hippolytus had two stages, baptism for the remission of sins, and a laying on hands for conferral of the Spirit.

responsible before God for the exercise of his authority over the local church.[72] At certain points one detects the vehemence of Cyprian's disagreement with Stephen. Yet unity and communion represented a more important value than uniformity of practice. In other words, in the wake of disagreement, even when the other was assuredly wrong, Cyprian stands for communion within pluralism. I shall return to Cyprian for a fuller characterization of the church at Carthage in the mid-third century.

DESCRIPTION OF THE PRE-CONSTANTINIAN CHURCH

These authors provide a certain amount of information about the development of the early church prior to the Constantinian move of imperial recognition. What follows summarizes this data, first, by addressing the church's response to the problems outlined at the head of this chapter. In response to the question of identity I gather together the various institutional forms that gradually arose to structure the expansion and complexification of the church as it moved out into the Mediterranean world at the end of the New Testament period. I also characterize the way the church understood and acted out its relationship to the world, that is, the Roman empire. Then, second, I outline Cyprian's pre-Constantinian Western church in Carthage, about which we have significant information from the bishop's perspective.

Response to Historical Crises

The historical problems that the church encountered during this critical period provided the occasions in which many of its basic institutions took shape. These correlate with the internal life of the church and its negotiation with its environment.

Unity and identity. The embryonic church of the first century developed clear and lasting institutional forms during these two centuries. To cast these against the problematic of internal unity and

---

72. "In this matter, we do not apply force to anyone, nor do we give any law since each prelate has, in the administration of the church, the free will of his own volition as one who will render an account of his action to his Lord." Letter 72.3.

identity does not of course tell the whole story. But simply to enumerate some of the most important institutions against that background allows one to see their sociological function in close connection with the theological relationship the church bears to God.

First, regarding *worship and cult:* Troeltsch indicates that the most basic element that holds the Christian community together is faith in God as revealed in Jesus Christ. Ultimately, then, the Christian community is grounded in worship and, in institutional terms, assembly for worship. In Justin one sees a regular order of time and procedure for the ceremonies of Sunday morning worship. In Hippolytus one has an order, i.e., a set of rules, for baptism, ordination, and eucharist. The *Didascalia Apostolorum* shows a community with a highly developed, self-identifying language, a firm sense of roles in the community, and moral exhortation for a wide variety of situations. The community meets in a proper church building and has a strong sense of boundaries.

Second, the single most important unifying institution in terms of organization is the *bishop.* The development begun in Ignatius is completed. The bishop is truly monarchical: he leads the worshiping community at baptism, eucharist, ordination of presbyters and deacons, and penitential regimes; he is responsible for the teaching in the catechumenate and at the eucharist; he participates in the consecration of other bishops in neighboring churches; he is the reconciler who accepts people back into communion in the church; he is the administrator who is responsible for the community's finances along with his deacon delegates; he is the head of the presbyteral council; he is the link with the other churches. One can see in these actual functions which gradually accrued to bishops the historical, sociological, and political basis for the theological and doctrinal formulae that characterized the range of episcopal power, office, and authority as priest, teacher, prophet, and governor or ruler. In terms of the sociology of knowledge, function in the community became objectified and gave way to office. The experience of and belief in the action of the Spirit within the community provided grounds for the theological legitimation of the office. The office in turn exercised a measure of oversight and control over how the Spirit was encountered and became effective.

Third, during the second century the church developed a canon of normative *scripture* which included especially the New Testament. The ideology for these constitutive documents lay in their apostolicity, their quality of reaching back to the source of true Christian belief. When it was perceived that significant "apostolic" truth was encoded into these writings, they became a constitutional source, norm, and criterion of Christian truth. This helped to hold the single communities together in worship where they were read and in doctrine as a source for teaching. Scripture supplied the basis for rejecting error. Scripture thus became a common possession for the whole Christian movement in a canon which would eventually contain a definite number of writings; it held distant communities together by a common norm of faith even when the interpretation of them differed.

Fourth, another such norm was a *rule of faith* which would eventually become a common *creed*. Derivative from the baptismal formula, it was a summary of Christian belief, and it too bound Christians together in a common set of beliefs. No single, universally recognized symbol of faith bound the whole Christian movement together: but various churches had various versions of a rule of belief defining a common faith. Division on a rule of faith meant division within the community. A rule of faith defined the Christian community and their beliefs over against society. As a public statement of Christian belief, it provided a short formula of Christian identity.

Fifth, *ordered ministries* structured and helped to nurture the unity. They insured that ministry was always available. The tripartite ministries of bishop, presbyter, and deacon seen in Ignatius were solidified by the time of Irenaeus, Tertullian, and Hippolytus. Each of these orders had definite functions, and there were other orders as well. In general, then, one has a picture of a fairly well-defined structure of the community that was sacralized by ordination. The interesting exception to this is the martyr-confessor who had spiritual authority and ministry without ordination because he or she was proven to be filled with the Spirit of God. As Hippolytus put it: "For he has the office of the presbyterate by his confession" (AT, 10.1). These elements of a charismatic leadership in the community helped bring about the conflict in the church of Cyprian. Note that all of the last three elements are apostolic: scripture, rule of faith, and ministries insure apostolicity; closeness to the original source is the final norm of truth.

Sixth, the order of the community was also structured by routinized *patterns of behavior.* Hippolytus's work itself was an example of the regularized customs or rituals of the community. Like the primitive manual, the *Didache,* it expressed the need for established ways of doing things in the assembling of a worshiping community, its ministries, its formal actions. All churches have such manuals of order. Those of the early churches would gradually grow over the centuries into a body of canon law for the international regulation of the church. They emerged out of the past, out of praxis, and took on a kind of hallowed character because they claimed to rest on tradition.

Seventh, the *catechumenate* was an institution of instruction and initiation into Christian belief and as such a major source of social cohesion. The two or three year period that is indicated in Hippolytus tells of its seriousness; it provided members with a metaphysical vision of the whole of reality; it functioned as a defensive bulwark against the inroads of divisive heresy; it guaranteed the moral cohesion of the community.

Finally, the criteria and mechanism for *reconciliation* with the community was very significant for the self-definition of the church. An institution of second repentance reflected an acceptance of human fallibility. But only one second repentance meant that the ideal of moral purity was still operative. One can see here a tension in socially expanding and increasingly large communities. As numbers grow a community becomes less tightly knit and more impersonal, and the social pressure for a distinctive moral behavior decreases. This tension between the ideals of a moral life and the actuality of human finitude and sinfulness played itself out in the public lives of Christians. The church gradually moved from being a small community of mutually supported holiness toward becoming an institution of a salvation mediated by leaders and by objective sacred rituals such as baptism, eucharist, and penance.

The relation of the church to the world. How did the church see itself in relation to the world, the world in the sense of culture and society, and the world in the sense of the state? In both cases one sees an ambivalent or double relationship.

First of all, regarding the church's *relation to social culture,* on the one hand the church stood over against culture because of its relation to God. It was attached to another world, and one of its highest values was martyrdom. Some, like Tertullian, regarded Roman culture as thoroughly idolatrous; every aspect of social life was steeped in emperor worship, licentiousness, and the solicitation of evil spirits. The holiness of the church applied to the members of the church. It possessed a strict ethical code, and virginity, celibacy, and asceticism were seen as values. The practice of a second repentance and reconciliation with the church indicated a recognition of human weakness, but there was only one reprieve, and even it was resisted by many. In sum, the church was in an alien culture, one dominated by the demons; it experienced itself as a persecuted minority group; it could not help but define itself over against society.

On the other hand the church was in the world, and even Tertullian in his more moderate moments thought there could be points of encounter. Christians participated in all aspects of life save the idolatrous and licentious. Gradually Christians would begin to compromise their sense of being sharply differentiated from the world and begin to feel at home in Roman society. The theme of the holiness of the church is important for defining how the church viewed itself in relation to society.

Second, regarding the church's *relation to the state,* one finds again a double and ambiguous attitude. On the one hand the church accepted the state, the emperor and the imperial order. The emperor ruled by the appointment of God and the Christian obeyed. Christians accepted a view of natural law by which the world was governed under God. The state persecuted Christians, but the church accepted this with patience for the time being as ultimately unfolding within the mysterious and sovereign will of God. Indeed Christians prayed regularly for the emperor and in so doing were the greatest allies of the empire.

On the other hand, and at the same time, Christians saw the whole empire as idolatrous; in fact the political order was under the control of the evil spirit-gods that were thwarting God's will. God is God and above the state; the emperor is the emperor but not God; the church is under God first. Thus a radical countercultural force within the church, both in its consciousness and in the empowering actuality of God as Spirit, allowed it to stand over against the state and to withstand persecution.[73]

One cannot find the theme of the church transforming society in this period in the sense achieved in the late modern period, except perhaps in the sense of "spreading out" and "absorbing by conversion." Many factors disallowed the possibility: the state was already ruled by God; to those lacking historical consciousness, society appeared immutable in its structures; and sociologically the church was too small a social force to contemplate the possibility.[74] The exception here was the domain of family life; the church stood against divorce and infanticide. And care for the sick and the poor within the church was an institutionalized value. Love for one another was translated into care for the poor, and this was one of the responsibilities of the bishop. The agape meal also concretized this active concern. Stark believes this practical love was a factor in the numerical growth of the church.[75]

Finally, then, one can look upon the church in this period as a parallel society, one that was not integrated into the empire. It provided an alternative way of life in an alternative society within society. It had structures that resembled those of the empire: resident governors in bishops, law, provincial or regional synods, an emerging priesthood

---

73. One finds in the early church a new understanding of the state that did not exist prior to Christianity, and it is well articulated by Tertullian in his *Apology*. The Christian citizen is obedient to the state, but the state no longer has divine sanction in all its actions, is no longer sacred. The Christian's higher allegiance to the supreme ruler, God, gives the Christian leverage against the state even as one is loyal to it. Hans von Campenhausen, *The Fathers of the Latin Church* (London: Adam & Charles Black, 1964), 15.

74. "The rise of Christianity altered profoundly the moral texture of the late Roman world. Yet in moral matters the Christian leaders made almost no innovation. What they did was more crucial. They created a new group, whose exceptional emphasis on solidarity in the face of its own inner tensions ensured that its members would practice what pagan and Jewish moralists had already begun to preach." Brown, *Late Antiquity*, 24.

75. Stark, *The Rise of Christianity*, 73–94.

and sacrifice.[76] It did not as yet have an emperor, however, but only the supreme ruler of the universe, God.

Description of a Pre-Constantinian Church

I return to Cyprian's church in Carthage during the 250s for a concluding characterization of an ecclesiology that developed during the second and third centuries.[77] Granted that this leaves us far short chronologically of the Constantinian peace, and that the church expanded greatly during the last half of the third century. But this is offset by the detailed picture of a church that one is able to retrieve from Cyprian's writings. Although Cyprian was no systematic theologian, the combination of the problems and controversies he encountered and his extensive correspondence stimulated a body of writing on his church and the church at large which yields a fairly coherent and comprehensive ecclesiology, the most detailed in the pre-Constantinian period. Cyprian's church is Western and Latin speaking, and as a particular church does not represent other churches; historically, it differed with Rome on significant issues, not to mention Eastern churches. Yet it may still be taken as an example of church self-understanding and illustrative of the kinds of problems faced by other churches in the second half of the third century. In any case, Cyprian's personal influence and his writings made his church of more than merely local significance.

The bishop. Cyprian was a bishop, and everything he wrote about the church was written from an episcopal point of view. The bishop held the preeminent position in the church in Cyprian's ecclesiol-

---

76. Robert Grant uses the phrase "a state within a state" to describe the church; "the pattern of government within the church was close to that of the larger state around it." Grant, *Early Christianity,* 43. Synods or local councils were assemblies of bishops in a given area who met to discuss and decide common policies. They were prevalent in various areas, not least North Africa in the third century. They will be discussed in connection with Cyprian's theology of the episcopacy.

77. No common ecclesiology defined the self-understanding of all the churches. "The church could be identified as anything from a local community of believers to a cosmic assembly that united celestial and human beings in praising and serving God" (Wagner, *After the Apostles,* 236–37). The church could be conceived as a school that preserved and taught God's saving truth, or a community marked by obedience to God's rule of life. Cyprian's was a coherent ecclesiology, but it was not the only one at the time.

ogy. "Each community had only one bishop, who served for life. The bishop was elected either by the community or by the bishops of neighboring churches with the consent of the community he would govern; he was then installed by other bishops. The election could be considered an expression of divine choice of a particular candidate."[78] That God chose the bishop, working through human processes, preserved the sacred character of the office. The relevance of the single bishop will appear more sharply in the statement of the mission of the church. The defining responsibilities of the bishop were both local or internal, with reference to his own church, and collegial, involving responsibility with other bishops for the whole church.

The bishop's duties at home included administration, judgment, and leadership in liturgical activity. The bishop governed the church; he had ultimate authority over church funds. "The bishop was also the principal judge in his church. He interpreted the behavioral demands of the gospel to the community and punished those who failed to fulfill them. He supervised the repentance and reconciliation of sinners, acting as he claimed in the place of Christ until the last day and final judgement. ... The ritual life of the community also revolved around the bishop, who himself presided at the eucharistic service in imitation of Christ and authorized the presbyters to do likewise. Through the imposition of hands, he admitted newly baptized members and readmitted penitents. Thus Cyprian would portray the local bishop as Peter, the rock upon which the community was founded."[79]

Although the bishop in Cyprian's church enjoyed the fullness of authority, he exercised it in a consultative manner. Cyprian consulted with the presbyters, with the confessors, with the laity at large. There were decisions that the bishop should not make alone, such as who should be readmitted to the church (Letter, 17.1.2), or whether or not members of the clergy were unworthy and subject to deposition.

---

78. Burns, *Cyprian*, 15. This whole synthetic account draws heavily from the work of Burns. The process of election is discussed by Paul J. Fitzgerald, "A Model for Dialogue: Cyprian of Carthage on Ecclesial Discernment," *Theological Studies* 59 (1998): 241–47.

79. Burns, *Cyprian*, 15.

The laity were part of the instrument by which God chose a bishop, and they could be instruments for their recall.[80]

The bishop stood at the head of a structured clergy. "The other clergy were distributed through several grades, including presbyters, deacons, subdeacons, acolytes and readers. Each had age requirements, specific duties and assigned compensations. The clergy as a whole worked under the supervision of the bishops; the deacons may have been at the disposal of individual presbyters."[81] "The relationship of the bishop to his clergy is that of a magistrate to his clerks: presbyters are to be paid a modest salary by the bishop in the name of the community."[82] In sum, relative to the church in the town or city, the bishop constituted the centering presence and authority within the community with oversight relative to every facet of the church's common life.

Besides being responsible for the local church, however, the bishop also was a member of a unified episcopate which as a body had responsibility for the whole church. The episcopate relative to the whole church was single: "a single power was held in common by all and only those bishops joined in the unity of the episcopal college. Thus he linked the authority of the bishops, the unity of the episcopate and the unity of the church."[83] "Local churches were never autonomous units but always part of a whole, since they were dependent upon the leaders of neighboring churches for the establishment and removal of their bishops. Individual bishops actually held and exercised their power to judge and sanctify in union with their colleagues."[84]

The large or great church was also one. But it was made up of many bishops whom Cyprian consistently claimed had full authority in their own churches. "Though Christ's great flock was indeed

80. Fitzgerald, "Model for Dialogue," 247–50. "Cyprian claimed significant authority for the bishop but recognized the community's right to choose, advise and, in extreme circumstances, depose its leaders." Burns, *Cyprian*, 49.

81. Burns, *Cyprian*, 16.

82. Paul J. Fitzgerald, "St. Cyprian of Carthage and Episcopal Authority: The Rule of God," Unpublished Paper at the Conference on the Teaching Authority of Bishops, The Jesuit Institute, Boston College, November 30–December 2, 2001, 8.

83. Burns, *Cyprian*, 159.

84. Ibid., 163.

one, it had many shepherds. Each of them had been assigned a portion of the flock to govern and would answer to the Lord for his stewardship. Though none was to intrude on the work of another, all were jointly responsible for the whole and even for each of its parts. Thus the theory of the unity of the worldwide church contained conflicting elements whose balance was achieved by negotiation."[85] The negotiation was accomplished by a steady flow of communications: meetings in synods and local councils, correspondence through letters and personal messengers, participation of bishops in the election, installation of bishops, and removal of unworthy bishops. Common policy was constantly discussed broadly. This negotiation was real and not always smooth. For synods could put pressure on individual bishops to follow a common policy, and bishops could support laity in other dioceses and regions in overthrowing the bishop.[86]

The church in North Africa during this period did not recognize a jurisdictional authority over itself. The bishop of Rome was not accorded any universal authority. The original function of Peter was understood to be exercised on the local level by the bishop of each church. Cyprian and his colleagues "consistently rejected the Roman bishops' claims to authority on the basis of apostolic foundation."[87] The primacy of one bishop of a region over others that developed in the fourth and fifth centuries, the patriarchal system, would be a consistent development from the time of Cyprian, as he and other bishops had leadership roles in their regions. "Cyprian and his councils tended to see their churches as equals to that of Rome, as a younger sister to an older when both reach maturity."[88] The bishop of Rome is *primatus,* and plays a vital role in the universal church, but he does not possess direct jurisdictional authority over other churches in other provinces. "The unique role of the bishop of Rome

---

85. Ibid., 151. There was one episcopate, and it was realized in the many churches. Not even a synod was binding on a bishop: Christ alone was the bishop's judge. Hans von Campenhausen, *Ecclesiastical Authority and Spiritual Power in the Church of the First Three Centuries* (London: Adam & Charles Black, 1969), 275–79.

86. "Although Cyprian and his colleagues regularly insisted that individual bishops retained the right to dissent from common decisions, they did not hesitate to reprimand deviants, particularly where common discipline was jeopardized." Burns, *Cyprian,* 153. Fitzgerald, "Episcopal Authority," 12–13, discusses the collegiality of the episcopate.

87. Burns, *Cyprian,* 165.

88. Fitzgerald, "Episcopal Authority," 13.

is to be the agent of universal communion by a unique universal exercise of charity and of communal prudential judgment, but not of command."[89]

Members of the church. Not only the clergy but also the members of the church, the laity at large, were ordered. "The widows and indigent were enrolled to receive financial support. The dedicated virgins were an established order within the community, whose bodily integrity was especially important for the church as a whole. These women retained their property but they refrained from marriage and were not to associate closely with men. They were especially honored as symbols of the church's separation from the Roman world."[90] Catechumens prepared for admission through the ritual of baptism; public sinners entered the group of penitents who pursued a course of prayer, fasting, and almsgiving under the supervision of the clergy; sinners who refused public penance were excommunicated; clergy who failed in their office could be reduced to the lay state. Also the ranks or designations of confessor and martyr were highlighted because of the persecution. We have seen how lay members of the church participated in and had a voice in various facets of church life. I will take up the members of the church below in terms of the relationship of the church to Roman society.

Mission of the church. The question of the goals of an organization or the mission of the church closely intersects with the nature of the church and how it understands itself. Theological self-understanding bears particularly upon the church's mission. This comes to a particular focus in Cyprian's church in an understanding of the church as a eucharistic community with the bishop as priest.

"The church was a concrete unity, a particular group of people sharing eucharistic fellowship and exclusive faith in Christ, under the leadership of their elected and recognized bishop."[91] Two things are important in this shorthand definition of the church. On the one hand, there could be only one such church in any town, and this unicity, a single church, correlates neatly with the integral unity of the community and the role of the eucharist in it. On the other hand,

89. Ibid., 14.
90. Burns, *Cyprian*, 16.
91. Ibid., 98.

the bishop or head of this one eucharistic assembly is the bishop as priest. "The bishop is always the principal priest in the local church," and as such he is "leader of the liturgy, preacher of sacred scripture, teacher of the tradition, and judge of the faithful."[92] The primary definition of the church, then, falls to the local, eucharistic community in which the bishop or head of the church is primarily not administrator or judge, but mediator of the divine power of unity in liturgy and sacrament.

If this designation is correct, then one can understand the mission of the church to be a community of eschatological salvation. "In Cyprian's way of thinking, the local church was a specific social group with an identifiable membership, sharing eucharistic fellowship under a bishop. To refuse to adhere to such a community under the leadership of a legitimate bishop was to be outside the church and by implication ineligible for participation in the kingdom of Christ."[93] Since there is only one such church in any given locale, and since there is no salvation outside this church, it follows that the chief mission of the church is to bring people into this historical community which can in turn enable their eschatological salvation. The church is a community of salvation.[94]

Sacraments. The mission of the church correlates nicely with the theology and function of the sacraments. In Cyprian's theology of baptism, for example, the boundary of the church "marked off insiders from outsiders, those who were allowed to participate in the eucharist from those who were not. This social boundary was assigned a heavenly as well as an earthly significance: because it specified the limits of the presence and operations of the Holy Spirit, it also determined who might gain access to the kingdom of heaven."[95] The eucharist has the same function of nurturing the community on earth in preparation for its inheritance of the kingdom of heaven. The sacrament of reconciliation, especially in the Cyprianic revision that

---

92. Fitzgerald, "Episcopal Authority," 7, n. 24. Presbyters are also priests in Cyprian's church, but they are so as extensions or agents of the bishop's priesthood. Ibid., 9.

93. Burns, *Cyprian*, 97.

94. The distinction made by Malina differentiating the goal of Jesus' community and Paul's community has hardened. See chapter 2 above, p. 95, n. 65.

95. Burns, *Cyprian*, 128.

allowed the bishop to readmit sinners to the eucharist for strength in the face of persecution, emphasized the mission of the church to prepare people for eschatological salvation.[96]

The church and the world. A description of the Carthaginian church would note that it consisted in Christians with a strong sense of identity, separated from the religious culture of the empire, and forming a fairly tightly bonded group. "Baptismal profession required the renunciation of all other religious practices, and in particular the avoidance of contact with the demonic idolatry which permeated Roman imperial society."[97] Yet the people were not cut off from society; rich and poor at their own level interacted with society where they could in conscience. And one would expect a gradual accommodation to society and a loosening of some of the boundaries that set Christians apart.

Cyprian's writings suggest in the church of Carthage a tension between Christian behavior that transcended the general morality of society, a virtuous Christian standard of life that stood above society, and a compromise of that high standard, a gradual relaxation into a more morally mediocre and sinful church, with a greater recognition of the mercy of God. On the one hand, if the numbers of Christians who defected were as large a Cyprian indicated, and if his reasons for the compromise were accurate, then one has to say that the quality of Christian life began to move in the direction of society at large; one sees a leveling of ethical ideals as expectations were drawn less over against those of society. However, in tension with this, the Cathaginian church still represented a parallel society, quite distinct from the empire. The church had developed clearer, stronger, and more elaborate boundaries; it remained self-sufficient and persecuted; and it still embraced the eschatological ideal of martyrdom.

One way of analyzing the development in the churches as they gradually became acclimated or inculturated in the environment of the Roman empire can be measured in the category of holiness and how it is predicated in the church. We saw earlier that holiness in

---

96. See J. Roldanus, "No Easy Reconciliation: St. Cyprian on Conditions for Reintegration of the Lapsed," *Journal of Theology for Southern Africa* 92 (1995): 23–31.

97. Burns, *Cyprian*, 13.

Tertullian seemed to refer quite pointedly to the members of the church as a group. Tertullian expected that the church would stand over against society by the power of the Spirit that was manifested in the moral integrity of the members of the church. In Cyprian's view, probably in the light of the lapse of so many of the members of the church, but perhaps because of social-spiritual conditions that explain the defection itself, the church at least required holiness in its ministers. This applied most directly to bishops.[98]

In an analogous discussion Burns uses the categories of boundaries separating the church from Roman society and culture. The contrast between Cyprian and a Novatian rigorist position also serves as a marker of change from a smaller, more closely defined community over against society to a community growing larger and accommodationist relative to social patterns. The Novatians insisted on purity in minister and member in an absolute egalitarian way; those who sinned grievously were excluded from the community. The shift with Cyprian was much more nuanced and included trust in the efficacy of reconciliation and, in the case of ministers, removal from office but not communion.[99] Cyprian's ecclesiology seems like a compromise when placed between the Novatian rigorist views and the laxist views recommended by those who admitted the lapsed without public accountability. "Cyprian might seem to have inaugurated a mediating position for preserving the holiness of the church by restricting to the clergy the purity requirement which had extended to the whole assembly: he argued that penitent apostates could be admitted to communion without polluting the entire congregation accepting them; yet he insisted that the sanctifying power of the church depended upon the holiness of the clergy, particularly their freedom from all taint of idolatry, apostasy or schism."[100]

One way of summing up the ecclesiology that emerged out of Cyprian's church in Carthage would be to see the correlation between its several key elements: episcopalism, communion, Spirit, unity, holiness. Any one of these symbols could be used to organize a synthesis

---

98. Evans, *One and Holy*, 57–58.
99. Burns, *Cyprian*, 67–77.
100. Ibid., 132.

of the church's self-understanding as it appears in Cyprian. The primary referent of the term "church" is the eucharistic community united organizationally and in terms of leadership around the bishop. But church also points to and can refer to the whole Christian movement. It is held together in unity by the unity of its bishops who as a group exercise responsibility for the whole. We saw how this communion worked out in practice: it involved practical mechanisms of sharing information, of granting autonomy to each bishop thereby setting up the conditions that allowed for pluralism, but at the same time active interference when a consensus of various voices indicated a serious breech of Christian truths or morality. Autonomous local churches were "built into the full flock of Christ through equally concrete alliances of their episcopal leaders, all of them in succession to the original apostolic community, all meeting to deliberate on the good of the whole. The Holy Spirit had been conferred upon Peter and the other apostles and passed to their successors, who in turn shared the Spirit within their local communions."[101] The unity and holiness of the church were due to the presence and activity of God as Spirit within it; the reason why sacraments were efficacious lay in the presence and power of the Spirit within the community. On the deepest theological level Cyprian's understanding of the church could be called a Spirit ecclesiology.

Peter Brown elicits a series of points that show the measure in which the church as a whole movement had entered into a new relationship with the empire by the close of the third century. The general persecution of Christians in 250, 257, and 303 signaled that things had changed. The empire as such took notice and was no longer leaving the matter in local hands. Several factors defined the public perception. The church had become a large public body united across a vast expanse of territory with a recognizable hierarchy of prominent leaders. This was noted, because the persecution targeted the leaders. The one thing that unified Christians was the common scripture, a canon, which appeared to outsiders as a common law and which, coming from God, claimed an uncommon loyalty. Christians were beginning to build churches and thus public spaces for

---

101. Ibid., 129.

assembly. These churches brought together a variegated group that transcended class and rank. Social differences were not leveled, but people were brought together in a deeper unity. The churches across the empire were plural and different. But this pluralism stood in tension with a sense of belonging to a larger extensive movement spread around the empire. Christian groups had a strong sense of belonging to a network of similar communities which spanned the Roman world.[102] Christians shared a common anthropology consisting of a sense of sin and salvation. But the church offered still more in the form of a transformation of the self as in a school of virtue. In baptism and a life of faith and moral fortitude the church proposed to transform the human person into a new being. The life of the church was communitarian and integrated into social life. One manifestation of this was the practice of giving alms for the remission of sins which Christians inherited from Judaism. This expanded the network of sustaining those in need into one of helping other communities, so that the churches emerged as remarkably cohesive and solvent bodies. The church offered a complete place of belonging. Religion appeared to consist in a complex of rituals, a cult of the gods; schools offered philosophy; morality was taught in the home. In the church, however, all three were integrated. The church held forth a complete, integrated vision and praxis of human existence.[103]

PRINCIPLES FOR A HISTORICAL ECCLESIOLOGY

A series of principles that will be helpful in understanding the church as such may serve as a conclusion to this interpretive description of the church in the second and third centuries. These descriptive characterizations of the church from a historical, sociological, and theological perspective combine an aspect of a general principle with an aspect of concrete instantiation since they are drawn from the

---

102. One has to read the bonds that united the churches, the insistence on apostolicity, the concern for succession and tradition, and other criteria of truth and right practice, dialectically against the background of pluralism and difference. To stress either side without the other would distort the evidence.

103. Brown, *Rise of Western Christendom*, 62–71.

churches in this period of the church's development. A list of such principles could be greatly expanded.

Unity as a Highest Value

The early church placed an extremely high value on unity; this appears true across the board in Ignatius, in Irenaeus, implicitly in Hippolytus's manual, in the *Didascalia*, and in Cyprian. This applies mainly to the local community, also to the regional church, and less strongly to the whole Christian movement. The concern for unity really never goes away. And when it appears diminished with schism or fragmentation into different churches, it asserts itself more strongly and explicitly as a negative experience of contrast. The local church is and can only be one. In Cyprian, however, one also sees a concern and responsibility for the unity of the whole Christian movement.

Cyprian's ecclesiology also allows for some measure of pluralism. We are dealing here with classical culture, and one should not read postmodern historical consciousness into the situation. But despite Cyprian's near obsession with unity, because it enfolds within itself so much of his ecclesiology, he can pragmatically affirm communion across differences. More would have to be said about the status of the issues debated in particular cases. For example, sacramental theology and practice were serious issues because so much was at stake in them. But Cyprian would not break communion over divergent sacramental customs and patterns. One can draw several lessons from this case, but the following ecclesiological principle seems reasonable: despite disagreement, even on basic issues, there can be communion among Christians because of everything else that they share in common.

Of course, the loose structure of the unity of the whole church made Cyprian's solution easier. In the middle of the third century the structure of the universal church could be characterized as episcopalism and intercommunion. Although the bishop of Rome was regarded as possessing a primacy of honor as a successor of Peter's episcopacy, no universal papacy existed; the bishop of Rome did not exercise juridical authority over the whole church. Rather intercommunion among monarchical bishops, reinforced by regional synods and collegiality, was the official political and institutional structure of unity. But the historical ecclesiological pattern of the third century could also be used to urge other forms of the unity of the whole church that would protect pluralism. In other words, the normative value of third century unity with pluralism could suggest to the present time new patterns for the world church.

Functional Development of Institutions

The analysis of the church's genesis provides the primordial witness to the development of ecclesial institutions. But development did not stop there. Some important further developments included the following:

Episcopal succession. Neither the New Testament nor historical evidence and critical reconstruction support the idea that bishops were the direct successors of "the twelve apostles." Yet in the course of the second century the concern for apostolicity became focused on the idea of a succession of bishops reaching back to the apostles and thus to Jesus. Across church history thereafter a monoepiscopal structure of the churches became central to church polity and today is regarded by some communions as a divinely established organizational institution without which a fully authentic church cannot exist. Do the last two chapters shed any light on this issue?[104]

The development of monoepiscopacy from the New Testament period to the end of the third century should be understood in a

---

104. Francis A. Sullivan, in his *From Apostles to Bishops: the Development of Episcopacy in the Early Church* (New York and Mahwah, N.J.: Newman Press, 2001), addresses this problem from a Roman Catholic perspective in two steps: (1) Historically, the institution of monoepiscopacy developed either through a college of presbyters establishing a bishop as their leader or though a man who had oversight in a region (as in the Pastoral Epistles) settling in a particular church which accepted him as its bishop. In both scenarios the man would have had links back to the apostles (2) Theologically, this historical development is interpreted as representing the will of God, so that through it the monoepiscopate is divinely established. Such a judgment is analogous to that which determined the writings that made up the New Testament canon. Just as the Spirit guided the church in the discernment of its sacred books, so too did the Spirit guide the judgment that monoepiscopacy is an essential and divinely willed structure of the church. See especially pp. 217–30. This theological interpretation and theory successfully legitimates an understanding of monoepiscopacy as a legitimate ecclesial structure. But it does not succeed in justifying it as a church-dividing structure. The theory does not establish that other developments or arrangements that might serve to guarantee apostolicity would not also be legitimate and divinely willed.

simultaneously historical and theological way, with a theological imagination that is guided by and emerges out of the historical and social developments. One must be careful not to impose juridical categories or theological conclusions from a later period upon the earlier historical data. When this historical-theological lens is applied to this issue, the emergence of monoepiscopacy appears to be a quite natural and spontaneous development, whatever were the actual events that engendered it. The problems of internal dissension and divisiveness during the course of the second century and a Spirit-inspired desire for unity within the churches and across the churches and the regions together account quite well for the development of the strong authority that the office of bishop achieved in the churches just examined. This development was historical and functional: it met a particular crisis and continued to preserve the church's unity. This office can be understood theologically, therefore, as divinely willed in a non-exclusive way. This means that, just as the Spirit of God impelled this particular organizational structure as a way of ensuring the church's well-being at this time, so too might the same Spirit inspire another arrangement for the church's well-being in other circumstances, as the New Testament proposes.

Reconciliation. Relative to the question of the "whence" of offices and ordered ministries, this early period shows that the sociological understanding of a functional response to needs accurately describes the emergence of ministries in the church, for example, deaconesses, and the expansion of certain powers of a given order of ministry, for example, second repentance and reconciliation within the church. But this sociological interpretation should not be separated from a theological analysis. The example of the deaconess is instructive: there the need for such an order was felt, it was established on the pragmatic grounds of need. But the position of deaconess was a sacred order involving social relationships that were described in sacred or theological language. A functional analysis and an ontological analysis are not antithetical to each other. This leads to a simultaneously historical, social, and theological conception of the church as a Spirit-filled community, normed by a memory of Jesus, that has within itself the wherewithal to "create" ministries for its well-being. The historical data of emerging new ministries are coherently theorized or correlated with a dynamic ecclesiology from below.

Another area of the development of sacramental or cultic action concerns ritual forgiveness and readmission into the church after sin that either excluded or placed one in a marginal state relative to the community. This consideration bears a direct relation to the question of holiness. One can easily recognize here the tensive existential relationship between institutional form, in this case ritual form, and the actual historical life of the community as the community adjusts its public discipline to the real-life exigencies of human frailty and sinfulness. This takes on a dramatic quality in the decision of Cyprian, in the face of renewed persecution, to shift the ritual practice and invite penitent sinners back to eucharistic communion for the purpose of nurture and fortification in the face of the expected trial. Theological development in this case clearly follows in the wake of praxis, in this case ministerial decision and practice. One sees in the action of Cyprian a change in a deep *habitus* of the Carthaginian community that reached back through Tertullian. The change became irresistible under the pressure of new circumstances and events.

Priesthood. The emergence of priesthood in the pre-Constantinian church provides another area in which this principle comes into play. We saw that priesthood was not a category applied to ministry in the New Testament church. Yet by the end of the third century Christianity has an order of priests, at least in its bishops. From where did this come? The response must be "historical development." This development can be schematized in two stages, the first an application to the bishop as the principal president or leader of the eucharist, the second an extension to the presbyter as communities grew and the presbyter shifted from an occasional delegate of the bishop to the eucharistic leader of a distinct subgroup.[105] It was a function of both

---

105. Cooke explains that, while the bishop is firmly established as priest by the end of the third century, the idea that a presbyter is a priest is very rare prior to Nicaea, despite the fact that the presbyters substituted for bishops at the eucharist. In the pre-Nicene period, priests as a group shared in the *sacerdotium* of the episcopacy without being designated priests. Cook, *Ministry*, 537–39. See also Paul Bernier, *Ministry in the Church* (Mystic, Conn.: Twenty-Third Publishing, 1992), 58–81 where he traces the development of presbyteral ministry into the ministry of priesthood.

the growth and complexification of the communities, of inculturation, and of theological reflection. As early as Paul the eucharist was
associated with Jesus' passion and death. As Jesus' saving mediation
was interpreted through the metaphor of a sacrificial offering to God
in a thoroughly Jewish way, and as the eucharist commemorated and
recapitulated this redemptive act, the bishop presider at the eucharist
gradually became understood in terms of the priest or high priest who
offered the ritual act of sacrifice in the community. This was certainly
intelligible in the Graeco-Roman cultural context where there was no
shortage of priests or cultic sacrifices.

To say that Christian priesthood was and is a product of historical
development and interpretation of the second and third centuries,
and thus of human freedom and construction, does not mean that it
is less than a God-willed or God-given ministerial office. The reasons
for this have been amply explained. Cyprian provides an example of
how one can understand God's will and choice for history being made
through the processes of human deliberation and agency. But it is
important to register the shifts in understanding that occurred. The
bishop became associated with the Aaronic high priesthood both as
chief celebrant of the eucharistic sacrifice and the "principal penitential and disciplinary minister."[106] One also finds in Cyprian language
of propitiating God on behalf of the people. This phrasing is quite distant from the New Testament period in which there were no priests
in the Christian community because only Christ held that position.
This also marks a shift toward a greater divide between bishops and
other people, toward a ministerial order of the church that is sacred in itself, as it were, that mediates grace in the way the whole
community did earlier.[107]

Tension between Structure and Communitas

The church bears within itself a tension between official episcopal authority and unofficial spiritual authority in the community. Cyprian's
church exemplifies this well. At a time of crisis, when Cyprian was
still a new bishop, the recognized spiritual authority of martyrs and

---

106. Jay, *The Church*, 57.
107. Ibid., 57–58.

confessors clashed with the institutional authority of the bishop. One can see the tensions between structure and *communitas*, or office and charism, being played out in concrete persons dealing with specific issues. It seems important, at least in this case, to refrain from judgments about who was right and who wrong, and to recognize that such conflicts are constitutive of a historical church, an organization that makes its way through new time and changing circumstance.

To conclude, the second and third centuries witnessed dramatic changes, and developments of the community of Christians called church at the end of the first century. The historical development during this period provides indispensable lessons for the construction of a historically conscious ecclesiology from below that uses a genetic method. The principles at work then can be related by analogy to problems facing the church at any given time. Yet through the course of these changes one can always discern a lived substance of the church that conforms to the definition that was drawn from the genesis of the church in the first century. The church consists of disciples of Jesus, those who have encountered God's salvation in him, so that their faith in God is structured by him. They form a community on the basis of this faith. They are united by faith and by the organizational and political structures of the community into a church, which is thus one on the basis of Christ, Spirit, and office. The centering activity of this church is Sunday worship: it is thus anchored in word and sacrament which are themselves intimately connected with ethics. The fellowship in the Spirit also transcends the local community. All the Christians of the Roman empire are one; together they stand over against the demonic elements in society.

Chapter 4

The Post-Constantinian Church: 300–600

In its prolonged genesis from the death and resurrection of Jesus into the second century and its further development through the second and third centuries, the church gained its substantial identity. This can be measured in terms of social organization, or by the various boundaries of a religion, and on the basis of theological self-understanding. Some of the responses to historical crises that helped constitute that identity were the decision not to limit membership in the community of faith by Jewish circumcision, the formulation of an understanding of the divinity of Jesus, a monoepiscopal organizational structure, the formation of a canon of scripture, and an internalized conviction that unity within and among the churches was among the highest of their values. At the end of the third century one could have said that the church had reached the term of its essential development. Yet a comparison of this church with the church at the end of the sixth century reveals another period of development as "substantial" as the first half of its life. In terms of size, extension, complexity, cultural identities, members, self-definition of its faith, sacramental theology, organizational structure, relation to the "world," and ideals of the spiritual life, the church went through another period of transformation. This chapter tries in a short space to synopsize these many developments historically, socially, and theologically, and from this picture retrieve perennial tensions and formal principles for understanding the church that might have relevance for an ecclesiology at any given time.

The analysis, consequently, is divided into four parts. The first is narrative; it recalls the story of the church and introduces the authors chosen to represent this period. The second part turns to

those key witnesses who in their lives and texts recorded the social and theological developments that had significant bearing upon
ecclesiological self-understanding. The third consists in an interpretive description of the church along the lines of the dimensions of a
social organization outlined in chapter 2. The fourth draws principles
for a historically conscious ecclesiology from the life of the church at
this time.

HISTORICAL DEVELOPMENT

In the overview of the rise of Christianity during the second and third
centuries it made sense to distinguish the imperial context from the
church developing within it. With Constantine, however, church and
empire begin to run together and become entwined. I therefore divide
this overview roughly by centuries. The narrative aims not at adequate historical reconstruction but at setting up a historical matrix
for interpreting the community and important theological persons,
texts, and events in it. Key areas of ecclesial development guide the
selection of what is highlighted in this representation. Among the
most important are these: the evolving relationship between church
and empire and, within that context, the increased differentiation
between the Eastern and Western churches; the unity of the church
across this expanding territorial reach, including the gradual emergence of the papacy; the rise of monasticism in the East and its spread
to the West; the development of central christological and anthropological doctrines, the refinement of sacramental theology in the West,
and, finally, the character and ideals of Christian life.[1]

---

1. The following works have been useful in the analysis of this historical development: Peter Brown, *Religion and Society in the Age of Saint Augustine* (London: Faber
and Faber, 1972), *The Cult of the Saints: Its Rise and Function in Latin Christianity*
(London: SCM Press, 1981), "Eastern and Western Christendom in Late Antiquity: A
Parting of the Ways," *Society and the Holy in Late Antiquity* (Berkeley: University of
California Press, 1982), *Late Antiquity* (Cambridge, Mass.: Harvard University Press,
1998), *The Rise of Western Christendom: Triumph and Diversity, AD 200–1000* (Oxford: Blackwell, 1996, 2003); Henry Chadwick, *The Early Church* (London: Penguin
Books, 1967), *The Church in Ancient Society: From Galilee to Gregory the Great* (Oxford: University Press, 2001); Bernard Cooke, *Ministry to Word and Sacrament: History
and Theology* (Philadelphia: Fortress Press, 1977); Jean Daniélou and Henri Marrou,
The First Six Hundred Years (New York: McGraw-Hill, 1964); Robert Evans, *One and*

The Fourth Century

At the dawn of the fourth century Christianity underwent the most violent and protracted persecution of its history. At the end of the century it was the official religion of the empire. No single individual is more responsible for that development than Constantine.

Constantine and Eusebius. In July of 306, on the death of Constantius, the supreme general of the western segment of the empire, his troops proclaimed his son, Constantine, emperor of the western territories. But Constantine was in Britain, and the position still had to be won militarily. Not until 312 did Constantine enter Rome victorious, having won the final battle in the name of the Christian God. The empire in the West suddenly found itself with a Christian ruler. In the years following, Constantine gradually solidified his position to the point where he defeated the Eastern emperor and established himself as sole ruler. In 330 he moved his capital to Constantinople, the "new Rome," where he reigned until his death in 337.

Several of Constantine's actions laid down the framework of all future developments. "His reign witnessed perhaps the most important change in the history of the church before those of modern times."[2] Constantine ended the persecution in the West. In 313, together with the Eastern emperor, he issued the so-called Edict of Milan declaring freedom of religious worship. He thus legitimized the church in principle. The change in the political state of affairs as well as the psychological turn about were dramatic. "The Church had passed quickly from a situation in which leading and honored bishops had been martyrs to one in which her leaders were the emperor's table guests and court advisors."[3]

Constantine then became the church's advocate: he heaped upon it power and responsibility within the civic realm. He gifted the church with properties; he built churches; he exempted the church and the

---

Holy (London: SPCK, 1972); W. H. C. Frend, *The Early Church* (Philadelphia: Fortress Press, 1982), *The Rise of Christianity* (Philadelphia: Fortress Press, 1984); Robert M. Grant, *Early Christianity and Society* (San Francisco: Harper & Row, 1977); Eric G. Jay, *The Church: Its Changing Image through Twenty Centuries* (Atlanta: John Knox Press, 1980); Jaroslav Pelikan, *The Christian Tradition,* 1, *The Emergence of the Catholic Tradition (100–600)* (Chicago and London: University of Chicago Press, 1971).

2. Daniélou and Marrou, *Six Hundred Years,* 235.
3. Evans, *One and Holy,* 78.

clergy from taxes thus giving them civic status.[4] He charged the church with civic responsibilities such as care of the poor and granted jurisdiction to church tribunals for settling certain legal conflicts. The church became an instrument in the running of society.

Constantine also assumed leadership in the church in addressing some of its most important religious crises, especially ones impacting the unity of the empire, and he supervised their settlement. He summoned the parties involved in the Donatist conflict to the Council of Arles, tried to impose the theological resolution, and finally attempted to close the issue by imperial force. He believed this to be part of his divinely authorized function. He convened the ecumenical Council of Nicaea and followed its deliberations closely. Under the rule of Constantine, orthodoxy, always a concern among the churches, became as well an imperial ideal. In the end, Constantine created with his actions an entirely new relationship of church and empire.[5]

Eusebius, bishop of Caesaria in Palestine, has been depicted as an intimate and counselor of Constantine. He was neither: he lived at a distance, exchanged letters with Constantine, but probably met him only four times.[6] But the historian, theologian, and panegyrist of Constantine who had lived through Diocletian's persecution grew thoroughly attached to him. For Eusebius Constantine represented the new Moses, and he formulated these reactions into an imperial political theology that operated for centuries thereafter and remains ever available when new situations seem to demand it.

During and after the rule of Constantine, the church's organizational structure solidified into the mold of the empire. Ecclesiastical regions largely coincided with those of the empire. "In the majority of cases the capital city of the eparchy [or province] became the see city of the bishop who had primacy over other bishops within the eparchy."[7]

---

4. Grant, *Early Christianity and Society*, 44–65, 151–54.

5. In Peter Brown's view, emperors were not merely concerned with maintaining peace and unity in the empire, but in drafting the bishops as a symbiotic network of power to help in reasserting imperial authority. Brown, *Religion and Society*, 317–24.

6. Timothy D. Barnes, *Constantine and Eusebius* (Cambridge, Mass.: Harvard University Press, 1981), 266.

7. Jay, *Church*, 75.

Developments in the East. The church in the East and in the West each offered distinctive contributions to the whole. Beginning with the East, the theological tradition and the monastic movement deserve to be highlighted.

Theology and doctrine. Although theology was surely not the exclusive preserve of the East, Greek-speaking theologians led the way to the formulation of classic doctrines concerning Christ and the trinity in the fourth century. A tradition already existed in the writings of Justin, Irenaeus, Clement, and Origen. When the subordinationist views of Arius, the Alexandrian presbyter, became public in 318, they touched off an extensive debate that would have consequences well into the future because of the far-reaching spread of his ideas. The simplified version of Arius's view, that the divine Logos generated by the Father and incarnate in Jesus was ultimately a creature, does not distort it. Since Constantine had responsibility for the unity of the empire, it was within his mandate to make sure the religion of the empire did not further divisions. He summoned the council that met at Nicaea on May 20, 325. Approximately 230 bishops, almost all from the East, signed on to the creedal doctrine that the Logos or Son incarnate in Jesus was consubstantial with, of the same stuff as, the Father. It remained ambiguous whether "same" meant strict numerical identity or identity of kind.

Although it may have been clear to many that, taken at the letter, Arius was wrong, it was by no means clear to all that Nicaea was right. Much of the doctrinal and institutional history of the fourth-century church in the East revolves around the various pro and anti-Nicene factions which distrusted, misunderstood, or simply rejected the other side. Moreover, Arian or semi-Arian conceptions of Jesus Christ were spread by missionary movements to the north and northwest. Athanasius, the great defender of Nicene orthodoxy, was able to serve his patriarchate of Alexandria only sporadically when it was politically feasible. The Cappadocian fathers, Basil, his brother Gregory of Nyssa, and Gregory of Nazianzus, were largely responsible for putting in place a set of terms and a vision that clarified the way Christians could talk of the relationship between God as Father, the Son, as well as God as Spirit. They prepared the way for the Council of Constantinople of 381 at which approximately 150 bishops, mostly from Syria and Asia Minor, clarified the meaning of the consubstantiality of the Son with the Father. It did not mean that they were numerically identical. They also expanded on the role of the Spirit as "Lord and giver of life." Insofar as this was taken as the equivalent of consubstantial with the Father and the Son, the doctrine of the trinity was effectively in place. In 382, the Council of Rome made the doctrine of the trinity explicit.[8]

When Constantine established his capital in Constantinople, he understood it to be the new Rome. In one of its canons, Constantinople I recognized the primacy of the see of Rome, but claimed a second primacy of honor for Constantinople as the New Rome. The claim established a certain role of leadership in the East but was not accepted in the West.[9]

Monasticism. The roots of monasticism in terms of an ascetical tradition and radical Christianity extend back into Judaism and the New Testament, but the movement blossomed in the East during the fourth century.[10] Social hard times as well as the religious quest for salvation helped account for it. Clement and Origen had described distinct levels of religious life and encouraged attachment to the higher realm of spiritual reality. To be fully open to the transcendent order one needed discipline and *ascesis*. But more importantly monasticism had an impact on people's imagination. The prestige of the monk, especially the hermit or desert father, lay in his lonely and focused commitment. "He personified the ancient ideal of singleness of heart."[11] Gradually many different ways of joining the ascetical movement and fulfilling its ideals evolved and took some institutional form.

---

8. Pelikan, *Christian Tradition,* 172–225; Daniélou and Marrou, *Six Hundred Years,* 249–67.

9. "The bishop of Constantinople shall have the primacy of honor after the bishop of Rome, because the same is the New Rome." Nicaea, c. 3, in H. J. Schroeder, *The Disciplinary Decrees of the General Councils* (St. Louis: B. Herder, 1937), 65. The canon suggests that primacy is a function of the political status of Rome, which Rome rejected in principle.

10. Daniélou and Marrou, *Six Hundred Years,* 269–79; Chadwick, *Early Church,* 174–83, *Church in Ancient Society,* 394–410; Brown, *Rise of Western Christendom,* 80–84.

11. Brown, *Late Antiquity,* 52.

Antony (250–356) became a religious hero in his own lifetime during the early part of the fourth century in the desert of Egypt. He embodied a spirituality of combat as he battled the demons. It is important to remember that people took the existence of these demons literally. Demons "could be held responsible for social and economic ills, while martyrdom...was regarded as a figurative goal to be accepted 'in intention' by the monks fighting spiritual rather than temporal foes."[12] The region of the Nile delta became home to monasteries known for their ascetic extremes. Pachomius, however, founded monasteries in the region of the upper Nile which combined prayer and work at a useful trade. This style of monastic community became a center of or interacted with a larger rural community. The monks took vows of stability, and thus the monasteries contributed a sense of order to village, town, and wider community.[13] Monasteries following Basil's rule in Asia Minor were relatively small with thirty or forty monks. Basil also adapted them to the town or city so that monks could work in orphanages, or schools, or hospitals; they could also do intellectual work. Basil's monasticism "aimed at changing society and transforming organized religion into a social as well as an individual creed."[14] Monasticism thus offered a variety of spiritualities.

The origins of women's religious life also begins in the East in tandem with monasticism. The "orders" of virgins and widows were well established in the second century. Along with men's groups, Pachomius wrote a rule for his sister Mary and her monastery of nuns. The sister of Basil and Gregory of Nyssa, Macrina, presided over a monastery of religious women. Religious life for women in the West has a beginning in the fourth century when educated Roman women, fired by stories of the desert father and mothers, began their own distinctive form of religious life in community. Women such as Marcella, Melania the Elder, Paula, Melania the Younger combined

---

12. Frend, *Rise of Christianity,* 575.
13. Frend associates Pachomius with "the beginning of a more ordered community asceticism which was to extend its influence throughout the Greek world, and ultimately provide a model for the monasteries in the west." Frend, *Early Church,* 192.
14. Frend, *Rise of Christianity,* 631.

prayer, work, and study of scripture. Paula worked closely with Jerome and founded monasteries for men and women in Bethlehem. Also, Augustine's sister served as the superior of a monastery of women in Hippo. After her death, in the event of a dispute over community organization, Augustine wrote a letter that detailed his vision of religious life. This letter is the basis of the "Rule of St. Augustine."[15]

Developments in the West. The developments in the Western empire and church unfold within the framework of the new legitimacy and imperial sponsorship of the church. The growth in numbers and the complexity of new relationships burst all previous bonds. For the first time Christianity could be the religion of convenience. At the same time some significant Roman citizens became Christians, and deeply so, resulting in a gradual formation of a Christian aristocracy. This is a time of prominent converts, many of whom withdrew from public life; Augustine was the archetypal example. But others remained loyal to the pagan tradition of Rome. Three reference points mark areas of significant social development: Donatism, the papacy, and theology.

Donatism. Donatism provides a model of schism in which the trivial and the profound are tied together in the hardest of knots. In the Diocletian persecution leaders were forced to "hand over" the scriptures. Within the framework of Cyprian's theology, any minister remotely associated with such an act was literally a *traditor* and a traitor of the Christian faith. After the persecution a new bishop of Carthage was consecrated by three bishops in 312. But when one of them was suspected of being a *traditor*, the rival faction of bishops from Numidia refused to recognize the newly consecrated Caecilian, held a council, and elected a bishop of their own. In 313 the faction of the rival bishop sought imperial mediation, and Constantine obliged by appointing a tribunal that judged in Caecilian's favor. When the splinter faction, now led by Donatus, appealed, Constantine called the Council of Arles in 314 and once again the judgment went against the Donatists. Moreover, the Cyprianic practice of rebaptizing

---

15. Patricia Ranft, *Women and the Religious Life in Premodern Europe* (New York: St. Martin's Press, 1996), 1–13.

heretics was condemned, and the bishop of Carthage, Caecilian, was forced to accommodate Roman practice.[16]

The differences that Cyprian was able to tolerate in churches on the opposite sides of the Mediterranean now became pivotal points for competing churches in all the towns of North Africa. By the end of the century Augustine confronted a rival church deeply identified with North African traditions. Early on Constantine again tried to settle the problem by force, by seizing Donatist property and exiling their leaders, but it did not work, and by 320 the Donatists were beginning to flourish. Their fortunes would wax and wane, but they remained an integral part of North African Christianity until the arrival of Islam.

The papacy. Trying to determine when the office of the papacy began is analogous to deciding when the Jewish Jesus movement became autonomous and then finally came into possession of a corporate or organizational self-identity. The church of Rome became monoepiscopal some time in the second century. When did the primacy that Irenaeus refers to begin to be asserted? and recognized? by whom? and in what matters? The bishop of Rome was recognized in the second and third centuries as having prestige and primacy, but when did he begin to exercise administrative and juridical authority? What was the radius of that authority? And was such an exercise of authority charismatic, or a function of Rome's political position, or a function of the office of bishop of Rome? The successive papacies of Damasus (366–84) and Siricius (384–99) represent a significant increase of what would become papal power and authority.

People remembered the papacy of Damasus for, among other things, the extravagant character of its open display of wealth; he fused "the old Roman civic and imperial pride with Christianity."[17] At the same time his episcopacy included the development of an administrative bureaucracy. In 378 emperor Galerius, responding to a request of a Roman council, granted the pope the right to hear appeals from bishops relative to decisions of their metropolitans. This

---

16. The background, origin, and history of Donatism are recounted and analyzed by W. H. C. Frend, *The Donatist Church: A Movement of Protest in Roman North Africa* (Oxford: Clarendon Press, 1971).

17. Chadwick, *Early Church*, 162.

extension granted by the emperor expanded the bishop of Rome's jurisdictional power. Damasus also commissioned Jerome to translate the bible into a uniform Latin version, which would ultimately provide the West with a common text of its foundational document. In 382, the Roman Council that appropriated the teaching of Constantinople I of the previous year also challenged any claims to primacy of that see by stating the primacy of the Roman church over all churches by reason of the pope's Petrine authority and not because of any conciliar decision.[18]

Damasus's successor took up where he left off. Siricius was an administrator, and he wrote letters to bishops "in Gaul and Spain in the same tone as he used toward his own suffragan bishops," that is, in a style of the imperial chancery including threats for lack of obedience.[19] Here one finds actual administrative power. These popes began to exercise authority in western Europe, if not in North Africa, in a new way.

Theology. The fourth century, especially during its second half, shines as a "golden age" of the Fathers of the church.[20] The list of important theologians in the East and West who flourished or were born in this period is remarkable. Theology in the West was advanced significantly through Ambrose and Augustine. Ambrose was the governor of the provinces in the north of Italy when, in 373, the people of Milan drafted him to be their bishop. A Roman aristocrat from a strongly Christian family loyal to Nicaea and not yet baptized, he accomplished in a matter of days the steps needed for consecration as bishop of Milan. Ambrose became the acknowledged leader of Christianity in the West in the last quarter of the fourth century, and most notably he embodied a relation of the church to the empire that stands in marked contrast to Eusebius and the East generally.

In 383 Ambrose found himself in a situation in which Julianna, the regent mother of the emperor and an Arian, demanded a basilica for Arian Christian worship. Ambrose refused by claiming that he simply was not able to alienate what is God's to Caesar. Some years later, in the wake of the punitive massacre of seven thousand people

---

18. Frend, *Early Church,* 219–20; Chadwick, *Church in Ancient Society,* 318–22.
19. Frend, *Rise of Christianity,* 628–29.
20. Daniélou and Marrou, *Six Hundred Years,* 301–8.

in Thessalonica ordered by emperor Theodosius, Ambrose succeeded in invoking the spiritual authority of the bishop over him as a member of the church. Theodosius did public penance rather than suffer excommunication. The symbolic power of these confrontations transcends legal precedent. The occasional overlapping of spiritual and temporal spheres of authority was inescapable, and confrontation between them in a variety of issues became typical of the church-world relationship in the West.

Augustine will be treated at greater length in the next section of this chapter, but the outline of this famous life should be chronicled. Augustine was born in the colonial town of Thagaste in Northern Africa in 354 of a Christian mother and a pagan father. Unbaptized, he received a classical Latin education in Carthage and became a professor of rhetoric. In his early quest for wisdom and truth he aligned himself with the Manichaeans for nine years. In 384, after a year in Rome, he was appointed professor of rhetoric in Milan where under the influence of Ambrose and others he underwent a focused conversion experience in the summer of 386. Having already set aside his common-law wife, he was baptized in 387 and returned to Africa in 388 intending to lead a sedate life as a Christian philosopher. In 391, however, he was ordained a priest and in 395 consecrated bishop of Hippo. Immediately after his conversion Augustine began a prolific career as a philosopher theologian.

As bishop of Hippo Augustine was immediately thrown into the conflict with the Donatists. Later, after the invasion of Rome in 410, Augustine encountered the ideas of Pelagius, instinctively reacted against them, and began to form them into a body of doctrine which he attacked and hunted down practically speaking to the end of his life. But his public fame was based on the Christian classics, *The Confessions, The City of God,* and *On the Trinity.* He lived a long and active life well into the fifth century and died with the Vandals at the door of his town of Hippo in 430. This single most important Christian theologian in the West profoundly shaped Western Christianity's basic anthropology, its sacramental theology, its self-understanding as church in the world. His frustration with Donatism also generated a rationale for political persecution and suppression of religion.

The Fifth Century

The overwhelmingly most significant external factor in the development of empire and church during the fifth century consisted in the gradual, or sometimes sudden and interruptive, migration of peoples from the north and northeast. From within, under the pressure of Christianity, the religious substructure of the empire was gradually being abandoned. In 391 Theodosius outlawed pagan sacrifice and other religious rites. What Tertullian saw as a whole culture tainted with pagan meanings was being depaganized and remythologized with Christian symbols. Then from the outside came people of an alien culture who with their military might took control of the social and political structures. As imperial structure withdrew, gradually everything changed, not in violent social upheaval, but in a sharp and complete "downsizing" as the political power from the Roman center disappeared.[21] In the East the invasions were less radical, the emperor more in control, Christianity more consolidated and resistant. In the West the borders grew porous and could not hold. The church reacted to the influx of new peoples in a variety of ways. In some respects the church accommodated the new situation. The church also evangelized the new peoples, and where they had internalized an Arian Christianity from the East fought against it. The church absorbed the incoming tribes in the sense that ecclesial organization remained in place, survived, and in fact was strengthened. In the first half of the fifth century the papacy grew stronger with a series of able administrators. Throughout the century and across the cities and provinces the social position and role of the church and the powers of bishops were greatly enhanced. In the West the local church "became the 'fixative' which held whole populations in place."[22] The bishops became wealthy; they built churches; they poured money back into the erection of shrines and the support of the poor. Able bishops were elected from the Christian aristocracy or came from the new monasteries.

Monasticism in the West. The monasticism that had emerged in the East gradually made its way into the sphere of Latin Christianity. Martin of Tours was dedicated to an ascetic life before becoming

---

21. Brown, *Rise of Western Christendom*, 97–104.
22. Ibid., 107.

bishop in 372; he founded a monastery outside the city overlooking the Loire. Jerome and Pelagius were in their distinct ways defenders of an ascetic Christian life. Augustine's clergy lived a common life. The monastery of Lérins was founded on the little island by that name along the Mediterranean coast near Cannes in 410. Others too were founded in the early years of the fifth century. The founder of Lérins later became the bishop of Arles, and one can read in that event a common pattern to come: monasteries as training ground for leaders in the church.

John Cassian. John Cassian played a key role in the development of monasticism in the West. Cassian's dates are close to Augustine's: born around 360, probably in the region west of the Black Sea in modern Romania, he died in the 430s. As a young man he joined a monastic community in Bethlehem and took an oath to remain there. However he traveled to Egypt and became completely captivated by the Christian asceticism and monastic life that he found in the Nile delta. Intending to stay, he was released from his former promise. But around the years 399–400, during a controversy among the monks in Egypt and an episcopal campaign against Origenists in which many were forced to leave, Cassian turned up in Constantinople where he was befriended by John Chrysostom. Cassian accompanied the deposed and exiled Chrysostom in 403–4 and subsequently acted as his envoy to Rome in 404. Cassian next appears in Marseille at St. Victor as its founder some time during the second decade of the fifth century. He also founded a monastery for women. Among his writings are his *Institutes*, which are rules and regulations for community life in a monastery, and his *Conferences*, which communicate the tradition of the hermits through anecdote and dialogue. Cassian wrote at the request of other monasteries in the process of being established and intended to pass on the gathered wisdom of the Egyptian tradition. Cassian's writing thus provided the bridge over which the theory of Eastern asceticism crossed into the West, and the ideas found in his texts exerted influence in the Western tradition right up into the present time.[23]

---

23. Columba Stewart, *Cassian the Monk* (New York, Oxford: Oxford University Press, 1998), 3–26.

The christological problem.[24] In many respects the doctrinal formula agreed upon at Chalcedon in 451, that Jesus Christ is consubstantial with God and with human beings, defines the central Christian belief. But it is a doctrine filled with tensions. Historically it came as a compromise formula that welded together two quite different appreciations of Jesus Christ. In creating a hybrid of two linguistic-conceptual frameworks, it satisfied many in the middle, but alienated Nestorian and monophysite Christians at the extremes. One may measure its fairness by the fact that both extremes accused it of favoring the other; the test of its success is the fact that it lasted. On the ecclesial level, however, the doctrine represented differences and produced tensive relations among the Eastern churches and between the Eastern and Western segments of the great church. This can be seen at two points.

First, like the debates surrounding the Nicene creed, the christological debate was largely Eastern. The main protagonists carrying the discussion forward were Greek-speaking theologians. The councils at Ephesus and Chalcedon had only a token number of representatives from the West. But in the case of Chalcedon the influence of Leo I played a major role and really carried the day. His letter or "Tome" addressing the issue of simultaneous humanity and divinity provided the dialectical imagination and language that was needed for the resolution. The exclamation that Peter had spoken through Leo showed recognition of a major theological achievement and enhanced the office of the papacy immeasurably.

Second, one can also discern growing differences between the Western and Eastern churches in the aftermath of the council. Politically, socially, and culturally the West enjoyed less stability than the East, but the church remained constant in its Nicene and Chalcedonian beliefs. The church in the West grew more self-defined organizationally and theologically. It staunchly defended its reaffirmed Nicene faith against Arian inroads. The movement toward distinct regional churches began in the fifth century as the power of the empire receded. By contrast, while the East appeared

---

24. The christological debate is extensively reviewed in Aloys Grillmeier, *Christ in Christian Tradition, 1, From the Apostolic Age to Chalcedon (451)* (Atlanta: John Knox Press, 1975).

more culturally stable, christological debates continued on into the next century and divided churches. Eastern Christianity was more internally volatile in theological matters than the Western church.

The church at the end of the century. By the end of the fifth century Christianity was in a far different position relative to the Roman empire than at the end of the third. It was the dominant cultural religion of the eastern portion of the empire; it was deeply entrenched in many of the cities, towns, and regions of the West. In the East there were still divisions within the church ostensibly over Chalcedonian and anti-Chalcedonian interpretations of Jesus Christ. The West had deeper political, social, and cultural problems of integrating the various waves of migrating peoples. Generally speaking the church was able to absorb the upheaval because of the depth of people's faith, supported by an episcopal and parochial organization that held up, and a number of leaders who had been prepared for the task in monasteries such as the those in Lérins and Marseilles. The ability of the church to draw the new peoples into itself was symbolized in 508 by the baptism of Clovis, king of the Franks, along with his son and many members of his army.

The differences between the church of the West and the East were growing more defined. The year 476 marked the end of the Western empire when the last Roman emperor was deposed by a Germanic ruler who proclaimed himself king and was recognized as such by the emperor in the East. In 484 the East and the West broke communion when a Roman synod excommunicated the patriarch of Constantinople ostensibly over Leo's "Tome" and christological interpretation. But the real issues underlying the thirty-five-year schism had more to do with differences of Christian culture.

Pope Gelasius. An aspect of these differences appears in the exchange at the end of the century between Pope Gelasius and emperor Anastasius in the East over the issue of spiritual and temporal authority. The emperor was interested in reconciling the churches; the pope communicated his views to him on the relation between the two authorities: "There are in fact two [powers], emperor Augustus, by which the world is sovereignly [*principaliter*] governed; the consecrated authority of the bishops and the royal power. Of these, the responsibility of the bishops is the more weighty, since even for the rulers of men they will have to give an account at the judgement seat of God."[25] The language may not seem new, but it defines a new context. Prior to this time the emperor had summoned and played a role in councils, among them Nicaea and Chalcedon; he had directed the external course of church expansion, including authorizing the expansion of the jurisdiction of the bishop of Rome. In the East an old imperial theology accorded the emperor a divine and even sacral role in protecting and managing the external history of Christendom.[26] Galasius's response symbolizes a broad encompassing view that is sharply different: the two spheres are distinct; they exist in competitive tension where they overlap; and in a Christian framework, the spiritual is the superior authority to which the temporal owes obedience.

The Sixth Century

Three areas continuous with the past mark points of incremental change in the life of the church in the sixth century and bear significance for its future. Three people represent these social developments. The first is Benedict in both his rule and his movement. The second is Justinian and his accomplishments in law and culture. The third is Gregory, the last of the great popes of antiquity.

Monasticism in the West: Benedict. Benedict began his ascetical life as a hermit in solitude but abandoned it and founded a monastery at Monte Cassino, south of Rome, around 520. He formulated a rule of life: "It followed Basil, Augustine, and above all, John Cassian, but running through it was an element of practical good sense and understanding of what could really be expected from the average postulant who became a monk."[27] It combined work and prayer with the focus on worship; although it left little leisure time, it did not emphasize ascetical practices; it fitted a full life of the Italian peasant of the time. Benedict added a vow of stability which bound the monk to his community for life as to an extended patriarchal family.

Others established monastic retreats during the sixth century, sometimes people of wealth and property who wanted to remove

---

25. Frend, *Rise of Christianity,* 810–11.
26. Ibid., 811.
27. Ibid., 882.

themselves from an active "secular" life and dedicate themselves to various formulas that combined work, worship, service in a certain locale, and regular prayer. Toward the end of the century Columbanus came from Ireland to Gaul and created monasteries there, thus combining missionary work with the foundation of stable monastic communities. With a rule more severe than Benedict's he proposed a spirituality of self-negation and obedience. From Gaul he moved eastward to Switzerland and crossed the Alps into Lombardy. In the course of the seventh century, however, Benedict's rule proved to be more successful and gradually became the standard for monastic life.

A significant landmark in the history of women religious is "The Rule for Nuns," the first known monastic rule written exclusively for women. This rule was composed by Caesarius, bishop of Arles, early in the sixth century for his sister's monastery. Dependent on Cassian and "The Rule of St. Augustine," and thus not distinctive in ideology, it insisted on enclosure for the nuns. Enclosure encouraged single-minded piety by isolating the sisters from family and the everyday concerns of secular life, and it protected them within a city environment during a time of invasions. The rule provides a glimpse of the poverty, literacy, work, and prayer of a community of accomplished women which also served as a school for girls.[28] But the most famous religious woman prior to the High Middle Ages was undoubtedly Bridget of Kildare whose life spanned the fifth and sixth centuries. As abbess, scholar, and even bishop, she left a legacy that inspires women to this day.

Before shifting attention to the East, one should note a book written in the first half of the sixth century that had a significant influence on medieval thinking, Boethius's *The Consolation of Philosophy*. Its author was an official in the civil administration of Theodoric, Ostrogothic king of Italy; he was accused of misconduct and sentenced to death. He wrote the book while awaiting execution in 523–24. It described a hierarchical vision of reality that provided a framework for scholastic thinking. So did the writings of an unknown theologian known as Dionysius, the convert of St. Paul, whose writings appear to date from the sixth century. His reflections on

---

28. Ranft, *Women and the Religious Life,* 19–21.

mystagogy and knowledge of God were translated into Latin in the ninth century, had a considerable influence on medieval theologians, and will be considered in the next chapter.

Byzantine Christianity: Justinian. In 518 Justin became emperor, and his son, Justinian, served in his shadow until 527 when he assumed full authority. His rule lasted until his death in 565. The impact of his almost half-century of imperial service dominates the century. A list of some of his accomplishments only suggests their cumulative effect. First of all, Justinian codified Roman law; he launched the project that resulted in a single body of law for the whole empire, more complete, comprehensive, and up to date than the Theodosian Code. It was published in 534 and would serve as a bridge between the Roman empire and the resurgence of law in the middle ages.

Justinian reestablished imperial rule in the East and then in North Africa and Sicily; he extended his reach even to parts of Italy and Rome in an attempt to reunite the empire. This grand scheme, of course, failed as his military power became weaker the further west it extended. The plague, which struck in 543, and war with the Persians on an eastern front, severely curtailed his military strength. But his solidification and unification of the East, the restoration of cities and economic life in North Africa, and the general rebuilding of churches and public structures were major achievements.

Justinian oversaw a reassertion of Byzantine art and religious culture. He commissioned the rebuilding of Hagia Sophia between 532 and 537, and it served as a kind of model for the Byzantine church. The altar was no longer set in the apse, but under a great octagonal dome which rose up from the center of the four wings of the Greek cross supported by multiple pillars. The dome of heaven was ruled over by Christ, and mosaics represented the descent of his rule through "archangels, angels, evangelists to earthly rulers, and thence to the faithful themselves."[29] This became a standard for the Byzantine churches in a religious culture that teemed with clergy and monasteries.

---

29. Frend, *Rise of Christianity,* 835.

In all of this Justinian was the leader; he "saw church *and* state as part of a single organism with himself as their earthly director."[30] He epitomized Constantinian political theology. He aggressively suppressed paganism. People regarded the emperor as "the living embodiment on earth of Christ in heaven, carrying out a fixed calendar of ceremonial in which he was associated at all times with the patriarch of Constantinople. Church and state were completely integrated. Religion now pervaded almost every aspect of life in the empire."[31] Bishops were integrated into the political as well as the religious system. As a position of prestige, it attracted talented men.

All of this represents Justinian from his eastern vantage point. How did he relate to the church at large? At the start of his father's rule, Justinian participated in the healing of the Acacian schism. He took an official position recognizing Chalcedon as one of the foundations of the empire, even though his own religious preferences were monophysite. Under his reign the monophysite sectors of the church grew independent and stronger, and the conflicts between Chalcedonians and anti-Chalcedonians could not be mediated. Justinian summoned the fifth ecumenical council, Constantinople II, but it settled little in determining that the two natures of Christ subsisted in one single divine hypostatic actor. This doctrine was acceptable in the West, because it was always interpreted in terms of Leo's "Tome," but it did not unite Chalcedonians and monophysites in the East.[32] Nonetheless, Justinian left behind a vibrant Byzantine religious culture that in many respects transcended these sharp christological differences.

Gregory I. While the sixth century Eastern church grew in a unified Byzantine culture, the church in the West became territorially fragmented but strong in each region. Brown highlights two episcopates in Gaul which represent the development. Caesarius of Arles, a product of Lérins, led the church in southern Gaul for forty years,

---

30. Ibid., 830.
31. Ibid., 870.
32. Between 542 and 578 the monophysite bishop of Edessa, Jacob Baradaeus, "took the fateful step of ordaining an entire monophysite counter-hierarchy," thus constituting a parallel church in each city. Brown, *Rise of Western Christendom*, 186.

from 502 to 542. Formed in Augustine's theology, he integrated the northern tribes into a rural, peasant church ever more distant from Rome. At the other end of the century Gregory of Tours led his church from 573 to 594. Northern Gaul had become a Frankish kingdom, and Gregory never experienced a Roman empire. He and his fellow bishops were drawn from educated Frankish-Roman land owners. They held a central and powerful role in their cities.[33]

Roman society and culture at the end of the century during the pontificate of Gregory I was anything but unified or homogeneous. Rome, in fact, survived in a state of crumbling decay with a population of fifty thousand. Western imperial rule had ceased the century before, and only briefly had Justinian been able to extend his rule as far as Rome. Gregory had been a secular public official before being ordained deacon; he then served as a pontifical legate in Constantinople. Made pope in 590, he became the central figure in the West. The style of this efficient administrator was "hands on," for he looked after the details.[34] Besides the sphere of episcopal coordination, he oversaw a world of agricultural businesses in the papal estates scattered among the provinces of the West. As the leader of the Western world, he also kept in touch with the emperor and the patriarchs in the East. His papacy is more fully described in the next part of this chapter.

Frend provides a conclusion to this narrative when he describes the church at the beginning of the seventh century in its two great blocks of East and West as reaching a certain equilibrium. Like a peaceful coexistence of cousins raised in different cultures, he sees "two different civilizations reflecting distinctive interpretations of the Christian faith, . . . two different ways of life and thought that permeated every level of their respective societies growing apart, with resultant tensions, misunderstandings, and conflicting ecclesiastical claims. . . . The Byzantine state church was based on principles

---

33. Ibid., 145–65.
34. His registry contains 866 surviving letters, those chosen by him as representative. Brown estimates that twenty thousand letters were written in his fourteen-year pontificate. Sixty-three percent were responses to requests for rulings or other administrative matters. Brown, *Rise of Western Christendom* (1996), 144.

of collegiality that conflicted with the monarchical ideas of church government represented by the papacy."[35]

SOCIAL AND THEOLOGICAL ANALYSIS

I pass now to social and theological analyses of developments in the church during this period. These developments arose out of the historical context just described, and some measure of concreteness is preserved by analysis of representative authors and texts. Still more selectivity is reflected in the choice of issues discussed. Augustine dominates this period, even though his influence was felt predominately in the West. Together with him several other developments significantly shaped the history of ecclesiology: the formulation of a political theology; the Donatist conception of the church and the Augustinian response to it; Augustine's views on sacraments, the human condition, and the repression of heresy; monasticism's spread to the West; the solidification of the papacy in Leo I and Gregory I.

Political Theology

The political theology that arose in Europe in the last half of the twentieth century rests on the suppositions of the modern secular state, the separation of religion and government, and the principle of religious liberty. The political theology of the fourth century presupposes no separation between religion and state and operates in a world in which gods, angels, demons, the Christian God, and human agency all collaborate in the production of history. Imagining these premises helps in the appreciation of this theology. More characteristic of the Eastern church than the Western at this time, this political theology depended on a concatenation of events and beliefs and exemplifies well how the coherence of any theology rests on historical

---

35. Frend, *Rise of Christianity*, 891–92. Brown thinks of the Eastern and Western churches as existing within a common Mediterranean culture, which appears when contrasted to its neighbors to the east and to the north. Without this view one can think of these two churches as too far distant and fail to recognize their shared landscape. He argues that "the unity of a Mediterranean civilization exerts a constant, discreet pressure to blur such stark and convenient contrasts [between overwhelming antitheses of two societies]." Brown, "Eastern and Western Christendom," *Society and the Holy,* 174. The common culture was a commixture of Christianity and classical culture; the churches of the East and West reacted differently to the synthesis.

plausibility. As represented by Eusebius, it can be summarized in four points, all of which presuppose that in this political theology the religious and political spheres run together in one unified history.[36]

First of all, historical events in the empire at the outset of the fourth century encouraged a political theology: the sympathy of Constantine to Christianity before entering Rome, his conversion to and bias toward the Christian church after his entry into Rome, his building of churches and lavish material support of Christianity, his political endorsement of bishops and clergy generally, his assumption of leadership in the church in a constructive way to heal divisions, all of this against the background of Diocletian's long and severe persecution produced a certain Christian euphoria.

Second, Christians had believed from early on that the emperor was a legitimate authority; he ruled, sometimes in inexplicable ways, by the will of God. Eusebius's political theology raised the stakes at this point: God was ruling through the emperor. The supreme God in heaven had an invincible warrior here on earth, a servant, who acted in God's stead; the emperor served as "the prefect of the Supreme Sovereign."[37] God was at work through Constantine, "cooperating with him" as he destroyed polytheistic worship and restored the houses of Christian worship (Praise, IX.14).

Third, opening up the vision still further, Eusebius looked back to the beginnings of the church and saw the confluence of the forces that came together to form the Roman empire and the emergence of the Christian church. This generated a deep sense of providential design and a conviction that church and empire, divine metaphysical agency and historical agency, were aligned and cooperating in a grand plan. "And as the knowledge of One God was imparted to all men and one manner of piety, the salutary teaching of Christ, in the same way at one and the same time a single sovereign arose for the

---

36. Entering a distinction between religion and politics distorts the meaning attached to historical events in this period. God was directly at work in all human affairs; the question was whether it was the right God. H. A. Drake, *In Praise of Constantine: A Historical Study and New Translation of Eusebius' Tricennial Orations* (Berkeley, Los Angeles, London: University of California Press, 1976), 13–14.

37. Eusebius, "In Praise of Constantine," VII. 13, in H. A. Drake, *In Praise of Constantine*, 97. References in the text are to this translation of the work by chapter and paragraph.

entire Roman empire and a deep peace took hold of the totality. Together, at the same critical moment, as if from a single divine will,
two beneficial shoots were produced for mankind: the empire of the
Romans and the teachings of true worship."[38] The power of Christ
and the power of the Christian civil ruler were working in tandem
but on two different levels. The power of Christ destroyed polytheism and the polyarchy of the demons, and heralded the kingdom of
God to Greeks, barbarians, and people at the ends of the earth. At
the same time the Roman empire destroyed the multiple fractious
governments of the world "in order to merge the entire race into one
unity and concord. Already it has united most of the various peoples,
and it is further destined to obtain all those not yet united, right up
to the very limits of the inhabited world" (Sepulchre, XVI, 6).

A fourth element of this political theology lies in the still larger
imaginative framework which, as it were, drew the prior elements
up into a coherent whole. The biggest picture represented monotheism and monarchy. The one God ruled supreme in the universe; and
monarchy was the one true form of government modeled on God's
rule. God ruled in the metaphysical world through the Logos; God
ruled in history through the emperor, the monarch (Praise, III, X).
This metaphysical picture yielded the key element in this theology,
namely, that in this cooperative agency of God with history the political civil rule occupied the wider and more inclusive space. The
church in history operated within the framework of imperial rule.
This appeared in both the practical and theoretical order. Practically,
the emperor possessed universal power and authority. As the Christian sovereign, he exercised actual universal jurisdiction within the
empire and within the church. As the monarchical sovereign, the
emperor, acting "in imitation of the Higher Power [Logos], directs
the helm and sets straight all things on earth" (Praise, I.6). On a
metaphysical level, the imperial theology was legitimated within the
framework of monotheism and the goals of unity, peace, and reconciliation under one encompassing rule. The commanding perspective of
Eusebius's "In Praise of Constantine" was a monotheism that could

---

38. Eusebius, "On Christ's Sepulchre," XVI. 4, in Drake, *In Praise of Constantine*,
120.

also appeal to pagans who were not polytheists and that extolled Constantine's reign in terms of the comprehensive unity of God's reign.[39]

This theology seemed plausible in the East during this period. It would be taken up again in the West quite spontaneously by Charlemagne and other rulers throughout the Middle Ages. It is still operative in various forms in religious cultures other than Christian. But we pass now to the issues embedded in Donatism.

Donatism

Representing the complexity of Donatism in a short space risks caricature. Clarity on the perspective of this interpretation thus assumes some importance. Given Christian pluralism today, it is less meaningful to describe Donatism as a schism or a heresy than to look at the ways in which it exemplifies some permanent or perennial characteristics of the church. The approach to Donatism here is "objective" to the extent that it aims at portraying a distinctive church by using the categories of social science and theology: its background, self-understanding as a community (goals), structures, sacramental theology and ethics (activities), and understanding of itself in history (environment). This will allow for a parallel development of Augustine's views on the church, for much of Augustine's legacy to ecclesiology came through his reaction against the Donatists.

The background of the Donatist church goes a long way in explaining its distinctive character. Donatism designates a North African Latin church in the tradition and under the inspiration of Tertullian and Cyprian that then spread out from Carthage to the more remote towns and thus took on a local or indigenous character. From Tertullian and Cyprian it imbibed the spirit of standing over against the pagan culture of Roman society, the tradition of the small community in a larger hostile society. It maintained the tradition of a piety that included moral uprightness in which identity was reinforced by standing apart from common social behavior. This was reinforced by

---

39. "In Praise of Constantine" consistently compares Constantine to Christ. "The empire of Constantine is a replica of the kingdom of heaven, the manifestation on earth of the ideal monarchy which exists in the celestial realm." Barnes, *Constantine and Eusebius*, 254.

a cult of martyrs as the bearers of the highest values of the community and the ideal of suffering for the truth of Christ. The ideal of martyrdom was a deep tradition of heroism, sanctity, and the full realization of human existence.[40]

The self-understanding of the Donatist church might be summed up as the communion of saints, at least as a designation of what it aspired to be. Donatism has become synonymous for a kind of puritan, heroic, or perfectionist Christianity. But this should be taken as a statement of ideals, for surely the Donatists, while striving for perfection, recognized that the community contained sinners. It is doubtful that the Donatist communities appeared much different than the Catholic communities. But the Donatist also knew what he or she was called to be. The church followed Cyprian in conceiving itself "a spiritual brotherhood, with the Spirit manifesting himself in the righteousness of the individual members of the priesthood, encouraging all to martyrdom and self-denial, abiding in them as they administered the sacraments."[41]

The structures of the community more closely conformed to this self-understanding. Whether or not each member was holy, the representatives, leaders, and ministers of the community had to be free from public sin. No mere formalism, this was supported, first, by Cyprian's theological understanding of the church as a community of the Spirit and, second, by his insistence on the bishop's authority in the community and its dependence on legitimate succession. The activity of God as Spirit in the community became dynamically effective in and through the lawful structures of the community. A Donatist could not imagine a sinless or holy church with sinful, unholy leaders; structures had to correspond with the nature and goal of the community. It thus became a community's duty "to separate itself from a sinful priest, under pain of risking contamination in sin."[42]

---

40. Evans, *One and Holy*, 67–68.
41. Frend, *The Donatist Church*, 141.
42. John Anthony Corcoran, *Augustinus contra Donatistas* (Donaldson, Ind.: Graduate Theological Foundation, 1997), 46. The so-called Catholic church of Africa was not the true church because its bishops at the time of the great persecution had handed over the scriptures, an act equivalent to idolatry. And these bishops spread a contagion of guilt to all who are in communion with them. Evans, *One and Holy*, 68–69.

This self-understanding and these structures correlated with Donatist sacramental theology and practice. Most notably, Donatists generally continued the practice of rebaptizing converts from other churches or apostates seeking readmission into the Donatist church. Without reviewing Cyprian's sacramental theology, it should be recalled that that sacramental theology was coherent within the set of premises and traditions shared in the church of North Africa at the time. A minister could not confer a specific grace of the Spirit if the minister and his church did not possess it.

These features of Donatism left this church in a distinctive relationship to its environment, one that carried forward the tradition of being over against the world. But it also stood over against other Christian churches, or the church throughout the Mediterranean world. The Donatist church embodied Christianity in its pure form, "the closed garden and the sealed fountain."[43] In so doing, it took on the self-designation of being the church of North Africa, a church inculturated especially but by no means exclusively in the countryside. It thus represented the very antithesis of the political theology of Eusebius: this church stood over against the empire and Roman culture and the universal church as the true and holy church of Christ. This was emphatically and paradigmatically illustrated early on by its rejection of the decisions at Arles.

Augustine

Augustine's contribution to the self-understanding of Christianity in the West dwarfs most others, and this makes it more difficult to restrict the presentation. This synopsis of Augustine's conception of the church also considers his theological anthropology which he developed in opposition to Pelagius because it greatly influenced spirituality and conceptions of the Christian life.

Church. Augustine's ecclesiology and other teachings developed in the course of his engaged and prolific life.[44] Relative to the Donatists, he was dependent for much of his argumentation on Optatus

---

43. Corcoran, *Augustinus,* 47.
44. F. van der Meer, in *Augustine the Bishop: The Life and Work of a Father of the Church* (London/New York: Sheed and Ward, 1961), presents Augustine in his workaday world.

of Milevis, a theologian who served as a bridge between Cyprian and Augustine. It is also important to note that Augustine's language about the church shifted as he took on new problems. One can see a drift from a christocentric basis to more emphasis on the role of the Spirit. This portrait of Augustine's teaching on the church roughly correlates with the last section in order implicitly to draw the contrast with Donatist ecclesiology. Augustine's *De Baptismo*, his major anti-Donatist work, provides the main but not exclusive source for this account.[45] In contrast to Donatist ecclesiology generally, Augustine exhibits a length in the framework of his thinking, a depth of metaphysics, and an expansiveness of world-historical and cosmic vision that are breathtaking.

Theological self-understanding. The center of Augustine's theological understanding of the church lies in the metaphor of the body of Christ. As Augustine develops it, the image has a mystical dimension which brings out the intimate union between Christ and his members who make up his extended body in history. Augustine reasons this way: "If he is the head, he evidently also has a body. His body is the holy church, of which the Apostle spoke this way: 'You are the body of Christ and his members.' Christ whole and entire, therefore, consists in a head and members, as in a complete person."[46] Borgomeo stresses the realism and intimacy of the union

---

45. I have drawn from the following sources of Augustine: *On Baptism, Against the Donatists, Nicene and Post-Nicene Fathers*, 4, ed. Philip Schaff (Peabody, Mass.: Hendrickson Publishers, 1994) [Bap]; *De Catechizandis Rudibus*, intro., trans., and commentary by Joseph Patrick Christopher (Washington: Catholic University of America, 1926) [DCR]; *The City of God* (New York: Penguin Books, 1986) [CG]; *Enchiridion: On Faith, Hope, and Love*, in *Augustine: Confessions and Enchiridion*, ed. Albert C. Outler (Philadelphia: Westminster Press, 1955) [Enc]; *Grace and Free Will*, in *The Fathers of the Church*, trans. Robert P. Russell (Washington, D.C.: Catholic University of America Press, 1968) [GFW]; *Letters, Fathers of the Church* (New York: Fathers of the Church, 1951–89) [Let]; *To Simplician — On Various Questions*, in *Augustine: Earlier Writings* (Philadelphia: Westminster Press, 1953) [Sim]; *The Trinity*, trans. Stephen McKenna (Washington, D.C.: Catholic University of America Press, 1963) [Trin].

46. Pasquale Borgomeo, *L'Eglise de ce temps dans la prédication de saint Augustin* (Paris: Etudes Augustiniennes, 1972), 210, citing Augustine on Ps 138. Several other studies have been helpful in this synthetic interpretation of the church: Peter Brown, *Augustine of Hippo* (Berkeley: University of California Press, 1969); Yves Congar, *L'Eglise: De saint Augustin à l'époque moderne* (Paris: Editions du Cerf, 1970); Tarsicius J. van Bavel, "What Kind of Church Do You Want? The Breadth of Augustine's Ecclesiology," *Louvain Studies* 7 (1979): 147–71; J. Patout Burns, "Christ

between Christ and the church, between head and members: this is where the power of the image lies and its particular relevance as a preached word. So strong is some of Augustine's language on the union between Christ and the church that Christ appears, but only appears, to be the very subject constituting the church. This coheres with Augustine's theology of the sacraments.

This one, integral, and total Christ is animated by the Spirit, the same Spirit by which Jesus was constituted the Christ: the Holy Spirit. In being in the body of Christ the Christian lives in the Spirit of Christ. The tangible sacrament of the table of the Lord and communion in the body and blood of Christ are seen as the means by which the faithful themselves become the very thing they celebrate, namely, the body of Christ. This theological conception directly relates to the spirituality Augustine preached to his people.[47]

Members of the church. Augustine's theological understanding of the church, one could say "from above," becomes more complicated in the several layers of meaning the term "church" assumes in different contexts. Distinguishing the referents of the term "church" helps sort this out. Three distinct meanings of the church can be seen by correlating the church with different segments of its members.

First of all, the term "church" refers to the heavenly community which encompasses all the angels and saints worshiping God; it is the heavenly community. It includes all the angels and all the saved stretching back before Christ. It is made up of the elect destined to fill up the places of the fallen angels (Enc 16.62); it is an otherworldly eschatological community. The church in Augustine's imagination transcended the historical; it was a metaphysical reality. "One can

---

and the Holy Spirit in Augustine's Theology of Baptism," *Augustine: From Rhetor to Theologian,* ed. Joanne McWilliam (Waterloo, Ont.: Wilfrid Laurier University Press, 1992), 161–72; Michael A. Fahey, "Augustine's Ecclesiology Revisited," *Augustine,* ed. McWilliam, 173–81; Eugene R. Fairweather, "St. Augustine's Interpretation of Infant Baptism," *Augustinus Magister* (Paris: Etudes Augustiniennes, 1954), 897–903; Gérard Phillips, "L'Influence de Christ-chef sur Son corps mystique suivant saint Augustin," *Augustinus Magister,* 805–15; M. Réveillard, "Le Christ-homme, tête de l'Eglise: Etude d'ecclésiologie selon Enarrations in Psalmos d'Augustin," *Recherches Augustiniennes* 5 (1968): 67–94; Eugene TeSelle, *Augustine the Theologian* (London: Burns and Oats, 1970).

47. Congar, *L'Eglise,* 13. See also Bavel, "What Kind of Church?" 155–59.

never insist too much on this point: the city of God is, of itself, essentially a heavenly reality, and the angels are its first citizens."[48]

Second, the term "church" also refers to the institutional society on earth, the empirical church. This church is a mixed community; it contains both good and evil people, the elect and saved and those neither elected nor saved, wheat and tares. "Thus there are two cities, one of the wicked, the other of the just, which endure from the beginning of the human race even to the end of time, which are now intermingled in body, but separated in will, and which, moreover, are to be separated in body also on the day of judgment" (DCR, 19.31).

Third, church also refers to an inner church, a church within the empirical church, of the elect or the saints. These are the people truly touched by grace and who live by charity and love. Augustine called this church "the Dove," the group of wheat amid the tares, the spiritual church, "the one uncorrupt, holy, chaste dove, which has neither spot nor wrinkle" (Bap IV.4.5; III.17.22; III.18.23; III.19.26). These still constitute a pilgrim church, living in this world, not perfect but moving toward perfection, and ultimately they will be saved.

Augustine saw an intercommunion between the heavenly church and the church on earth; they were two parts of the same church. "By the church here we are to understand the whole church, not just the part that journeys here on earth . . . , but also that part which, in heaven, has always, from creation, held fast to God, and which never experienced the evils of a fall. This part, composed of the holy angels, remains in blessedness, and it gives help . . . to the other part still on pilgrimage" (Enc 15.56).

With this expansive and layered framework for thinking about the church, Augustine could be both fluid and nuanced in speaking about it. For example, the church existed from the very beginning, and historically it encompassed both Jewish and Christian history (Bap I.15.24; I.17.26). People inside the church of the new dispensation in Christ, that is, the empirical, historical church, might be outside

---

48. Congar, *L'Eglise*, 18. One should not confuse the city of God with the earthly church as though they were synonymous. The basic rule here is to recognize that Augustine uses the term "church" in different contexts with different emphases and one cannot simply equate the empirical church of this world with the rich theological concept of the city of God. Ibid.

the inner or spiritual community; those outside the empirical church may be inside the spiritual community (Bap V.27.38; V.28.39). The rock-bottom criterion for salvific membership lay in God's grace and the human response of faith and charity and perseverance. These distinctions help explain various extremes in the way Augustine spoke about the church: on the one hand the church was the pure bride of Christ, on the other hand Augustine explicitly named the kinds of sinners one found in the church when he warned candidates for baptism against scandal (DCR, 7.11; 25.48). They were not few. Augustine was a realist; he had a radical doctrine of sin; the empirical church was not a holy community. At best it was a hospital; it housed the sick; it provided a framework for healing and perhaps progress in holiness, but not perfection.[49] Compared to the early church, the understanding of the church had changed significantly.

Structures. Throughout the towns of North Africa, the structures of the Donatist churches looked more or less the same as those of the Catholic churches. But Augustine was revolted and scandalized by the division and hostility between them: this was wrong; it sinned against charity. It was natural enough to have different views on everything, and even some variance in the possession of the truth; but to divide church unity was always evil (Bap II.5.6). Augustine appealed to Cyprian: he had disagreed but retained communion with Rome. For Augustine the church was catholic, that is, geographically encompassing the known world, one across this expanse. He could not imagine within this framework a true church cut off from the whole church.[50]

Augustine emphasized structures which reinforced this expansive unity of the whole church. Scripture was the absolute authority of the whole church, and then, in a kind of ascending order, he cited the authority of local councils depending on their size and scope, and finally world or ecumenical councils. Augustine both recognized the primacy of the pope and at the same time seemed comfortable within

---

49. Brown, *Augustine,* 365.
50. Augustine thus used Cyprian against the Donatists: "Wherefore, if the communion of wicked men destroyed the church in the time of Cyprian, [the Donatists] have no source from which they can derive their own communion; and if the church was not destroyed, they have no excuse for their separation from it." Bap III.2.3.

the episcopalism of Cyprian (Bap II.3.4). But when things went bad in Africa, he could appeal to the jurisdictional authority of the pope.[51]

Sacramental theology. In Cyprian and the Donatists the holiness and efficacy of the sacraments were in some measure linked to the holiness and moral integrity of the minister and to the church's possession of the Spirit. One cannot give the Spirit if one does not possess it. Augustine proposed an alternative view, resting on different premises, which can be summed up in three basic distinctions.

The first concerns the objectivity of the sacraments. Augustine was a neo-Platonist, and for a Platonist the idea that transcendent value existed as a function of the minister did not set right. Everything in creation participated in and shared in the creator; the creator was the immanent source of the intelligibility of everything that is. The whole of creation overflowed with signs of God's presence. The sacraments, which were instituted by God, were holy in themselves, objectively and independently of the subjectivity of the minister. God did not need the holiness or the moral purity of the minister to confer grace. Involved in the sacraments, then, were God, the receiver of God's grace or saving influence, and the sign through which this was mediated. "Christ himself is acting in the sacraments of the church, and all the sacraments are his property."[52]

The second nuance in Augustine's sacramental theology distinguishes between the holiness of the minister and the effectiveness of the sacrament. On the basis of the objectivity of the sacrament, real and valid sacraments existed outside the true church. The moral quality or state of the minister did not affect the offer of God's grace nor on that level the effectiveness of the sacrament.[53] Baptism, therefore, wherever administered, effectively bestowed a permanent indelible seal or character on the recipient. In his most telling point Augustine argued this way: if this were not the case, even within the

---

51. Evans, *One and Holy*, 88.
52. Bavel, "What Kind of Church," 155.
53. "But the baptism of Christ, consecrated by the words of the gospel, is necessarily holy, however polluted and unclean its ministers may be; because its inherent sanctity cannot be polluted, and the divine excellence abides in its sacrament, whether to the salvation of those who use it aright, or to the destruction of those who use it wrongly." Bap III.10.15.

Catholic Church, every time one doubted the motives of the minister, one would have to be rebaptized. Ultimately one could never be sure one really received baptism or ordination.

But, third, the sacraments could not be fruitful in the subject receiving them unless dispositions were right, unless they were received in authentic faith. The distinction here lay between the objectively effective and what was profitable, or fruitful, or subjectively effective. In short, with this distinction, one could have a sacrament truly given and objectively effective, but not received because of inappropriate dispositions of the subject. In baptism, if the recipients' faith were not authentic, sin was not forgiven, or it reverted back upon the self (Bap III.13.18). Thus, outside the church sacraments were not fruitful because they were received in a state of schism, and therefore love and charity with respect to other Christians was lacking. Augustine always presupposed that schism and division in the church meant a lack of charity. Within the church, the effectiveness and fruitfulness of the sacraments were also mediated through the prayers and holiness of the saints, the intercessory power of the Dove.

The distinction between the objective effectiveness of Christ's action in the sacraments and the action of the Spirit who brings it to fruition provides a clue to how Christ and Spirit combine in an economy that also describes the function and purpose of the church in history. The church is the body of Christ and Christ acts in the sacraments. "It is the Holy Spirit who is the principle which actualizes the church in its reality, that is to say in equivalent terms, in its *unitas*, through *caritas*."[54] The Spirit constitutes the unity and charity of the sanctified within the church, and the group of saints functions as the medium of grace to the others.[55] Thus God's power

54. Congar, *L'Eglise*, 17.

55. Burns sees Augustine working out the relation between Christ and the Spirit in his theology of baptism in relation to the Donatists. By itself baptism by Christ is not sufficient for sanctification. "By using the notion of charity as a key, he linked together the gift of the Spirit, the unity of the church, the efficacy of intercessory prayer, and the power to forgive sins. On that base he constructed a new hypothesis which would allow Christ to baptize without the sanctifying effects of the Holy Spirit. Christ baptizes through the minister; the Spirit forgives sins through the saints." Burns, "Christ and the Holy Spirit," 167.

and presence in the church operates through an economy, a process that involves Christ acting through the ministry of the clergy and the Spirit who gives the gift of charity which constitutes the unity of the church; that group within the church who indeed live out this charity act as agents of God's grace in history. The personal gift of the Spirit and "grace" and its effect of charity in the human person are reciprocal concepts.[56] Even Augustine's defense of infant baptism did not rely solely on the objectivity of Christ's work in the sacrament. The authenticity of infant baptism completely depends on the solidarity of the community in grace. "It is the bond created by the Holy Spirit, who dwells in the sponsors, and comes to dwell in the baptized, that makes it possible for others to stand for the child before God."[57]

The drift toward an emphasis on the Spirit in ecclesiology without any abandonment of the central metaphor, the body of Christ, comes with Augustine's concern with the effectiveness of the church in history. He too had a view of Christ and the Spirit deifying the human. But his tendency was to turn the divine gift to human beings into moral and ascetical applications.[58] This will become clearer in the treatment of the church in history and Augustine's anthropology.

Environment: church and world. One would not expect a simple conception of the relation between the church and the world in Augustine. Distinguishing three layers of his thought indicates its complexity and serves as a context or background for his statements: the eschatological, the world historical, and the present social (Let 138.3.17). The relationship between city of God and the worldly city varies in each context.

Eschatologically the two cities were radically opposed alternatives. A city or a group might be regarded as a people, a social unit, a corporate assembly bound together in agreement in the things they love or have set their hearts on.[59] The final city of God is the eternal

---

56. Augustine's Pauline formula to this effect is as follows: "The love which comes from God and which is God, in a proper sense, is the Holy Spirit, through whom divine charity is diffused into our hearts, through which the whole trinity lives within us." Trin 15.18.32.

57. Fairweather, "Infant Baptism," 903.

58. Phillips, "L'Influence de Christ," 811–14.

59. "Now what is a state but a multitude of men bound together by some bond of accord?" Let 138.2; CG, XIX.24; TeSelle, *Augustine the Theologian*, 271

heavenly communion of angels and saints in the love of God (CG, XIX.20). The earthly city in its raw human condition constitutes the antithesis of this; here there is no unity except in the love turned in on itself that generates discord and self-destruction.

Shifting now to the context of history, and addressing generally the church and the world, the empirical church does not equal the city of God, for as a mixed community it shares in its measure of sin. But it harbors the Dove, the elect whose love is turned away from self to love of God and neighbor.[60] The human city, as was said, represents the opposite of the kingdom of God. Like Tertullian, Augustine believed the Roman empire to be under the control of demons worshiped as gods (CG IV.1).[61] But the human city is not completely negative: it represents the sphere of ordinary human life, and government has a constructive role in maintaining order and peace. The church which unfolds within civil rule also benefits from times of peace. Augustine was able "to think at a *proximate* level about the positive aspects of the justice and peace achieved in the political order."[62]

In the concrete world of here and now, therefore, Augustine's attitude to civil rule is ambivalent. Obviously, civil authority is not absolute, it can be corrupt, but it can also serve and protect the common good.[63] And in its turn, the church can have a salutary effect on social existence in this world because of the virtues taught by the Christian church. On the one hand, then, Augustine could place the standard of the city of God in judgment upon the society and civil authority. On the other hand, he could envision making deals with the empire for the good of the church and the removal of public obstacles

---

60. The title of Augustine's work is misleading because the idea of a city appears to refer to a political entity. In reality he means the title as a translation of "the communion of saints." Brown, *Religion and Society,* 25.

61. Brown, *Religion and Society,* 119–46.

62. TeSelle, *Augustine the Theologian,* 274.

63. Peace in the world is salutary for the church. Augustine took it for granted that the purpose of the state or empire was to preserve the interests and goals dictated by the church (Brown, *Religion and Society,* 44). But Augustine's view of the relation of the church to the empire in many ways contradicts that of Eusebius: "The ultimate destiny of Catholic Christianity is [in principle] not in the slightest degree tied to the fortunes of the Roman empire." Evans, *One and Holy,* 112; also 122–23.

to salvation.[64] Thus he explicitly justified the use of imperial force to suppress the Donatist churches.

This presentation does not purport to represent the fullness, depth, or nuance of Augustine on the church, but it provides the broad lines of an ecclesiology that guided the church in the West through the Middle Ages. Augustine's teachings on the status of human existence before God complement and fill out his ecclesiology.

Anthropology. Augustine's considerations of the doctrines of human sin and God's grace delineate in a classical way, at least for the Western church, a Christian anthropology. Taken in their amplitude, one could consider them central to his thinking. They have bearing on the Christian vision of reality as a whole, on the nature and role of the church in history, and on individual and corporate Christian spirituality. Corresponding to the import of each symbol, sin and grace, it will be helpful first to distinguish the negative or pessimistic side of his teaching and then the constructive and uplifting.

All human beings are born into a condition of sinfulness and guilt from which human freedom completely lacks the power to extricate itself. Augustine was convinced that, if this were not the case, the redemptive logic of the incarnation of Christ would be compromised. Along the way he virtually created the version of original sin that understood it as a condition inherited from Adam and Eve and disseminated by procreation.[65] Yet Augustine's phenomenology of the effects of sin in the human subject is compelling: human freedom acts like a prisoner to itself; this spiritual reality is curved in or bent back upon itself in self-seeking. Every apparent self-transcendence really promotes self-aggrandizement. This initial condition has gradually hardened through social conditioning and constant acting out. The pessimism of Augustine really lies in the fact that in his view this condition will never be overcome in the overwhelming majority of human beings. The absolutely gratuitous grace of Christ for final

---

64. TeSelle, *Augustine the Theologian*, 277–78.

65. This was not a creation out of nothing. See Tatha Wiley, *Original Sin: Origin, Development, and Contemporary Meaning* (New York: Paulist Press, 2001), chaps. 1–3. She argues convincingly that the doctrine of original sin had the function of explaining the practice of infant baptism.

human salvation becomes a relative rarity. The church did not follow Augustine's doctrine of predestination to the letter, but after Augustine the effect of baptism and Christian initiation was increasingly understood in terms of remission of original sin.[66]

The positive side of the picture appears in Augustine's brilliant description of the operation of God's grace. While one may imagine that most Christians conceived themselves in these terms, for Augustine the story actually belonged only to the church's inner elect. The existential drama can be schematized in terms of a neo-Platonic ascent. All human existence inherently yearns for transcendence through the media of the attractions of beauty, goodness, truth, and being itself. God's grace, which is the work of the Holy Spirit, works within this human dynamism by planting impulse and desire and power to release spiritual freedom from itself (Sim 1.2.21). Grace not only frees human freedom, it cooperates with it and empowers it to perform salvific acts.[67] The church's mission consists in mediating the availability of this grace to history.[68] In eternity, in the final heavenly city of God, the human spirit "will be freed from all evil and filled with all good, enjoying unfailingly the delight of eternal joys" (CG XXII.30). This fundamental imaginative framework controlled the understanding of the church until the time of Luther.

Monastic Spirituality: Cassian and Benedict

Cassian brought the wisdom of monastic life to the West in the early fifth century, and his writings provided a rationale for the monasteries that were being founded in Europe. In the sixth century Benedict designed a rule that would eventually become the standard for Western monasticism. They are taken together to represent the theory and

---

66. Bernard Cooke, *Ministry to Word and Sacrament: History and Theology* (Philadelphia: Fortress Press, 1977), 264.

67. "God, then, works in us, without our cooperation, the power to will, but once we begin to will, and do so in a way that brings us to act, then it is that he cooperates with us." GFW 17.33.

68. One could summarize Augustine's ecclesiology around this conception of the church's mission. The church was a universal society that acted as God's instrument for claiming people of every nation as God's elect. It had the nature of a communion of people whom, through the sacramental mediation of grace, God drew forward toward final union in God's life in eternity. See Evans, *One and Holy,* 81.

practice that grounded monastic spirituality in the Western church. The term "spirituality" as it is used here refers to the way persons or groups lead their lives, together with its reflective principles, all within the context of a relationship to ultimate reality or encounter with God. In terms of this understanding of spirituality, these two authors complement each other, with Benedict providing a rule for living out principles articulated by Cassian.

Cassian on monastic life. The tradition which Cassian communicated in his *Conferences* wedded deep theological grounding and long-lived practical common sense in a psychologically sophisticated body of wisdom.[69] Although it may not be called systematic, it operated out of consistent principles and maxims. A sense of this can be communicated by considering the framework of monastic or ascetic life and how its goals are achieved in community and by a life of solitude.

Eschatology and teleology. Cassian explains the aims and goals of monastic life in a masterful and seamless blend of eschatology and teleology. The baseline perspective is Christian eschatology. The end time, defining a point of view Cassian and his mentors simply took for granted, cannot be overemphasized. "He explores the temporal and experiential disjunction between present experience and future hope, and he places the monk on the frontier between them. . . . His belief in heaven and his attendant conviction that monastic life is entirely oriented toward preparing for heaven shape everything he writes."[70]

Teleology, a sense of ultimate goals and of means to achieve them, formed the substructure of Cassian's representation of monastic life. He keeps going back to the distinction between means and ends in order "to shift the monks' outlook from earth to heaven," to put meanings in a broader eschatological framework. "Cassian's great

---

69. John Cassian, *John Cassian: The Conferences, Ancient Christian Writers*, 57 (New York: Paulist Press, 1997). Cited in the text by conference and paragraph. These were written by Cassian in the 420s. They were preceded by *The Institutes* in which Cassian described the external regulations of monastic life and the spiritual battle against the vices to attain purity of heart and perfection in community. See also Owen Chadwick, *John Cassian* (Cambridge: University Press, 1968).

70. Stewart, *Cassian*, 40.

contribution to monastic theology . . . is a relentless insistence on the long view. He finds the reason for every action and aspect of the monastic life in the striving to reach its goal and end."[71] The ultimate goal of monastic life was eternal life. The immediate goal made this possible, and it consisted in "purity of heart," without which one could not enter the kingdom of God (I.2–4). Purity of heart, which defined holiness, consisted in a permanent orientation or direction of one's intention to the higher goals toward which the whole of life was directed (I.5).[72] The highest value in this life, as a proleptic participation in the end, consisted in divine contemplation.[73] The backdrop of eternity relativized life in this world, including even all service dedicated to alleviating human need. In the kingdom of heaven contemplation constituted the fulfillment of life. The monk strove to anticipate this on earth (I.10).

Monastic life in community. Obedience dominated the purpose of life in community, the destruction of self-will and pride through submission to the rule, to the superior of the community, and through them to God (XVIII.10). Self-denial marked life in community, and Cassian told the story of the monk who, when slapped and humiliated publicly, accepted this quietly and modestly (XIX.1–2). But asceticism and discipline were means, and they had always to be subordinate to charity and purity of heart (I.7). The whole life of the monk found meaning in prayer.[74] The monk in community lacked the hermit's solitude that is conducive to rapturous experience of the divine (XIX.9), but he had no temporal anxieties, as did the hermit, and he could concentrate on cultivating and leading a life of the

---

71. Ibid., 44–45.

72. "Cassian's teaching on purity of heart has three main aspects: ascetical purification, a theological equation of purity of heart with love, and the experience of liberation from sin in tranquility of heart. . . . He anchors both goal and end biblically with Romans 6:22, 'having then your fruit in sanctification, the end (*finis*) is eternal life.'" Ibid., 43–44.

73. "The Lord, you see, placed the chief good in divine contemplation. All other virtues, however necessary and useful and good we deem them, must be placed on a lower plane because they are sought for the sake of this one thing" (I.8).

74. The goal of prayer is "that the mind may every day be lifted beyond the material sphere to the realm of the spirit, until the whole life and every little stirring of the heart become one continuous prayer" (X.7).

virtues in obedience to God's will (XIX.14). In all this Cassian provided the basic logic for what came to be the traditional three vows of religious life: freedom from property and wealth or poverty (XVIII.5), chastity in order to love God totally (XI.18), and surrender of one's will to another in obedience (XIX.8). The three supplied the means to purity of heart in one's love of God.

The hermit. The goal of the hermit's life consisted in purity of heart and contemplation of God. Through solitude and asceticism the mind became freed from the world and from the body so that the human spirit might completely unite itself with God in intention. "The hermit aims at freeing his mind from all earthly thoughts, and to unite it with Christ so far as his human weakness allows" (XIX, 8). But this was a life of struggle on one's own. The hermit actually entered into combat; this was an aggressive and even heroic spirituality that directly confronted the demons who were a, if not the, source of evil in this world. Life in community was considered preparation for this higher life of asceticism and contemplation in solitude and, when one could no longer stand its rigors, one might return to community (XIX.3). These themes, especially the thematic of community life, were influential in the construction of Benedict's rule.

The Rule of Benedict.[75] Benedict's rule contained an exhortatory prologue and 73 chapters or canons or rules that were practical, concrete, specific, and quite detailed. They appear to be the fruit of traditions of practice and common sense, and were geared to dealing with everyday issues and preventing problems before they arose. One can almost describe the communities in organizational terms from the rule. The goals of the community represented in Cassian generally speaking remain constant in Benedict's rule; here the focus falls on the monks and the organization of their lives.

Who could join a monastery? According to the rule, they were rich and poor although the rich had to alienate their property and wealth; they were old and young including boys; they were predominately lay but priests could enter; some were educated, others illiterate; some

---

75. "The Rule of Benedict," in *Western Asceticism: Library of Christian Classics,* XII, ed. Owen Chadwick (Philadelphia: Westminster Press, 1958), 290–337. Cited in the text by number of the rule or canon.

talented or skilled, who with supervision might be allowed to exercise their trade. They promised obedience, stability, and membership for life: leaving carried the threat of damnation (58). The main virtues of a good monk were obedience, silence, and humility.

The structure of the community was monarchical with the abbot, elected unanimously, at its head. The large monastery had priors and deans and other minor offices such as the porter. The prior was appointed by the abbot. The rule called for community assemblies so that the abbot could listen to the community as a whole. It stipulated a certain seniority among the monks according to time in the community, but generally encouraged fraternal relations, forbade fighting, and provided for a full range of punishments for minor deviations from the order of the day, infractions of the rule, or more serious offenses. These ranged from slight public humiliations to imprisonment and corporal punishment on to excommunication.

The order of the day and regulations for everyday life filled every nook and cranny. The community assembled for singing the psalms seven times during the day and once in the middle of the night. Meals, worship, reading, silence, and sleep were scheduled; food, clothing, comportment toward each other were regulated. For example, main meals were two, including a pound of bread a day, no meat, and some wine. Some thought that wine was not for monks, but Benedict said "it is hard to persuade modern monks of this" (40). The monk had no private possessions; all was held in common; but each received according to his needs. Communication with the outside world in letters or gifts was overseen. Trips outside the monastery were regulated.

These seemingly exhaustive regulations still left plenty of room for adaptation to different environments. Members in different cultures and climates and language groups were different. Monasteries adjusted to the seasons. The constituency and leadership would generate a distinctive tradition. The kind of work that occupied monasteries would help determine their character. Also, monasteries offered hospitality and in varying degrees would be open to the environment in which they might play a major social role. Indeed, the monastery became one of the most important catalysts in Western history right up to the sixteenth-century Reformation.

Papacy: Leo I and Gregory I

The expansion of administrative capability during the papacies of Damasus and Siricius in the late fourth century enabled an increasing breadth of jurisdictional authority. In the mid-fifth century and at the end of the sixth century two great popes reveal the growing authority of the office.[76]

Leo I. The papacy admits of inspection from two distinct points of view, its relation to the emperor and empire and its relation to the churches in the Christian world. Regarding the first, becoming the religion of the empire in the West raised the question of the autonomy of the church, and the theology of the papacy was the answer, that is, it guarded the identity of the church. Leo's task was to define the papacy not against an anti-Christian empire but as a distinct spiritual rule vis-à-vis a Christian emperor, "in parallel with" but "autonomous from." Leo viewed the church as in a sort of partnership with the empire in directing the unfolding of history. Each possessed its own God-given authority; each contributed to the task something the other did not. Besides maintaining civil order, the emperor also had the role of guarding and defending the church, but not ruling over the church. This last point was especially delicate with regard to the right of the emperor to summon councils.[77] When the Council of Chalcedon reaffirmed Nicaea's assertion that Constantinople enjoy a primacy after Rome as the New Rome, Leo simply rejected it.[78]

Regarding Leo's papacy with respect to the churches in the Christian world, Leo's signal achievement consisted in establishing a rationale for papal authority. His position consisted in a two-step argument establishing that the pope is Peter, and then that Peter is Christ.[79] The first move rests on a juridical argument from Roman law, rendered theological, that the pope is the heir to Peter. According to Roman law the heir continues the deceased. "Legally, therefore,

---

76. William J. La Due, in *The Chair of St. Peter: A History of the Papacy* (Maryknoll, N.Y.: Orbis Books, 1999), 40–61 charts the expansion of the papal office during this period.

77. Evans, *One and Holy*, 129–36.

78. Council of Chalcedon, c. 28, in Schroeder, *Disciplinary Decrees*, 125–26.

79. What follows draws on the analysis of Walter Ullmann, "Leo I and the Theme of Papal Primacy," *The Journal of Theological Studies* 11 (New Series) (1960): 25–51. References in the text are to pages of this article.

there is no difference between the heir and the deceased: the latter is literally continued in the former" (34). The concept also involves a clear distinction between the heir as individual or person and the heir of the office. The pope has inherited the office, but not the personal qualities of Peter. "To the pope the office, function, and power of St. Peter have been transferred *via successionis*, but not his personal merits — how could they?" (35)

The second move was to define Peter as the vicar of Christ. Leo did this by interpreting the commission of Christ to Peter in juridical terms. "One may even go so far as to say that the exclusively legal complexion of Peter's position suggested in fact operating with legal means in order to clarify its essence and the continuation of Petrine powers in the pope" (41). In this framework one then reads the text of the New Testament exegetically in terms of a legal commissioning.

Ullmann sums up Leo's reasoning succinctly in this way: "It was the judicial nature of the office which led Leo I to conceive the Petrine commission in proper legal categories and secondly to utilize the Roman law in his clarification of the relationship between him *qua* pope and Peter *qua* office-holder: and his further penetration — in truly Roman lucid simplicity — resulted in the equation of Christ = Peter = pope, all of which has nothing to do with the charisma, but merely with the *officium*" (43). Thus the monarchical principle for the whole church is established, and "the care of the universal church should converge toward Peter's one seat, and nothing anywhere should be separated from its Head."[80] The logic that Leo thus established would last.

Gregory I. Gregory did not advance the theory of the papacy: "His pontificate certainly made little impact on the development of the papacy as an institution."[81] But in his letters and their implied authority one can get a more concrete image of how the papacy functioned. One way of portraying this in a brief space is simply to enumerate the many different relationships that defined its operations, without

---

80. Leo I, Letter 14.12 in *Leo the Great and Gregory the Great, Nicene and Post-Nicene Fathers*, 12, ed. P. Schaff and H. Wace (Peabody, Mass.: Hendrickson Publishers, 1994), 19.

81. R. A. Markus, *Gregory the Great and His World* (Cambridge: University Press, 1997), 203.

too much attention to the multiple problems that occupied Gregory in each aspect of his job.

From inside the church, looking outward, Gregory dealt first of all with the emperor and his exarch in Ravenna. He was usually deferential wherever he could be, but did not fail to represent his disagreements where necessary. Second, Gregory had to arbitrate problems between the church and the various rulers of the places where the church was well established. He was a court of appeal for various local problems. Third, there were various rulers in the West who were beyond the sphere of the empire, in Spain and Gaul, for example, with whom Gregory negotiated and tried to retain an influence. And, fourth, Gregory spent no small amount of time protecting the church from its enemies, principally the Lombards who had free reign in Northern Italy. Wherever he could Gregory acted as the protector of both church and civil order in Italy.

Looking inward to the governing of his own church, an array of different relationships occupied his attention. First, he had to define and maintain his relationship with other patriarchs in Constantinople, Antioch, Jerusalem, and Alexandria. Gregory may have believed that he had some jurisdictional authority relative to these churches, but far from exercising it, he tended to insist on their autonomous local authority.[82] Second, he related to those within his sphere of jurisdiction in the West as would a metropolitan, solving problems of elections and other disputes, appointing and removing people from office, and enforcing church discipline. Third, Gregory was the head of a vast system of papal estates and oversaw a whole corps of rectors and other officers who managed the properties and collected the revenues. These revenues were spent on the salaries of clergy and

---

82. Gregory fiercely resisted the Patriarch of Constantinople's appropriation of the title "Universal Bishop," and in his appeal for support in this from other patriarchs he conceded to Antioch and Alexandria a Petrine connection that supported their autonomous authority: three seats of one Petrine ministry. In the name of humility and communion Gregory did not insist on universal jurisdictional prerogatives. See Gregory I, *Register of the Epistles of Saint Gregory the Great*, Book VII, Letter 40, in *Leo the Great and Gregory the Great*, 229. Gregory's letters are cited by book in the Register and number of the letter in it. See also Letter VIII.30 where Gregory rejects the title "Universal Pope" and his power to issue commands to the Patriarch of Alexandria.

other officials of the church, maintaining church buildings, ceme-
teries, monasteries, nuns' convents, hospices, and welfare agencies,
distributing food to the poor, and caring for widows and orphans. The
Roman Church was the richest landowner in Italy.[83] Gregory's business managers were normally monks or clerics, and they served as his
liaisons and ambassadors to the far-flung churches in the provinces,
allowing him to rule from afar.[84] Fourth, Gregory sent Augustine,
a monk of his monastery in Rome, with a group of companions to
Britain to reestablish the church there. He sent them through Gaul
to gain support for the mission and to strengthen his relationship
to France (Letter VIII.30). Fifth, Gregory related to the people in all
the churches as a kind of court of appeal. His letters are full of his
attending to isolated cases of every kind. Gregory, the humble monk,
may have worn his authority lightly, but he possessed an extraordinary amount of it and used it extensively. His successor, Gregory VII,
will do the same in a time four and a half centuries later that called,
he thought, for more heavy-handed insistence on jurisdiction and
penalty.[85]

DESCRIPTION OF THE
POST-CONSTANTINIAN CHURCH

Development in a historical institution is continuous; no gaps or
leaps to completely new forms interrupt the steady process; everything stumbles forward in the mixture of social causality, sin, and
graced freedom. But two portraits of the same institution at different times of its life can show in an almost visual way significant

---

83. Markus, *Gregory the Great and His World*, 112–24.

84. See Gregory I, Letter I.1 to all the bishops of Sicily, informing them that he has
made "Peter, subdeacon of our See, our delegate in the province of Sicily." In Letter I.18
to Peter Gregory gives him orders to regulate matters in the churches there.

85. One of the legacies of Gregory concerned the use of power, whether by pope
or bishop, abbot or king. He provided a model for the Christian exercise of authority
which he learned from the abbot in Benedict's rule. On the one hand, it was absolute
power that expected unhesitating obedience. On the other hand, it required of the ruler
absolute integrity of purpose, clarity of aim, knowledge of the subjects, and orientation
to the salvation of souls. In emphasizing the responsibility of the ruler for the souls of
his subjects, Gregory coined a language for the governing elite of Europe. Brown, *The
Rise of Western Christendom* (2003), 142–44.

changes. This section attempts a description of the church as it took shape from the fourth through the sixth centuries. Contrast with the church in the second and early third centuries would highlight the historical changes that occurred. The categories for considera-tion roughly correspond to the elements of any organization: the self-understanding of the church, its members, its mission or pur-pose, the activities in which it engages, and its relationships to the environment. It will be noted that the description leans toward the Western church.

Nothing influences the development of an institution more con-sistently than change in its environment. The three centuries just surveyed saw the division of the empire in two, East and West, the breakdown of the empire in the West, and the increased weight upon the church to provide a certain social cohesion in Latin lands.

During this time the church grew numerically: the communities became more numerous and each one larger. As the church be-came more established, conversions of convenience increased and, generally, intentional faith commitment on the average weakened. Tertullian's characterization of the church community vis-à-vis Latin society no longer described local communities but became at best the expression of the ideals of the past. Any given church could be wealthy or poor, but the churches of Rome and Gaul, for example, commanded considerable wealth, even though its people and lower clergy might be poor. In terms of the distinction between sect and church of Ernst Troeltsch, the sect had become a church. Sociolog-ically speaking, the monasteries took the form of sects within the boundaries of the wider church.

The Unity and Self-Understanding of the Church

The unity of the church is defined both organizationally and theo-logically. The organization of the local and regional churches was set at the beginning of the fourth century; the basic institutions ran parallel to the organization of the empire. A bishop led local com-munities; clergy and laity were clearly distinguished in a hierarchy: bishop, priest, deacon, subdeacon. Lower orders, and the status of widows, consecrated virgins, and other offices distinguished people from ordinary laity, but they were not clergy. In principle, the people elected bishops; often the choice was determined by local clergy or neighboring bishops, or by appointment of the metropolitan; politics would play a part when civil rulers or wealthy patrons or relatives had a say. Above the bishops in the towns was the metropolitan, usually the bishop of the principal city in the province. Above the groups of provincial churches and metropolitans were the patriarchs, the bishops of Alexandria, Rome, Constantinople, Antioch, and Jerusalem.[86] Regional councils were a regular feature by the end of the fourth century, and their decrees began to provide prescriptions for a developing canon law.[87] Nicaea ruled that two synods be held annually in each province (c. 5), and this was reiterated at Chalcedon (c. 19).

Organizationally, a communion of bishops and a communion of patriarchs held the whole church together. But this was no longer the collegial episcopalism reflected in Cyprian. The post-Constantinian church became structured in a descending, hierarchical, jurisdictional order with patriarch exercising some control over metropolitans, and metropolitans over bishops. In the West, with the rise of the papacy, more and more churches became drawn into the jurisdictional coordination, if not direct authority, of the pope in Rome.[88] But whatever content the Roman popes gave to their claims of primacy, the bishop of Rome never actually possessed, in the sense of exercised, direct jurisdictional authority over the Eastern churches of Alexandria, Jerusalem, Antioch, and Constantinople. Only Constantine and some other emperors actually possessed universal jurisdictional authority in the church.

---

86. This all encompassing organization is reflected in cc. 4 and 6 of the Council of Nicaea. See Schroeder, *Disciplinary Decrees*, 26–33. Nicaea, c. 4, prescribed that bishops be elected by the bishops of the province. The East tended to be suspicious of episcopal elections because of political interference; in the West the laity continued to participate, at least nominally, in episcopal elections into the twelfth century (Schroeder, *Disciplinary Decrees*, 27). Because one finds "no formal rule about the participation of the believing people in the choice of a bishop, although the whole of patristic literature presupposes this participation as an ecclesial requirement," one has to conclude to a great variety of practices that were not universally regulated. Edward Schillebeeckx, *The Church with a Human Face: A New and Expanded Theology of Ministry* (New York: Crossroad, 1985), 148.

87. Daniélou and Marrou, *The First Six Hundred Years*, 239–40, 309–19; Cooke, *Ministry*, 79, 429–30.

88. Jay, *The Church*, 76.

On a theological level, Augustine was just as concerned as Cyprian for the unity of the church. The true church makes itself known by its four marks: it is one, holy, catholic and apostolic. Catholicity here means universality; the church represented the kingdom of God and was intended by God to be a universal society, the instrument of God for claiming God's chosen from every nation. The church now understood itself as coterminous with the empire, until it broke down in the West, and thus with all of society and the world. But this institutional aspect of the church did not reflect the center of Augustine's decisively theological vision of the church. The church is the body of Christ in heaven and on earth. It is authentically so on earth in those animated by the Spirit who is pure divine love and the cause of faith and love within the church. The Spirit is the point of distinction between Catholic and Donatist churches for, although they have Christ effective in the sacraments, the Spirit is not present in Donatist churches. But the idea of the presence and absence of the Spirit of love and charity also functions *within* the Catholic Church. In a post-Constantinian church one must distinguish between the visible organizational church and the invisible church where the Spirit was effective. This is the church within the church. The institutional church is a mixed community, but within it were those who were really moved by the Holy Spirit.

Augustine's understanding of the church surpasses Cyprian's in nuance, depth, and realism. He maintains a certain balance between objective and subjective dimensions of the church. Ironically, he preserves the tradition of a holy community, in its members, secretly within the wider church. Christ and the Spirit work in tandem through the church. On the one hand the church is the objective institution which is the means or medium of God's grace. On the other hand, the saints within it are still sinners but struggling because they live under the power of the Spirit of love.

The Church in Its Members

The Augustinian understanding of the church correlates neatly with the new social condition of the extended communities. His negative anthropology and his view of the small number of the elect influenced his conception of the members of the church. The great majority of the members of the church were quite decisively understood to be sinners; only a few were holy and blessed. We saw that he posited three aspects of church corresponding with three sets of members: the eschatological church and, in this world, the whole church of inscribed members and the inner circle of the sanctified. The inner circle was small. Surely this conception of things conformed to the world he witnessed around him. It is a dark picture. Perhaps most people imagined or hoped they would be among the saved, and this mitigated the pessimism. But the broad impact of this conception makes holy fear one of the driving forces of membership in the church.

A second development in the understanding of the church and its members lay in a displacement of the quality of holiness from the general run of its members to the institution itself. This process implied a certain objectification of the holiness of the church. Loosely reflecting a metaphysical way of thinking inspired by neo-Platonism, the church became holy because it participated in the holiness of Christ. As finite, this-worldly reality participated in the world of perfect ideal reality, so too the church on earth was the body of Christ by participation: Christ was the head of the church, and Christ lived in the church as its ground of holiness.[89] This objectification was not complete, however, for within the larger church of sinners the Dove, those few who were animated by the Spirit of charity, converted this metaphysical holiness into existential, historical life.

This broad imaginative framework for understanding the church and its members commands attention in two respects. First, it clearly represented the empirical church that actually existed in its now numerous members: no more perfectionism and high moral standards of a church of the few, but the church of everybody, of common everyday citizens and slaves, the church of the masses. The second feature, equally sharp and significant, lies in the degree of difference between this characterization of the church and the one of the late second and early third centuries. This was not the church of Hippolytus, Tertullian, or the *Didascalia.* Augustine's conception of the whole church on earth was far from Donatist ideals. But this represented no gratu-

---

89. Evans, *One and Holy,* 84.

itous change in ecclesiology; it was the church which changed, and Augustine's portrait of it merely caught up with the changes. On becoming the religion of the empire the church began to be conceived in legal, political terms; it was the legitimate religion of the empire. Its political privileges urged it toward institutional totality and regimentation. Increasingly church life became more passive and centered in liturgical cult and devotional practices.[90]

Goals and Mission

By the end of the fourth century, Christianity was the official religion of the empire and had spread to the cities and towns. Even in the West, where the church maintained its autonomy from imperial organization, the church became more and more entwined with civil society by becoming a major agent of social services, organization, and even protection. The great popes, after they insisted on the church's autonomy and spiritual integrity, did not hesitate to speak of the union of interests and complementarity of goals between church and empire. One could speak of a Christian empire under a Christian emperor. As a description, however, this language was far more appropriate to the East than the West because the migrational movements in Europe destroyed the military and political unity of the Western empire.

One can view the mission of the church on the local level and within the context of a larger historical vision. In terms of Augustine's Western ecclesiology, the mission and function of the church could be interpreted as medicinal: what was done on the social level with its social services the church also accomplished on the religious or spiritual level with its sacraments. The key for understanding the phrase "the church as the sacrament of salvation" rests in the negative sin-ridden anthropology proposed by Augustine in reaction to Pelagius. As sacrament the church mediates God's grace to the peoples who make up the congregations in the cities and towns. But this role easily expands to become a theology of history. The church of Christ provides the means by which God's providence and grace

---

90. Schillebeeckx, *The Church with a Human Face*, 142–43.

touch people in history for their salvation. God's plan for creation assigns to the church the mission to be the historical vehicle for the restoration of the eschatological or heavenly church. The church became hypostasized. Augustine did with the church what Paul did with Jesus: as Paul viewed Jesus as the cosmic Christ, so Augustine saw the church in cosmic eschatological terms.[91]

This understanding provided a strong rationale for missionary activity. The impulse for spreading the gospel now included but exceeded sharing the good news of salvation through Jesus Christ, inviting people to share one's religious experience and faith. Salvation became dependent upon ecclesial membership. Only baptism would forgive the sin unto death into which each is born. This meaning transcends the contextual meaning of the phrase "no salvation outside the church," as used by Cyprian with reference to Christian schism. It is now cosmic and embracing all human history. In an Augustinian framework, granting exceptions according to God's providence and grace, salvation is absent where the church does not mediate it.

Activities of the Church

Two areas of activity help to delineate the church of late antiquity: one is liturgical practice and its correlation with sacramental theology, another is the rise of the cult of the martyrs and saints.

At the end of the fourth century the eucharistic liturgy was celebrated everywhere on a daily basis, but more solemnly on Sundays and feast days. Two poles structured the liturgical year: Easter, which was celebrated on different dates in the East and the West, and the nativity of Jesus. In the East the nativity of Jesus was celebrated as a feast of incarnation and epiphany on January 6; in the West the feast emerged early in the fourth century and was celebrated on December 25 as Christians coopted "the birthday of the sun-god at the Winter solstice."[92] The church in each city, led by its bishop, assembled on Sundays in the basilica; this was its public space.[93] The

---

91. Cooke, *Ministry.*, 77.
92. Chadwick, *The Early Church*, 126–27.
93. Depending on the size and wealth of the town, the basilica might be surrounded by a complex of buildings with different functions. See van der Meer's reconstruction of Augustine's church and others in North Africa in *Augustine the Bishop*, 20–25.

hierarchical order of members was reflected in the approach to communion: "bishops and clergy first, then the continent of both sexes, and, last of all, the married laity. In a specially designated area at the very back of the basilica, furthest from the apse, stood the 'penitents,' those whose sin excluded them from active participation."[94]

Augustine's sacramental theology became the final Catholic formula: the church is God's holy institution distinct from subjective or personal holiness of the members. While this makes no sense empirically or historically, it makes good sense sociologically and theologically. In Troeltsch's categories it typically pertains to a church as distinct from a sect. This formula, as Pelikan says, will last for a thousand years.[95]

Objective sacramental theology raises the question of how it was implemented in liturgical practice. Bradshaw describes succinctly the changes that occurred in the language and performance of baptism and the eucharist as a result of the influx of large numbers into the church after the legitimation of Christianity.[96] In this new situation "the baptismal process became instead the means of conveying a profound experience to the candidates in the hope of bringing about their conversion. In order to accomplish this new role, the process became much more dramatic — one might even say theatrical — in character" (22). The candidates were not fully instructed in the faith; prior to baptism beliefs were cloaked in secrecy; after baptism, in a post-baptismal instruction period called mystagogy, they were led by instruction into the faith they had embraced. The idea was that the elaborate ceremonies would help produce the religious fervor and faith that might otherwise be lacking. Another development consisted in increased "focus on the invisible transformation that was believed to take place in baptism rather than to look for visible

---

94. Brown, *Late Antiquity*, 40. "A public system of penance remained current throughout the period. Excommunication involved public exclusion from the Eucharist, and its effects could be reversed only by an equally public act of reconciliation with the bishop." Ibid.

95. Pelikan, *The Emergence of the Catholic Tradition*, 312.

96. Paul Bradshaw, *Early Christian Worship: A Basic Introduction to Ideas and Practice* (Collegeville, Minn.: Liturgical Press, 1995). References in the text are to pages in this text.

changes in the conduct of the newly baptized" (23). Thus the metaphor of the seal from the New Testament began to be taken literally or metaphysically.

Relative to the eucharist, the second half of the fourth century witnessed a major change in eucharistic practice corresponding with "the emergence of an attitude of great awe and fear directed toward the eucharistic elements, together with a decline in the frequency of the reception of communion" (64). The style of eucharistic celebrations changed. "They became much more formal and elaborate; they used such things as ceremonial actions, vesture, processions, and music in order to make an impression on the congregation; and in word and action they stressed the majesty and transcendence of God and the divinity of Christ present in the eucharistic mystery" (64).[97] Concerned about the declining standards of Christian life, ministers placed greater stress on the need for a worthy life as a condition for communion. The result was that many "preferred to give up the reception of communion rather than amend their lives. Thus began the practice of non-communicating attendance at the eucharist" (66). The effect of this was a break between eucharistic action and receiving communion, so that assisting at the eucharist without reception of communion became an integral act. And this in turn led to the idea that the eucharist was something that the clergy did for the laity, whether or not they were there, rather than a community activity. Further still, the eucharist "not only ceased to be a communal action, but was not even viewed as food to be eaten. Instead, it became principally an object of devotion, to be gazed at from afar" (67). From small church with more intimate eucharistic gatherings these assemblies developed into something closer to theater in which one was less actively engaged.

Another major development in the devotional life of people in the Western church consisted in the rise of devotion to saints, especially to martyrs, and to their relics, and generally a belief in the miraculous.[98] First of all, the saints. The saint provided a concrete

---

97. Bradshaw cites Chrysostom's language: he speaks of a dreadful sacrifice, and a "terrible and awful table" that has to be approached with fear and trembling. Ibid., 65.

98. Peter Brown, in *The Cult of the Saints: Its Rise and Function in Latin Christianity* (London: SCM Press, 1981), describes these developments. References in the text are to pages in this work.

link, a local *axis mundi*, between heaven and earth, especially at his or her grave site. The saint in heaven also was present on earth, located at his or her grave, and operative. The inscription on the tomb of St. Martin of Tours says it bluntly: "Here lies Martin the bishop, of holy memory, whose soul is in the hand of God; but he is fully here, present and made plain in miracles of every kind" (4). These are not mere heroes to be emulated, but live intimates of God able to intercede and protect. The logic of this phenomenon was demonstrated by Paulinus of Nola in his written life of his patron Saint Felix.[99] Paulinus attributes to Saint Felix "all the sense of intimate involvement with an invisible companion that men in previous generations had looked for in a relationship with the nonhuman figures of gods, *daimones*, or angels" (55). The relationship took the shape of the patron and friend from Roman culture, enhanced with the power that comes from friendship with God, softened by the status as another human being. Saints were private and public, based on a personal relationship or on a relationship with a particular place or church. They helped bond a community together. This has to be read against the background of a corporate pessimism, sense of sin and judgment, together with a growing ascetic movement. People needed help and heavenly patrons provided direction and support.

In the fourth and fifth centuries belief in miracles at the tombs or in connection with the relics of martyrs exploded across the Mediterranean world "with geyserlike force" (75). The roots of this lie in belief in the resurrection and the power of the patron in heaven. The martyrs were especially close to God because their martyrdom itself was not an act of human courage but a manifestation of the power of God. Like the presence of the saint or martyr at the tomb, the relic as a piece of the saint's body forms a localized linkage between heaven and earth; like a sacrament, it makes the resurrected saint present in a focused way.

Double Relationship to God and World

The double relationship of the church to God and to the world constitutes an a priori formal structure for understanding the church. In

---

99. Brown believes the work merits for Paulinus "a place alongside the mighty Augustine, as founder of Latin Christian piety." Ibid., 55.

the pre-Constantinian period, especially as this is reflected in Tertullian, this double relationship set up a tensive bearing toward the world of Roman society and culture: the church was within Roman society and culture but not of it. This tensive relationship provided an existential coloring of Christian life itself.

By contrast, as the church as a whole became more and more the church of the Graeco-Roman empire, the two terms of the double relationship in some respects were differentiated and institutionalized. A radical relationship to God, once lived out in an absolute way in martyrdom, became institutionalized in monasticism and symbolized in clerical celibacy. The relationship to the world was institutionalized in the bishop's role in city and town and the second-class spirituality of ordinary Christians.

In relation to God. There will always be Christians who are singlemindedly intent in living out their relationship to God in an almost exclusive way, and various forms of monastic and conventual life provide recognized and structured opportunities for this commitment. Monasticism institutionalized the ancient tradition of Christians being countercultural and otherworldly. Here was serious Christianity, in the spirit of the martyrs, in continuity with the early Christian ethic and ascetic struggle against the demons and the forces of idolatry in the world.[100] Monastic life was highly reflective and consciously developed, so that Christian spirituality as such was in some measure coopted by various forms of monastic or religious life. The life of the laity, in the world of everyday concerns, appeared less religious and less spiritual by comparison. Bishops who had spent time as monks advocated a type of spirituality for the people that was "essentially monastic in character" and in that measure also essentially alienating.[101] This new division departed from the idea of a single ordinary Christian life lived with degrees of perfection across the board. It represented, rather, the beginning of distinct ways of

---

100. Gregory I had a tendency, although he never formally held this, to equate those in monastic life with the elect in Augustine's view of the church. "The antithesis of elect and reprobate within the Church, conditioned as it is by ascetic and perfectionist spirituality, is not unlike the antithesis of Church and world in Tertullian and Cyprian." Evans, *One and Holy*, 151, 148–49.

101. Bradshaw, *Early Christian Worship*, 74.

life and a double standard in measuring Christian vocation and per-fection. There were two types of Christian life: the one was heroic in its ideals, uncompromising with the world and imperial society; the other was life in a sinful society, one compromised by the world and marked by the mediocre morality of the masses. This was not a distinction between clergy and laity, but the intrinsically uneven contrast between monastic ideals and actual life in the world.

But this does not subtract from the vitality of the religious and spiritual values of monasticism and hermetic life, not to mention the positive contributions to society of the monasteries and individ-ual monks. At first, this mode of life was not really accepted in the West; its ideology was considered strange and bizarre. But it gradually became a dynamic force in the church and remained so continuously through many reforms right up to our own time, a development manifested in a variety of different religious associations. On the one hand, then, monasticism gradually raised up in the church in the West a cadre of solid, active, and responsible Christian leaders schooled in a deep spirituality.[102] On the other hand, this tended to minimize the estimate for the possibility of the sanctity of Chris-tian life "in the world." This tension lived on in the church during the course of its history; it exists today, but to a decidedly greater degree in some churches than in others since the sixteenth-century Reformation.

The question of Christian ethics cannot be separated from the holiness of the church and its relation to the world. Whether one considers this period as a diffusion of the church into the empire or an absorption of the empire, the transition entailed a lowering of the standards of Christian morality. Against this background Pelagius has to be considered an honest but sociologically and theologically outmoded reaction. As Christianity began to become a religion of the masses, Pelagianism represented the ancient ascetic ideals. In a more

---

102. Monasticism, Brown insists, was not simply for illiterate, rural, anticultural individuals. A monastery could also be a center of education where young talented people were dedicated to service of God and trained, to reemerge as abbots or clergy who were learned and disciplined. This constituted in effect a new form of education based in liturgy and bible, quiet and order, in the presence of God. Brown, *Late Antiquity*, 56–59.

progressive way so did monasticism, and it is not at all strange that Pelagianism found some allies among the monks.[103]

The discipline of clerical celibacy reflects a conception of sexuality but also a conception of the relation of the Christian minister to God. A universal practice of ministerial, clerical, or priestly celibacy did not exist in the early church. But by the fourth century the chastity of clerics was a universal concern. The Council of Nicaea bluntly states that higher clergy, bishops, priests, and deacons should not allow women to live in their houses except those who are above all suspicion.[104] Celibacy was also discussed at Nicaea, and although the council refused to make celibacy obligatory, it forbade marriage after receiving orders.[105] But since ministers were generally recruited from among married men, preferably those of a certain age when sexual ardor had cooled, the discussion of celibacy focused on sexual continence or abstinence from all sexual activity rather than the state of marriage.[106] This took different forms in the East and in the West.[107]

---

103. For example, Cassian tried to chart a middle course between Augustine and Pelagius consisting of a more generous estimation of the extent of salvation among human beings, the fate of unbaptized infants, and some role of human freedom in the possibility of turning toward God. See Cassian, XIII, 7, 8.4, 9, 11.1, 16.1.

104. Nicaea, c. 4 in Schroeder, *Disciplinary Decrees*, 21.

105. Edward Schillebeeckx, *Celibacy* (New York: Sheed and Ward, 1968), 33.

106. Celibacy "was usually adopted in middle age and would later be imposed on priests after the age of thirty." Brown, *Late Antiquity*, 33. There were many who were willing to abstain from sex after a fully active sexual life in their youth, in order to represent the church and become engaged in the public order. Continence among the clergy demonstrated the church's distinction from society. Ibid., 33–34.

107. In the East, the discipline moved in the direction of excluding marriage after ordination; bishops who were married were to live continently; later it was decided that they separate from their wives; priests and deacons could remain with their spouses and have normal sexual relations (Schillebeeckx, *Celibacy*, 35–37). In the West, several documents in the fourth century representing the church in Spain, North Africa and Rome prescribe continence for bishops, priests, and deacons. These sources and a host of others are analyzed by Christian Cochini, *Apostolic Origins of Priestly Celibacy* (San Francisco: Ignatius Press, 1990), 3–17 and passim. Leo I and Gregory I permitted priests to live with wives as brother and sister, but "the practice of continence remained for the most part a dead letter until the eleventh or even the twelfth century" (Schillebeeckx, *Celibacy*, 41). The point is that one must assume that the practice was uneven throughout the church, so that one cannot point to a universal *practice* of clerical celibacy in the West "prior to the reform movement directed by Gregory VII in the eleventh century" (Cooke, *Ministry*, 558). Even after the Gregorian reform and through the Middle Ages practice was uneven.

Sexuality and religious ritual observance are frequently linked, and the motivations for continence were many. Not a few bore a relation to the New Testament: the church is the bride of Christ and the consecrated virgin lives this relationship explicitly, so that the unmarried condition is most intensely Christian;[108] continence was a gift or charism; it was connected to contact with God in prayer, as though love of God and love of spouse were competitive; it promoted complete freedom, an angelic response to God; it had ascetic merit of fostering self-control and the focusing of one's life; it mirrored Mary's virginity and total availability for God's will; it had an eschatological aim. More specifically relative to ritual ministry, sex was impure and was to be avoided by one who offered the eucharist. It directed the minister's attention back toward the self, family, and procreation.[109] Afterward the influence of Augustine became important insofar as sexuality, which as a created reality was good, became reinterpreted as an area in which the sinful or fallen condition of human existence forcefully manifested itself. The heat and passion of sex were no longer considered as part of its overall function, but as the material, bodily, sensual side of the person breaking out of the control of mind and will and signaling a self radically divided against its authentic being and God.[110] For a variety of reasons, then, sexual continence was an explicit ideal attached to ordained ministry.

In relation to the world. Here "world" refers to civil society both in its public institutions and as the state or governmental structure. In some ways the church remained a parallel society within the empire, distinct with its own autonomy, and thus continuous with the pre-Constantinian period. The tension between pope and emperor

---

108. Schillebeeckx, *Celibacy*, 30.

109. Ibid., 55–57. Some phrases of a decretal issued by a Roman synod in the fourth century illustrate this: "Would an impure man dare soil what is holy when holy things are for holy people? ... If commixture is defiling, it is obvious that the priest must be ready to carry out his celestial functions — he who has to supplicate on behalf of the sins of the others — so that he himself not be found impure" (See Cochini, *Apostolic Origins of Priestly Celibacy*, 15). Frequently one finds an appeal back to the prescriptions for the ritual purity of priests in the Old Testament. In the monastic reasoning of Cassian, celibacy was the principal marker of the monks' social distinctiveness, and "the physical and psychological processes of growth into chastity [became] a privileged language expressing the monks' relationship to God and to other human beings." Stewart, *Cassian*, 62.

110. Brown, *Late Antiquity*, 71–74.

ensured this in the West. But momentous shifts completely altered the situation. In general the transition ran from being over against society toward integration with society. This integration was most complete in the person of the bishop. The power and standing of bishops in society, in both the East and the West, gave him a central role in city and town. So much part of society was the bishop that, in Gaul at the end of the sixth century, "no one could hope to become bishop without laying down a substantial sum in gratitude to the lay prince who made it possible."[111] He would recoup his outlay by fees levied on candidates for ordination. The problems that would be addressed in the Gregorian reform had their beginnings in late antiquity.

To sum up here, three large propositions may serve to conclude this rapid portrait of the church of late antiquity. First, the church's development over these three centuries was generated by a dialectical interaction of social forces and the church's own inward life. The church both conformed to the social and political patterns that characterized these centuries in the East and West, and at the same time retained an autonomy that grew from within. Second, throughout the period the bishop continued to be the main centering and consolidating institution of the church, and this position was strengthened in different ways in the East and the West. Pope and patriarch exercised important roles in holding the churches together, but in the concrete life of the church their importance remained secondary to the bishop. Third, the stratification of religious life and ideals into two large classes, professionally serious Christians committed to some form of ascetic life and those people who lived in the world, had a major influence on the meaning of Christian life that would also last in the West until the sixteenth-century Reformation.

PRINCIPLES FOR
A HISTORICAL ECCLESIOLOGY

In his *The Varieties of Religious Experience* William James lays down the principle that one can best study the nature of human responses

---

111. Chadwick, *Church in Ancient Society*, 663.

by considering extreme forms; in his case this meant powerful examples of religious experience. This chapter provides an overview of
a period of history in which the church underwent major changes; in
some cases from one extreme to another. What formal principles can
be derived from these material developments to serve a general ecclesiology? The points which follow are hardly exhaustive, and many are
reiterations, but take on a fuller meaning with every new historical
instantiation.

Development: Emergence of the Papacy

The first and single most important premise for understanding the
church in history is the dynamic of development itself. A comparison
between the church in the year 300 and the year 600 will bear that
out: in those three centuries the church moved from being a minority religion to being the established religion of the empire, and from
being more like Troeltsch's sect type to a church type of Christianity. And those shifts include a number of areas in which significant
adjustments occurred.

An example of such historical development is the emergence of
the jurisdictional power and authority of the papacy. From as early
as the second century, the church and bishop of Rome held a certain "primacy" of position among the churches and an ability to
receive appeals and arbitrate disputes. Like all metropolitan sees,
the bishopric of Rome held authority relative to the churches in
its sphere. Gradually the jurisdictional power and authority of the
bishop of Rome expanded in the Western, Latin speaking region.
The extension of bureaucracy and administrative capacity provided
an intrinsic element enabling the actual exercise of religious authority by the pope in Rome. In popes Leo I and Gregory I one can see
how the development of administrative system and a theology of
a Petrine office combine to establish and solidify the institution of
the papacy. But whatever the claims of individual popes, they never
actually enjoyed universal juridical power.

The developmental principle takes on significance when one tries
to reformulate the theology of the papacy. Understanding the office
of the papacy has to take place within the context of historical development. Most biblical exegetes argue against the historicity of Jesus

setting up a Petrine ministry as that came to be understood, and this forces a shift in the imaginative framework for appropriating the language that was traditional up to the sixteenth century.[112] In other words, the office developed. The assimilation between pope and Peter consists in symbolic language mediating a religious understanding of the role of the pope; that religious perception and theological judgment were authentic. But the linkage between Peter and pope cannot be made in terms of a historical transmission of religious and ecclesial jurisdiction or exclusive divine law. Rather the development of this institution was a historical development, for the good of the church, impelled and ratified by God as Spirit from within the community, and open to further development.

Inculturation

One could isolate a number of different developments that occurred during this time span and analyze them under the aspect of an adjustment to a new social and cultural setting. Certainly a major, and perhaps the most important, of such inculturations were the doctrinal formulas developed at Nicaea and Chalcedon in which the conciliar Fathers rendered the basic confessions of Christians in Greek categories derived from philosophy in response to the questions of an intellectual culture. These doctrines reflected a universal Christian experience of salvation in Jesus the Christ. When the formulations of the central doctrines of Christianity are recognized as examples of inculturation, they no longer appear as absolute or a-historical propositions, but as classic and paradigmatic examples of the principle of inculturation which cannot be bypassed because of the role they continue to play in defining the church's beliefs.

The development of sacramental theology provides another example of inculturation. This may be more pointed because both terms of the development, *a quo* and *ad quem*, were plausible in their context. Tertullian's church was still small. Cyprian's sacramental theology made sense in his church, at least up to the time when the crisis of a persecution showed some need for adjustments in practice.

---

112. The supposition at this point is that the leadership of Peter among the disciples and a Petrine ministry in a Christian church are two very different matters, even though the second may have in part developed from the first.

By and large, the theology of sacramental efficacy based in the dynamism of the Holy Spirit fit a relatively small church standing over against society. It was coherent with actual practice, with the self-conscious identity of the community, and with its need for discipline and high standards of morality. But Cyprian's theology made no sense in the empirical, established church of Augustine's time. The actual church as it existed then urged a different practice and demanded a new theology. One could not count on the moral purity of the minister in a large established church. The polarity between the ideal and the actual sheds light on this development of sacramental theology: it describes accurately one of the lines along which the understanding of the metaphysics and functioning of the sacraments occurred. Metaphysically and ideally the sacraments mediated Christ's grace. But Augustine could look out on his congregation and say with certainty that, although the sacraments are always objectively efficacious, they were not always fruitful or subjectively effective. The church in history is the history of the ongoing inculturation of the movement or community into ever new history.

Commixture of Conservative and Progressive Forces

Change stands over against "more of the same"; it consists in moving from one state of affairs or structure to another, a point "from which" and a term "toward which." History always involves movement and is thus characterized by continuity and change. Conservative forces are aligned with continuity; progressive forces with adjustment to the novel or different aspects of new situations. Both forces exist within a society or group, and they may be understood to exist in a polar or tensive relationship with each other. This formal polarity can function as a heuristic lens to identify forces and thus illumine the dynamics of a changing church.

It is interesting to consider the place of Augustine in this particular developmental framework. Because he was so influential in setting the course of the Western church for succeeding centuries, he usually appears to be traditional, a conservative rather than a progressive force. But in some rather fundamental ways Augustine was a progressive innovator. He appears as such in relation to the Donatists who were striving to preserve the traditional ideals so clearly and authoritatively articulated by Cyprian. Augustine was sensitive to this and did in fact preserve much of Cyprian, but he did so by reinterpreting and reappropriating him. Similarly, Pelagius preserved the values of ascetic Christianity, and Augustine's doctrine of sin was innovative.[113] Now both of these observations need more discussion and nuance, but even on the face of it the reversal of this "location" of these figures shows that one must understand things contextually. What seems conservative from one perspective may appear innovative from another.

Moreover, the commixture of these forces shows that their dialectical interaction can be regarded as a positive catalytic structure. A postmodern situation provides a wider perspective from which one can see how these two forces can coincide. A positive evaluation of pluralism allows for the coexistence of groups which represent and even institutionalize conflicting traditional and progressive values. Postmodernity, not to mention modern notions of religious tolerance, makes it difficult to appreciate the reasons why a Donatist church could not have subsisted within a larger institution. The Catholic and the Donatist churches separated. Yet in the analogous case of monasticism, the monastery was able to exist within a local church's administrative unity, even though it set up a significantly different way of Christian life. In some elemental ways, just as Augustine's concept of the hidden spiritual church within the church carried forward Donatist ideals on a theological level, the monastic movement carried forward the spiritual ideals of the Donatists in an institutional way within the church's organizational structure. Development shows the extent to which accommodations are possible at any given time.

Institutional Objectification

The church is an objective historical institution. The Christian has to believe that human institution in no way exhausts the reality of the church; but one can neither deny or minimize the objective dimensions of the church, the patterned behavior and the contractual

---

113. Paul Ricoeur, "'Original Sin': A Study in Meaning," *The Conflict of Interpretations*, ed. Don Ihde (Evanston, Ill.: Northwestern University Press, 1974), 269–86.

or legal structures. The existential, living, communal dimensions of the church, the actual interactions of human beings, always coexist with the objective dimensions. This period provides examples of this polarity on a variety of different levels.

Robert Evans calls attention to the development, from the second to the fifth centuries in the Latin church, of how or where the quality of holiness applies to the church. Tertullian advocated an existentially "holy" church manifested in the high moral tone of the whole community. In Cyprian and the Donatists religious and moral purity was expected at least in the ministers. By the time of Augustine the holiness of the church takes on a more objective sense: the membership as a whole is hardly holy, and the clergy may or may not be so, but the church as objective institution is still the holy church in its doctrine, sacraments, and sanctified core. The sacramental theology of Augustine provides a clear example of how the objective sacraments, because they belong to Christ and are his instruments of grace, convey their spiritual and religious effects whether or not the minister is worthy or the faith and love of the members subjectively receives it.

Objectification also applies to offices and authority. We saw earlier how charisma becomes routinized into contractual or standardized functions, and how this process also sets up a permanent tension between objective and subjective dimensions of an office. A leader who holds an office may also be charismatic, but the leader also may be an uninspiring administrator or, worse, incompetent and dysfunctional. Yet the office may bear an authority despite the office holder. It will become clear in the course of the following chapters that, without this distinction, the office of the papacy would never have survived its incumbents.

This distinction, therefore, bears considerable importance in understanding the church. Because of its ambiguity or polar character it can lead to paradoxical assertions and even abuse. For example, how can one say that a church is holy when it is overtly sinful in its members or its leaders or both? Or that a pope has authority when what he says bears little religious claim on members of the church? But there is a sense in which the church can symbolize and mediate transcendent power despite its constituency and office holders at any given time.

A perspective that reduces the tension between an objective and an existential understanding of the church to either side cut loose from the other will inevitably become a *reductio ad absurdum*. On the one hand, objective holiness with no holiness among the members is no holiness at all. And on the other, the development of the church during the early centuries shows that one cannot count on the subjective holiness of the community to sustain itself in history without objectification.

Distinction between the Empirical Church and the Sanctified Within

This distinction by Augustine became a source for several analogous distinctions in the history of ecclesiology, not all equally clear nor equally recognized. Even though Augustine's distinction as straightforward as it seems could be abused, it may also serve a worthy purpose. However inseparable they may be, one has to be able to distinguish the church as external collectivity and institution from its inner life which the church confesses to be subject of the influence of God within it. For Augustine, these two were not mutually extensive; the sanctified constituted a minority within the great church. Those lines will not be able to be so clearly drawn in later ecclesiologies, but it is essential to distinguish the human and the divine within the church even when they remain inseparable, the one mediated by the other. This distinction allowed Augustine distance from the institution; it enabled him to distinguish between elements that were human and sinful from those that were divine; it allowed him to speak realistically about the institutional church; it gave him the tools to think dialectically about the church and to make statements that seemed to be opposed: the church is the body of Christ, and the church is sinful. This distinction needs to be used carefully, but without some form of it the institutional church could idolize itself.

The Dialectic of Whole and Part

The dialectical principle of whole and part can be stated simply, but its relevance varies. The principle says that the whole church exists in any given part: any local church can embody the whole church. But at the same time, the whole or universal church consists of a communion of churches. This means that the object of ecclesiology is always the whole Christian movement; no single church exhausts the church, even though the church subsists in principle in every church. But no one belongs to the whole except in and through a local church. This principle will take on more significance as the church becomes more divided. But the principle itself may be illumined by reflection on the split between Catholicism and Donatism, and the beginning of the drift apart of the Western and Eastern churches.

Donatism provides an interesting case of division within the church. On the one hand, the originating events seem somewhat ordinary. The tendency in retrospect is to think that the counter-positions should have been subject to negotiation and compromise. Yet they generated a deep and bitter rift that ran all through Christian North Africa. The conflict was so intractable that interpreters have to find a number of deep rivers that somehow explain the lasting character of the turbulence on the surface. Whatever the deep causes, however, Donatism raises the ecclesiological question of whether this division was necessary. Donatism, in other words, raises the question in more general terms of what the merits of such a division were and whether the reasons that supported the division in the past would be applicable today. The point is not to respond to these historical questions with historical answers, but simply to raise them against the background of the historical consciousness and acceptance of pluralism that characterizes postmodern intellectual culture. The division between Donatists and Catholics in the post-Constantinian church may be a negative interlude providing a positive lesson: this sort of thing can be avoided.

The Eastern and Western church will "officially" part company in the eleventh century, but one can already see the two Christian cultures gradually drifting apart, beginning particularly with the move of Emperor Constantine to his new capital in the East. It is remarkable that they held together for so long. But if these two churches did recognize each other over such a long period despite the various schisms which were healed and the widening gaps in their self-understanding, ethos, and practice, once again, do we not have fertile ground for understanding how these churches were also substantially continuous with each other, and for grasping the unity of the whole church

across and within the significant differences among the parts? The
history of the church continually displays a process of inculturation,
whether or not it is consciously intended. But this inevitably means
differentiation among the parts. Historical ecclesiology continually
looks for the substantial unity of the church across its historical dif-
ferentiations, that is, by appropriating them where possible and not
immediately raising them up as obstacles to unity.

The Relation of the Church to State and Society

Finally, the relation of the church to the world names the place where
the greatest change occurred in the transition from a pre- to a post-
Constantinian church. The contrast between the second century
church and the sixth century church is complete: the one consists
in tiny conventicles cowering in cities around the empire, the other
is the state religion, in some places charged with running many basic
civic functions over and above its explicitly religious function. It was
not possible for the early church to be constructively engaged in society; it was not possible for the church to avoid such responsibility
after the emperors in effect "established" the church, directed it to
respond to concrete human needs, and delegated to its leaders some
of their own authority. We have noted along the way that part of the
growing differences between the church in the East and the West were
bound to different realizations of the synergy of church and state.
Once again, then, one can discern in these developments a maxim:
the church will assume different relationships with society and state
according to the time, place, and sociopolitical constellations of the
distribution of power. There is no hard and fast concrete norm for
the relationship between church and society and state.

Part III

THE CHURCH IN THE
MIDDLE AGES

Chapter 5

The Gregorian Reform and the
New Medieval Church

One wonders whether Gregory I would have recognized the church as the same as the one over which he presided if he had been transported to the Fourth Lateran Council in 1215 and witnessed Innocent III in the chair of Peter. The church had come a long way in those six hundred years, and laying the two churches side by side provides a striking example of historical analogy. The church in the high and late Middle Ages in many ways differed as much from that of Gregory I as his did from that of Ignatius of Antioch.[1]

The next two chapters describe and analyze the medieval church, with special attention on the Western church. This narrows the focus of this historical ecclesiology but is inescapable if the work is to be kept within some limits. In principle, a historical ecclesiology should be open and inclusive in its scope. But still other sharply restricting factors are at work. One cannot really tell the story of the development of the church from 700 to 1500 in a few pages. The narrative here proceeds on the basis of a selection of certain key persons, historical situations, events, and texts as a way of schematically representing what is contained in a sea of historical literature. This is done with an eye to portraying some of the distinctive features of the medieval church in Europe which was unlike anything before it or after it. Chapter 5 traces the church into the thirteenth century

---

1. Peter Brown writes: "The seventh century, and not the inconclusive political crises that we call the 'Barbarian Invasions' of the fifth century, witnessed the true break between the ancient world and what followed." "'Our' Christianity was created in the seventh century and not before." Peter Brown, *The Rise of Western Christendom*, 2nd ed. (Oxford: Blackwell, 2003), 219, 220.

when it reached the apogee of its power in Europe, and chapter 6 describes the church up to the beginning of the sixteenth century. Many characterize this latter period as one of decline, but that judgment often refers to the political power and moral probity of the popes. Throughout this period the church continued to have an impact on the lives of people.

This chapter follows a now familiar strategy. The first part comments on some key historical developments that helped define the age and the church within it. Given the context, the second part analyzes more closely persons and texts that witness to the self-understanding of the church during this period. In this light the third part offers a descriptive characterization of the church as a whole, as a massive religious organization. The chapter will conclude by drawing to the surface some principles or axioms that are at work in the church at this time and which will be useful for a constructive and historically conscious interpretation of the church.

HISTORICAL DEVELOPMENT

Any attempt at characterizing the development of the church into the High Middle Ages in a short space is reduced to answering this question: what historical events and what people would be included in a short list of the key factors that defined this social reality? In what follows, the key organizing event is the protracted process of the Gregorian reform during the second half of the eleventh century. With that as a centering event, one can tell the story of this period in three stages: the period leading up to and setting the stage for the Gregorian reform, the representation of it as a kind of turning point in the history of the church, and the flowering forth of the Western church as Christendom in the twelfth and thirteenth centuries.[2]

---

2. Sources for this historical section include the following works: John Binns, *An Introduction to the Christian Orthodox Churches* (Cambridge: University Press, 2002); Uta-Renate Blumenthal, *The Investiture Controversy: Church and Monarchy from the Ninth to the Twelfth Century* (Philadelphia: University of Pennsylvania Press, 1988); Peter Brown, *The Rise of Western Christendom: Triumph and Diversity, AD 200–1000*, 2nd ed. (Oxford: Blackwell, 2003); Yves Congar, *L'Eglise: De saint Augustin à l'èpoque moderne* (Paris: Editions du Cerf, 1970); Bernard Cook, *Ministry to Word and Sacrament: History and Theology* (Philadelphia: Fortress Press, 1977); H. E. J. Cowdrey,

The European Church from Gregory I to the Eleventh Century

When Gregory I died in 604 the church was expanding into Europe. And by the time the Gregorian reform was completed, virtually all of western Europe was Christian on the surface, with the exception of the minority of Jews who lived alongside Christians and the Muslims who lived with Christians in Spain. This long period of transition could be looked upon as a massive process of inculturation where the church took on a symbiotic relationship with society and political structure so that Europe itself became Christian. But who swallowed whom in this synthesis? Beginning with the Gregorian reform, a constant balancing of power between popes and secular rulers created a tension on the macro-political level. But the deeper cultural integration began much earlier. The rise of Islam in the seventh century provided a backdrop for the extended process of development. As Islam spread, suppressing Christianity in Northern Africa and moving into Spain, cutting deeply into the territories of Eastern Christianity, it set up a fairly clear external boundary of the European church. The very presence of Islam, at times an aggressive presence, continually exercised an influence on the self-understanding and often equally aggressive behavior of the church.

The development of the early church into the Roman empire showed the degree to which what might be called secular or general social-political history controls the shape of the church at any given time. The story continues in the early Middle Ages. The invasions caused a breakdown of the unifying structure of the Roman empire. The administrative structures and agencies, the law and government, the systems of communication and trade that linked elements of wider European society yielded to the emergence of a

---

The Cluniacs and the Gregorian Reform (Oxford: Clarendon Press, 1970); Eric G. Jay, *The Church: Its Changing Image through Twenty Centuries* (Atlanta: John Knox Press, 1980); David Knowles, with Dimitri Obolensky, *The Middle Ages* (New York: McGraw-Hill, 1968); Joseph H. Lynch, *The Medieval Church* (London, New York: Longman, 1992); John Meyendorff, *The Orthodox Church: Its Past and Its Role in the World Today* (New York: Pantheon Books, 1962); R. W. Southern, *The Making of the Middle Ages* (New Haven: Yale University Press, 1959); Brian Tierney, *The Crisis of Church and State 1050–1300* (Englewood Cliffs, N.J.: Prentice Hall, 1964); Ernst Troeltsch, *The Social Teaching of the Christian Churches* (New York: Harper Torchbooks, 1960); Walter Ullmann, *A Short History of the Papacy in the Middle Ages* (London: Methuen, 1972); Timothy Ware, *The Orthodox Church* (London: Penguin books, 1997).

feudal system of society. Centralized government by law gave way to private and personal relationships, largely dictated by individual wealth and power. In the place of common adherence to an objective body of laws, the political relationships among people became more a function of strength and power. The structure of any given locale could be understood in terms of bilateral relationships between the powerful and the less so, the lord and the vassal, the guarantor of order and protection and those offering service and taxes. This shift in the structure of society involved three developments for the church.

One significant development consisted in the emergence of proprietary churches. During the seventh and eighth centuries individual churches became private property; they belonged to the lord who built and owned them and were regarded as a piece of real property; a church could be bought, or sold, or divided among heirs. This was not the result of a sinister conspiracy, but occurred as a natural development. The owner of a large farm, which constituted a rural community, for example, might build a church for his or her tenants and thus own the church. But this resulted in the priest becoming the employee or the dependent of the owner. A church could be owned by a king, a prince, a private individual, a bishop, or a consortium. These churches, usually with land and income attached, thus became part of the feudal system, and the ministers in the churches related to their owners within the feudal structure.[3]

A second development left bishops in possession of temporal power. The career of Gregory I in some ways foreshadowed the basic structure of this transition. In the breakdown of central authority and the vacuum of power left by the invasions, the bishops naturally filled the need for leadership with an organizational basis. Children of wealthy families with access to education became bishops, and bishops became local authorities; they governed cities and administered justice.[4]

Third, with the breakdown of the empire the church north of the Alps remained distant from any concrete or practical administration

---

3. Knowles, *The Middle Ages*, 51–55.
4. Ibid., 29–30. This development was already in full progress during the sixth century in France. See Brown, *Western Christendom*, 145–65.

from Rome. The pope never related to churches of the north the way he did to the churches in Italy. General social disorder, if not chaos, prevented any easy communication across Europe that might allow such a relationship to develop. Thus the church of the West sorted itself into more or less self-regulating regional churches. Rome did not control the development during this period, and church structures tended to blend into the fabric of society. In the course of the seventh and eighth centuries "Christian churches had become profoundly regionalized. Christianity was a patchwork of adjacent, but separate, 'micro-Christendoms.'"[5]

The Carolingian period and its aftermath. In the year 750 the pope sanctioned the takeover of the kingship of France by Pippin, and from then on the pope tended to identify with the West rather than the East, in some respects over against the emperor in the East. The Western church thus moved further along its way toward establishing a distinctive self-understanding and identity. In the year 800 Pope Leo III crowned Charlemagne, the Frankish king, Emperor of Rome, an event which some call the most significant single incident of the whole Middle Ages. It established a precedent: emperors of the West, Roman Emperors, were constituted by papal coronation.

The rule of Charlemagne solidified the integration of the European church with feudal society. He created a large territorial church which was effectively ruled and governed by the king himself. This is not to be understood in terms of competition with Rome or the pope or with the bishops. Charlemagne followed the imperial model established by Constantine, Eusebius, and Justinian. Indeed the church provided an instrument to bind the empire together: politically Charlemagne ruled through "a 'managerial aristocracy' composed of powerful laymen, bishops, and great abbots."[6] Bishops became the administrators of the kingdom; they were counselors, legates, educators, administrators. Charlemagne appointed bishops, called synods, legislated on

---

5. Brown, *Western Christendom*, 364. The work of missionaries such as Willibrord (658–739) and especially Boniface (675–754) are important for understanding the process by which the church expanded in Europe and began to penetrate the countryside.

6. Ibid., 437. Charlemagne used church institutions to integrate his empire politically, legally, educationally, and, finally, culturally as he promoted Latin, the language of the Roman Church. Ibid., 437–52.

doctrinal and liturgical matters. At this point, the situation appears radically different than that of Leo I and Gregory I: though Gregory I was socially and politically an integral part of the functioning of the empire, in church affairs he enjoyed autonomy and leverage relative to imperial authority. In the Carolingian church a sharp distinction between the church as an institution and the state as an institution scarcely existed. One Christian society was ruled by a Christian king or emperor with the bishops.

The period after Charlemagne's death in 816 was one of gradual disintegration. He divided his empire among his sons, they fought one against the other, and the administrative unity that Charlemagne forged fell apart. This crumbling of the Carolingian empire during the course of the ninth century also marks the beginning of the darkest days of the papacy. With some notable exceptions the popes during the end of the ninth and all through the tenth and into the eleventh century were little more than local bishops placed in power by an emperor or by one of the rival families of Rome. Scandalous stories of individual popes abound. With the rise of the German kings in the tenth century, the pope became a pawn in the rivalry between the Romans and the German kings who succeeded to the title of Roman Emperor. The German emperors, in exchange for coronation, appointed and deposed popes and received the oath of fealty from popes. In short, Rome became a territorial church. The German emperor ruled a feudal empire of which the Roman Church was a part. "In fact, between 955 and 1057 there were 25 popes, of whom no fewer than 12 were straight imperial appointments and the others creations of the Roman aristocracy, while five popes were deposed or dismissed by the emperors."[7] This situation prevailed up to the beginning of the Gregorian reform.

---

7. Ullmann, *Papacy in the Middle Ages*, 128. "Sentimentally Rome was still the heart of Europe, but from an economic and administrative point of view it was a heart which had ceased to beat" (Southern, *Middle Ages*, 135). Southern depicts a city overgrown with vegetation, strewn with monuments from the past. "Within the walls, which had once housed over a million people, a small population was gathered in clusters in the lower town, along the banks, and on the island between the banks, of the Tiber" (135). Yet it had hundreds of churches and its main industry was pilgrimages. People visited the center of spirituality and relics. The pope "presided with patriarchal dignity in a position where a legislator would have been frustrated and where an administrator would have found nothing to administer" (136).

General renaissance. The Gregorian reform was part of a much more general rebirth that began more or less around the year 1000.[8] The date is arbitrary and corresponds to no single event. Many factors helped nurture this renaissance with reference to the church. Not least among them was monasticism which underwent a resurgence during the tenth century. The Abbey of Cluny, quietly begun in the year 909, exemplified a monastic reform based on political independence and religious authenticity. The key to its success lay in its autonomy and its loyalty to Rome. Its founders set it up as independent from all lay or episcopal control, and directly dependent on the Church of Rome. It could thus flourish with purely internal elections of abbots and pursue a reformed religious life. The movement spread rapidly and was accompanied by other monastic revivals in England, Normandy, and Germany. From these monasteries would spring both the ideals of the Gregorian reform and the actual reformers.[9]

Gradually schools and centers of study began to reappear. Charlemagne had set up a system of schools in the monasteries and in the cathedrals and reestablished a curriculum of learning. These waned with the collapse of his empire, but began to emerge again around the year 1000. Education, the study of grammar and other basic skills of learning, as well as the study of theology, was a factor of the rebirth of society and the church. In the middle of the eleventh century there arose a serious controversy concerning the nature of the eucharist which could count as marking the beginnings of a distinctive medieval theology.

But more significant for the life of Europe generally and of the church in particular was the growth of the study of law. Throughout the disruptions of the past, the bureaucracy and the archives of Rome and other centers remained intact and in them a wealth of documents

---

8. The social, economic, and political factors contributing to the cultural renaissance supply the basis for a realistic appreciation of what went forward. As an example, see the account of the evolution of the medieval city in Joseph and Frances Gies, *Life in a Medieval City* (New York: Thomas Y. Crowell, 1969), 1–22.

9. Cowdrey shows how Cluny, the papacy, and the Gregorian reformers helped each other. The two reform movements had different goals, but they complemented and reinforced each other. During the course of the Gregorian reform the freedom of Cluny exemplified an ideal. "When the Gregorians aspired to achieve the liberty of the church, Cluny above all other institutions henceforth provided a pattern of which they approved." Cowdrey, *Cluniacs*, 51; also xxiv–xxv. Congar agrees in *L'Eglise*, 91.

survived. Study focused both on old Roman law and the laws of the church. Gradually a body of law to which one could appeal as to an objective authority began to exercise influence. In all of this study, the basic medium of learning was the text. It was renaissance: a looking back and learning from the wisdom of the past and a bringing forward and applying in the present. Argument was interpretation of past texts; the logic began with and rested on authority and precedent. Nowhere was this more apparent than in the letters of Gregory VII.

None of these simultaneous developments occurred spontaneously; they were intricately dependent on social-historical expansions in Europe. The broadening of the economy, the increase in travel and trade, and the growth of towns provided the social matrix in which these other developments occurred. The massive symbiosis of church and society would be stunningly realized in the appearance of gothic architecture. The cathedral symbolized the Christian vision in stone, and the physical structure "incarnated" a *mythos* for town society. The cathedral united an imaginative portrayal of Christian narrative and doctrine with the economy of the place. The physical church housed believing people as they assembled for liturgy and festival; work and worship were joined; the cathedral established local identity and forged relations with other cathedral towns. But this lies ahead.

The Gregorian Reform

The Gregorian reform, named after its most prominent protagonist, Gregory VII, was roughly coterminous with the second half of the eleventh century. Whether reform or revolution, it was animated from the top as popes confronted secular rulers and European bishops. The half-century teems with legislative acts, symbolic events, and spiritual power plays that in many fundamental ways completely transformed the Western church on a structural level and in its basic outlook. The events here take on significance in the light of the issues, and the issues assume a meaning and importance within the heuristic framework one uses to interpret them.

Interpreting the Gregorian Reform. No single perspective on the Gregorian reform can encompass the full meaning of what happened and why. But distinguishing two different broad interpretations may serve the purposes of an ecclesiology from below: a historicist inter-pretation, not without theological import, and a particular theological interpretation of the logic of the events.

The historian views the Gregorian reform as a change in church administration and organization that was brought about by the so-cial, economic, and political changes in western Europe.[10] The shift in theology and church structure thus bears analogies to the shift that occurred from Cyprian to Augustine. Several factors enter into this point of view. First, one has to see the reform in the context of land, income derived from land, and the legacy of the Carolingian empire. The point of departure is the proprietary church system where own-ership of church and church property is real and uncontested. But this system and paradigmatic way of viewing things was dying and something new was taking its place. Second, in the old system every-one thought that the secular ruler had the responsibility or privilege of filling ecclesiastical office with the right person.[11] The idea was not to give it to the wrong or least qualified person. Henry III began the Gregorian reform out of concern for the church by appointing the right person as pope.[12] Third, in the course of the conflict the church, in the sense of its clerical leaders, sought to protect its prop-erty which it needed in turn to protect its integrity. But the result was a change in a worldview. Earlier divinely appointed rulers and clergy together governed church property in a system that gave each a more or less equal footing. The concept that clergy alone could appoint to church office created a new and different system. Then, fourth, once this paradigm was in place, investiture appeared to be synonymous with simony and the whole practice was treated as an abomination: hence the strong language against it in the latter half of the eleventh century.

---

10. Southern, *Middle Ages*, 118–34.

11. "The king was no ordinary layman. Instead, he was the ruler elected by God, who had not only the right but also the responsibility to intervene in the church, since protection and supervision of the church in the sense of lordship were part of the *ministerium* God had bestowed on him." Blumenthal, *Investiture*, 34.

12. In the common view the lord, like Charlemagne, felt responsible for the church and appointed appropriate bishops, pastors, and chaplains. "No doubt it was wrong to give a church to an unworthy person for money: but it was foolish to give it to a stranger for nothing." In the old system, they were not "selling holy things — they were dealing only with the temporalities attached to holy things." Ibid., 124, 125.

The theological interpretation grew in the course of the Gregorian reform itself around the slogan *libertas ecclesiae.* In this view, what was at stake in the reform most generally was the freedom of the church.[13] The leadership of the church at every level was entangled in secular society. The papacy, an object of contention between the emperor and Roman aristocracy, was unable to exercise its authority across all of Europe. Bishops functioned as temporal feudal lords, or vassals of lords, or administrators who, at worst, had bought their office. Priests outside the cities frequently functioned and lived like serfs, part of someone's private church, ordained peasants who served at subsistence levels. This situation did not reflect a plot of lay rulers nor a planned strategy; as a product of historical development this simply represented the way things were. But the system needed reform at three specific points.

The issues of the reform. Reforming the church overtly revolved around three points. The first was simony, the "sale and purchase of clerical offices, estates, or functions."[14] How widespread this practice was is not clear. In any case, since a bishop was also a temporal ruler, it seemed to many proper that the one assuming temporal rule pay one's lord for the position according to feudal practice.[15] But at the same time, the system clearly put the church's freedom at risk; a bishop was controlled by the lord from whom he bought the office. Moreover the office of the bishop would be easily degraded if positions went to the highest bidder.

A second issue was celibacy which was far from settled in the patristic period. Concubinage and marriage of priests were fairly widespread, and this compromised a long-standing ascetic ideal, despite the fact that it was acceptable behavior in society at the time.

---

13. "Liberty in the Middle Ages could only be conceived in the context of lordship, which was an ideological reference point" (ibid., 51). Royal protection meant liberty of church or monastery from intervention by the aristocracy; papal protection or lordship meant liberty from interfering or land grabbing bishops or nobles, and so on. The ideal of liberty of the reformers thus had layers of meaning from the reclaiming of dominion over church property to the level of freedom to elect men to church ministry on the basis of spiritual and religious criteria.

14. Ibid., 48.

15. Once again, practices differed according to locale. "The *servitium reale* can in no way be compared with the sums of money that were changing hands in the trade of bishoprics or abbeys in the south of France." Ibid., 49.

But the monasteries were setting new standards of Christian life. The monastery provided the model of Christianity for a region. "It was from the monasteries that the countryside learned its religion."[16] Monks thus encouraged reform of the clergy, so that the clergy in turn could have more spiritual leverage on society. Other social issues involving inheritance and alienation of a lord's or a church's property through inheritance to sons complicated things. Lay lords generally preferred to keep priests celibate.

The practice of investiture became the most serious issue of all. Investiture, which had been authorized by popes in the past, involved several compromising elements. The secular ruler appointed the bishop, and only afterward was he approved by the metropolitan and the people. In the ceremony of installation, the ruler received an oath of allegiance in return for the bestowal of the symbols of authority *before* the person was consecrated or ordained bishop. The whole system allowed a secular ruler to retain loyal nonhereditary co-rulers in place over against competitive lay lords or princes whose power increased with hereditary successors. But speaking generally, one should note that the relation between bishops and rulers varied among the regional churches. Thus the investiture controversy and negotiations with Rome took somewhat different forms in Germany, England, and France. Since these issues were systemic, changing them involved upsetting balances of power and elaborate patterns of social behavior.

The reform movement. The Gregorian reform, which left a legacy of fierce struggle between popes and emperors, began in the year 1049 at the instigation of the German emperor Henry III. In that year he appointed a German pope, a relative, Leo IX. Leo brought with him to Rome several able reform-minded men whom he made cardinals, that is, his counselors and administrators. Working with them he condemned the crime or heresy of simony and clerical concubinage and then traveled into Europe to hold local synods and enforce the decrees. He also established a system of legates, resident representatives of the pope with full papal powers. Leo IX died in 1054, the year of the break between the churches of the East and the West. The

---

16. Southern, *Middle Ages*, 158.

zeal for reform and assertion of papal power extended to the East and formalized a breach which lasts to this day despite several attempts to restore unity.

The movement toward reform continued in 1059 when Pope Nicolas II published a decree on the election of the pope. The pope would be elected by the cardinal bishops, supported by the other cardinals, and approved by the clergy and people of Rome. This amounted to a declaration of independence of the papacy from the emperor and the Roman families. In the same year the pope issued a decree condemning the practice of investiture. Another declaration of autonomy, this one proposed a hierarchy of the church free from control by wealthy or powerful rulers.[17] With these decrees the basic ideas of the reform program were in place. The significance of Gregory VII is that he moved the reform ideas into action; he enforced them.

Hildebrand was born between 1020 and 1025 in Tuscany and became a monk. When Leo IX was appointed pope by the emperor in 1049, Hildebrand was the youngest of the reformers whom he brought with him to Rome. He acted as treasurer of the Roman Church and as a papal legate and was influential in the election of his predecessors. In 1073 on the death of the currently reigning pope, Gregory was first elected by popular acclaim in Rome and then canonically.

His twelve years as Pope were marked by his historic struggle with Henry IV of Germany. In this colorful conflict, Gregory VII first gained the upper hand by his excommunication of the king and the suspension of his kingship.[18] But after he lifted the excommu-

---

17. Papal reformers and imperial powers could have cooperated in a struggle against clerical marriage and even simony. But the reform gradually turned into a struggle against lay influence in the church. Cardinal Humbert of Silva Candida, one of the original reformers, was the main theorist and protagonist in this turn: both simony and investiture were seen as usurpation of ecclesiastical prerogatives by lay people. He related simony to secular powers enriching themselves through church property and investiture as a complete reversal of a canonical process of electing bishops. The sources show a more complex picture. Blumenthal, *Investiture*, 87, 89–91.

18. Gregory VII's excommunication and deposition of Henry IV had major symbolic significance. It changed the Gelasian doctrine of two parallel authorities into the supremacy of one over the other. Gregory's act "turned the ancient concept of the duality of church and monarchy upside down, introduced profound changes, and destroyed forever the medieval ideal of the one Christian *res publica*, although Gregory VII himself was still entirely wedded to this concept." Ibid., 124.

nication, the tide turned again toward Henry, and in the end he drove Gregory out of Rome before the latter's death in 1085. But by this time the pattern of autonomous papal leadership had gained a foothold.

What did the Gregorian reform accomplish? Simony was raised to the level of heresy and high crime. The ideal of clerical celibacy was reaffirmed and would be legislated further at the Lateran Councils over the next two centuries. Regarding investiture, however, the reform resulted in a compromise or a *modus vivendi*. The reformers insisted that a secular ruler could not appoint a bishop; he had to be canonically elected by the clergy of the place and received by the people. They were to be consecrated by other bishops with the approval of the metropolitan. The king or ruler could not invest a bishop with authority. A bishop's office was spiritual and thus distinct from lay investiture. All those who were invested by a lay ruler were not legitimate bishops. These reform measures, however, were not and could not have been accepted by any secular ruler, because *in fact* bishops possessed both spiritual and temporal authority. The office had become and remained a position within the civic order and involved temporal rule. Because of the confusion of powers in the person of bishops, the two lines of power could be conflicted, especially relative to property. The bishop was responsible to the church law and obedient to metropolitan and pope; as lord he was responsible to his lay ruler. As far as lay rulers were concerned, to accept the reform measure would be to surrender actual temporal authority to the church.

In the end this conflict was not really settled, but a compromise reached at the Diet of Worms in 1122 allowed the parties to live within a tension of competing interests. In other words, bishops were elected canonically, and rulers continued to influence or determine these elections. The concordat basically managed a reconciliation between emperor Henry V and the papacy. The provisions were as follows: "The emperor renounced investiture with ring and crosier, thus allowing free canonical election and consecration. The pope, in turn, conceded for German bishoprics and abbeys elections in the presence of the king or his representatives. The king had the right to intervene in disputed elections, and most important, the emperor could invest candidates for German sees before consecration with the *regalia* (not defined in the document) of the diocese, using the sceptre instead of ring and crosier."[19]

The Emergence of Christendom

The Gregorian reform provided a basis and a social historical impulse for the creation of Christendom, a unity of church and society throughout Europe. One may qualify the comprehensiveness of this unity in various respects. But even the ongoing rivalry and conflict between *sacerdotium* and *regnum* unfolded under or within a unified religious framework in which all conceded divine authority to rulers. What follows tries to reflect the scope of this synthesis by enumerating several of the institutions that gradually came to reinforce it in the course of the twelfth and thirteenth centuries. A fuller synchronic description of the church will be offered in the third part of the chapter.

The papacy grew stronger with a series of capable popes. The Gregorian reform completely transformed the office of the papacy. Thereafter strong and competent leaders furthered the interests of the church during the twelfth and thirteenth centuries and enhanced the office. The often fierce resistance of secular rulers frequently elicited more resolve on the part of popes.

Toward the end of the reform movement, in 1095, Pope Urban II preached the first crusade, launched to free the holy places from the hands of Islam. Crusades thus began at the end of the eleventh century and continued into the fourteenth. The first crusade caught the religious imagination of the whole of Europe; it both exemplified and solidified a direct, symbolic authority of the pope over the whole Western church. In a way the first crusade was the climax of the Gregorian reform.[20]

---

19. Ibid., 173.

20. Chenu notes that the Old Testament fed the imagination in conceiving of the church as the kingdom of God. Since the church in the New Testament did not provide models for a people of God integrated with the structures of society, it was natural to turn to the Jewish scriptures. A clear case in point were the crusades: "It was clearly in the Old Testament that the crusade, that distinctive enterprise of all Christendom, found its inspiration, its basis, its rules, and all the ambiguities concerning worldly messianism that form a usual part of the imagery of the prophetic books."

The popes continuously exercised their authority by letter and decree. But they also consolidated their power and exercised their authority through councils. The council was a way of legislating in a public way for the whole of Christendom. Four Lateran Councils were held in Rome during the twelfth and early thirteenth centuries; during the rest of the medieval period councils were held outside Rome in various sites for various reasons. Each of the Lateran Councils passed a good deal of general or universal legislation, especially the Fourth Lateran Council in 1215.

Law continually expanded through conciliar legislation and papal decree. And, more generally, law continued to be studied and codified. Interpreting law and reconciling conflicting laws made this study an increasingly complex and significant discipline. More than theologians the canonists mediated the fundamental vision of the church. Law objectified the norms of discipline as they were set in writing and standardized in codes. As the body of law grew, it reached more widely to cover more aspects of life, both narrow ecclesial life and broader social life.

With law arose new offices of administration. The governing of all aspects of the church simply grew and became more complex. The growth of the bureaucracy at the center in some measure reached down the line to dioceses, towns, and monasteries.

By and large society looked to the church as the provider of education. The church thus served as the socializing agency of society through the mediation of general and higher education. This began to shift during the thirteenth century with the growth of cities and the emergence of universities. But church authorities exercised oversight of these universities. Moreover, the church's theology entered a significant new phase with the development of a medieval synthesis that would shape the self-understanding of Christians, especially Catholic Christians, through to the middle of the twentieth century. Added to this was the common language of education, Latin, which served as another bond unifying all of western Europe.

Marie-Dominique Chenu, *Nature, Man, and Society in the Twelfth Century* (Chicago: University of Chicago Press, 1968), 158.

Education as a socializing agency reflected and communicated to the elite the theological grounding of Christian civilization. One looked at the world theocratically and saw it organized hierarchically. The cosmos was understood to be arranged in orders or levels of being that were related in a descending pattern ranging from the higher to the lower. Authority came from the top, from God, and descended as it were through the ranks. For example, theocratic assumptions underlay the fact that both popes and kings justified their authority on the basis of God's will as mediated through revelation.

The Inquisition was organized early in the thirteenth century. It reflected a unified Christian culture where heretics were feared and hunted down within church and society and treated as criminals. The Inquisition was delegated in various places by the center, by the pope, and thus became another arm of papal control. To contradict papal teaching was enough to constitute heresy. Peter Brown's reflection on an earlier culture is apropos: "We should remember that in the late-Roman *quaestio* [inquiry], torture was not an end in itself: it was applied only to gain the truth. The dramatic dialogue between judge and culprit carried with it a sincerity that pain alone could guarantee."[21] Although the Inquisition inspired fear and terror, no public outcry was raised against it. The institution fit into the religious culture and society of the time.

A great expansion of religious life occurred during this period, especially through new foundations of religious orders. The Franciscans and the Dominicans, founded early in the thirteenth century, were apostolic, that is, not stable, isolated, and contemplative but reaching out to people in society with special functions of preaching and ministering in one or another specific way. Even monastic life, although primarily dedicated to God, formed an integral part of society. As institutions, for example, monasteries contributed to society by their agricultural activity and their role in education.

The church functioned principally to minister salvation. The phrase "ministry of salvation" refers to the concrete sacramental ministry of the church to the people. The church through its clergy

---

21. Peter Brown, *The Cult of the Saints: Its Rise and Function in Latin Christianity* (London: SCM Press, 1981), 109.

mediated salvation to each person in society. Troeltsch points to confession and forgiveness of sin as a vehicle of influence on the general populace. Penitential practice became universal during the Middle Ages and consisted in private confession, reconciliation, and an increasingly standardized assigned penance for sins committed. The ability to withhold salvation by excommunication was the bedrock of hierarchical authority.

Art and architecture helped mediate integration of life experience on the imaginative level. The building of churches and cathedrals were town and city projects that occupied people over long periods of time and worked their way into an integrative imaginative framework through social action. The cathedrals were focal points for the economic life of towns.[22]

Chenu describes the contrast between the religious and the scientific imagination which began to arise in the twelfth century concern for nature. He refers to modes of inquiry which sought the causes of things. Science was connected with a discovery of nature as a universal sphere of reality that operated according to laws. Science consisted in fitting things into this pattern of necessity: "It was no longer the extravagant occurrences that interested them, those marvels which entranced their forebears and rapt them into a world all the more real in their eyes for its very capriciousness. On the contrary, they were interested in regular and determinate sequences, especially in the area of vital activity."[23] This interest in explaining things gradually made its way into the area of theology. Chenu traces the evolution of the discipline as practiced by a corps of Masters of Theology who taught in the cathedral schools in the twelfth century. Through them theology gradually became professionalized as they questioned the meaning of sacred texts, found different answers, and developed standardized methods of resolving the conflicts. Interest grew in producing summaries or *summae* of Christian knowledge such as Peter Lombards's *Summa Sententiarum*. The transition from

---

22. J. and F. Gies, *Life in a Medieval City*, 135–53, tell the story of the discovery of the techniques which led to the building of gothic cathedrals and how their building functioned economically and sociologically.

23. Chenu, *Nature, Man, and Society*, 18.

monastic theology to the theology of the universities in the thirteenth century passed through the vital activity of the twelfth.[24]

Aristotle's philosophy fit well with this concern for nature and provided a tool for a new ideological and theological integration of church and world. Aristotle's logic provided a path for reasoning, and then his philosophy of nature and metaphysics at the end of the twelfth century focused attention with new precision to the idea of nature. Aristotle was recovered through contact with the Islamic world, translated into Latin and introduced into the schools and universities that began to be formed around the year 1200.

The thought of Aristotle reflected and enhanced the new mode of thinking. Instead of explaining everything in relation to God, either in a mystical meditative way or on the basis of the authority of revelation, Aristotle explained reality in terms of the intrinsic natures of things. Everything that exists has an inner or intrinsic principle of intelligibility and a way of behaving or operating that is proper to itself, to its nature. The intrinsic nature of things explained why they operated in this way instead of that way. Aristotle thus became the basis for the medieval synthesis developed in the theology of the schools. This theology possessed an objective quality as it sought to understand things "in themselves" through an analysis of their natures and on the basis of the causes which produced them. The writings of Thomas Aquinas provided the grandest example of scholasticism. For Aquinas human nature was a nature, but one that also possessed a capacity for and a dynamism toward completion by God in the supernatural order of revelation and grace. Grace built on and was teleologically integrated into the natural order of reality. Thus the whole Christian dispensation was seen as perfectly responding to, complementing by fitting into, and fulfilling the natural Aristotelian world.[25]

This enumeration of various institutions and aspects of Christian society in the High Middle Ages does not portray the dynamic life of Christians within it. That picture will be sketched further on. But it is enough to differentiate sharply the church of medieval Europe

---

24. Ibid., 270–309.
25. A generalized and abstract treatment of this is provided by Troeltsch from a sociological point of view in *The Social Teaching*, 257–80.

from the church of the empire of late Roman antiquity. The German emperor had coopted the name Roman, but the regions north and west of the Alps provided energy and growth in all areas of church life. The church was bound together by communion with the bishop of Rome who held the whole thing together by symbolic authority and legislated discipline, but increasingly the center of gravity was the whole of Europe with its balance of regional powers. And as the Roman Church became more European, it grew more distant from the Greek Church.

The Greek Church

The foundation of Constantinople by Constantine initiated a process in which the church in the East and the church in the West began to take on distinct identities. Justinian consolidated a Greek Christian culture the spiritual center of which was the Greek Church. This brief description of the Greek Church in the early Middle Ages focuses on Constantinople as distinct from other Eastern churches that remained on an Antiochene or Alexandrian side of the Chalcedonian formula.

The rise and spread of Islam during the seventh and eighth centuries transformed the Roman empire in the East into the Christian empire of Byzantium. Political control of Egypt, Palestine, Syria, and large parts of Turkey were lost to Islam. Christians did not cease to exist under Muslim rule, but over time the people were gradually absorbed into the new Arabic culture and religion. "At the center of a drastically simplified society, Constantinople stood alone. Other cities had become mere fortresses and market-towns. But even Constantinople was a depleted city. Its population had shrunk to around 60,000."[26] It also gradually became isolated from the increasingly autonomous Roman, Latin, European West. After Avars and Slavs began migrating into the Balkan peninsula in the late sixth century, "Illyricum, which used to serve as a bridge, became . . . a barrier between Byzantium and the Latin world."[27] The distinctiveness of this Eastern church can be roughly characterized by three large, temporally

---

26. Brown, *Western Christendom*, 386.
27. Ware, *The Orthodox Church*, 45.

extended events: the iconoclast crisis, the missionary movement, and
the schism between the Eastern and the Western churches.

The Iconoclast crisis (726–843). The iconoclast conflict mirrors
the two sides of the dialectical character of the religious symbol or
sacrament which both points away from itself to the transcendent
reality of the sacred and makes that holy sphere present by embody-
ing it. The iconoclasts were impressed with the transcendence of
God and feared idolatry; iconodules experienced the immanence of
God to the world and reverenced, not adored, sacred images because
of what they stood for. Nevertheless, Emperor Leo III inaugurated
the smashing of images in 726; Empress Irene suspended it fifty five
years later, and the Council of Nicaea II (787) upheld the place of
icons. But a second wave of iconoclasm was ordered by Leo V in 815,
and it lasted until 843 when icons were reinstated permanently.

These bare facts scarcely convey the religious depth of this controversy; some of its results at least point to what was at stake. First
of all, the outcome helped to establish some basic principles in Eastern Christian spirituality. The world of matter, physical reality, is
symbolic; by the incarnation it has been drawn up into the power
of God's salvation so that it can participate in and convey transcendence. Such is the icon. By mystagogy, the drawing of the human
spirit and consciousness into the sphere of transcendence, symbols
can dialectically represent the divine.[28] When the crisis was finally
over, pent up energy was released, and religious art, liturgy, and devotion to relics rekindled spirituality. Moreover, on a political level,
the position of the patriarch vis-à-vis the emperor was strengthened.
After the ninth century the emperors "were no longer in a position
to impose their doctrinal will on the Byzantine Church."[29]

The Greek Orthodox Church refers to itself as the church of the
seven councils, that is, the first seven ecumenical councils whose

---

28. "In former times God, being without form or body, could in no way be represented, but today, since God has appeared in the flesh and lived among men, I can
represent what is visible in God. I do not worship matter, but I worship the creator
of matter who became matter for my sake and who through matter accomplished
my salvation." John of Damascus, *Apology* 1.16, cited by Binns, *Christian Orthodox
Churches*, 101–2.

29. Meyendorff, *The Orthodox Church*, 23.

last was Nicaea II; in them the foundational ecclesiology, spirituality, and "doctrines of the faith were set out and accepted by the
western as well as the eastern parts of the church."[30] A summary
of some of those basic principles will help to underline its unique
character, especially in relationship to the Western church. First, and
almost presupposed as basic and essential, are ecclesiological principles drawn from Ignatius of Antioch and Cyprian before Nicaea
(325): with respect to the one, the centrality of the bishop in each
local church, his role as eucharistic minister, and the central place
of the eucharist in constituting the church community; with respect
to the other, the unity of the episcopate, the regular assembly of the
bishops of a region in synod, and the communication among bishops broadly. Second, the doctrinal content of the councils define the
central beliefs underlying this ecclesiology: the person and nature of
Jesus Christ as incarnate Son of God; the divine Spirit at work in
the church at large and animating its synodal gatherings; the doctrine of the trinity as expressed in the Nicene creed of the Council
of Constantinople (381). Third, conciliar canons establish the five
patriarchs which the church thought of as "constituting a Pentarchy.
The five patriarchs were invested with a kind of collective primacy
in the church and consecrated the metropolitans in their respective
areas."[31] Of the five patriarchates, however, Rome enjoyed a primacy
understood not in terms of power or jurisdiction but more vaguely
as a trusted court of appeal. One can perceive in these broad principles a church whose primal unit is constituted by the bishop and
whose overall unity is defined less by juridical bonds than by synodal
gatherings and trust in the Spirit working within them. Fourth, the
church encompassed the whole of life, and "there was no rigid line
of separation between the religious and the secular, between Church

---

30. Binns, *Christian Orthodox Churches*, 62. "The Orthodox regard the period of
the ecumenical councils as a *normative* period. It was then, by and large, that the
dogmatic and canonical norms of the Orthodox faith were laid down, as we know
them today...." Meyendorff, *The Orthodox Church*, 31–32.

31. Ibid., 64. "The five patriarchates between them divided into spheres of jurisdiction the whole of the known world, apart from Cyprus, which was granted
independence by the Council of Ephesus and thus remained self-governing ever since."
Ware, *The Orthodox Church*, 26–27. Pentarchy was not conceived against Rome;
rather it "translated the sense of church in the East, collegial and synodal, a form
of communion of the churches singing the same note." Congar, *L'Eglise*, 79.

and State: the two were seen as parts of a single organism. Hence it was inevitable that the emperor played an active part in the affairs of the church."[32] During these early centuries the balance between these two distinct powers, temporal and spiritual, oscillated between patriarch and emperor.

The missionary movement. The missionary movement, begun effectively with the work of Cyril and Methodius in the 860s, provided another defining moment in the development of the Greek Church. The story is simple, the effects profound and lasting. Moravia petitioned Constantinople to send missionaries who could carry the Christian message to the area in a language understood by the people. Constantine, who took the name Cyril at the end of his life, and his brother Methodius, raised in Thessalonica, knew a Macedonian brand of the Slav language. Along with it they created an alphabet and translated gospel passages and the liturgy into what would become "Church Slavonic." Although in the end the Moravian mission was undercut by German missionaries who introduced the Latin rite, the disciples of Cyril and Methodius turned to Bulgaria where they replaced the Greek language, unintelligible to the Bulgars, with Slavonic forms. The mission took off.

The spread of a combination of Byzantine, Slavic, and indigenous Christianity in Serbia and Russia was analogous to that of Bulgaria.[33] The Bulgarian Church enjoyed a patriarch beginning in 927 and became autocephalous in 1235; the archbishop of the Serbian Church was autocephalous in 1219 and became a patriarch in 1346. The conversion of Russia, after tentative steps in the ninth and early tenth centuries, leapt forward when, around 988, Prince Vladimir of Kiev (980–1015) "was converted to Christianity and married Anna, the sister of the Byzantine Emperor. Orthodoxy became the State religion of Russia, and...Vladimir set to in earnest to Christianize his realm: priests, relics, sacred vessels, and icons were imported; mass baptisms were held in the rivers; church courts were set up, and ecclesiastical tithes were instituted."[34] The Russian Church became

---

32. Ware, *The Orthodox Church*, 40–41.
33. Dimitri Obolensky, in Knowles, *The Middle Ages*, 302–18, provides a brief account of the formation of the Bulgarian, Serbian, and Russian Churches.
34. Ware, *The Orthodox Church*, 78.

autonomous in 1448, a patriarchate in 1589. The significance of the work of Cyril and Methodius far transcends their immediate results: they were responsible for introducing a whole linguistic group into Christian sources and provided the foundations for their medieval culture;[35] they symbolize the universal relevance of the Christian church by its inculturation into particular historical churches thus creating the possibility of a pluralistic family of churches.

The East-West schism. The schism between the Eastern and the Western church should not be understood to have occurred in the mutual excommunications that ended the mission of Cardinal Humbert to the Patriarch of Constantinople, Michael Cerularius, in 1054. That event was only one factor in a much longer and larger story involving cultural, political, and theological factors. For example, the formula, *Filioque,* was first added to the Nicene Creed in Spain to counteract Arian tendencies in Visigothic Christianity; from there it infiltrated France and Italy. Charlemagne made much of it and pressed the point against the Greek Church. But "Popes Hadrian I (772–95) and Leo III (795–816) defended the Council of Nicaea and formally rejected the interpolation in the Creed."[36] Next, a dispute between Patriarch Photius and Pope Nicholas I during the 860s involved two theological issues: the universal jurisdiction of the pope implied in his ability to decide by his own authority between two contending claimants to the patriarchal office, and the formula *Filioque* which German missionaries were bringing into Bulgaria prior to the mission of the Greeks. This dispute was resolved by events, but it placed the two main theological issues on the table. Evidence shows that Rome began to adopt the *Filioque* in the early eleventh century in its liturgy and that this was noticed by the Greek Church. And the failed mission of 1054, which was also politically motivated, did not help relations between the Greek and the Roman churches. But few today doubt that it took the sack of Constantinople in 1204 by Crusaders finally to seal the breach between the two churches:

---

35. Obolensky, "Cyril and Methodius and the Moravian Mission," in Knowles, *The Middle Ages,* 25.

36. Meyendorff, *The Orthodox Church,* 43.

"Eastern Christendom has never forgotten those three appalling days of pillage."[37]

In the end, however, many think that, although the schism is complicated by all sorts of political and cultural difficulties, the fundamental problem remains theological: "theological causes are at the root of the matter because all attempts at conciliation and reunion have been frustrated by the failure to overcome these hurdles."[38] These theological problems can be reduced to two: the theology of the Holy Spirit represented by the unilateral interpolation into the Nicene Creed of the *Filioque,* and the theological conception of the church's nature and structure. The difference in ecclesiologies can be seen in the contrast between a pope with universal jurisdiction and a combination of patriarchal superstructure with an episcopal and synodal communion ecclesiology analogous to that found in Cyprian.

SOCIAL AND THEOLOGICAL ANALYSIS

The brief commentary on the historical development of the church during the first half of the Middle Ages provides an outer face of the life within. The analysis now shifts to interpretation of some key figures as they appear in texts from the period. These figures are witnesses to what was going on around them. They are in some measure representative: while others could be chosen, these persons and texts entered into the historical construction of the church. They reflect a great variety of influences at diverse levels. Gregory VII was a pope who so carried forward the reform of the church in the eleventh century that he gave his name to the movement; legislative councils of the period institutionalized the order of the medieval church; Pseudo-Dionysius was a much earlier figure who, upon retrieval, helped shape the imaginative framework of the self-understanding of the whole church; Bernard of Clairvaux exemplified the role of monasticism in the age as he crystallized basic spiritual values that should have grounded the operation of the church from top to bottom; Francis revived and in some respect crystallized a revolutionary development in the spirituality of the church; Thomas Aquinas stood at

37. Ware, *The Orthodox Church,* 60.
38. Meyendorff, *The Orthodox Church,* 40–41.

the summit of the university theologians who articulated a synthetic and integrating understanding of the world of Christendom.

Gregory VII

Reading the letters of popes in order to understand the church in a certain period mixes in a unique way dimensions of ecclesiology from above and from below.[39] On the one hand, one witnesses at a literary first hand the exercise of authority and power from above. Many of the documents are executive papal directives. On the other hand, one enters into this world through the subjectivity and the experience of the one exercising this power and authority. The letters give an intimate internal view of the working of the church though the man who as pope was trying to gain control over the whole Western church. Gregory VII's letters reflect a global view of what is going on in Christendom. As in the case of Gregory I the range of issues to which Gregory VII attends is astonishing: from a decree deposing the king of Germany to trying to straighten out the marriage of a knight that appealed to him in Rome. The scope of persons, positions, subject matter, and concerns that Gregory dealt with gives an insight into the litigious character of medieval Europe and the complexity of the administrative bureaucracy or curia of the Roman Church.

What can be said of the person of Gregory? In a sense this is irrelevant to ecclesiology, but few can resist taking a position on Gregory's character. At the two extremes, he is viewed as either a power-hungry temporal ruler or a religiously driven saint. Others try to unite the two extremes in a composite picture.[40] Some personal qualities are reflected in the letters. He gives spiritual and pious exhortation. He complains at the burden of his office and has feelings of inadequacy even while he is taking on the leaders of the whole of Western society. He is pessimistic about the world and about the church itself in its members. In all his actions one sees a basic fairness; in some cases he allows legates to be open to the reality of the local situation and

---

39. The letters of Gregory VII that provide the basis of the synthetic account which follows are found in *The Correspondence of Pope Gregory VII: Selected Letters from the Registrum*, ed. and trans. Ephraim Emerton (New York: Columbia University Press, 1932) and *The Epistolae Vagantes of Pope Gregory VII*, ed. and trans. H. E. J. Cowdrey (Oxford: Clarendon Press, 1972).

40. For example, Tierney, *Crisis*, 46, and Knowles, *The Middle Ages*, 177–78.

shows a willingness to hear arguments that might justify seeming disobedience, but generally he valued uniformity. The human being often shines through the autocrat. Thus in judging both the man and the office it will be important to enter into his world and concede the fact that Gregory believed what he said. The following account of the content of Gregory's letters according to various themes aims at characterizing the exercise of controlling authority by the man at the top of a hierarchical structure and the conception of the church that is implicit in them.

The political relation of the church to the secular world. The letters show the church and especially the papacy as not only deeply involved in affairs of state, but as being a commanding authority. Gregory writes to distant kingdoms claiming authority over Christian lands which are bound by loyalty to the Apostolic See. The Roman Church contains the single uniting authority over all of Europe. Gregory also exercises military authority; he organizes military power to solve political and religious problems. He elicits a desire to conquer the East militarily and subject this church to papal rule. Gregory urges bishops to call kings or temporal rulers to account. The church is free, and in moral issues its loyalty to kings should not prevent it from correcting the abuses of kings.

More strikingly, Gregory threatens kings with deposition and actually deposes Henry IV. His arguments for this authority are found in a letter to Bishop Hermann of Metz.[41] Ultimately the logic is quite simple: the supposition for the view is the unity of Christendom, one single and integrated Christian society. This society contains two spheres of rule, temporal and spiritual. But intrinsically the spiritual and religious sphere is superior to the temporal. Therefore the temporal is subordinate to the spiritual.[42] This logical argument finds backing in the order of God as stated in scripture. Gregory understands the power to bind and loose given to Peter as applying to the whole sphere of history and society, both temporal and spiritual. The

---

41. This letter is found in Emerton, *Correspondence*, 166–75. A portion of the letter along with others in the exchange with Henry IV and a commentary is presented by Tierney, *Crisis*, 53–73.

42. It is often noted that the error lies here: higher does not imply subordination, for the two could exist in parallel, as in the Gelasian teaching.

whole of society then is to be governed by God's law. Peter, the pope, is the highest authority, and all Christians owe him obedience. The pope can depose a king if the king is disobedient to papal authority.

The church and society. The theme of the relation of the church to society is not the subject of any particular letter of Gregory, but the supposition, the horizon, and the background of all of them. Put simply, the church suffuses society. The church is a religious society, and Christian Europe constitutes the one church. Prior to the Gregorian reform the church may have been collapsed into social patterns in a way that compromised the spiritual character of ecclesial leaders. Bishops were temporal rulers; priests were vassals of temporal lords. Gregory now presupposes the spiritual freedom and integrity of the church and its God-given spiritual and moral control over all social relationships.

Church organization. At least in its most general structure church organization consisted in a hierarchical society. The pope was at the top in a centralized position of authority with an administrative curia. A body of cardinals now made up an upper level administrative staff and the bishops among them were the electors of the pope. There were local archbishops in major centers and bishops dependent on them in the smaller cities. Priests ordained by bishops were dependent on them. Then there were the monasteries, dependent on or autonomous from the bishop and obedient to a higher office. Most important for holding the whole thing together was the system of legates in various regions who regularly communicated back to Rome and acted in place with the authority of the pope.

The structure of church authority. One of the most interesting aspects of the letters lies in the structure and extent of Gregory's authority and the various ways in which he exercised it. One should note some of the suppositions of papal authority. First of all, the church was one. There was only one church, and unity here tended to translate into uniformity. The letters show Gregory's insistence on uniformity. Second, the church was governed by law. The traditions of law went all the way back to the primitive manuals. Third, the pope was the supreme authority. In fact, the whole church of the West was governed by the pope in a way that a bishop in the third century governed a local church. Gregory enforced this in the Western church in an unprecedented manner. Fourth, there was no salvation outside the church. Unity with the pope defined unity within the church on which salvation depended. Fifth, therefore, the power to excommunicate was the pope's ultimate weapon and lever of power. He wielded spiritual power that concerned one's salvation. These are not merely Gregory's suppositions but the shared beliefs of the whole church of the West.

   The extent of papal authority. What were the claims of the pope? These are found in the document called the *Dictatus Papae* in the form of a short list of propositions.[43] They are generally accepted as expressing Gregory's thought. All were more or less "traditional," except the power to depose emperors and kings. But the power of the document consists in the placing together in a terse direct form a whole series of scattered claims from different times. Together the propositions add up to something close to absolute authority over church and ultimately society. It should not be assumed, however, that all of these claims were universally accepted.

   The method of governing. Fundamentally Gregory governed by legislation, the issuing of decrees; he appealed to the traditions and precedents of past law, and he created new law. His law was universally binding because he had universal governing power. He had a staff. "The pope's chief assistants were the cardinals who included at this time (1073) seven bishops, twenty-eight priests, eighteen deacons and possibly twenty-one subdeacons."[44] His two tools of government were the local council and legates. Councils were held twice a year, during the first week of Lent and, when that was not sufficient, again in November. With a system of legates, especially the legate at large with plenipotentiary power, he brought the system to the problems themselves.[45]

   The letters show how he enforced the law. He would personally rebuke bishops or summon them to Rome to appear before his synod. In cases of overt disobedience he would threaten excommunication and finally would actually excommunicate. He would appeal to bishops against princes, and to princes against bishops, and to clergy

---

43. Tierney, *Crisis*, 49–50.
44. Southern, *Middle Ages*, 143.
45. Ibid., 145–51.

and the people against bishops. He would release people from oaths of fealty. He would threaten with excommunication those who supported an already excommunicated bishop, or those who assisted at the services of a noncelibate priest. In one letter Gregory granted general remission of sins to all those faithful to Rome against a rival bishop.[46] At other times Gregory governed by appeal to the ordinary lord-vassal or feudal contract, or through personal appeal. Often one sees a combination of personal appeal and official authority. What was the scope of Gregory's authority? Put most simply, it extended to every imaginable area of life.

Finally, popes summoned councils. In the twelfth and thirteenth centuries they assembled six.

Councils of the High Middle Ages

The six councils of the High Middle Ages were Lateran I (1123), Lateran II (1139), Lateran III (1179), Lateran IV (1215), Lyons I (1245) and Lyons II (1274). Together they provide a certain window into the dynamics of church life. That does not mean that the laws enacted by these councils were immediately translated into actual practice; a good portion of this legislation was ignored by many, or followed in partial or irregular ways in different places. One sees in these documents, therefore, not a description of church life on the ground, but the way in which law and legislated systems grew to form a legally structured organization or society. Once on the books, the conciliar legislation enshrined ideals, provided rules for resolving cases or problems as they arose, and helped to fashion the ethics of the church. One can also get a glimpse of some of the problematic aspects of church life, as through a photographic negative, at least at a formal level and without any statistical idea of how prevalent the abuses might be.

Most of the conciliar legislation was disciplinary. Virtually everyone in western Europe north of Spain except Jews were members of the church, so that conciliar legislation affected all. The hierarchical structure of offices in the church was fundamentally in place and legislation touched on all ranks. In the early twelfth century the

---

46. Emerton, *Correspondence*, 134.

conciliar legislation tended to strengthen the gains of the Gregorian reform; by Lateran IV, the whole range of life in church and society was in view. A growing complexification of law and official juridical procedure appears right on the surface of the canons.[47] Yet the laws codify the social dynamics of life in the church. This descriptive report on the church as seen through these councils is organized into three areas: first, the various memberships of the church regulated by the canons; second, the more general relation between church and society that is reflected there; and, third, the mission and goal of the church as it appears functionally in these councils.

On various functions in the church. The issues around which the Gregorian reform turned continued to be addressed during the twelfth and right into the thirteenth century. The analysis here aims at capturing how the ideals of the reform were solidified within the organic institutional life of the church through legislation that touched various persons or groups.

On the pope. During the course of the twelfth and thirteenth centuries the process of electing a pope was refined. Some think that at Lateran II the role of electing the pope was restricted to the cardinals, thus eliminating the ratifying role of the lower clergy and people of Rome that was also stipulated in 1059.[48] Lateran III then decreed that a valid papal election required a two-thirds majority of the electors present (c. 1). But that could at times be difficult to achieve, and prior to the election of Gregory X in 1272 the office was vacant for two years and nine months. Thus Lyons II instituted the conclave which virtually locked the cardinal bishops up until they did their duty, gradually cutting back on their food if they took too long (c. 2).

---

47. For example, Lateran IV, canon 8 lays down three procedures which can be undertaken in order to redress or have recourse against clerics who abuse their power or otherwise break the law. These are "accusation," or the bringing of official written complaints to superiors, "denunciation," or (after private admonition) the making known of a crime to the superior, and "inquiry," or an investigation based on complaints. "Till the French Revolution this decree was of considerable importance in both ecclesiastical and civil criminal law." H. J. Schroeder, *Disciplinary Decrees of the General Councils* (St. Louis: B. Herder, 1937), 250, commenting on the canon in question, 248–50. Reference to the canonical decrees of the councils in the text by council and canon are to this work.

48. Schroeder, *Disciplinary Decrees*, 196.

On bishops. The councils loosely protected the office of bishop from unqualified men by various regulations. A man had to be thirty years old to be elected bishop, and had to receive orders within a certain period of time after election. Bishops were forbidden from taxing excessively and even their entourages were regulated lest too many horses during a visitation cause an impossible burden on the visited community (Lat III, cc. 2–4). Lateran IV urged that bishops initiate reform in their own offices and in the general morals of their subjects (c. 7). The same council showed a certain concern over episcopal elections: it warned that secular interference would render an election void and warned against unworthy candidates. This legislation does not describe general practice for some centuries to come.

On priests. Lateran I continued the struggle for the freedom of priests and their tithes from lay control: all assignments of priests had to have episcopal approval (Lat I, c. 18; Lat III, c. 19). Priests are not to receive a church from a lay person (Lat III, c. 14). Celibacy is reaffirmed, with a citation of Nicaea, and marriage and concubinage are forbidden: it is unbecoming that a cleric be associated with "marriage" or "impurities." The laity are urged to shun masses of priests associated with women (Lat I, cc. 3, 21; Lat II, cc 6, 7; Lat IV, c. 14). Sons of clerics are barred from the priesthood (Lat II, c. 21). Simony relative to priestly office and ministries continues to be condemned (Lat III, c. 7). A priest should only care for a plurality of churches and ecclesiastical titles by dispensation (Lat III, c. 13; Lyons II, c. 18).[49]

Lateran III decreed that no one should be ordained without a title to some income unless he had means of his own (c. 5). Edward Schillebeeckx sees in this canon the influence of a momentous shift that was occurring in the understanding and practice of priesthood: away from ordination into and on the basis of attachment to and leadership of a community toward "absolute" ordination, i.e., independence from a concrete community. The perception depends on a feudal context, the movement away from proprietary churches, and is reflected in the general problem of vagrant priests. The canon in question does not positively affirm absolute ordination, but it fails

---

49. The abuse did not consist in overwork due to shortage of priests but in an accumulation of wealth due to avarice.

to uphold Nicaea against the prevailing drift toward absolute ordination.[50] This trend was supported by theologies of the eucharist and a priesthood defined by reception of a sacred power to consecrate.[51]

Lateran IV contained a series of decrees regulating the life of the priest, from a screening of candidates to a whole series of activities that were unbecoming the priest, such as frequenting taverns, hunting, gaming, carousing, and finally to ways of suspending unworthy priests through provincial synods (Lat IV, cc. 15–20, 27–31). Decrees such as these may be taken as providing by contrast some indication of possible patterns of behavior more or less prevalent in the villages and towns. Lyons II decreed that a priest must be at least twenty-five years old and have the proper knowledge and morals (c. 13).

On monasteries and monks. One cannot exaggerate the role of monasticism in the development of the church in the Middle Ages: monasteries prepared leaders of the church, helped in the development of rural Europe, and provided a religious centering in many areas. The rise of the Dominicans and Franciscans in the thirteenth century correlated with the growth of towns and cities and the general increase in mobility. Monasticism in many ways constituted a religious system parallel to the episcopal and diocesan government, especially when monasteries possessed some autonomy or exemption from episcopal control, and this set up the possibility of a tension between authorities or influences that could be either creative or unproductive. This tension is represented in some of the conciliar legislation, but it is systemic and lasts to this day.

Two major legislative moves occurred during the course of the thirteenth century. Lateran IV stated that "we strictly forbid anyone in the future to found a new order" (c. 13). The background for this was a proliferation of religious groups which required no official approval. But shortly after Lateran IV, first the Dominicans and

---

50. Nicaea, c. 15, and the Council of Arles before that in 314, legislated that bishops, priests, and deacons should not move from one city or church to another. They had a spiritual bond to the community for which they were ordained.

51. Edward Schillebeeckx, *Ministry: Leadership in the Community of Jesus Christ* (New York: Crossroad, 1981), 52–58. Lat IV, c. 1 contains a creed in which the notion of transubstantiation first appears in a conciliar document. Ordination to the priesthood conferred the power to effect this transubstantiation of bread and wine into the body and blood of Christ.

then the Franciscans were officially recognized by the Rome.[52] At Lyons II mendicant orders founded after Lateran IV which had not been officially approved by the pope were abolished, and those which were approved were not to receive new members but left to die out. The constitution spared the Dominicans, Franciscans, Carmelites, and Augustinians (c. 23). The decree reflects the tension between religious orders and the more direct line of episcopal authority.

On the laity. A good part of conciliar legislation directed toward the laity carried forward the effort at freeing church office and property from any lay control. Thus all churches and church tithes were to be returned to bishops, even if they had been given to lay people. "We command also that laymen who hold churches shall either return them to the bishops or incur excommunication" (Lat II, c. 10). No one was to claim through heredity any "churches, prebends, deaneries, chaplaincies, or any ecclesiastical offices" (Lat II, c. 16). In general, all alienation of church property by laypeople without legitimate sanction was forbidden (Lat IV, c. 44; Lyons II, c. 22). Secular rulers were not allowed to grab the revenues of churches or monasteries during transitions of leadership (Lyons II, c. 12). More positive concern for laity appears in the following considerations of the impact of the church on society.

The relation of church and society. The conciliar legislation of this period reflects the distinctive relationship between church and society during the Middle Ages. From the perspective of the institutional history of Europe the period is famous for the battle of the popes, and sometimes bishops, against emperors, kings, and secular rulers. But from the general perspective of society and culture, church and society appeared to be simply one. Unlike emperors, these councils legislated for all of Europe. This is not to suggest that everyone accepted church legislation without murmur. But the decrees reflect the symbiosis on three distinct levels: public spirituality, the social order, and the broadest sphere of an appeal for the common action of a united Christendom.

---

52. Strictly speaking Lateran IV legislation tried to prevent the proliferation of religious rules. The Franciscans argued that Francis's first rule was approved earlier by Innocent III, and the Dominicans argued that their's was the rule of St. Augustine and thus not new.

Beginning with the stage of public spirituality, the real impact of the church occurred within the churches at the liturgies in the rural communities and towns. The councils reached this grass roots level by urging a general reanimation of the faith of Christendom and charging bishops to preach, instruct the people, and make sure that the sacraments were being administered (Lat IV, c. 10). Lateran IV legislated yearly confession and communion (c. 21). It also regulated preaching, oversaw various aspects of popular piety such as the use of relics and the granting of indulgences, and protected against simony (cc. 62–63). The church was where people came together, and Lyons II decreed basic decorum: entrance into churches should be humble and devout. "Where the divine services are celebrated with peace and quiet, let no one create disturbance, excite commotion, or commit violence" (c. 25). The imagination can reconstruct the scenes that elicited this legislation.

The impact of the church on society was basic and extensive. In a society marked by some violence, the church was an instrument of law and order in legislating the "truce of God," which many lay rulers helped enforce by assuming responsibility as guarantors of safe travel in their territories. Church laws promoted protection from bodily harm of clerics, innocent travelers, and those going to market. Excommunication was used to curtail fighting and banditry (Lat II, c. 12; Lat III, c. 21–22). The church also tried to outlaw popular tournaments (Lat II, c. 14; Lat III, c. 20). It forbade marriages within certain degrees of blood relations (Lat II, c. 17; Lat IV, c. 50). It proposed severe penalties on arson, a common and devastating means of destroying an enemy (Lat II, cc. 18–20). It frequently condemned usury or lending money at interest (Lat II, c. 13; Lyons II, cc. 26–27). It promoted education in cathedrals, monasteries, and all the churches, and encouraged free education for clerics and for the poor (Lat III, c. 18; Lat IV, c. 11).

On the larger level of the ability of the church to channel the course of European life, both of the councils of Lyons contained extensive deliberation and provision for another crusade to the Holy Land (Lyons I, c. 18; Lyons II, c. 32). Lyons II was called at least in part to forge a reunion with the Greek Church. Even though both of these projects ultimately failed, it exemplified the ability of the church to commit all of Europe to a common project not as an outside authority but drawing on a common Christian identity.

The functional mission of the church. How might one characterize the mission and goal of the church in functional terms on the basis of these six councils of the twelfth and thirteenth centuries? The mission has a number of dimensions to it. First and foremost the mission of the church that is implicit but unstated in these councils takes form in the daily and weekly religious activity of the parishes and monastic communities. The church provided the media of salvation in its liturgical assemblies, sacraments, and general parochial life. All the superstructure functions relative to this; organization has its ultimate telos in leading people to the salvation of eternal life. Second, the church also sought to preserve the message of the faith. Lateran II reaffirmed an earlier synodal condemnation of a specific heresy (c. 23). And Lateran IV begins with a fairly elaborate creed and a short catechetical treatise on the trinity (cc. 1–2). Third, the church acted as the conscience of society, the preserver of morals, the guardian of values, and even an enforcer of law and order under the threat of religious sanction. The church was the spiritual regulator of social order as canon law spilled over into the general functioning of society. And, finally, the church drew the boundaries between Christendom and non-Christians. It provided legislation that aggressively marginalized the Jews and aimed crusades at driving back the Saracens (Lat IV, cc. 67–69).

We pass now to a set of texts which were influential in shaping the cosmic worldview which contained and in some measure justified or legitimated this practical legislation.

Dionysius the Areopagite

Luke says that after Paul preached in Athens a certain Dionysius the Areopagite believed, and a late fifth and early sixth-century Greek author, perhaps a Syrian monk, wrote a series of mystical works in his name. Pseudo-Dionysius had an impact on John Damascene's support of the use of icons; he was translated into Latin by John Scotus Eriugena in the mid-ninth century and again in the early thirteenth by Robert Grosseteste. Dionysius was read in the twelfth and thirteenth centuries and had a significant influence in the areas of mysticism, spirituality, epistemology, church, and society.[53] These texts, then, are read with a medieval eye and in the context of the period after the Gregorian reform, which included the unity of church and society, a more or less stable sacramental system in rural, town, and city churches, and a hierarchical ordering of the church. If the question was, what would such a hierarchical ordering of church and society have meant?, Dionysius provided an answer that influenced many. This section lays that out briefly in terms of what a hierarchy is, how it is structured, and what it does.[54]

Dionysius defines a hierarchy as "a sacred order, a state of understanding and an activity approximating as closely as possible to the divine. And it is uplifted to the imitation of God in proportion to the enlightenment" (CH, 153). Hierarchy is an ordered arrangement of tasks and duties and functions and orders or levels of reality and understanding. In these orders each member imitates God and as far as possible becomes a fellow worker with or for God according to specific differentiated roles: some are purified and some purify; some receive illumination and some cause it; some are perfected and some bring it about. Thus members actually imitate God in the way that is suitable to their role (CH, 154). But these characterizations of hierarchy fall short of the range of the term. Hierarchy for Dionysius is an analogous concept with plural applications that enjoy a common character.

Every hierarchy has a threefold structure: "the most sacred operation of the sacraments, the godlike dispensers of the sacred things,

---

53. Chenu specifies how study of pseudo-Dionysius became quite intense in the second third of the twelfth century. Three aspects of his works were especially influential: the hierarchical structure of reality, the symbolic structure of reality, and the theme of negative knowledge of God (Chenu, *Nature, Man, and Society*, 80). The notion of "hierarchy" is especially important as a background theory whose influence is all pervasive. "From the middle of the century on, the 'hierarchical' conception of the universe would cast over men's minds a spell comparable to that cast by the scientific *mythos* of evolution in the nineteenth century. The key to the understanding of the universe, and of man in the universe, was taken to be the ordered, dynamic, and progressive chain of all beings — a chain in which causality and meaning fall together, and in which each being is a 'theophany,' a revelation of God. . . . " Ibid., 23.

54. References to Dionysius are to *Pseudo-Dionysius: The Complete Works*, trans. Colm Luibheid (New York: Paulist Press, 1987). I draw mainly from *The Celestial Hierarchy* and *The Ecclesiastical Hierarchy* which will be cited as CH and EH respectively with reference to pages in the Paulist edition.

and those guided by them, according to capacity, toward the sacred" (EH, 235). This view of earthly hierarchy thus revolves around sacraments: there are (a) sacraments, (b) those who are inspired by God to understand and administer them, and (c) those who are initiated into their sacred mystery (EH, 233).[55] Moreover, each of these three members of a hierarchy are themselves differentiated in a threefold manner. Sacraments, for example, each have three powers or dimensions. The sacrament purifies, it illumines and initiates those who are purified, and it perfects those who receive it (EH, 235).[56]

Those who administer the sacraments form a threefold hierarchy differentiated by function and rank: the highest order is the hierarch, who is as it were the keystone of the arch, for the other orders descend through him by the power of consecration and are perfected by him (EH, 236–37). The term "hierarch" refers to "a holy and inspired man, someone who understands all sacred knowledge, someone in whom an entire hierarchy is completely perfected and known" (EH, 197).[57] The order of priests is light-bearing and illuminating; it guides initiates and makes known the works of God by explaining and leading into contemplation (EH, 237). The role of deacons is to purify. The order of deacons "has the task of purification and it uplifts those who have been purified to the clear sacred acts of the priests" (EH, 238). This threefold order thus represents symbolically and mediates the threefold activity of God: purifying, illuminating, and perfecting. The threefold division thus provides "an image of the ordered and harmonious nature of the divine activities" (EH, 238; also 239).

Those who enter the orders of clerical ministry also make up a threefold hierarchy. Lowest are those who remain at the level of purification. The middle order are those who share in the sacred vision and are thus illumined and contemplative. "The order of those made perfect is that of the monks who live a single-minded life. Thus, our

---

55. There is also a threefold structure in the celestial hierarchy, but it consists in three groups of higher beings and does not revolve around sacraments.

56. Also, the different sacraments can be understood and classified according to their predominate functions of purifying, illuminating, or perfecting.

57. At this point the hierarch is synonymous with the bishop. But bishops are never mentioned, nor is there reference to the church. In the mind of the author, church may exemplify hierarchy, but hierarchy is understood in a broader philosophical, epistemological, and religious framework.

own hierarchy is blessedly and harmoniously divided into orders in accordance with divine revelation and therefore displays the same sequence as the hierarchies of heaven" (EH, 248).

The payoff of Dionysius's elaborate vision lies in the role and function of hierarchy, what hierarchy does. The triune God is the source of hierarchy, and its goal or purpose is to communicate salvation to rational beings through a process of divinization that is extended through the hierarchy. The divinization of the saved consists in becoming like God and being united with God (EH, 198). God "has bestowed hierarchy as a gift to ensure the salvation and divinization of every being endowed with reason and intelligence" (EH, 198). The whole point of hierarchy, then, is economy, the divine process of mediating God's saving power in heaven and on earth. The hierarch cooperates with God in mediating God's threefold saving activity of purifying, illuminating, and perfecting (CH, 155).

On earth, this saving process unfolds by way of symbolic mediation. Symbols are images or realities within the sphere of the perceptible by which rational creatures are uplifted into the sphere of the divine (EH, 234). The heavenly hierarchy is superior, higher, incorporeal, not perceptible, but transcendent and conceptual. Hierarchy in this world is perceptible and given in a plurality of forms. These perceptible forms are symbolic because they lift us upward toward and into the unity of the divine sphere. They are mystagogic, that is, they lead or draw one into divine mystery. For humans beings on earth "it is by way of the perceptible images that we are uplifted as far as we can be to the contemplation of what is divine" (EH, 197). A platonic distinction between above and below, between the divine and the creaturely, accounts for the need of symbolic mediation, and hierarchy functions as the great medium or structure of symbolic media. This is not a dichotomy but a bridge precisely because of the symbolic mediation and economy of hierarchy. The hierarchy of this world is "symbolic and adapted to what we are. In a divine fashion it needs perceptible things to lift us up into the domain of conceptions" (EH, 199).

It is important to take cognizance of the level at which Dionysius makes his proposal. This is not in the first instance ecclesiology, even though it was seen to fit most congenially with the church after the Gregorian reform. This is a platonic vision of reality in terms of the Christian imagination and economy of salvation. The vision is conceived in cosmological and epistemological terms.[58] Hierarchies are not static structures but dynamic; they do not represent, they function. Hierarchies are structures of symbols and offices that mediate God's world and draw people back to God. Through the initiative of God the earthly becomes symbolic of the heavenly, the transcendent, the divine. The cathedral of Chartres shows that the people who built it knew exactly what Dionysius was talking about. And Bonaventure's description of Holy Orders in the mid-thirteenth century shows how this metaphysical imagination was applied to ecclesiastical thinking: the power of orders is ranked; power over power is higher and more excellent; perfection of power exists in those who can confer power on others. "And because excellence is diluted as it descends and is unified as it ascends, there are many bishops, fewer archbishops, and very few patriarchs, and one father of fathers who is rightly called pope, the one, first and greatest spiritual father of all fathers, and on the other hand of all the faithful, the distinguished hierarch, the single spouse, undivided head, highest pontiff, vicar of Christ, fountain, origin, and ruler of all ecclesiastical principalities. From him, the highest of all, ordained power is derived even down to the lowest member of the church as the great dignity in the ecclesiastical hierarchy requires."[59]

Bernard of Clairvaux

Bernard of Clairvaux was a monk and a mystic, abbot and founder of monasteries, counselor of kings and popes, theologian and spiritual

---

58. Dionysius the Areopagite's viewpoint "is completely dominated by the quest for spiritual knowledge. His entire enterprise is fundamentally an epistemology, whether it concerns the divine names, the biblical symbols for the angels, or the liturgical symbols of the ecclesiastical tradition" (Paul Rorem, *Pseudo-Dionysius: A Commentary on the Texts and an Introduction to Their Influence* [New York: Oxford University Press, 1993], 93). It is also metaphysical. "The integration — at once ontological and noetic — of all the beings it contains in its hierarchical order implies a 'continuity' that is at once dynamic and static in principle. Between each of these beings in their separate ranks exists an intimate bond: the greater intensity of the superior being exerts an attractive force upon the one next below it and draws it upward toward its own higher level; and out of this attraction arises the fulfillment of the lower being, or, if it is a spiritual being, its happiness." Chenu, *Man, Nature, and Society,* 24.

59. Bonaventure, *Breviloquium,* trans. E. E. Nemmers (St. Louis: B. Herder, 1946), VI.12.5, 209–10.

writer, preacher of the second crusade to the Holy Land, and leading churchman of his time. Born in 1090, Bernard joined the newly
founded monastery at Cîteaux at the age of twenty-two. Three years
later he was sent as the abbot of a new foundation at Clairvaux and
he remained there until his death in 1153. He became the inspiration of the remarkable spread of the Cistercians. His extraordinary
experience and prominence make him a good witness to church life
at the middle of the twelfth century. His advice to Pope Eugenius, a
former monk of his monastery, provides some insight into some of
the problems of the church, what an ideal pope would look like, and
an example of monastic spirituality and theology.[60]

Problems in the church. Bernard described several problems in
the church in his appeal to the pope's responsibility for the church.
These were essentially abuses which he thought could be remedied
by papal administrative power. Five such problems stand out, the
first of which was heresy. Heresy generated fear because it was an
enemy within and, although local, like disease it could spread. The
major case in point at this time were the Cathars who were a notice-
able presence in southern France. Bernard was also concerned with
reunion with the Greeks, a recurring issue of the Middle Ages (III,
2–5, 81–85).

The system of appeals to the pope represented a systemic abuse.
Decisions at a local level were consistently appealed at a higher.
Appealing episcopal decisions to the pope gradually undermined episcopal authority. Popes tended to encourage this to strengthen their
own power. Many of the appeals according to Bernard were not in
good faith. On this issue Bernard asked Eugenius point blank: "How
long will you ignore or turn away from the complaints of the whole
world? How long will you sleep? How long will your consideration
fail to keep watch over the confusion and abuse of appeals" (III, 7,
87 [III, 6–12, 85–93]).

The system of exemptions also seems to have been widespread.
It consisted in releasing a particular level of authority from the

---

60. Bernard of Clairvaux, *Five Books on Consideration: Advice to a Pope, The Works
of Bernard of Clairvaux*, 13, trans. J. D. Anderson and E. T. Kennan (Kalamazoo,
Mich.: Cistercian Publications, 1976). References to this work in the text are by book,
paragraph number, and page.

immediately higher through direct attachment to the Holy See. In this way the immediately higher authority was deprived of authority and revenues. "Abbots are freed from the jurisdiction of bishops, bishops from that of archbishops, archbishops from that of patriarchs or primates. Does this seem good?" (III, 14, 97) The pope could do this, but should not, for he was appointed "not to deny, but to preserve the degrees of honor and of dignities and the ranks proper to each . . . " (III, 14, 98). The result was that the party exempted became haughty and independent, and the one from whom exemption was granted became enraged. Not a good situation (III, 16, 100). Bernard saw this as attacking hierarchy, that is, the ranking of the orders, the organic system. Just as there is order in heaven among the angels, so too on earth "the primates or patriarchs, archbishops, bishops, priests or abbots, and all the rest are arranged under one supreme Pontiff" (III, 18, 103).[61]

Bernard complained that church laws were not enforced. For example, relative to the age requirements for ecclesiastical promotion and clerical dress, the sanctions of suspension or deprivation of benefice were ignored or simply neglected (III, 19–20, 104–7).

Finally, Bernard deplored the wealth and luxury of the Roman church. His sarcasm spilled out. "The life of the poor is sown in the streets of the rich. . . . In the midst of all this, you, the shepherd, go forth adorned with gold and surrounded by colorful array. What do the sheep receive? . . . Doubtless Peter engaged in the same practice, and Paul amused himself thus! You see the entire zeal of the Church burn solely to protect its dignity. Everything is given to honor, little or nothing to sanctity" (IV, 5, 115). He also accused the leadership of the church of avarice, although he spared Eugenius of that charge.

---

61. Note how the need and positive function of papal protection through exemption in the days prior to the Gregorian reform had been reversed in a new situation. Cluny flourished because of this exemption. In the course of time a positive practice developed into an abuse. "But, who is unaware that situated in various dioceses there are some monasteries which have belonged in a special way to the Apostolic See from their very foundations by the wish of their founders. But there is a difference between a privilege granted to devotion and one which ambition, impatient of restraint, strives to obtain" (III, 18, 103). Conciliar legislation addressed the problem, it was a question of enforcement.

But the main motive of many who led the church was avarice (III, 13, 93–96).

An ideal pope. One can draw a thin sketch, not a full portrait, of what an ideal pope might look like from Bernard's advice. This is important for a couple of reasons. One is that Bernard's reflections had considerable weight into the future. Another is that historians frequently depict the papacy during this period in terms of the struggle with temporal rulers for power. Bernard's counsel shows sympathy for a more complex office.

First of all, Bernard's ecclesiology centered on the papacy. The two structural elements that held the organizational church together were the pope and the bishops united with him. "The great prop and stay of the church as a whole is the pope. . . . Next after the pope come the bishops who are 'columns of the church of God.'"[62] Bernard had an exalted view of the pope's power and authority. In his view the pope was the high priest, Supreme Pontiff, prince of bishops, with the power of Peter, a vicar of Christ by anointing. He endorsed the argument that the pope was Peter, the one shepherd to whom the unity of the whole flock was entrusted. The pope's purview was not a local church but the universal church. The pope had universal responsibility for souls and universal jurisdiction, that is, over the whole church and all the churches (II, 15–16, 66–68). "The power of the others is bound by definite limits; yours extends even over those who have received power over others. If cause exists, can you not close heaven to a bishop, depose him from the episcopacy, and even give him over to Satan?" (II, 16, 68)[63]

Bernard was concerned that the pope balance an exhausting and consuming administrative responsibility with a personal, moral, and

---

62. G. R. Evans, *The Mind of Bernard of Clairvaux* (Oxford: Clarendon Press, 1983), 194.

63. This organizational view of the church had a theological conviction underpinning it. "Bernard's certainty about the nature of the church's authority rests upon his conviction that behind every act of the church is Christ" (ibid., 192). Bernard also took up the image of the two swords (Lk 22:36–38), and his views carried some weight. "Bernard argues that both belong to the pope, but the pope cannot commit the acts of violence which are the work of the temporal sword, even when it is justly wielded in a just war. He must entrust the work to someone else. So the soldier's sword belongs to the pope, but, although it may be drawn from its sheath at his command, it must not be drawn by his own hand." Ibid., 198.

spiritual life. Bernard believed that the demands of the job, the overwhelming administrative detail, would depersonalize the man, harden his heart, deaden or render callous a "sense of just and useful pain" (I, 3, 27). The work of a pope involved dealing with an enormous number of cases, appeals, litigants, to which there was no end. But the responsibility also required time for leisure and spiritual concerns. A pope must reserve time for himself (I, 4, 29; I, 6, 34). He should not get bogged down in details, but take time for consideration (I, 7, 36; I, 8, 37).

Perhaps the main point that Bernard drove home was that the office was a ministry and not a position of dominion; it conferred a stewardship and not a possession (II, 9, 56). The charge was to administer, serve, provide counsel, but not to be a lord or owner or ruler (III, 1–2, 80). It entailed responsibility and not a static position of glory and wealth (II, 10, 57). "This is the precedent established by the Apostles: dominion is forbidden, ministry is imposed" (II, 11, 59). A pope should be humble; the humbler he is, the more he is raised above ordinary people (II, 13, 63).

Relative to a pope's running of his curia and household, and relative to the problems of incompetency and corruption, Bernard's message was simple: the pope should have good, proven, and trusted men in his curia. Generally an international team was required for universal operations. If the people in the offices were good, everything would take care of itself (IV, 9–16, 120–29). As for the pope's household, he should not concern himself with those details, but should chose a person and give that person absolute authority (IV, 17–21, 130–35).

Monastic spirituality and theology. Bernard provides an excellent counterpoint to the development of the mobile and apostolically engaged mendicants and the flowering of the theology of the universities of the thirteenth century. Bernard radiates the tradition of Cassian in his spirituality and a contemplative spirit in his theological understanding.

With regard to spirituality, Bernard balanced the responsibility and power of the pope on the one hand with the consideration of him as a person on the other. The spirituality appeared as a consideration of the kind of person a pope is called to be. The pope must remember that he is creature, called into existence out of nothing; he must consider whether as a person he embodies the basic Christian virtues, whether he is prone to act out of wisdom and virtue, whether he seeks the mean between idleness and frivolity, whether he is discerning in judging the people he deals with (II, 17–23, 69–78). Bernard thus draws upon basic monastic principles rooted in psychological discernment, the cultivation of the virtues, and the formation of a person in terms of self-knowledge and reflection.

Despite the pope's active life, Bernard does not hesitate to remind him of the mystical tradition. There are three modes of ascent to things above. The first is through the life of the senses, or through the sensible contact with things of this world. This is the practical way. The second is through the use of philosophy and reflection and may be called scientific. The third is occasional, when one soars in contemplation to the sublime, "not by gradual steps but by sudden ecstasies." The third way is called speculative. The first two lead to the third which consists in tasting the divine and is more mystical in character (V, 3–4, 141–43).

Bernard's conception of theology is not far removed from the spiritual life. He speaks of three ways of investigating God and angels. These three ways of ascent to the transcendent sphere of reality are like three ways of doing theology. The first is by opinion, the second by understanding, the third by faith.[64] Bernard frequently cites scripture, sometimes as mere dressing, a borrowing of words, at other times proposing an argument from precedent or example.

In this work, Bernard develops a rather elaborate angelology, a full description of the world of angels and how they are arranged according to their ranks of dignity and function. The whole thing gives an idea of how theology was done in the monastery as a contemplative exercise based on various sayings or passages of scripture (V, 7–12, 146–54). He also briefly develops a contemplative theology of God

---

64. "Faith is a kind of voluntary and sure foretaste of truth not yet evident; understanding is a sure and manifest knowledge of something not seen; opinion is to hold something as true which you do not know to be false. . . . Even though faith is no more uncertain than understanding, still it is wrapped in mystery which understanding is not" (V, 6, 145). Representing this faith-filled contemplative theology illustrates the kind of theology done in a monastic setting and the degree to which university theology was a new turn.

and trinity (V, 13–19, 155–64). This theology of God is a descriptive account of God that appeals to scripture and is structured by a series of questions about God. For example, what is God? Where is God? If all things are in God, where is God? What are God's attributes, such as God's simplicity? What is to be said of God's unity and trinity? Does number apply to God? By responding to these questions Bernard lays out the tradition of the Christian conception of God as it is found in the scriptures, the Fathers, and within the monasteries.

Francis of Assisi

Both Francis and Dominic rode the tide of an evangelical awakening that transpired during the twelfth century. Issuing from the Gregorian reform, it harkened back to the teachings of Jesus, especially relative to poverty, and to an early church less encumbered by society. It appealed to the literal senses of the gospel stories and teachings of Jesus, thus making it radical at certain points. The revival was a town phenomenon that, unlike the Gregorian reform, involved laity as much or more than the clergy.[65] "The lay apostolic movement developed in this new urban class, tied to the economy of the market and of trade, not without resentment against feudal society."[66] It also engaged students and the intellectual "clientele of the rapidly growing urban schools of which the University of Paris would become, early in the thirteenth century, the prototypical fulfillment."[67]

Francis was not a university student, but he was inspired by the evangelical movement. The barest facts of his life are these: born in 1181 into an Italian family that was not poor, he underwent a lengthy process of conversion in his early twenties. By 1206, at the age of twenty-four, Francis was committed to living an ascetic life of poverty. Two years later, in 1208, he received a further inspiration from the gospel that he was to be apostolic, that is, to undertake a ministry of preaching. He was then joined by his earliest companions. By 1209 they formed a group of twelve for which Francis wrote a short rule in life which was approved by Innocent III in Rome. The Franciscan movement was thus officially underway, and it grew rapidly.

---

65. Chenu, *Nature, Man, and Society,* 258–59.
66. Ibid., 243.
67. Ibid.

The next significant events occurred at the beginning of the 1220s. Francis had resigned as executive head of the order, but was asked to write a more adequate rule for a much larger movement; no longer a small group of 12 ascetic preachers, the Franciscans had become an expanding religious order. The first attempt at a new rule in 1221 was not approved; the second attempt of 1223 was. Also a so-called Second Order of women Franciscans had been formed under the leadership of Francis's friend Clare. The remaining years of Francis were characterized by his mystical experiences, his lingering illness, and then his death in Assisi in 1226 at the age of forty-five. He was declared a saint a little over a year later but recognized as one during his lifetime.

The impact of Francis does not lie as much in what he did in the sense of achievements as in the ideal that he exemplified in his life. He embodied an evangelical existence that was simple and clear, and it attracted the attention of everyone. Mother Theresa in the late twentieth century occupied a position analogous to that of Francis. The ideals of unadorned evangelical preaching were in the air during the twelfth century, sometimes in heretical form. Francis gave these themes a new legitimacy, especially when his order was officially accepted by the church. The person of Francis, what he stood for, and his acceptance by the pope all combined to touch the imagination of all and give new impetus to a movement. The ideal he projected was in fact so simple and radical that it caused conflict among the Franciscans themselves during his lifetime. He called for real poverty. But the attempt to routinize real poverty in a large institution proved to be difficult. Thus almost from the beginning a tension appeared which ended up in eventually dividing the so-called spiritual Franciscans and the more compromising element of the order.

One can capture the spirit of Francis from a few of the classic texts that came from his pen or were attributed to him. They are all short, but they capture the ideal that he stood for. One is *The Rule of 1221*, the first extended rule that Francis wrote but was not accepted at Rome. His earliest rule from 1209 is not extant but is thought to be embedded in this rule of 1221. His *The Testament of Francis* was composed just before he died. It contains a certain tension between rule and ideal for, at the close of the text, Francis forbids any interpretation of this document or the Rule itself. Another important Franciscan document is Francis's *Letter to All the Faithful.* This contains Francis's conception of general Christian life. His ideals were not simply meant for his order. Thus one finds in *The Rule for the Third Order,* which was not written by Francis but is often attributed to him, an attempt to institutionalize a Franciscan spirituality well beyond the borders of the religious order itself. Already in the twelfth century groups of laity had formed around values of asceticism and service. Thus Francis's *Letter to All the Faithful* and the principles formulated in *The Rule for the Third Order* further inspired a religious spirit already in place, shaped it according to Francis's spiritual ideals, and helped mediate it into society at large.

How might one describe this spirituality? Five themes, basic enough to imply many others, characterize the spirit of Francis.[68] The first is *poverty.* Francis expressed what amounted to a hatred of money. The Franciscan is not to touch it. On the other side of this repugnance, poverty is idealized and personified as "Lady Poverty." Poverty functions as a medium for identification with Christ.

The second is *humility.*[69] Humility offers another way of identifying with Christ. It is the typical Christian virtue. Implied in it is a suspicion of all the things that cause pride, for example, office or learning. Very early on, if a Franciscan was to be a scholar, he would have to have books and a situation in which to study. But this seemed to compromise absolute poverty. This exemplifies the inbuilt problems attached to the ideals as members of the order took up various forms of ministry.

The third is *simplicity.* Simplicity characterizes a Franciscan's life and the Christian message preached. Francis's texts urge a kind of literal evangelical piety of discipleship, of following Jesus' own path. Franciscan spirituality embodies a return to certain New Testament ideals relating directly to zeal for communicating the gospel.

---

68. The best translation of the texts of Francis are found in *Francis of Assisi,* 4 vols., ed. Regis J. Armstrong, J. Wayne Hellmann, and William J. Short (Hyde Park, N.Y.: New City Press, 1999–2002). The characterization of Franciscan spirituality which follows is drawn from the four texts mentioned above.

69. See John R. H. Moorman, *Saint Francis of Assisi* (London: SPCK, 1976), 25–27.

The fourth is *prayer.* Francis himself was a mystic. He could easily have retired from the world in a hermetic way of life. But he
channeled prayer into ministry. Added to this attention to prayer are
practices of asceticism and self-discipline.

The fifth Franciscan virtue might be called *mobility* in contrast
to monastic stability. Francis did not originate this; itinerant preaching had arisen more than a century earlier. But here mobility was
formulated into the way of life of a religious order. Shared by the
Dominicans, this created a major new kind of religious life in
the church: the itinerant religious, apostolically commissioned to
achieve specific goals in society, directly reaching out to people across
the boundaries of parish or monastery, exempt from direct episcopal
control and thus contrary to Bernard's counsel, yet peculiarly appropriate in the newly expanding cities in Europe. Religious orders
such as the Franciscans and the Dominicans, which were directly
answerable to the pope or the center, exercised a kind of catalytic
energy that transcended the boundaries of dioceses. Preaching would
pick up in the parishes when the mendicants demonstrated how it
could be done. They helped actualize the church's adapting to the
new vitality of European culture.

Thomas Aquinas

Thomas of Aquino in Italy was born in 1225 or perhaps earlier and
as a youth was exposed to the thought of Aristotle, perhaps at a
young age in Naples where Aristotle was being translated, and later
as a Dominican under the tutelage of Albert the Great. In any case
Thomas joined the Dominicans, studied in Paris, and taught there
during two extended periods as well as in Italy. He was in Italy when
he was summoned to Lyons II but died en route in 1274. Thomas
Aquinas represents the high-water mark of medieval theology.

One can discern the broad lines of Augustine's ecclesiology in
Aquinas: "church" in Aquinas has different meanings when viewed
from different perspectives. At one limit, the church transcends time
and space; it has its fullest realization in heaven; its members transcend people in this world: the church of glory, the heavenly church,
the triumphant church. Church membership on earth includes
those in the empirical church, but it also transcends Christians;

it encompasses all who are saved, inside or outside the empirical church, angels and human beings.[70] Despite this Augustinian doctrine, Aquinas's theology of the church completely transformed that of Augustine when that teaching was received into a new, theological framework. The contemplative theology of the monasteries underwent a thoroughgoing transition with the formation of the cathedral schools, the recovery of Aristotle's logic, the formation of the universities around the beginning of the thirteenth century, and the introduction of Aristotle's philosophy of nature and metaphysics into theological language. As a result Aquinas exemplified a new, socially constructed, intellectual culture that transformed Augustine's theological understanding of the church. Some of the distinctive elements of Thomas's theology were his use of Aristotelian logic and metaphysical language, his realistic epistemology tied to sensible data, his projection of teleology into each individual nature or kind of being, his conception of nature as a teleologically oriented principle of action, his appropriation by analogy of a supernatural sphere, his definition of the virtues as oriented to action, his principle of the necessity of a worldly mediation of grace, his understanding of salvation being played out in ethical human behavior, his Dionysian conception of a hierarchy of the orders of reality, his exalted notion of monarchy as a form of government and of papacy, his view of Christ as head of the church, the congruence of the church as the body of Christ and the sacrament of the eucharist, and the neat correspondence of his ecclesiology with the medieval town, and with a Europe after the Gregorian reform.[71]

Thomas Aquinas bears no small importance for understanding the Christian church for two reasons. The first lies in his ecclesiology as such; it represents well the theological dimension of church self-understanding at the apogee of medieval theology. The second consists in the larger theological synthesis that Aquinas achieved; it

---

70. Avery Dulles, "The Church according to Thomas Aquinas," *A Church to Believe In* (New York: Crossroad, 1982), 151–52.

71. For an account of the recovery and integration of Aristotle's works into Western schools and universities see Fernand Van Steenberghen, *Aristotle in the West* (Louvain: E. Nauwelaerts, 1955). Marie-Dominique Chenu, *Toward Understanding Saint Thomas* (Chicago: Henry Regnery, 1964), provides a guide to the form and logic of Thomas's thought.

extends well beyond his ecclesiology and exemplifies the whole age of the theology of the schools.

The church in Thomas Aquinas. Congar synthesizes Thomas's ecclesiology around three major themes: "The church can be considered as Spirit-centered and ethical, or as Christ-centered, or as institutional and sacramental."[72]

First of all, the church is the Spirit-filled and Spirit-animated congregation of the faithful. Aquinas shared the conception, also common to the canonists, that named the church the *congregatio fidelium* (E, 231–32). The Spirit of God dwells in the church, in the individual members, and through them in the whole, making it a kind of living organism. Although not an entity, still the church is more than a sociological reality, as the Spirit constitutes a bond of unity. The Spirit at work in the members also operates as a principle of holiness. In those members animated by the virtues of faith, hope, and love, and moving toward God in their lives, the church possesses a more than merely objective holiness. The idea of the telos of grace comes into play here: "Only God can lift us up to the life of God; only a 'dynamic' principle genuinely divine can direct and move us towards the objects of the divine life" (MC, 58). Aquinas's ecclesiology bears a strong anthropological and ethical element that complements the theocentric perspective: human beings return to God by living ecclesial lives. The church embodies a dynamic historical role.

Second, Aquinas's ecclesiology also has a christocentric dimension. Harkening back to the New Testament images of a cosmic Christ and Christ the head of the whole church, and drawing these images forward from Augustine, Aquinas holds that all grace has its foundation in Jesus Christ. All who receive saving grace do so in dependence upon and by participation in Christ's grace. "Nothing exists in the economy of return to God that does not spring from Christ, that is not produced in us by him and first known and willed

---

72. Yves Congar, "The Idea of the Church in St Thomas Aquinas," *The Mystery of the Church* (Baltimore and Dublin: Helicon Press, 1965), 72–73. Aquinas never composed a full systematic discourse on the church, so that his ecclesiology has to be reconstructed from pertinent material scattered throughout his writings. Avery Dulles does this in the essay cited above. So does Yves Congar in the essay just cited and in *L'Eglise*, 232–41. I draw the synthesis which follows principally from Congar and cite his two works in the text respectively as MC and E.

by him, that does not have its pattern in him and assimilate to his perfection as image of the Father" (MC, 62).

Third, the "inward" and "outward" dimensions of the church are bonded together to form a single entity. This proposition serves the function of keeping together the mystical or theologal dimensions of the church and considerations of the church sociologically and as a juridical organization. The fusion of the inward or spiritual and the outward or material dimensions of the church are summed up in two theses by Congar: "(1) the Church-as-Institution is the very existing form of the Mystical Body and of the new life in Christ; (2) it is, further, the sacrament and the ministry — in a word, the concretion — of the Mystical Body" (MC, 66).

The church as society, as an organization of mutual help or organized collaboration under a hierarchical authority structure "is not a different reality from the living Body given new life in Christ, with the Holy Spirit as its soul. The latter is the inward dimension of that which appears outwardly as a community organized and ruled by the hierarchy" (MC, 67). This identity carries over to the role of ministry and sacraments: these are the behaviors which render actual the inner theological life of the church. "The church visible and institutional is the ministry of faith and of the sacraments of faith, by which human beings are grafted into Christ and upbuild the Mystical Body which is the church's inward identity" (MC, 70). The eucharist assumes a central role here. This is the centering sacrament that constitutes the church most strongly; the realism and depth of eucharistic understanding gives to the church as the Body of Christ a realistic and almost literal theological dimension (E, 235). In sum: "The whole purpose of the church, as Saint Thomas conceives it, is to unite with God. This union takes place primarily through sanctifying grace, which is effectively communicated by the sacraments."[73]

Other aspects of Aquinas's ecclesiology reflected his period. Aquinas saw in the body of scholars and teachers that arose in the High Middle Ages a source of authority. Thus there were two *magisteria*, or authorities, not competitive but in concert, the one of those who

---

73. Dulles, "The Church according to Thomas Aquinas," 158.

possessed the power of office to teach, the other of those with the expertise of critical knowledge (E, 241–42). He had an exalted notion of the papacy that paralleled his view that monarchy was the highest form of government. Essentially the pope in his conception was the bishop of the whole church with direct jurisdictional authority.[74] Aquinas also provided a way of thinking that led eventually to the view that the pope was infallible. Most agreed on the infallibility of the church. Thus, on the basis of the role of the pope in the church, Aquinas reasoned to a charism of office that implied infallibility (E, 244–48).[75] Relative to the balance of papal authority and civil rule, Aquinas struck a moderate position that recognized with Aristotle the natural or intrinsic right of a people or society to its government.

The impact of the Thomistic synthesis. More influential than his ecclesiology was the synthesis of theology that Aquinas produced. His *Summa Theologiae* exemplifies in the best and most comprehensive way the massive adjustment in theology that occurred during the Middle Ages. It thus became a system, or it typified one, and became a reference for a theological language that through the centuries shaped the Western church, continuously in Roman Catholicism, and to some extent by reaction in the churches of the sixteenth-century Reformation. This language, which was inspired by Aristotle, carried various forms of the medieval synthesis within Catholicism through the councils of Trent and Vatican I right up to Vatican II.

DESCRIPTION OF THE WESTERN CHURCH IN THE HIGH MIDDLE AGES

The strategy of this chapter calls for increasing abstraction. The first level bypassed social history and charted some of the great events of the developing church. The chapter touched down in some fashion through an analysis of influential and representative authors. The

---

74. "Saint Thomas was concerned with the worldwide church united under the primacy of the pope. He looked upon dioceses as administrative districts or portions of the people of God rather than as churches in the theological and sacramental sense of the word." Ibid., 167.

75. A classic reference for this in Aquinas is *Summa Theologiae*, II-II, 1, 10 where he discusses the authority of the pope in deciding issues relative to the creed.

present section presents a broad description of the church of the medieval period into the thirteenth century with some specific reference to the church in England. Only the aim of this organizational and theological analysis could possibly justify it, and that is implicitly to compare and contrast it with what went before and what will follow. The medieval church, the same church as the early church and the church of late antiquity, was also a *novum*, a church that was unique and will never be again.

Organizational Structure

This analysis employs the categories of organizational structure, but unlike the early church, where the referents were tiny house churches, here the church is a massive organization that was split off from the eastern half of the church and encompassed western Europe. The place to begin is the organization's structure, for in a hierarchical world this sacred organizational structure dominated the understanding of the church. The hierarchical organization of the church was constituted by its orders of administration and ministry.

Papacy. The first function of the papacy relates *ad intra*, to the governance of the church.[76] At the beginning of the eleventh century the church was in desperate need of reform, and only the pope could have effected that reform. David Knowles makes the point explicitly. The emperors of Germany could not have effected a reform because western Europe was divided in its temporal rule. They did not relate to the papacy in the manner of the monarch Charlemagne. The church was under lay control and only the pope had the potential for spiritual and symbolic power and universal jurisdiction. Reform had to come from the center if it were to effect the whole church; it had to come from the papacy.[77]

---

76. The function of the papacy *ad extra* appears under the heading of church and world.

77. Knowles, *The Middle Ages*, 168. This topic deserves more discussion; historians are divided; but this statement is minimal in its intent. I wish to highlight two things: the first is that the Gregorian reform was truly a reform, despite the fact that the former system was not intrinsically wrong and that the reform entailed some negative results. The second is that, although the reasons for it were diffused among changing social conditions and a variety of agents, the papacy led the reform.

In spearheading the reform Gregory gave birth to the "modern" papacy, that is, what did not exist before him and would last to the present. The claims he made were made before him, but he actualized them in the West. Through the movement that he, more than anyone else, carried into action the papacy gained control over the entire Western church. Its claims would become even more exaggerated, and the headship would be seriously challenged in the conciliarist movement. But by then papal authority had become so ingrained that it would survive the severest test. The unity of Christendom symbolically rests in the papacy. Symbolic causality refers to the influence that is enabled by the religious attachment or identification of significant people with the pope over and above juridical authority. In a sense the pope established his pan-European religious authority when he summoned the first crusade in 1095. The crusades represent an exercise of leadership that transcended all regional authority and rallied Europe as a whole.[78]

Cardinals. Together with the jurisdictional and symbolic authority of the pope, the Gregorian reform further developed the administrative centralization of the church. The structuring of the cardinalate into an international administrative council which also controlled the election of the pope facilitated the process. Not only did this form of election begin to give the papacy some independence from secular control, it also marked the beginning of an effective administrative system. The bureaucracy collected taxes, and through legates it reached into regions far off. It would be expanded in its efficiency during the fourteenth century. But even back in Gregory's time one can see the pope governing the universal church in a way analogous to Cyprian governing his regional church. The pope had become Cyprian's bishop governing the whole church through letter, synod, and decree.

Bishops. The investiture controversy came to an end in compromise and mutual understanding in 1122. But the agreement did not mean that secular rulers no longer had any influence on the selection of bishops, nor did it mean that the bishops ceased being secular

---

78. André Vauchez, *The Laity in the Middle Ages: Religious Beliefs and Devotional Practices* (Notre Dame, Ind.: University of Notre Dame Press, 1993), 48.

rulers or their agents. What was new was the increment in papal authority and power: bishops were attached to Rome jurisdictionally, and all things being politically equal, the pope could remove a bishop or undercut his authority. The church had become a large and relatively tight organizational entity in an extraordinarily new way.

Being a bishop in thirteenth century England entailed multiple relationships and activities. "Life was very full, for a bishop had to combine with his pastoral duties the responsibilities of a landowner and feudal lord, judge and magistrate, Kings's Counselor and Member of Parliament."[79] Most of the income for the diocese came from church properties which had to be administered; the bishops of England during the thirteenth century were frequently deep in debt because of the cost of an episcopal household and the services it provided as against the difficulty of collecting tithes (CL, 171–76). The main duty of a bishop was to attend to the parishes. He did this principally through parish visitation, "an occasion for inspecting and examining the parish and its clergy [and] an opportunity for the bishop to address his clergy and people" (CL, 194). A bishop thus spent much time traveling with his entourage, visiting parishes and religious houses in his diocese and attending to his secular responsibilities.

Parish and priests. One of the fruits of the Gregorian reform was the final emergence of the clergy as a clearly identifiable class over against the laity. "In the course of this campaign," Knowles writes, "there emerged in the West, for the first time, an organized class, the clergy or great body of clerks, tightly bound together under bishops who themselves were tied tightly to the bishop of Rome, with a law and interests that separated them from the laity, who were to occupy a lower place."[80] This represents a quantum jump from the hint of

---

79. John R. H. Moorman, *Church Life in England in the Thirteenth Century* (Cambridge: University Press, 1955), 179. Cited in the text as CL. Since it is impossible to profile in any detail the bishop or priest across Europe, I turn to studies of the English church in the thirteenth century. Besides Moorman, I appeal to Colin Platt, *The Parish Churches of Medieval England* (London: Secker & Warburg, 1981) and Frances and Joseph Gies, *Life in a Medieval Village* (New York: Harper & Row, 1990). These are cited in the text as PCME and LMV respectively.

80. Knowles, *The Middle Ages*, 169. Congar sees evidence in various liturgical practices in Charlemagne's time that people had already begun to think of the church as constituted by the clergy. Congar, *L'Eglise*, 57.

a distinction of roles found in *1 Clement* at the end of the first century. The context is the whole Western church with a strong central government. A theology of absolute ordination, bestowing the sacred power to consecrate the eucharist, generated an understanding of priesthood that further distances it from being a function of a particular community. Priests thus form a group who alone possess a sacred spiritual power above the temporal sphere, and who are unified by being tied through bishops to the center. In a way this development naturally and logically follows the outcome of the dispute between spiritual and temporal power. As the church in its higher clergy gradually freed itself from lay control, so too did its lower clergy gradually become distinguished as a class with sacred power.

This process, moreover, needed time before it influenced parishes in the villages. About 90 percent of Christians in thirteenth century Europe lived in villages (LMV, 1). The average English parish covered a large area which included the center of population and the surrounding farms, villages, and hamlets. There would be chapels in outlying areas covered by a priest chaplain who possibly lived there. A parish church was both the physical church and the land and revenues that were attached to it.[81] A rector of a parish might live in the parish and assume charge of its ministry, or he may be absent for a variety of possible reasons. A vicar took the place of an absentee rector and shepherded the parish for a salary. During the thirteenth century more rectors were absent than present, and "the proportion of those who were in priest's orders was often no more than 20 or 25 per cent"; other clergy, the majority, were deacons or subdeacons who never advanced to the priesthood (CL, 48).[82] A regular practice that emerged in the twelfth century called "appropriation" entailed the assigning of the income of the parish to a monastery which in

---

81. As a result of the Gregorian reform bishops assumed control over the parish churches, and lay patrons encountered more difficulty in claiming their profits. The proprietary structure did not disappear all at once; kings and landowners still asserted rights of appointing priests, but by the end of the twelfth century in England "the privately owned church had become a rarity." PCME, 6–9, cited at p. 9.

82. There was also a clergy glut in England as too many men were living off the system. It has been estimated that 2 percent of the population were in orders. Moorman supports this rough figure: of a population of three million, "there were at least forty thousand secular clergy in this country as well as nearly seventeen thousand monks and friars" (CL, 52).

turn salaried a vicar, usually not a monk, for the ministry therein.[83] The vicarage system was regularized in the thirteenth century when vicars were guaranteed the "security of tenure and a minimum wage" (CL, 45). Before that they often lived in poverty. The rectors or vicars who served the rural parishes tended to be local men of artisan or peasant class and thus not well educated; absentee rectors tended to be educated sons of the wealthy or landowning classes who enjoyed a substantial part of the income of the parishes (CL, 24–51). Although the clergy mirrored class in society, a person with talent could advance within the clerical system. A number of bishops who came from humble origins prove this (CL, 158).

Relative to the education of the priests, Moorman reckons that "the vast majority of those who served the parishes in the thirteenth century must have been only very partially instructed, while some were undoubtedly practically illiterate" (CL, 90). A bit more precisely, one can see a gradation: in or near the towns, a young man might obtain a basic education in a school and the clergy might be more educated; in the isolated villages one would have only a smattering of knowledge learned by apprenticeship from the "sympathetic but perhaps ill-educated priest" (CL, 109).

By the thirteenth century the bishops lived according to the dispensation of celibacy, but in the villages among the lower clergy the discipline was far from uniformly followed. While some priests lived celibate lives, others were publicly married, or lived with a woman but were not married, or had promiscuous relationships with women parishioners (CL, 62–67). There was severe criticism of the morality of the lower clergy during the thirteenth century by evenhanded critics (CL, 214).

The relation of the priest to the people was complex. On the one hand, the "thirteenth century parish priest was more closely associated with his people than the modern clergyman can ever hope to be" because of the common, isolated, compacted life together in community (CL, 83). But at the same time, the priest exacted tithes from

---

83. "By the end of the thirteenth century there is no doubt that at least half of the parish churches of England had been thus appropriated, by far the majority having gone to the religious houses" (CL, 42). Village life generally and the life of the parish priest in it is recreated in some detail by the Gieses in LMV, especially pp. 155–71.

his generally poor people and these were constantly contested or fell short and thus provided a source of friction (CL, 83, 138; PCME, 55–56).

   Councils, synods, and law. Law, regular Roman synods, and general councils structured and supported the symbolic authority of the church, rationalized it, and channeled it into administration. The post-Gregorian church possessed a unity that increasingly approached a uniformity governed by universal law. The principle of unity lay in the head, the pope, who reflected the headship of Christ from whom all grace flowed. The pope claimed universal jurisdiction which in varying degrees could be exercised in actual governance, extending outward from the center in a universal discipline. This was not a church that consciously tolerated unity amid differences, but a unity reinforced by at least a formal respect for a growing body of law. In a postmodern, pluralistic situation marked by individualism a stress on law may appear repressive. But in relation to a fluid if not chaotic feudal system based on individual power and physical force objective law provided the seedbed for civilization.[84]

Members of the Church

Members of the church include pope, bishops, priests, and a host of subdistinctions among deacons and other minor orders. Also many monks were priests; and religious women were set apart from life in the world. The collection of all other than clerics under the category "members of the church" is thus arbitrary.

   Monks. The High Middle Ages seem like a golden age of monasticism. First, the Cluniac movement of the tenth and eleventh centuries nurtured the Gregorian reform. The twelfth century saw the remarkable spread of the Cistercians. The rapid growth of these successive movements reflected the spiritual ideals of the time: more

---

84. Troeltsch points out that the medieval church was itself the first example of a modern state. It became an institution that was sovereign, with a body of appointed or elected officials and an administration, using a formal written law and supported by obedience and allegiance, a collective unity with a will fashioned out of individual wills, with respect for individual rights. Before the church there was no sovereign state, no body politic to which people owed allegiance as to an ultimate spiritual value. The church became the model of the values incorporated into the modern state. Troeltsch, *The Social Teachings,* 252, 325–26.

or less withdrawal from the world, but not total isolation, rather dedication to work, prayer, and public worship.[85] The status of the monk was neither extraordinary nor countercultural: he had a recognized position in society. Yet the taking of vows and the habit were the equivalent of a new birth and a serious commitment. Monasteries had many social functions, from agricultural development to social stabilization.[86] But the deepest reason why they existed consisted in public prayer. The monk's life was structured by liturgy; the monastery was where prayer was done correctly. Behind this lay the religious and cultural conviction that prayer worked and that people could assist one another and the whole of society through prayer. In a religious culture, a society steeped in a religious outlook and set of behaviors, monks and nuns "were acknowledged to be living the most holy form of life accessible to human beings."[87]

The rise of the mendicants and their engaged apostolic life represented a new development in organized religious life, and the Dominicans and the Franciscans, along with other groups, flourish to the present day. Less withdrawal, more engagement in society; more urban and less rural; less stable and more mobile. This spiritual adrenaline affected the hierarchy, theology, cities, and parishes through the concrete activities of the members of these orders and through the ideals and values which they represented.

Women and women religious. The profound changes in church and society between the eleventh and thirteenth centuries affected women and women's religious life. Today's discussion of these changes always involves two distinct issues. One question involves what women did in the church, for the church, and for society

---

85. Vauchez, *Laity in the Middle Ages*, 97.

86. Religious and nonreligious factors joined to stimulate the expansion and viability of monastic life. Speaking of monasticism in the tenth and eleventh centuries, and thus prior to Cîteaux, Southern describes it as not a life of retirement from the world, not a life of poverty, and not a life of ascetic self-denial. The gentry who founded a monastery did not want to find "marks of poverty in the buildings, dress or equipment of the monks" (*Middle Ages*, 161). That is not why the monastery was founded. The monasteries did not represent escape from the ideals of society but their religious expression. A good percentage of monks were conscripts, given to the monastery as children; some found their vocation there as they grew up. But it was not a hard conscription because it was a noble life highly valued socially. Southern gives a brief characterization of life in a Burgundian monastery that is religiously and humanistically attractive. Ibid., 163.

87. Lynch, *The Medieval Church*, 130–31; Knowles, *The Middle Ages*, 117–28.

through the church. Another concerns what the church did for women. Both of these issues are in play in three aspects of this complex development.

First, the religious life of women underwent a resurgence prior to and during the period of the Gregorian reform in terms of numbers and foundations. Also, a certain diversification meant that more options for different styles of religious life appeared. For example, the Gilbertines in England opened up the possibility of the religious life of lay sisters to poor and uneducated women.[88] Other groups, founded either independently or in association with other religious orders, such as the Premonstratensians and the Cistercians, freed the religious life of women from the hegemony of the Benedictine rule. Religious life provided women with an option apart from marriage which was respected by church and society and which developed women's talents and contributed to society.

Second, one of the most significant of developments during this period began at the end of the twelfth century. Arising out of twelfth century movements, lay women gathered into groups in order to perform works of charity in society under the inspiration of the gospel and Christian values but without the restrictions of monastery or formal religious vows. The distinctiveness of such groups, who had different inspirations and names in different places, lies in the manner in which these groups forged a kind of middle way between formal religious life and an ordinary lay state. The beguines are perhaps the best example. The etymology of this word is debated, but it refers to women who "set themselves apart from the world by living austere, poor, chaste lives in which manual labor and charitable service were joined to worship (which was not, however, rigidly prescribed as it was in convents). Initially, at least, their practice contrasted sharply with traditional monasticism, since they took no vows and had no complex organization and rules, no order linking the houses, no hierarchy of officials, no wealthy founders or leaders."[89] The beguines

---

88. Patricia Ranft, *Women and the Religious Life in Premodern Europe* (New York: St. Martin Press, 1996), 52–54.

89. Caroline Walker Bynum, *Holy Feast and Holy Fast: The Religious Significance of Food to Medieval Women* (Berkeley: University of California Press, 1987), 17. Ranft offers this description of the beguines: "In their immediate world the beguines offered

drew from "the new bourgeoisie or from a lower nobility associated with the towns."[90] The life appeared as a new and attractive alternative to the more traditional cloistered life. For many of the young women "it was the presence, not the absence, of a prospective bridegroom that activated desire for perpetual chastity."[91] Virginity was not escape from family, but "was seen by both men and women as a positive and compelling religious ideal."[92]

A third phase of development in the role of women in the church consisted of the influence of the third orders. We saw earlier that Francis reached out to all Christians in his *Letter* and that his spirit was used in the composition of the rule for what came to be called third orders. These tertiaries were lay women who remained squarely in the world and who were associated with the life of the twelfth-century religious orders dedicated to apostolic activity. The third orders had their roots in movements among the laity that went back to the eleventh century. They represent both church support to lay apostolic activity and, in another sense, a monasticization of the laity.[93]

Laity. Since the Carolingian period the church more or less encompassed the whole of Western European society with the exception of the Jewish minority and the Muslims in Spain. In the distinction between the clergy and the laity, therefore, the laity refers to everyone else, the whole of society. The common perception says that in the wake of the Gregorian reform the gulf between the clergy and the

---

women an orthodox equivalent to heretical *vita apostolica* groups. Second, they were groups that women themselves directed. They were outside the bounds of monastic control and, originally, of diocesan control; beguines were independent women. Third, some beguines were powerful beyond their own circle of women. . . . Fourth, they offered women a type of religious life that was adaptable to the new urban environment of the day. In southern Europe the male mendicants met this need [along with women's groups like the beguines but with different names in the south], but it was female beguines who supplied the solution in the north. Last, the beguine movement was at its birth and remained until its final days a *via media*, a life for women somewhere between that of a nun and a laywoman." Ranft, *Women and the Religious Life*, 74.

90. Bynum, *Holy Feast*, 18.
91. Ibid., 20.
92. Ibid.
93. Vauchez, *Laity in the Middle Ages*, 72. It should be noted that "the tendency of later historians to identify pious women with a particular order has obscured the extent to which, especially in the thirteenth century, institutional affiliation and structure were, to women, unimportant or constantly changing." Bynum, *Holy Feast*, 24.

laity widened.[94] But this generalization would probably have to be nuanced in the light of sociological differentiation. Such a differentiation proposed in the eleventh century divided society into those who prayed, those who fought, and those who worked.[95] If one allowed for a growing class of landed aristocracy who did not fight along with an educated class of bureaucrats and tradespeople, one might work with three distinct groups of laity.

Surely the masses of Christians on the farms and villages of Europe who lacked education stood sharply over against the clerical administration of the church as passive consumers. But they grew in conscious participation in ecclesial life during this period. Gregory explicitly appealed to laity against priests who flouted celibacy. The crusades drew many of these people into active participation in a "holy" venture. This group of people actively participated in the heretical movements of the day. But only the clergy had access to scripture and, even if they were not well educated themselves, a veneer of Latin culture and exposure to theology were enough for them to look upon the faithful as theologically ignorant.[96] At the same time, one might suspect that in the rural areas the gap between the people and the clergy applied more to the bishop and other higher clergy than to the parish priest.

In the twelfth and thirteenth centuries a number of movements involved segments of lay men and women who assumed an active role in the common life of the church. The penitential movement consisted in laity who sought to live a kind of religious life without leaving life in society and work at their trades; they internalized a penitential ideal and strove to conform to it.[97] Vauchez chronicles the lives of a number of saints in the twelfth century who won their

---

94. "On the one hand, the church fought for its autonomy and won it progressively by affirming its independence from the emperors and kings whose power it desacralized. But on the other hand, it accentuated the tendency of the clergy to consider the church as their own and to identify with it. The laity, relegated to their temporal tasks, in this view represented nothing but the simple object of the pastoral ministry of the clergy." Vauchez, *Laity in the Middle Ages*, 43.

95. Ibid., 30.

96. Ibid., 101–2.

97. Ibid., 119. Penitence in this case refers to an attitude and way of life. "It meant assuming a humble and repentant attitude, the only one suitable for a sinner before God who wished to be joined to Him through love." Ibid., 122.

reputations for sanctity precisely as lay people dedicated to a certain asceticism, work with pilgrims, and other charitable works.[98] Other examples from the thirteenth century, such as the beguines and those who took up lives as tertiaries, indicate a sector of the laity that were active in the church.

Finally, relative to the other class of those who fight, the crusades and monasticism were married in various militant orders of knights, the Knights of the Temple or Templars being the most famous. These knights swore to be poor, obedient, and chaste, and were dedicated to the protection of the Holy Land. These orders also accepted women who did not fight but performed charitable works among other monastic duties.[99] In sum, in the aftermath of the Gregorian reform the clergy assumed a clearer sense of identity and position in the church. While the uneducated masses may have remained passive, the period also witnessed a good deal of growth in active lay spirituality and participation in church life. Thus the religious life of the laity might be more accurately understood variously in terms of social differentiation than simply by reference to clerical dominance.

Self-Understanding and Mission

Although Thomas Aquinas did not write a treatise called "the church," he had a well developed theological understanding of it. The thinkers most concerned with the nature of the church were canonists, but their legal reflections were shot through with theological suppositions.[100] Ecclesiological reflection was thus quite developed in the High Middle Ages, but it remained unsynthesized. The idea of the church as the *congregatio fidelium*, or community of the faithful,

---

98. Ibid., 51–72. These groups of laity thus predate the third order movement and show how the latter built on currents in church and social life that were springing up from below, so to speak.

99. Lynch, *The Medieval Church*, 208; Ranft, *Women and the Religious Life*, 57–58.

100. Congar discerns two distinct trends or types of thinking that he loosely relates to the theologians and the canonists: the theologians are more holistic and idealistic, the canonists more historical and realist. On the church as the body of Christ, the theologian focuses on the head and the line of authority from Christ to the pope that holds it together; the canonist tends to think of the body as a social reality. On church and state, the theologian tends to think of the unity of society which is differentiated; the canonist tends to be more dualist and historically conscious. Congar, *L'Eglise*, 178–79, 218–19.

provided the commanding metaphor for understanding the church as a whole. This allowed the church to be construed organizationally in the legal terms of the canonists and theologically as the body of Christ. But the legally structured institution was emphasized as never before. Congar notes how "Gregory VII sketched out the elements of a juridical ecclesiology dominated by the institution of the papacy. His action constituted the greatest shift Catholic ecclesiology had ever known."[101] He goes on to explain how this development was written into the logic adopted by the reformers. "Speaking generally, the reform of the eleventh century consisted in this: in order to free itself from the control of temporal rulers, and to get out of the ambiguous Carolingian situation where the church was identified with Christian society and empire, the church had to claim for itself its own law in a structure that was fully autonomous."[102]

Without reviewing Aquinas's theological construction of the church, one might ask how his view of it represented a distinctive medieval conception. It seems plausible to imagine that for the first time in history the term "church" could have had such a massive, clearly defined, international organization as its earthly referent. Its organizational infrastructure had ideological support in a metaphysical and divinely willed plan. In the hierarchical universe of Dionysius, the top-down structure originated in heaven, and the earthly structure symbolically schooled the imagination, informed the mind, and directed human behavior so that the church could lead human existence back to God. The word "church" in the medieval period, more than at any time before, referred to a universal hierarchical structure.

"Sanctifier of society" characterizes a way to understand the mission of the church in this period.[103] Its aptness becomes evident when one translates Aquinas's metaphysical understanding of the role of

---

101. Ibid., 103.

102. Ibid., 112. See also 92–98 for a fuller characterization of the ecclesiology of the reformers.

103. This brief formal statement will be developed further in more concrete social terms with the consideration of the activities of the church and its relation to society. But note that the phrase "sanctifier of society" does not imply that in fact all people participated in the church in a fervent manner. Even in the villages it is not clear that church participation was universal, active, and intentional.

the church into the descriptive terms of the church's actual historical existence. In Thomas's teleological understanding of reality human existence was called not only to a natural end of happiness but to supernatural union with God. He thus conceptually constructed a supernatural order of reality, mediated by Jesus Christ, with a portion of the human race participating in it; this included a Christian level of existence that shared in a new supernatural nature or principle of action constituted by habitual grace, and a life of supernaturally oriented behavior structured by supernatural or graced virtues leading to this blessed end. The church provided the historical medium of this metanarrative that structured all of history. But this grand vision was played out concretely in the church in each town and village. The sacramental system structured the whole life cycle, and the church mediated the sacramental system. Here was a mission as big as history itself and as concrete as baptisms at Easter, eucharist on Sundays, and Christian burial.

Activities

What did the church as an organization do? How did it perform its mission? In the church on the ground, a certain gulf obtained between bishops, especially of larger cities or dioceses, and the ordinary people, especially rural peasants. The institutional church took on flesh in the priests and monks in the parish communities. There they presided over the eucharist and administered the sacraments. In these activities one can visualize the influence on daily life.

Eucharistic assembly and worship. The celebration of the eucharist was the center of the church's existence: every Sunday in every church from the cathedral to the stone chapel with the dirt floor. The belief in Christ's presence in the eucharist in popular imagination tended toward a physical realism: Lateran IV supported this with the language of transubstantiation; the thirteenth-century feast of Corpus Christi, with its processions through the streets, confirmed it. To gaze on the host, at the elevation during Mass or at benediction, moved people; theologically it was a real spiritual communion. Understanding of the eucharist itself centered on a sacrifice linked with Jesus' passion and death. In celebrating Mass "the priest stood with his back to the congregation, often behind a screen that partly or wholly blocked [people's] view. He spoke in Latin and lowered his voice so as to whisper at particularly solemn moments in the mass. Lay people were encouraged to adopt an attitude of reverence in the presence of so awesome an event as the physical presence of the savior."[104] The sheer transcendence of the eucharist seemed to prohibit frequent communion. The legislation of Lateran IV on communion once a year at Easter time made this a centerpiece in the church's pastoral care of people.[105] More generally, despite the regenerating activity of the Order of Preachers and the Friars Minor, the quality of preaching in the parishes was not high. The aim was to inspire correct belief and correct behavior "by transmitting a few essential notions of doctrine and especially by recommending pious or devotional practices."[106] In addition to the doctrine of real presence, two other beliefs marked the piety of the period: consciousness of sin together with a fear of hell, and devotion to the Virgin Mary (CL, 74–77). At the same time, the life of the "medieval villager was full of superstition, some of which was clearly a relic of pre-Christian days" (CL, 82).

The other sacraments formed the framework of an entire life. By the Middle Ages seven sacraments were in place: baptism, confirmation, eucharist, penance, marriage, holy orders, and extreme unction. With baptism one was ushered into an ecclesial existence and a higher form of life; with a final anointing and a Christian burial one was supported through purgatory and toward heaven. Marriage was constituted by mutual assent, but the church's witness made it a sacrament and the church played a significant role in regulating marriages, often competing with the interests of families: alliances, inheritances, and general politics.

Ethics. The church had no small input on human behavior in society. Through theologians such as Thomas Aquinas, the church adapted much of Aristotle's social and virtue ethics into Christian teaching. On the practical level, the church acted as the conscience

---

104. Lynch, *The Medieval Church*, 281. Also Cook, *Ministry to Word and Sacrament*, 116–18.

105. Lynch, *The Medieval Church*, 283. See Bynum, *Holy Feast*, 50–67, for a description of eucharistic piety in the thirteenth century. I will describe eucharistic practice at greater length in the next chapter.

106. Vauchez, *Laity in the Middle Ages*, 104.

of society through the pulpit and the practice of confession. It bears repeating that the practice of confession provided the church through the priest with a strong measure of social control.[107] "A major function of the parish priest was that of instructing his parishioners. It was up to him to teach the children the Creed, the Lord's Prayer, the *Ave,* and the Ten Commandments" (LMV. 169). The rector might also instruct the people in the ordinary customs and morality of everyday life. "The priest's instruction of adults came largely through confession, in which he not only examined the penitent's morals but his religious knowledge" (LMV, 169). The priests used the manuals of confession as a guide to the examination of the penitent's conscience.

The needs of the poor were always great in rural parishes, not only in times of poor harvests, but also due to the lack of a social welfare system in case of accident, sickness, or death. The appropriation system exacerbated the problem by draining the parish funds, one of the main sources of social welfare, from the parish (CL, 43). The modest salary of the vicar did not allow him to help bear the burden of the poor. In ancient times the poor had a right to one quarter of what was paid in tithe; that was subverted by the appropriations system (CL, 138–39).[108]

Relation of the Church to Its World

As a preface to this discussion, it will be helpful to clarify what the term "world" meant in the medieval period. Can one assume that world and church designated distinct spheres? Troeltsch proposed that the church did not see itself "over against" the world, but rather simply as one with it. Church and world were coterminous; each one comprised the other; the idea that the church would set out to change society or the world simply never arose. Rather the world as creature was basically good. The structures of society were the product of natural law and more or less coincided with what God intended. This natural world was a potency for grace, for the supernatural, for revelation, and for the divinely revealed law which was

---

107. Lynch, *The Medieval Church,* 283.
108. "Under the system of 'appropriations' at least two-thirds of the income of many parishes went into the treasury of some religious house which might be many miles away." CL, 139.

mediated through scripture and the church. Thus one finds a vast integration, with Christianity fitting into society, nature, the world. But the church did not see itself or use its authority as an agency to reform the world or to alter it; it was not countercultural but the fulfillment of culture.[109] With this broad background, how does this relationship cash out in terms of state and society?

Church and state. The term "state" is ambiguous in the medieval period; no autonomous Roman empire loomed over the church as in the early centuries. Sovereign states in a modern sense began to develop more clearly in the fourteenth century. The term "state" thus refers here to the sphere of temporal power and authority exercised by individual rulers. Passing over regional complexity, and taking the popes' conflicts with secular rulers as defining a broad type, the investiture controversy showed Gregory claiming authority over secular rulers, emperors and kings in matters relating to the church, and popes who followed him did the same. To some extent they succeeded in gaining that authority. Almost all the commentators point out the irony of this development. In a sense the church did not set out to claim it. The traditional doctrine had been that there were two swords, spiritual and temporal, two authorities in parallel, each divinely authorized. But now the old doctrine existed in a new situation, one in which in fact the two powers were united in the person of the bishop within the context of feudalism.[110] Thus, when the papacy claimed the superiority of the spiritual and its intrinsic autonomy,

---

109. By and large Troeltsch rests his case on the theology of Aquinas and the actual society which was formed in the Middle Ages and which generated the Thomistic synthesis in the first place. See his long discussion in *The Social Teachings*, 257ff. In these grand, social and metaphysical terms, one can agree with Troeltsch. But his thesis should be balanced dialectically by recognition that life was hard, that nature could be cruel, that history was infected with sin, that is, not "good," and that the church did aggressively influence society and shape culture on a historical level. In both the early church and in our own day, as the church becomes a minority, the destructive and sinful character of the social structures of the world becomes more apparent. In such situations theology is more inclined to accept the countercultural role of the church and to react against sociopolitical arrangements from an eschatological perspective that allows the church to be critic of secular life.

110. In the situation created by Charlemagne's Christian society, the idea of the two authorities shifted with the sense of the identity of church and society. For Gelasius, temporal and spiritual power were distinct with respect to the world and the church; in Charlemagne's time, these were understood as two distinct powers *within* the church; rulers were understood to be legitimate rulers of the church. Congar, *L'Eglise*, 53.

in fact it was subordinating the temporal authority of episcopal civil rulers to its own. Gregory VII also claimed the right of bishops to correct and rebuke kings. If church leadership had been in the hands of the ruling laity, Gregorian claims moved it in the other direction. The application of an old doctrine in new circumstances often generates revolutionary results.

Several factors, however, exclude any idea that the church gained control of secular or temporal rule. The pope never claimed total power.[111] The resolution of the investiture controversy was a standoff, a compromise, and kings still exerted influence in the appointment of bishops. Secular power consistently guarded its own claims of ruling by divine right and authority. And pragmatically, while the pope claimed spiritual authority over civil rulers, this authority was never absolute but frequently could only be exercised in conjunction with political power. A common theology supported the exercise of authority in spiritual and religious matters. Many Christian rulers were simply obedient to the pope. But the extreme claims of the popes, and implicitly the church, over temporal rule were also constantly resisted. Thus one senses that without temporal *power* the church would not have been able to exercise *authority*. In fact, when the balance of power was tipped in the favor of kings, they took advantage of it to gain the upper hand in temporal affairs. The pope could not have survived as a spiritual authority without temporal power.

The unique position of the church vis-à-vis civil government in this period appears by contrast with modern Western states. In open and democratic societies marked by religious pluralism and the complete autonomy of civil authority from all religion, it is impossible for any church to use spiritual *power*. At best a church can appeal to reason and, on the basis of spiritual *authority*, argue to conclusions that themselves appeal to common religious experience and freedom. The distinction here is precisely between spiritual power and intrinsic religious authority. The medieval church, because it was coterminous with society, could exercise spiritual authority as dominating power. It combined both spiritual power, for example, to excommunicate, and sheer political power. Its authority in relation to the state was

111. Tierney, *Crisis*, 57.

more than purely religious or spiritual authority, that is, an appeal to spiritual freedom on intrinsically religious grounds; it was mixed with power of a political kind.[112]

Church and society. The single most impressive development of the Middle Ages according to Troeltsch was the creation of a single unified Christian society. This occurred in two stages: the first was the evolution into the state-church system exemplified in Charlemagne's empire which grew out of the proprietary churches and the regional or territorial churches. The church was not so much subjugated by the Carolingians as used as a medium of civilization. The second stage, after a period of decline, arose with the emergence of the papacy and through it a differentiation, but not separation, of the church's clerical organization from that of society, and a universalizing of church influence throughout western Europe. The papacy became the symbolic focal point for a united society.

Many factors helped solidify this unity. The church and society had become integrated. The differentiation of the church from temporal rulers did not mean the freeing of society from the church. Like a conscience, the church regulated society by its interior omnipresence. The church no longer served emperors and kings; it animated a unified religious civilization. The church helped fashion Western society in the Middle Ages through accumulated power of the many agencies through which it interacted with daily life. The church perceived itself as not only one with society, but as the guiding if not controlling influence on every sphere of human life: personal, family, social, moral, religious, economic, political. It exercised an internal governing pressure. The church exerted influence on the political, educational, religious, and ideological or symbolic levels. The church played a leading role in European politics. The church became the educator of Europe. The church controlled the media of salvation in a religious culture. Monasticism, which in the early church preserved the otherworldly values of Christianity and stood over against society, had a different character in the Middle Ages. It had become a

---

112. I discuss the categories of power and authority, and spiritual power and spiritual authority, in the last section of this chapter.

way of life within or alongside society, a recognized status and mission. The monasteries were the trainers of popes, the preservers of intellectual culture, educators, developers of agriculture, rural centers of activity. Ideologically, Troeltsch shows how the intellectual worldview of Aquinas, a system in which nature and grace interpenetrated, reflects the social world. To summarize in Troeltsch's words: "The total effect of these events was an interpenetration of church and state, of the spiritual and the temporal, of the ascetic and the sociopolitical aspects of life, which gave the church of the Middle Ages a quite different character from that of the early church."[113]

One reason why one hesitates before the idea that the church could ever control society may lie in the natural tendency to see the church as a separate social entity standing over against temporal affairs as in the modern period. In the thirteenth century no such separation existed: the church was internal to the body of society like a skeletal, muscular, and mental structure. It regulated from within as soul, utopic vision, motive, and source of energy, even though concretely in its actions it did not always live up to its own ideals. Medieval life was saturated with religion and church: religious symbols were everywhere. The church possessed the most impressive buildings and the influential people who were recognizable by all in the streets. Time was measured by the church: daily time by bells and the office, weekly time by Sunday worship, yearly time by religious festivals. There were times for fasting and for feasting; days of abstinence from meat, from work, and from sex. In sum, all of history was framed by creation, redemption, and the end time.[114]

PRINCIPLES FOR
A HISTORICAL ECCLESIOLOGY

In the Gregorian reform and the two centuries that followed it, the church in the West underwent a transformation only slightly less momentous than the Constantinian realignment. As a conclusion

---

113. Troeltsch, *The Social Teaching*, 223.
114. Lynch, *The Medieval Church*, 302.

to this representation of its life and self-understanding an enumeration of some of the principles and axioms that were operative in the church during this period will be useful for ecclesiology as such.

The Church in the High Middle Ages Was Unique

Of course, every historical period bears an unrepeatable identity. But any given time may be considered classic, a particularity whose contours exemplify norms that are missed in their passing and operate as ideals or goals for the future. The intricate interweaving of Christian religion and everyday temporal life can operate as a romantic ideal. It seems extremely important, therefore, to insist on what must seem obvious to many: the church of western Europe in the twelfth and thirteenth centuries is not normative, it represents no universal ideal of church organization and existence, and is not closer to the will of God than another particular historical manifestation of the church.

A simple contrast between the organizational form of the church in the High Middle Ages and the church in the great epochs before and after it show plainly enough that such a church never existed prior to that time and will never exist again as such in Europe. The points of contrast between the church described in the last section and the description of the church in the third century are striking. Yet from an ecclesiological perspective, one is not in any way "more" the Christian church than the other. And relative to the future, whereas the unity and homogeneity of Christianity and culture appear attractive from a narrow point of view, it would appear dominating and totalitarian in today's situation of de facto pluralism and a culture in which difference remains welcome as a value in principle. Already at the end of the thirteenth century one can identify elements in the European situation that are undermining the church's hold on society.

The Gregorian Reform Furthered and Strengthened Objectification of the Church

This proposition highlights one aspect of the new church created by the Gregorian reform. The term "objectification" runs parallel to routinization and is always operative in the historical life of an organization. But the Gregorian reform released a movement that harnessed a series of developments into a tight organization of massive size. The structure of the church consisted in a hierarchical organization of offices descending from the pope in Rome to the parish priest in the countryside. This church counted as its members the vast majority of people. The church constituted the one organizational structure that effectively encompassed all of western Europe. Theology and a metaphysical conception of hierarchical order supported the components of the structure. A developed body of law, studied and practiced by a large corps of canon lawyers, further structured the body. It possessed a developed bureaucracy to administer the organization in its complexity practically to its territorial limits. Offices now clearly transcended their incumbents. The Gregorian reform set out to "free" or at least differentiate the Western church in its offices and administration from the Carolingian form of symbiosis with secular life; in doing so it created a massive, autonomous religious institution. The primary referent of the term "church" in the Western church in the Middle Ages is the whole church with the pope as its earthly head, even though its primary theological definition was *"congregatio fidelium."* This stands in marked contrast to the primary referent of the term "church" in antiquity which was the local church as part of a worldwide movement. The large church in the West had changed from a communion of churches.

The Medieval Church Illustrates the Dialectical Relationship between Doctrine and Practice

The principle of institution and understanding being generated by practice and in turn regulating practice governed the development in the first and second centuries and thereafter. Its operation in the medieval church is no less instructive. The further development of the sacraments illustrates it clearly: the church's practices gradually solidified into seven distinct sacraments in the medieval church. A less obvious and more complex example can be seen in the medieval solidification of papal office and power. One can find papal claims to various powers prior to the Gregorian reform going back to the fourth, fifth, and ninth centuries. But it took a whole set of social and economic conditions, religious developments such as Cluny, new beginnings in education and the study of law, and so on, to set the conditions of the possibility of exercising these claims. More important still, the possession of authority depends on the ability to exercise it, and this exercise is administrative. The plausibility of papal claims to authority depended upon the administrative structures that allowed its exercise. In the West, these structures were really built up during the Carolingian period in which the church of Western Europe was unified on a Justinian model. Later popes were able to define and establish papal authority in and over the Western church in a new and distinctive way in the Gregorian reform and its aftermath. But the same papacy failed to establish its authority over the Eastern church. In an ecclesiology from below one must think of theological prerogatives as mediated through and conditioned by concrete historical possibilities.

Tradition Possesses Revolutionary Power in New Situations

Papal claims to spiritual authority illustrate this simple historical maxim. The traditional teaching was indeed that the spiritual realm was superior to and outranked the temporal and material. But in the past a kind of separation and balance of powers obtained: in the Gelasian formula the temporal was temporal and the spiritual spiritual. In the fourth and fifth centuries in the West, the church in varying degrees still stood over against culture. But in the Carolingian period the church became an instrument in the governing of the empire, leading to the frequent merger of the two kinds of authority or power in the one person of the ruler-bishop. For a pope or bishop to claim the superiority of the spiritual in this situation amounted to a subordination of the temporal to the spiritual which sometimes in a given case amounted to a claim to temporal rule itself. To repeat formulas from the past in new situations changes their meaning; the exercise of old precepts in new situations can have revolutionary consequences. One cannot simply repeat the past to preserve it; one must constantly reinterpret it. The church in fact necessarily does this, whether consciously or not.

The Papacy Exercises Various Kinds of Power and Authority

A study of the church in the Middle Ages shows that the pope exercise power and authority in a great variety of ways. The analysis of Gregory's letters shows that he would take a variety of tactical paths to accomplish his goals. Without going deeply into this question, some obvious and important distinctions appear on the surface of this historical period. The first is a distinction between power and authority; a second is an analogous extension of this to the spiritual and religious level, a distinction between a spiritual authority that is dominative and one that appeals to religious freedom.

Authority may be distinguished from power. Whereas power points to the ability to control the behavior of others by some form of coercion or external pressure that binds whether or not they freely accept it, authority may be regarded precisely as the ability to move others to act through an appeal to their freedom. The principle that genuine authority appeals to freedom is most apparent in charismatic leadership, but is not wholly lacking in a rationalized organization. Freedom may still characterize institutions in the collective consent to live by the rules. Analogously, religious or spiritual authority is exercised in the sphere or context of one's relationship to God. But such spiritual authority can be exercised in such a way that, within the context of organized religion, it coerces or relies only on the law, or it can appeal to freedom, inviting the subject's commitment. Religious authority is successful as truly religious and spiritual when it attracts freedom in a certain direction. In the first case authority becomes reduced to spiritual power or dominative spiritual authority. In the latter case, religious authority is genuinely spiritual in its appeal to freedom.

Given this particular polarity in understanding religious authority, one can see these two exercises of authority at work in the papacy, and also in other ecclesiastical offices. On the one hand, since all belong to the church, the church functioned as a necessary organization. It was socially difficult, if not impossible, not to belong to the church. In this context religious authority was often exercised as a kind of dominating spiritual authority, one that appealed to law rather than freedom, and within the boundaries of the law it could threatened with spiritual punishment. The clearest and most extreme example was the penalty of excommunication which could imply, by exclusion from the sacraments, final damnation. The strongest weapon in the papal arsenal was excommunication. By contrast, religious authority could appeal exclusively to freedom with appeals that enticed through perceived religious value. Such was the papal summons for the crusade, although that too entailed commercial values and may have appealed to some base instincts. The first kind of authority, which in its extreme is dominating, relies on the law; it is more objective and rationalized, depends more on the office than the personality of the office holder. The second kind of authority leans toward the charismatic, and may be called symbolic authority because it represents or mediates the values and ideals that attract freedom. Both of these kinds of authority were important to the papacy. In fact they intersected and combined. But it is noteworthy that dominating religious authority frequently appears to be the more esteemed or sought after, while symbolic authority is often neglected, minimized, or reduced to the confines of law. Both were operative during the High Middle Ages, and it is difficult to say which was more important.

The Gregorian Reform Produced Some Ambiguous Effects

The assumption of this observation is that by and large the Gregorian reform was a genuine reformation of the church. Some may, from various points of view, dispute that overall conclusion. Even the more optimistic judgment will normally allow for some negative aspects to what from certain perspectives seemed to have been either salutary or at least necessary. The liberation of the office of the priest from secular constraints provides a good example of this principle. For the church to command respect, it needed a leadership class that possessed some moral, educational, and spiritual stature. The sacramental principle that the effectiveness of the sacraments does not depend upon the personality of the minister would be reduced to absurdity if applied socially to a universally corrupt leadership class. But establishing a more distinct identity of the priest resulted in sewing the seeds of clericalism. Developments in the theology of the eucharist, and attitudes toward it, coupled with a theology of orders, and social conceptions of the social identity of priest all led to an objective ontological view of orders that loosened the tie of the priest to a particular community. A wide gap separates the notion of being a priest in the massive church of the thirteenth century and being a priest in a fourth century church. The bond of the ordained minister to his particular community of the Spirit was severely weakened in theory and practice. Itinerant priests were not only a theological problem but also a practical one. By contrast, the historical continuity and analogy of the early church and the medieval church appear most forcefully in the parish congregation when the pastor is actually ministering to the congregation.

The Categories Church and Sect are Useful for Understanding Unity and Division in the Church

In his analytical study of the church across history, Troeltsch introduces these categories after depicting the church in the Middle Ages.[115] It is not necessary to develop these well-known types here other than to say that the Catholic Church of the Middle Ages represents well, if it was not the model for, the church type. Churches identify with society and have a symbiotic relation to it. By contrast, in Troeltsch's usage, a sect is usually a small community, standing over against society, perhaps prophetic and concerned with its moral purity, and more egalitarian in its membership.[116] These categories are useful for discussing the division of the church into two separated "churches," the Eastern church and the Western church, and the ability of the one Western church to contain monastic movements within itself while rejecting Cathars and Waldensians as heretical.

It is fairly clear that the Eastern church and the Western church began drifting apart from the very foundation of the Eastern capital of the Roman empire in Constantinople in the fourth century. The split between these two churches in the eleventh century simply ratified something that was long a reality. The Western church, especially in and through its papal leadership, internalized a concept of universal jurisdictional authority that projected sovereignty over the whole Christian movement. As a matter of fact or pragmatically, the papacy has never been able to exercise such authority. In terms of

---

115. Troeltsch, *The Social Teachings,* 331–43.

116. The two types of Troeltsch are further developed by H. Richard Niebuhr theologically as distinct from sociologically in his *Christ and Culture* (New York: Harper and Row, 1951) where he distinguishes an extreme and a moderate form of each of Troeltsch's two types, and then proposes a bridging type of the church as the transformer of culture.

Troeltsch's categories, the patriarchal churches of the East and the Western church are all "churches," and it is difficult to imagine such clearly differentiated churches coming together in a single tightly knit organizational unity under one jurisdictional head.

By contrast, the monastic movements in the course of the development of the Western church share many of the characteristics of Troeltsch's sect type of church. At their start they often reflect a high degree of idealism and moral fervor, and often enough reflect some form of countercultural impetus, at least in the practice of withdrawal. They surely reflect a desire among the members to lead an intense Christian life. Yet these movements are completely contained within the confines of the institutional church in which they exist. If they contain a critique of the larger institution's accommodation with society it remains implicit. By contrast, the Cathars, in their attempts at moral purity, defined themselves outside and over against the Western Catholic Church, and the Waldensians were suspected of being so. The question raised by these distinctions concerns the criteria for deciding when unity is possible and when it must be broken. By the insights of current Western postmodern intellectual culture, with its appreciation of historical difference and pluralism, the standards of the Middle Ages do not appear very fluid. This represents another reason why the church created by the Gregorian reform can never be considered universally normative. But its integration with society will always provide a romantically seductive attraction for a Catholic imagination.

Chapter 6

Conciliarism and the Late Medieval Church

Some consider the fourteenth and fifteenth centuries a period of decline. With respect to the church, such a judgment may measure the prestige and authority of the papacy. But more generally with reference to Europe, these centuries saw the growth and solidification of nation states, as in France and England; arts and letters enjoyed a massive renaissance; the spiritual life of the church was enhanced by mysticism and new forms of religious life. There can be no doubt, however, that the stature of the papacy waned, and this had far-reaching impact on the life of the church and society at large. The consistent general desire for reform during this whole period correlated with the central leadership of the Western church losing a good deal of its strictly religious authority, a deteriorization that culminated in the renaissance papacy.

A historical narrative about the ecclesiology of this period finds a focus in conciliarism. Several reasons suggest it. First of all, the conciliarist movement flourished right in the middle of these two centuries. A major "event" that happened over a long period of time, conciliarism fully engaged the leaders of the church throughout Europe and left an impact on the church that lived on below the surface well into the future. Second, although conciliarism is often conceived as pitted against the papacy, because popes and conciliarists fiercely fought each other, it never strove to defeat or destroy the papacy. During the Western schism the goal of the conciliarist movement was to restore the papacy; in accomplishing this it saved the institution. As to the other goal of the conciliarists, reform of the church, it was less successful and ultimately failed. Third, although a Roman Catholic ecclesiology centered on the papacy tended thereafter to declare conciliarism a heresy and thus dismiss it on particularist doctrinal grounds, an ecclesiology from below must consider it a major historical movement in the life of the church, one which would be highly appreciated by other confessions. Fourth, some elements in conciliarism remain coherent and credible today, and one cannot pass up the possible relevance of lessons from another time.

Conciliarism thus forms a kind of center-point in the narrative ecclesiology and the analysis of texts which follow. They move forward toward conciliarism and then away from or beyond it to the end of the fifteenth century. The third part of the chapter describes the church in a language that transcends the conciliarist problematic, but the fourth part suggests that conciliarism contains several principles that would be very valuable for understanding the universal church today and at any given time.

HISTORICAL DEVELOPMENT

Life for many in Europe during this period was difficult. "Famine, plague, war, social violence, economic contraction, the failure of political and religious institutions and religious anxiety haunted Europe for more than 150 years."[1] A constant tension prevailed between popes and secular rulers. As in some giant zero-sum game, kings and other rulers gained more autonomy across Europe, and the papacy lost much of the universal scope of its power. The growth of national states remains in the background of this chronicle of two centuries as a movement in three stages: the events leading up to the Western schism, the conciliarism between 1378 and 1418 that enabled a resolution to that problem, and developments during the rest of the fifteenth century.[2]

---

1. Joseph H. Lynch, *The Medieval Church: A Brief History* (London and New York: Longman, 1992), 303.
2. This schematic narrative is drawn from a number of sources including principally the following: Bernard Cooke, *Ministry to Word and Sacrament* (Philadelphia: Fortress Press, 1976); Eric G. Jay, *The Church: Its Changing Image Through Twenty Centuries* (Atlanta: John Knox Press, 1977); Hubert Jedin and John Dolan, eds., *Handbook of Church History*, 4, *From the High Middle Ages to the Eve of the Reformation* (New York: Herder and Herder, 1970), cited hereafter as *Handbook*; David Knowles, with Dimitri Obolensky, *The Middle Ages* (New York: McGraw-Hill, 1968); Lynch, *The Medieval Church*; Francis Oakley, *The Western Church in the Late Middle Ages*

Tensions within Christendom

The metaphor of "tensions" offers a framework for broad statements about this dynamic period of church history that do not lose touch with concrete events. The tensions symbolized by Francis and the Franciscan movement provide a good place to begin. The spread of the active religious orders, especially the Franciscans and the Dominicans, captured and carried forward a movement of dynamic Christian vitality and idealism that arose before them and extended far beyond them. The new values, especially those surrounding the Franciscan ideal, functioned as a basis for internal criticism of the existing institutions of the church. Christlike poverty, simplicity, and humility stood in contrast to every show of wealth and power by the institutional church. Theologians like John Wyclif exemplified the way in which Franciscan ideals provided criteria for criticism of the structure of parish ministry in the English church.

The thought of Aristotle exercised a significant integrating role in European thinking generally and in the church's theology. But it also played a distinctly disintegrating function. Aristotle was subversive, and the church instinctively recognized this when it repeatedly condemned his thought during the thirteenth century. Aristotelians and Augustinians battled during Aquinas's tenure at the University of Paris. The reason for this lay in different imaginative frameworks for understanding reality: Aristotle's view of the "nature" of things as intrinsic principles of operation implied secularizing insights. The world was not purely sacral and not run by God directly; reasons for things lay within the natural sphere, and the mind could understand them clearly and convincingly. The appeal to the intrinsic causes of things, to natural law, to the natural right of a society to govern itself, and so on, did not so much deny a divine or ecclesiastical view as subvert it, or go around it, on the basis of new suppositions.[3] This development was most evident in its application

---

(Ithaca and London: Cornell University Press, 1979); John A. F. Thompson, *The Western Church in the Middle Ages* (New York: Arnold and Oxford University Press, 1998); Ernst Troeltsch, *The Social Teaching of the Christian Churches* (New York: Harper Torchbooks, 1960).

3. Brian Tierney, *Crisis of Church and State: 1050–1300* (Englewood Cliffs, N.J.: Prentice-Hall, 1964), 159.

to society and government as reflected in a line of thought stretching from Thomas Aquinas, through John of Paris, to an extreme form in Marsilius of Padua. William of Ockham parlayed an Aristotelian realism with a Franciscan sensibility for poverty into fundamental insights concerning the nature of the church.

These philosophical and theological tensions reflected social and political developments in the church and the political centers of Europe. One of the major factors for the beginning of the change in the fortunes of the papacy consisted in the further development of a counterpower and authority.[4] As the church had promoted the study of law and developed a system of administrative bureaucracies, so too nation states gradually responded to the exigencies of administration and developed rationalized governments. As the church learned from the state in the patristic period, here the church led the way.[5] The gradual growth toward nations, national centers with systems of law and administration, led to political power at the periphery to counterbalance the religious power at the center. But another reason for the beginning of the decline of papal power can be located in the very claims of popes to authority: they grew excessive and not quite credible. As the historical situation changed, the arguments did not correspond to reality as it was experienced in new contexts. As the social and political situation of Europe shifted, the sheer repetition of the claims of Gregory VII no longer seemed persuasive.

These factors were at work in the dramatic conflict between Philip IV, the king of France at the turn of the fourteenth century, and Boniface VIII, pope from 1294 to 1303.[6] The conflict began over the right of the local ruler to subject church property to taxes, and it gradually escalated into a test of the ultimate loyalty of the national hierarchy, to Rome or to the nation. The battle illustrates that the tension between a Roman center of the church and lay rulers at the

---

4. Ibid., 159–60.

5. Troeltsch, in *The Social Teaching*, 325, describes the medieval church as a model for an emergent modern state characterized by an institutional unity, with an administrative bureaucracy, a body of laws, and a collective will, dedicated to respect of individual rights and the common good.

6. See among the many accounts of this conflict Hans Wolter, "Celestine and Boniface VIII," *Handbook*, 267–81.

perimeter still obtained; this flare-up resulted in a defeat for the papacy. For his part, Boniface solemnly declared the most far-reaching claim to authority ever, and the whole medieval period of papal power reaches a kind of literary crescendo in the last sentence of the papal bull *Unam Sanctam* (1302): "Therefore we declare, state, define and pronounce that it is altogether necessary to salvation for every human creature to be subject to the Roman Pontiff." And for his part, the French king deliberately distorted the papal position in a public campaign of disinformation and had thugs attack and rough-up the pope physically. Some see the humiliation of the pope by the French king as a turning point in the political history of the papacy. "In a direct confrontation between a pope and a king, people who were subjects of both chose to support their king."[7] It thus encouraged lay rulers to assert more influence on the church locally.

Boniface VIII died in 1303 and was succeeded briefly by Benedict XI and then Clement V who transferred the papal court to Avignon in 1309 and summoned the Council of Vienne. Beginning in October of 1311, this council aimed at fulfilling a threefold task: to settle the matter of the Order of the Knights Templar, to secure aid for the Holy Land, and to consider ways of reforming the church and preserving its liberty. Although sometimes called a reform council, the real pressure for its convocation came from Philip IV. The king wanted the Templars, who were based in Paris, suppressed because of their wealth and control of the flow of money. He had been actively persecuting members of the order for several years. When the council, after an investigation, refused to suppress the Templars, Clement found himself caught between council and king and as a way out suppressed the order on his own authority in 1312.[8] In matters of church reform, this council produced no landmark legislation. Some of the topics it addressed and decisions it made were the following: it tried to settle the dispute between the Spiritual Franciscans and the more moderate faction among them; it addressed the tensions between secular and regular clergy; it suppressed the beguines, but they were given new life by Clement's successor, John XXII; it addressed abuses

---

7. Lynch, *The Medieval Church*, 322.

8. H. J. Schroeder, *Disciplinary Decrees of the General Councils* (St. Louis: B. Herder Book Co., 1937), 365–69.

in liturgical reverence and decorum; it coordinated the activities of the Inquisition and local episcopal tribunals; it tried to regulate the dress and lifestyle of clerics in minor orders.[9]

The story of the decline of the papacy continued during the residency at Avignon. No matter what the causes or reasons for the Avignon papacy, it was anomalous that the bishop of Rome rule the church from a fortified city north of the Alps and within the political sphere of France. Besides being referred to as a "Babylonian Captivity" (Petrarch) of the papacy,[10] the almost seventy years spent there were marked by a growth in the administrative bureaucracy of the papal court and in the efficacy in levying taxes to support itself.[11] During this same period, from 1347 to 1351, the black plague, introduced into Europe through sea trade with Russia, decimated Europe. Generally speaking, these were not joyous times.[12] Finally, in 1377, through the persuasive prodding of Catherine of Siena, Gregory XI moved back to Rome.

But 1378 was a fateful year, for Gregory XI died, and the 16 cardinal electors, with volatile urging from the Roman citizens, chose as his successor an Italian from outside the college of cardinals who was enthroned as pope at Easter. But in the months which followed the new pope apparently acted with intemperate abrasiveness against the cardinals and added Italians to their number. Lacking any canonical leverage over a pope, the non-Italians (eleven French and one Spaniard) left Rome and in August resorted to declaring the papal

---

9. Schroeder, *Disciplinary Decrees*, 372–442.

10. The seven successive popes at Avignon were all French, and they were surrounded by a predominantly French college of cardinals, and an increasingly French administrative bureaucracy. Of the 134 cardinals appointed during the Avignon papacy, 113 were French. See Thompson, *The Western Church*, 170; Lynch, *The Medieval Church*, 326.

11. See Karl August Fink, "The Curia at Avignon," *Handbook*, 333–44, for a concise account of the curial finances, administrative procedures, and courtly extravagance of the cardinals at Avignon. "The unceasing and inconsiderate demands for money and the defective administration of the system of benefices and finances gave scandal." "Every possibility for obtaining money [suspension, excommunication, interdict for fees not paid] was exploited ruthlessly." Ibid., 343.

12. For a brief account of the plague see Lynch, *The Medieval Church*, 306–11. The depiction of the "Dance of Death," a mural of skeletal death leading people of all social classes and positions, hand in hand, to their fate rimmed chapels and churches and communicated the mood of the period.

election unfree in the light of pressure from Roman citizenry. In September the cardinals elected one of their own French members as pope, and he moved back to Avignon. The result was two popes each canonically elected by the same cardinal electors. Approximately half of Europe was obedient to one pope and the other half to the other. The problem had no easy solution.

Things were further complicated with the Council of Pisa which assembled after thirty years of schism. Through various political negotiations the popes from the two lines almost came together to simultaneously resign. But ultimately they refused to meet, and the cardinals on both sides revolted, gathered in 1408, and announced that a general council would meet at Pisa in March of 1409. Both popes were summoned but did not attend. The council had a fairly large representation and proceeded to elect a new pope, Alexander V, after deposing the other two. But the two popes refused to be deposed, and large areas remained loyal to them, and thus three popes reigned with a distinct area of Europe loyal to each. Pisa, however, was not a complete failure. It paved the way for the Council of Constance by showing what could be done and what was to be avoided.[13] Ultimately, the schism would be healed by conciliarism.

Conciliarism and the Resolution of the Great Western Schism

Conciliarism represents a movement, a complex of ideas and initiatives, that grew during the thirteenth and fourteenth centuries and which was widely accepted during the great Western schism and well into the fifteenth century.[14] Viewing conciliarism as a more diffuse movement of thought and action allows it to be considered more objectively because less ideologically. I shall trace the movement of the ideas here, how they inspired action at Constance and Basel, and in the second part of this chapter the ecclesiology implied in them.

The prehistory of conciliarism begins when elements of conciliarist thought appear in the "Decretists," the canonists commenting

---

13. Thompson, *The Western Church*, 183.

14. Brian Tierney defines conciliarism in the following way: "Conciliarism is a doctrine asserting that a general council constitutes the supreme authority in the Church" ("Conciliarism," *New Catholic Encyclopedia*, IV [New York: McGraw-Hill, 1967], 109). In my analysis I consider conciliarism as a historical movement, part of which are various versions of the general theory of the supremacy of a council to a pope.

on the *Decretum* (1140) of Gratian, and afterward.[15] One finds these roots in responses to such questions as the following: can the pope be deposed? When? By whom? What if the pope is found to be heretical? Some of the answers to these questions were these: the pope could be deposed for heresy or serious scandal. Therefore his power is not absolute. The church cannot be considered simply a juridical entity based on an extension of papal authority; rather it is a corporation, a whole community, the Body of Christ. Office in the church does not exist for itself but in service of the corporation. These ideas existed in the canonical tradition, especially the idea of the unity of the whole church as a body of the faithful. This idea rose up more prominently when confronted by the schism.

The importance of Tierney's thesis is simple but foundational. If the other explanations are accepted, conciliarism appears as an anomaly, a freak accident, that arose suddenly and apart from tradition. Or it may appear as coming from outside the church. Tierney proves that it sprang from a tradition within the church.[16] It is important to remember that the canonists carried the tradition of ecclesiological reflection more extensively than the theologians.

Conciliarist themes continued to grow around the issue of the church in relation to temporal power. Tierney's thesis does not rule out other nonecclesial factors influencing the movement. The canonists themselves were riding the tide of eleventh and twelfth-century developments. During the polemics surrounding the question of church and state in the fourteenth century and the Avignon papacy conciliarist themes were developed on a broader level. For example, Marsilius of Padua developed the Aristotelian idea of the natural right of a community or society to have its government. For Marsilius the authority of the legislator really consists in society as a whole, or its

---

15. This is the finding of Brian Tierney in his *Foundations of the Conciliar Theory: The Contribution of the Medieval Canonists from Gratian to the Great Schism* (Cambridge: University Press, 1955), and it is important for explaining the origin of conciliarism. There are a variety of explanations of its genesis: some see it arising with the schism; some with Marsilius of Padua and William Ockham. Still others see it as a cultural by-product of constitutionalism in national governments. Tierney proves that it had roots in canon law and he traces them.

16. Tierney's thesis is seconded by Francis Oakley, *Council Over Pope? Towards a Provisional Ecclesiology* (New York: Herder and Herder, 1969), 78–83.

weightier part. These ideas were not exactly traditional, for they were influenced by society and culture and schooled in an Aristotelian conception of the nature of societies. But at the same time they are congruent with ideas from the canonical tradition. Authority comes from God, but this authority was beginning to be seen as channeled, as it were, from below, ascending to the leader through the people rather than directly descending from God to the leader.[17]

When the schism occurred, beginning in 1378, these ideas were applied to the church and the pope at its head. The problem was formidable. Both popes claimed legitimacy and Christendom itself was split. At issue, then, was the unity of the whole European church and how to restore it. Everyone presupposed that the church in fact was one, in itself and as the unifying ground of Western society. Moreover, the *very basis* of that unity resided in the papacy in a twofold way: first, symbolically, and this was reflected spontaneously through religious loyalty and affection; second, juridically, since the Gregorian reform. But in this situation it was the papacy that caused and constituted the division, even though the cardinals initiated it. The problem that the schism created for the church and the rulers of Europe was that it had to attack the institution on which the unity of the church and society was based in order to restore that unity and the very institution that was supposed to guarantee it.[18] This was the role that was assumed by conciliarism.

The period between 1380 and 1420 produced a good deal of discussion of conciliarist theory and strategies for ending the schism and implementing reform in the church. Analysis of the arguments will be taken up later, but how was the schism resolved? We have already seen that the Council of Pisa did not work because it elected a third pope before the peoples loyal to the deposed popes had pledged obedience to the new one. In the following years leadership for summoning another council was assumed by a layman in the person

---

17. William of Ockham, in many respects the archetypal nominalist and Aristotelian in his ecclesiology, was another "precursor" of conciliar theory. For a summary of his thought and its place in the first half of the fourteenth century see Erwin Iserloh, "Nominalism: The Universities between *Via Antiqua* and *Via Moderna*," *Handbook*, 344–55. I shall say more about Marsilius of Padua and William of Ockham in the next section.

18. Tierney, *Foundations*, 239–40.

of Sigismund, king of Germany, who worked through a reluctant John XXIII, successor of the pope elected at Pisa. The Council of Constance was convened in 1414, and between that year and 1418 the city of Constance acted as the capital of Europe.

The Council of Constance began on November 5, 1414, and ended on April 22, 1418, after forty-five sessions. Its stated purpose was to end the schism, to repress heresy, and to reform the church in head and members. It succeeded in the first task of restoring the papacy; it condemned many opinions of Wyclif and John Hus; it ultimately failed in the long term at reforming the church in either head or members; and it left enshrined in conciliar decrees the doctrine of the supremacy of council to pope.

On April 6, 1415, at its fifth session the council issued *Haec Sancta,* a decree affirming the council's legitimacy and authority over the papal claimants. Speaking in the name of the council the decree states: "First it declares that, legitimately assembled in the Holy Spirit, constituting a general council and representing the Catholic Church militant, it has power immediately from Christ; and that everyone of whatever state or dignity, even papal, is bound to obey it in those matters which pertain to the faith, the eradication of the said schism and the general reform of the said church of God in head and members."[19] On May 4 it condemned a series of propositions of John Wyclif. On May 29 it deposed John XXIII of the Pisan line. On July 6 it executed John Hus, who had been promised a safe passage, after a hearing, a condemnation, and his refusal to recant. On July 14 the council received the resignation of Gregory XII of the Roman line. In September–October of 1415 Sigismund and representatives of the council met with Benedict XIII of the Avignon line in Perpignan with no result. Only after receiving a pledge of loyalty to the council from his former supporters did it depose him in the 37th Session on July 26, 1417. But just as the way seemed clear for electing a new pope a new problem arose: Italy, Spain, and France wanted to elect a pope immediately; the English and Germans wanted reform, especially of the papal curia, before an election. The way forward

---

19. *Haec Sancta,* Council of Constance, Session 5 (April 6, 1415) in Norman P. Tanner, ed., *Decrees of the Ecumenical Councils,* I, *Nicaea I to Lateran V* (London and Washington, D.C.: Sheed & Ward and Georgetown University Press, 1990), 409.

included conciliar legislation intended to ensure that the new pope would attend to the reform. Thus on October 9, 1417, Constance issued the decree *Frequens* which required regular councils.[20] Then on November 11 the cardinals and other council members representing the nations elected Cardinal Otto Colonna as Pope Martin V.

Prior to the election of the pope, the council had issued a decree containing eighteen points of reform that should be addressed. After his election, Martin V responded to the topics with drafts of reform decrees for the council's action. From these drafts the council fashioned seven decrees, which mainly revoked the benefices and exemptions established during the schism and limited the pope's ability to impose general taxes.[21] Finally, in April of 1418 Martin V designated Pavia as the site of the first regular council five years from that date.

What is the canonical status or legality of *Haec Sancta*, the decree which affirmed the superiority of a council over a pope? This is a disputed question. On the one hand, the decree was never taken up and officially accepted or ratified by the newly elected pope, Martin V, whereas he did ratify other decrees of the council. And later popes, while they accepted the council generally, did so with the express reservation of any diminution of the rights of Rome.[22] Some hold it was a decree prepared to meet only a particular concrete situation; some cardinals had protested against it.[23] On the other hand, the council was a fully authoritative body, actually summoned by John XXIII, so that it did not have to be ratified and no one thought it did. Everyone, including Martin V who was a conciliarist, accepted

---

20. In the words of the council: "we establish, enact, decree and ordain, by a perpetual edict, that general councils shall be held henceforth in the following way. The first shall follow in five years immediately after the end of this council, the second in seven years immediately after the end of the next council, and thereafter they are to be held every ten years for ever." *Frequens*, Council of Constance, Session 39 (Oct. 9, 1417) in Tanner, *Decrees*, 439.

21. Discussion of reform abounded prior to Constance, and much was decided at the council itself, so that "the old and often repeated assertion that it did little for the reform of the church is completely unjustified." Karl August Fink, "The Council of Constance: Martin V," *Handbook*, 464.

22. Knowles, *The Middle Ages*, 421.

23. For example, Thompson holds that *Haec Sancta* was a purely *ad hoc* decree, to be understood only in its immediate circumstances. The council established itself as a superior authority only for that occasion. Thompson, *The Western Church*, 185.

this decree as valid. Even after Martin V the decree was accepted because the validity of the papacy depended on the validity of the council which deposed John XXIII. It was a canonically correct document.[24] Thus the question is still debated, but in fact it gradually became moot as conciliarism as a movement lost its power. But at the same time, conciliarist ideas lingered on and were operative in the sixteenth century when the church split again.

The Western Church at the End of the Middle Ages

The years following the Council of Constance represent a period of papal resurgence. Gradually popes gained the leverage to exercise their sovereignty in the midst of their struggle with conciliarists and actual councils, especially the Council of Basel. According to the decree, *Frequens,* a council was to be called in five years. It assembled in Pavia in Italy and transferred almost immediately to Siena because of plague. Meeting during 1423 and 1424 it accomplished very little and was suspended by Martin V because of poor attendance.

Seven years later, the Council of Basel opened in 1431. Eugenius IV was elected pope on the eve of the council in March, the month the council was to begin. It began slowly as delegates trickled in. It was made up of fewer bishops and more university people and lower clergy than previous councils. Strongly conciliarist and even antipapalist, Basel engaged in a constant struggle for power with the pope. In December of 1431, Eugenius issued a bull dissolving the council and convoking another for 1433 in Bologna to accommodate representatives of the Greek church who were seeking union. This unleashed antipapal and conciliarist sentiment within the council and abroad, and in the course of 1432–33 the council wore the pope down with threats and sheer political power. Finally, on December 15, 1433, the pope recognized the council. In the course of 1434–36 Basel proceeded to ratify Constance and the conciliarist principle over again, and on this basis proposed legislation that would further limit papal power. It also proposed a number of decrees in the direction of

---

24. For example, Fink declares that: "From the viewpoint of the contemporary political and intellectual situation, the Council of Constance in its entirety must be regarded as ecumenical and its decrees universally binding." Fink, "The Council of Constance: Martin V," *Handbook,* 467–68.

church reform, mainly of the Roman curia and its ability to raise revenues from the church at large. During this period as well negotiations with Constantinople continued, and both Eugenius and the Greeks favored a council of reunion in an Italian city.

Early in 1437 the Council of Basel began to divide into two factions, a majority for remaining in Basel and a minority for reconvening in an Italian city in favor of reuniting with the Greek Church. The majority consisted largely of doctors and lower clergy; the minority consisted largely of papal legates and bishops. On May 7 there was a shouting match in which the two factions "read their decrees at the same time."[25] In late December or on January 1, 1438, Eugenius ordered the Council of Basel transferred to Ferrara in Italy, and a minority faction that included many of the bishops transferred with it. It opened on January 8, and on February 15 the pope presided with 72 bishops present. This branch of the original council continued in Ferrara for a year, was then transferred to Florence (1439), and finally transferred to Rome (1442) where the last session was held on August 7, 1445. All of this time was spent dealing with the Greek Church in an effort toward reunion. From Florence in 1439 the decree *Laetentur Coeli* declared the reunion of the Orthodox and the Latin churches. However, desire for military support in resisting the advance of the Turks motivated the suit of the Greek Church for union with the West, and the doctrinal agreements were forced. In the end the Greek churches back home rejected the concessions that were made at the Council of Florence: there was no effective union.[26]

In the meantime, Basel continued until 1449. Among other things it deposed Eugenius as a heretic and elected an anti-pope. But in the end the Council of Basel was doomed to failure. In electing its own pope and thereby reintroducing schism it turned the world against itself. Ultimately the pope outmaneuvered Basel and, through the help of the Greeks, regained control over church and council. There

---

25. Schroeder, *Disciplinary Decrees*, 467.

26. Along the way, however, *Laetentur Coeli* responded to *Haec Sancta* by defining that, to the pope "was committed in blessed Peter the full power of tending, ruling and governing the whole church..." *Laetentur Coeli*, Council of Florence, Session 6 (July 6, 1439), in Tanner, *Decrees*, 528.

was no general support for conciliarist ideas among the rulers of Europe. The short decree of Pius II, *Execrabilis*, of 1460 is the final nail in the coffin of conciliarist government of the Western church.

The fifteenth century ended with the popes securely but sometimes scandalously in charge of the European church. The renaissance papacy is often regarded as another low point in the history of popes. They were generally more noted for their wealth, patronage of the arts, nepotism, and offspring than for their sanctity.[27]

This chronicle of the late Middle Ages has so focused on the papacy that one might suspect that no other aspect of the church was worthy of note. This is not the case. These centuries were marked by the appearance of such mystics as Meister Ekhart, Catherine of Siena, and others. The wave of nominalism in theology, with its attendant premise of the absolute transcendence of God, left a legacy that would reappear in the sixteenth-century Reformation. Nicholas of Cusa synthesized conciliarist principles in an expansive treatise on the church. Some consider the work of Juan de Torquemada, *Summa de Ecclesia*, of the fifteenth century the first systematic work in ecclesiology.[28] The lay piety which emerged as a movement in the twelfth and thirteenth centuries grew significantly in this period and took explicit institutional forms in the confraternities and other lay associations. The *devotio moderna* named a renewed wave of spirituality that affected clergy and laity alike and included a deep attachment to the eucharist. And the scholarship of the humanists stimulated a historical reappropriation of the scripture and the Fathers of the church. Finally, if there was one common sentiment that united the whole

---

27. "The popes must be regarded as monarchs, who differed from their lay counterparts only in the fact that their position was elective rather than hereditary." But family played a role in the elections. "Paul II was the nephew of Eugenius IV, Alexander VI of Calixtus III, Pius III of Pius II, and Julius II of Sixtus IV." Thompson, *The Western Church*, 226. For a brief history of the papacy during these two centuries see William J. La Due, *The Chair of Saint Peter: A History of the Papacy* (Maryknoll, N.Y.: Orbis Books, 1999), 135–82.

28. The work was written at mid-century and first published in 1480. It took a strong institutional and papalist point of view, and in this respect was influential in the 1560s when it was republished. There were other treatments of the church prior to Torquemada, for example, James of Viterbo's *De Regimine Christiana* (1301–2), but Torquemada dealt entirely with the church and with the entire church. It aimed at being a systematic *summa*. William E. Maguire, *John of Torquemada, O.P.: The Antiquity of the Church* (Washington, D.C.: Catholic University of America Press, 1957), 9–10.

church at the beginning of the sixteenth century, it was a desire for reform of the church in head and members.

SOCIAL AND THEOLOGICAL ANALYSIS

An analysis of some authors and texts representative of the late Middle Ages will specify more concretely the developments of the church and its self-understanding during this period. They are arranged chronologically. A good place to begin is the rise of autonomous nation states and the consequent shifting relations between church and state that lay behind the conflict between Philip IV and Boniface VIII. The political philosophy developing in tandem with events in this period had a direct bearing on ecclesiology.

Aristotelianism, Nation States, and the Church

The growth of naturalism reinforced by Aristotelian language communicated a point of view on reality that took on a life of its own. It can be seen at work in various authors and in different ways. In many ways Aristotle's metaphysics possesses a certain common sense character. One can trace its growing influence on conceptions of society over the period between the writings of Thomas Aquinas, John of Paris, and Marsilius of Padua, followed by Ockham.

Thomas Aquinas. On the issues of the state and the relation between church and state the ideas of Aquinas resembled those of Aristotle. They stood in contrast to the view, stemming from Augustine, that "civil government existed only because men had fallen into sin."[29] Thomas followed Aristotle in holding that civil government played an inherent role in human existence itself: human beings exist in solidarity, can achieve human goals only in community, and therefore need public authority to regulate social affairs. This intrinsic demand for social organization and thus natural origin of the state was complemented by distinctions between eternal, natural, positive, and divine law. "On Thomistic premises it became possible to construct a theory of an autonomous state, functioning justly according to its own laws and independent of ecclesiastical supervision."[30]

---

29. Tierney, *Crisis*, 165.
30. Ibid., 167.

Thomas held for a parallelism of spheres, authorities, and powers. "The spiritual and the secular power are both derived from the divine power; and therefore the secular power is under the spiritual only... in those things that pertain to salvation of the soul.... But in those things that pertain to civil good, the secular power is to be obeyed rather than the spiritual, according to the saying in Matthew 22: [21], 'Render to Caesar the things that are Caesar's.'"[31]

John of Paris. The dispute between Philip IV of France and Boniface VIII at the turn of the century stirred up the question of the relation of the powers of secular and ecclesiastical rulers to each other. Among the many views on this question at the time, many consider those of John of Paris among the most balanced. He was a Dominican Friar and teacher who died in 1306. His *Treatise on the Powers of Kings and Popes* incisively represented Aristotelian thinking. John advocated a kind of parallelism of powers, two spheres of rule each of whose authority is received from God. The spiritual may be the higher authority, but within the secular sphere, civil rule is autonomous. While this resembles the doctrine of the patristic period, four elements mark a distinct progression. First, Aristotelian underpinnings anchor John's position: solid arguments from the social nature of human existence. Second, although office bears an authority that comes from God, human beings negotiate the selection of the person in authority; this human action as it were channels the authority of God to both king and prelate, so that in some measure it depends on human agents. The pope does not delegate episcopal authority. As John puts it: "the power of prelates is not from God through the pope but immediately from God and from the people who elect or consent."[32] For John of Paris simple monarchy was not the highest form of government; highest was one in which all the people participated through chosen representatives.[33] Third, the ruler is responsible to the community. "The lord pope as head and

---

31. Thomas Aquinas, *Commentary on the Four Books of the Sentences* (1253–55), trans. E. Lewis, *Medieval Political Ideas* (New York: 1954), 566–67, cited in Tierney, *Crisis,* 171.

32. John of Paris, *Tractatus de Potestate Regia et Papali* (1302–3), text in Tierney, *Crisis,* 208. Cited in the text as *Tractatus* with the page reference to Tierney.

33. Tierney, *Crisis,* 197.

supreme member of the universal church is the general and universal administrator of all the goods of the churches both spiritual and temporal. He is not indeed the owner of them..." (*Tractatus*, 206). In this he reinforces an idea insisted upon by Bernard of Clairvaux.[34] Fourth, the ruler can be deposed for behaving criminally or bringing scandal upon the church. Neither secular ruler nor prelate can depose the other; but in the case of malfeasance, each can stir up the proper authorities or the whole community to cast the offender out of office.[35]

Marsilius of Padua. The political backdrop of the careers of both of Marsilius of Padua and William of Ockham involves the last major confrontation of pope and emperor of the medieval period. Ludwig of Bavaria was elected emperor in 1314, but not unanimously, and he did not militarily defeat his rival until 1322. Ludwig would reign as emperor until his death in 1347. Pope John XXII was elected in 1316. He refused to recognize Ludwig as emperor, and when he acted as emperor without papal confirmation, the pope excommunicated him in 1324. Thereupon Ludwig proceeded to Rome, had himself installed as emperor, and set up a rival pope there before returning to Germany in 1330. The dispute between the authority of secular ruler and pope, therefore, had a living context. There were other issues as well. Soon after his election Pope John XXII tried to resolve the ongoing conflict over matters relating to the role of poverty in Christian life, generally relative to the question of the church's ownership of property, and specifically with respect to Franciscan values. These questions deeply engaged Franciscan spirituality, but they far transcended asceticism in a political economy based on land.

Marsilius was born in Padua between 1275 and 1280. He studied philosophy and medicine at the University of Paris, was made

---

34. "John not only maintained that the prince in the state and the pope in the church existed to promote the welfare of the whole community in their different ways, but also that they were in a real sense responsible to the community. The withdrawal of consent by the people could be just as effective in deposing an evil ruler as the giving of consent was in establishing a good one. The pope, for instance, was steward of all the goods of the church and defender of the church's faith, but if he misappropriated the goods of the church or betrayed the faith of the church he was liable to rebuke and in the last resort to deposition by a general council or by the cardinals acting on behalf of all the people." Tierney, *Crisis*, 197.

35. Tierney, *Crisis*, 210.

Rector of the University in 1313, and taught there up until 1324. In that year he finished the *Defender of Peace*, which was quickly condemned, so that Marsilius was forced to leave. He took refuge with Ludwig of Bavaria in Rome, and eventually returned with him to Germany. This account looks at Marsilius from the particular vantage point of ecclesiology. He was bent on showing how the papacy had assumed temporal authority and power not its own and was responsible for general civil unrest. Marsilius was an important figure in the large arena of political and social theory. Relative to ecclesiology, his opinions helped to deabsolutize the Gregorian structure of the church, encourage conciliarist thinking, and provide alternatives in ecclesiological understanding that could be constructive in other situations.

The *Defensor Pacis* has a two-part construction, to which is added a brief summary-conclusion. The first part explains generally the nature and function of government with the help of Aristotelian reasoning. The second antipapalist part describes the strife caused by the claims of the church to authority in European society. Here he appeals freely to scripture. Gewirth summarizes Marsilius's vision of a peaceful harmonious society in this way: "The government is that part of the state which maintains such peace. It does so by judging disputes which are among the citizens, by assigning different citizens to different functions, and by regulating the performance of those functions. But in order that the government may not pervert this authority to its own private interests, it must be regulated in its function by law, and the law must be made by the people, the whole body of citizens.... Consequently, the government must be 'one' in the sense that all the governmental acts and commands emanate ultimately from one source."[36] But in fact there is no peace because the church confuses spiritual and temporal authority and attempts to exercise hegemony over temporal society.

One can, by oversimplification, isolate three broad positions that Marsilius takes against the reigning ecclesiology. These define a

---

36. Alan Gewirth, ed. and trans., Marsilius of Padua, *The Defender of Peace*, II, *The Defensor Pacis* (New York: Columbia University Press, 1956), xxiv. Cited in the text as DP with reference to part (or discourse), chapter, and number.

general framework for understanding the church. First, Marsilius operated within the Constantinian-Justinian-Carolingian framework of the single ruler of society who regulated the public life of the church. "Only the ruler by authority of the legislator has coercive jurisdiction over the person and property of every individual mortal person, of whatever status, and of every group of laymen or clergymen" (DP, 3.2.15). Gone is the parallelism and tensive balance between temporal and spiritual authority.

Second, Marsilius advocated a strong distinction between temporal and spiritual authority; priests had spiritual authority and no God-given coercive temporal authority. The essential authority of the priest is to administer the sacraments (DP, 2.7–10). "A bishop or priest, as such, has no rulership or coercive jurisdiction over any clergyman or layman, even if the latter be a heretic" (DP, 3.2.14). Moreover, the distinctions among priests according to office is of human and not divine origin. And what was humanly bestowed could be humanly taken away.

Third, Marsilius advocated a kind of republicanism in which society's legislator was the community itself or its weightier part. "Only the whole body of citizens, or the weightier part thereof, is the human legislator" (DP, 3.2.6). But this applied to both state and to the church which was comprised of the same people. Thus the government of the church was conciliar, and the community itself appointed the positions of authority in the church. "Only the general council of all the faithful has the authority to designate a bishop or any metropolitan church highest of all, and to deprive or depose them from such position" (DP, 3.2.32). A general council determined the articles of Christian faith (DP, 3.2.2).

One can find precedent for many of these views. But Marsilius wove them together into a tight, fiercely argued package that not only contradicted contemporary practice but seemed scandalous. The important thing here is not whether or not Marsilius's ideas had any chance of success at the time. Rather he witnesses to the cultural and political shifts of the period. He helped nurture conciliarist ideas which would flower in the later crisis. And he anticipated many ideas which became commonplace in the modern era.

William Ockham

Not much of the early life of Ockham is known. He was perhaps born in 1285 in Ockham, Surrey. He studied and taught theology at Oxford and had become a Franciscan by 1324 when he was summoned to Avignon to be investigated for some of his opinions. He was finally examined in 1328. In May of 1328, however, he and the Minister General of the Franciscans, who had also been summoned to Avignon, and a small band of Franciscans who opposed the teachings of John XXII, fled by boat down the Rhone. Ockham joined the retinue of Ludwig of Bavaria, first in Pisa, and then in 1330 returned with him to Germany and lived in Munich under Ludwig's protection. He was excommunicated by John XXII in 1328 almost immediately after leaving Avignon for doing so without permission and refusing to return when summoned. He wrote extensively in the areas of epistemology and philosophy as well as theology. He died in Munich in 1347 unreconciled with the church and was buried in the Franciscan convent where he lived.

Ockham's writings on the church are occasional, nonsystematic, and polemical. His ecclesiology is scattered through thirteen separate works which treat a wide variety of ecclesiological matters in an unorganized way. John Ryan calls it a "radical theology of the church which . . . testifies to the transitional nature of the era in which it was produced."[37]

Ryan interprets Ockham's ecclesiology as responding to a dilemma. On the one hand, Ockham accepted much of the traditional language of the church regarding its divine foundation, including the foundations of the papacy in Peter. On the other hand, he was convinced that the papacy at Avignon in the person of John XXII and his successors was in heresy. He needed an ecclesiology that could explain this (JR, 57).[38]

---

37. John J. Ryan, *The Nature, Structure and Function of the Church in William of Ockham* (Missoula, Mont.: Scholars Press, 1979), 3, 56. I rely principally on Ryan's interpretation of the logic of Ockham's ecclesiology. References to this work in the text are cited as JR and its page number.

38. In 1334 Ockham wrote a letter to the assembly of Franciscans in Assisi as an apology for his behavior and position. He explained that he was convinced that the pope was seriously in error and even heretical in many of his teachings. He provided a long list of these errors in propositional form. "Because of the errors and heresies written

Ockham's solution to the dilemma consisted in a distinction be-tween two aspects of the church and subordinating one to the other. In this way he did not deny the divine authorization of the hierarchi-cal structure of the church, but he set it in a broader context in which it was relativized (JR, 58). He explained the difference between the institutional structure of the church and its communitarian life as a congregation of the faithful. In its essence the church is the union of people in faith: "True belief appears to constitute for Ockham the common good of the church and its real nature. . . . [H]e does in fact subordinate everything else to the needs of faith. He may say that the church is a visible kingdom, but its only true bond is the invisible union of faith" (JR, 59). Ockham does not separate the visible and invisible, nor restrict the reality of the church to the invisible func-tioning of faith. "Ockham does not present two forms of the church, but rather two laws for the church, both intended to be taken as di-vine" (JR, 57). Ockham, therefore, affirms the divine establishment of the papacy and hierarchy, but he undercuts its absolute authority and attenuates it relative to the needs of the community (JR, 9–16).[39]

The distinction and tension that Ockham proposes operates be-tween two divine aspects of the church: institution and the wholeness of the believing community. These represent two aspects or distin-guishable spheres of operation in which the overall health of the living faith of the community takes priority (JR, 55–57). Although Ryan does not use this language, one can see the principle of func-tionality implicitly operative in what Ockham proposes: the structure

---

above and countless others, I withdraw from the obedience of the pseudo-pope and of all who support him to the prejudice of the orthodox faith." The errors were of such a nature that the pope was "deprived of the papacy and excommunicated by the law itself." The errors that Ockham fixed on most prominently had to do with the pope's teachings on poverty and on the question of the authority of church and civil rulers, or spiritual and temporal rule. See William of Ockham, *The Letter to the Friars Minor and Other Writings*, ed. Arthur Stephen McGrade and John Kilcullen, trans. John Kilcullen (Cambridge: University Press, 1995), 12–13. Cited as *Letter.*

39. "As we observe Ockham pursue the disengagement of the essential reality of the church from its structures, the bifurcation in his view of the church becomes more and more apparent. He sees its hierarchically structured institution as originating in Christ's action and possessing divine authorization; but at the same time he sees its inmost reality — the union of true believers — as having a divine guarantee which at any time might dissociate it from the divinely authorized structure." JR, 29.

is indeed God-given, but it is not absolute and is subject to the possibility of distortion or error. When it departs from essential belief, it must be judged in the light of the higher divine dimension of the living community, its faith life, which the institution functions to preserve.

Ockham in the end was neither a conciliarist nor a Marsilian, two positions with which he has been frequently aligned. Although he shared some views with both of these camps, he was not a conciliarist because he defended the divinely established and universal authority of the papacy. Although he held that this authority was not absolute and at certain times could be overruled or bypassed, he did not place supreme authority in a council. In other words, Ockham also deabsolutized a general council; councils are not infallible. Councils are legitimate vehicles of church teaching, but he did not make the conciliarist or Marsilian move of investing full authority in any particular office or group over against the papacy.[40] He also differed from Marsilius on another fundamental issue. Marsilius held that because of the contentious character of human beings the best form of government must be one in which all are subject to one sole authority. Ockham clearly distinguished himself from that position by holding a Gelasian dualism of spiritual and secular authority.[41] But, finally, both Marsilius's and Ockham's views were influential with the conciliarists.

John Wyclif

Wyclif was born in 1328, studied at Oxford, received the Master's degree around 1358 and became a Doctor of Theology in 1372. For a brief period he worked for the king but returned to lecture at Oxford. His views on temporal authority and the right of dominion over property, especially relative to the church, got him into trouble. He proposed that secular rulers should expropriate the church's property if it were sinfully managed. The theology behind this position involved God's dominion and human stewardship and the right to exercise it. However, he escaped condemnation. After 1378, the year

40. McGrade and Kilcullen, *Letter*, xx–xxi.
41. See Ockham, "Question III" of *Eight Questions on the Power of the Pope*, in *Letter*, 299–333.

of the beginning of the Western schism, Wyclif's writings become much more radical and especially antipapal. Among them were his views on the eucharist which attacked the doctrine of transubstantiation of Lateran IV. He lost some support of his fellow theologians on this issue and in 1382 retired to his parish where he died in 1384.

Besides the content of his writings, the significance of Wyclif lies in the actual influence these writings exercised. Wyclif himself was influenced by Marsilius of Padua and by St. Francis. In turn, John Hus carried Wyclif's thoughts and writings back to the continent. His ideas were prevalent enough for them to be condemned at Constance and for Hus to be burned for refusing to retract them. Wyclif's ideas and especially his desire for reform would be felt in the sixteenth century making him a precursor of the Reformation.

A short work by Wyclif, *On the Pastoral Office*, offers insight into the institutions of ministry in fourteenth-century England; one can recognize the structures of parish life described in the last chapter. The text provides both a severe criticism and a presentation of a positive ideal for the ministry and life of the clergy.[42] The reader of this text sees double: on the one hand, the description of institutional abuses allows one theologically to appreciate the aims of clerical ministry and spirituality. On the other hand, the high spiritual ideals of the Word of God and Franciscan spirituality lead one to estimate the degree to which they were compromised and the urgency of reform. This portrait of ministry unfolds in three stages: first, the premise; second, the ills; third, the reformer's conception of the form pastoral ministry should take.

This work rests on the premise of the spiritual character of the mission of the church. This picks up the theme sounded by Marsilius: a strong distinction between the spiritual and the temporal, and the sphere of the church separated off from worldly goals. Possessions, specifically property and wealth, threaten to corrupt the very nature of the church.[43] Within this framework Wyclif discusses

---

42. John Wyclif, *The Pastoral Office*, in *Advocates of Reform: From Wyclif to Erasmus,* ed. Matthew Spinka (Philadelphia: Westminster Press, 1953). Cited in the text as PO by part and chapter.

43. Wyclif is an example of one scandalized by the wealth of the church. "The magnificence of the papal court and the wealth of cardinals, bishops, and abbots were

the pastor, and by extension ministry in general, but with particular emphasis on the delivery of the Word of God on the parish level.

The main problems within the church, as Wyclif saw it, had to do with wealth. He laced into bishops, friars, canons, and monks (PO, 1.16); he explicitly attacked the religions orders, the Franciscans, Dominicans, Carmelites, and Augustinians, for their castles, abbeys, lands, and general wealth (PO, 2.6). The desire for worldly possessions had infected every level of church ministry.[44] Wealthy prelates who played the role of secular lords were a scandal and merited abusive language: they "are commonly gorged with inhuman and gluttonous feasts, and yet are satiated sumptuously without a qualm from the goods of the poor" (PO, 1.4). Even on the level of the parish, Wyclif gives the impression that many a pastor was fleecing his flock (PO, 1.7). He reacts against the system of the absentee curate who lives off the parish income while a vicar ministers to the congregation (PO, 1.11, 1.17, 2.8). Wyclif also testifies to clerical concubinage: "As for lust, many so-called curates are not content with a parish church unless they have a chapel attached thereto, or a wife sojourning with them or living sumptuously apart, yet near enough to be supported by parish funds. Yet they live outside of matrimony in open adultery..." (PO, 1.17). But greed outstrips lust as the corruptor of the clergy.

In reaction against the state of ministry in the church as he saw it, Wyclif constructs an understanding of ministry from below that aims at the effective mediation of the Word of God to the people. First of all the curate should be actually poor. Poverty guarantees the spiritual mission of the church, and this mission obliges the parish priest to poverty (PO, 1.2). The priest should relinquish treasure and temporal goods "beyond what is necessary for the fulfillment of his

---

in scandalous contrast with the Christianity of the New Testament." Jay, *The Church,* 133.

44. "There are three degrees to which clerics have lapsed from the poverty of Jesus Christ. The first degree is in occupying secular lordship. In this degree are the pope, bishops, abbots, and others in many ways disguised. In the second degree are those having only slightly anxious possession of so-called temporal movable goods. In the third degree are the clerics burning with desire for temporal goods, and others who have cast aside anxiety for the cure of souls and thrust their anxiety too much into the quest for the temporal goods of this world." PO, 2.11.

holy office" (PO, 1.3, 1.15, 2.10). What is left over should be used for benefit of the poor (PO, 2.8).

Describing the curate, Wyclif says he should be competent for parish ministry. The primary responsibility and quality required in a pastor is his holiness and integrity of life (PO, 1.1). He should be elected by the parishioners on the basis of merit alone and not appointed from outside. The curate should live on the basis of the support of the parishioners. Wyclif objects to the system of endowed parishes. The curate is responsible to the people of the parish, and such responsibility cannot be exercised from outside or through a vicar: "no curate can satisfy God through a vicar without in his own person incurring sin" (PO, 2.8). Pastors should preach; preaching the Word of God is the primary ministry. "Among all the duties of the pastor after justice of life, holy preaching is most to be praised.... Preaching the gospel exceeds prayer and administration of the sacraments, to an infinite degree" (PO. 2.2).[45]

Finally, Wyclif advocated the translation of scripture into the vernacular. In his view "Saint Jerome labored and translated the Bible from divers tongues into Latin that it might after be translated into other tongues. Thus Christ and his apostles taught the people in that tongue that was best known to them" (PO, 2.2). Wyclif was evangelically motivated in this: he wanted the Word of God in English so it could directly nourish the faith of the people. Translation would provide the faithful with leverage against the distortions of the friars. The norm for true faith and the principles for the spiritual existence lived in the pages of the New Testament.

Wyclif in some respects stood over against the whole system of the church, against church finances, official procedures, law, bureaucratization, administration, and institutionalized wealth, armed with

---

45. A good deal of preaching was prescribed during the late Middle Ages: on Sundays, feast days, during the week in Advent and Lent. It was a basic medium of instruction. But it was also neglected, especially in rural areas, and the quality of preaching was elementary and poor. One basic problem was the inadequate education of priests; a high estimate is that 20 percent attended university. Also, given the practice of absentee benefice holders, vicars were poorly recompensed. But there were no lack of numbers. I referred to a clergy glut in thirteenth century England in the last chapter (see p. 322, n. 82). Iserloh estimates that in certain cities in Germany during the late Middle Ages 10 percent of the population were priests and religious. Erwin Iserloh, "The Inner Life of the Church," *Handbook*, 567, 574–78.

simple evangelical convictions, namely, the spiritual mission of the church and its consequent call to poverty. He is a direct descendant of Francis and reflects the general desire for reform in the church at large.

Eucharistic Feast of Corpus Christi and Confraternities

While Wyclif complained about lack of attention to the ministry of the Word in parish life, eucharistic devotion flourished in the course of the fourteenth century through the development of the feast of Corpus Christi. The last chapter indicated that this feast has its origin in the thirteenth century. It stems from a recurrent visionary dream of Juliana of Cornillon (c. 1193–1258), who served in a leper hospital in Liège. The dream was interpreted as an urging from God for a eucharistic feast. This was communicated to her confessor, and through him to the bishop and the Dominicans who ministered to beguines. The bishop established the feast in his diocese in 1246, but he died within the year and his successor suppressed it. However, the feast was promoted by the Dominicans and others in Europe during the course of the thirteenth century. Finally, early in the fourteenth century the feast was fully recognized universally through the attention of John XXII.[46] It is generally believed that Thomas Aquinas was the author of the liturgy of the feast of Corpus Christi.

How was the eucharist understood during this period? Scholastic theology had generated a strong, realistic and almost physical understanding of Christ's presence in the sacrament. This was mediated to people through the parish. Manuals of fundamental doctrine, the "mysteries of the church," provided clergy with basic theological knowledge. In one such manual the author explains the eucharist in terms of "its foundation, its nature, the priest, conditions of worthy reception, in a succession of short chapters which resemble a series of practical questions and answers" (Rubin, 86). About half of it dealt with the eucharist (Rubin, 90). Besides the manuals for the clergy,

---

46. Miri Rubin, *Corpus Christi: The Eucharist in Late Medieval Culture* (Cambridge: Cambridge University Press, 1991), 164–85. This work is cited in the text as Rubin by page number.

fourteenth-century catechisms in the vernacular addressed the laity (Rubin, 98–108).[47]

The feast of Corpus Christi was a time for explicit instruction on the sacraments in sermons, especially on the eucharist. Rubin analyzes at length an early fourteenth-century didactic English sermon. It opens with a general statement about the feast and how it was founded and endowed with indulgences, and how all priests, good or bad, have the power of consecration effecting Christ's real presence. The sermon then goes on to describe four properties or effects of the sacrament. First, it mediates the redemptive power of Christ to humankind, to those alive and dead; second, it recalls the passion of Christ, the source of all grace; third, it is the token of love of God for humans and the return of love by human beings for God; and, fourth, the transubstantiation of the eucharist provides a test for Christian faith. "A short summary at the end of the sermon exhorts men and women to worship God's body with all their might and to love Him wholeheartedly" (Rubin, 222–24, cited at 224).

Another aspect of the social function of the eucharist appears in its relationship to the growth of fraternities during the fourteenth century. Fraternities or confraternities were voluntary associations organized around a variety of activities geared toward mutual help, nurturing common interests, or sociability. These fraternities increased at the middle of the century, some think because of increased lay piety, or dissatisfaction with the parish structure, or in response to the disorientation in the wake of the plague. But whatever the multiple reasons, one can "understand fraternities as providers of essential personal, familial, religious, economic and political services, [and] as providing security in some essential areas of life..." (Rubin, 233). Very often these fraternities were explicitly religious and, if not, they might still have involved religious activities.[48] Among the religious fraternities, many were explicitly thematized around Corpus Christi.

---

47. The manual, "Manipulus Coratorum," written by a priest, Guy of Montrocher, in 1333 and considered a classic in the fourteenth century, dealt with sacraments, penitential practice, the Our Father, and the ten commandments. I will discuss the question of theological knowledge and catechesis later in this section.

48. Thompson, *The Western Church*, 208–9. Basic Christian Communities, which flourished after Vatican II in Latin America, but with roots prior to that, display features analogous to the confraternities of the late Middle Ages.

"Corpus Christi fraternities exhibit traits which were common to most fraternities: they provided funerary services and relief to members and their dependents, and organized feasts and dinners; some provided legal support, and all indulged in para-liturgical activities, those religious practices which went beyond basic parochial requirements. Most Corpus Christi fraternities held their annual meetings on or around the feast day; these assemblies were often combined with commemoration of dead members. . . . Yet the eucharistic interests exhibited by the Corpus Christi fraternities never overwhelmed the basic routine of sociability and mutual help, but rather enhanced it" (Rubin, 234–35). Thus these associations might run a hospital, an almshouse, promote visitation to the sick, found a college; but these social concerns meshed with eucharistic and general religious interests.

The Corpus Christi procession. Corpus Christi was a summer feast, and the procession outside the confines of the church or monastery rapidly expanded during the second quarter of the fourteenth century. This may be seen as an outgrowth of the efficacy attached to looking upon the consecrated species that will be described more fully further on. With the procession, the public presentation of the eucharistic species grew into a far larger event in town and city. For example: "By 1336 the Milanese procession was ordered to include ecclesiastical dignitaries, hermits, friars, monks, secular clergy, and the archbishop on a white horse . . ." (Rubin, 244). "The Corpus Christi procession developed in cathedrals, religious houses and parishes, in clerical processions, or those which included both clergy and laity; there were village processions as well as processions arranged in craft-guild groupings" (Rubin, 245). By the end of the fourteenth century, these processions had become orchestrated by secular civic authorities, and thus involved a display of the hierarchy of political power intertwined with the central religious focus. Civic authorities, town councils, priests and/or bishop, the guilds of the crafts or trade associations, the fraternities as organizers or participants, were all involved in an order that was sometimes a cause for quarrel (Rubin, 248). The feast of Corpus Christi also inspired dramatic presentations in villages, towns, regions, cites, cathedrals (Rubin, 271–87).

Another eucharistic practice consisted in the exposition of the blessed sacrament. This devotion involved displaying the host in a monstrance in the church for the people's gaze. The practice had roots in the practice of elevating the host after consecration. The realism of the theology of the body of Christ "made access to it more problematical, and communion less easy and simple. Elevation offered a sort of substitute 'sacramental viewing,' which like communion was taught to affect one markedly" (Rubin, 63). The elevation of the consecrated species had a quasi-sacramental value attached to it; that is, it effected something (Rubin, 73). Given this theology, and in the light of the processions, exposition of the Blessed Sacrament fit neatly. Riding the tide of eucharistic piety, the practice spread in the course of the fourteenth century (Rubin, 288–94).

In sum: "The popular demand for looking was met from the fourteenth century by numerous eucharistic processions, expositions, and benedictions with the sacrament."[49] When one says that the eucharist played a central role in the life of the church in the late medieval period, the reference points to a multifaceted presence and function in the life of the community. The eucharist "performed" in various settings: in a worldview formed by the doctrinal narrative of salvation, in the daily and Sunday liturgy, prominently on the feasts of Holy Thursday and Corpus Christi, in processions, in fraternities organized to promote the devotion, in plays, in a symbolism that drew into its meaning the life of the whole community to become the body of Christ in its various levels of social, religious, and political organization.

Religious Experience and Religious Life

The fourteenth century "saw the greatest flowering of medieval mysticism, above all in Germany and the Netherlands but also in England and, though to a much lesser degree, in Italy."[50] A number

---

49. Iserloh, "The Inner Life of the Church," *Handbook*, 572. At this time too the effects or fruits of the Mass tended to become quantified. "Mass priests" did nothing but say Masses for specified intentions; the large churches contained multiple side altars for Masses; series of Masses were endowed at various degrees of ceremony. Ibid., 572–73.

50. Oakley, *The Western Church*, 90–91.

of significantly different mystical writers left a mark on the age. The Dominican Meister Eckhart preached and wrote of a mystical union with God that led to a process against his views. He died defending himself at Avignon in 1328.[51] John van Ruysbroeck lived a long life of eighty-eight years from 1293 to 1381. After ordination and an active ministry, at age fifty he withdrew with companions into a life of solitude and wrote a good number of works in mystical theology, as well as an explanation of the creed for priests.[52] Bridget of Sweden was a "mystic, author, prophet, politician, wife, mother, social worker, and theologian, [and] the founder of the Order of the Holy Savior, commonly known as the Bridgettines."[53] After twenty years of marriage and eight children, with the death of her husband and on the basis of mystical experience, she pleaded the case for her new order of women and men until her death in 1373. But perhaps the most famous of the mystics of the two centuries was Catherine of Siena who was a member of a Dominican laywomen's association and who died at the age of thirty-three in 1380. Her religious experience gave her courage; her activism for the reform of the church made her famous. She was responsible for persuading Gregory XI to return to Rome, thus bringing the Avignon papacy prior to the schism to a close.[54] Julian of Norwich was probably a laywoman who experienced a series of personal revelations or "shewings" that she later

---

51. Meister Eckhart, *Meister Eckhart: Teacher and Preacher*, ed. Bernard McGinn et al. (New York: Paulist Press, 1986).

52. Jan van Ruusbroec, *John Ruusbroec: The Spiritual Espousals and Other Works*, intro. and trans. James A. Wiseman (New York: Paulist Press, 1985). Thematic differences distinguish these authors, such as an emphasis on the intellectual or speculative character of experience or an emphasis on the will or affective experience. One may also see correlations between mystical experiences of God infinitely transcendent and yet near and the suppositions of the nominalist theology of the period, which will be discussed later. See Oakley, *The Western Church*, 89–100.

53. Patricia Ranft, *Women and the Religious Life in Premodern Europe* (New York: St. Martin's Press, 1996), 89; Bridget of Sweden, *Life and Selected Revelations: Birgitta of Sweden*, ed. Marguerite Tjader Harris (New York: Paulist Press, 1990).

54. Catherine of Siena, *The Dialogue: Catherine of Siena*, trans. and intro. by Suzanne Noffke (New York: Paulist Press, 1980). Bridget and Catherine both undertook a prophetic mission for the reform of the church. "Far from closing out the rest of the world, their mystical experiences thus led directly to a commitment to the salvation of souls." André Vauchez, *The Laity in the Middle Ages: Religious Beliefs and Devotional Practices* (Notre Dame, Ind.: University of Notre Dame Press, 1993), 246.

tried to communicate in writing. She died around 1416 or perhaps a bit later.[55]

Distinctive forms of religious life developed during these centuries among both men and women. Among women the numbers of so-called tertiaries and other groups of active people, more or less associated with religious orders but living outside of cloister and working apostolically in the world, expanded. Still more loosely defined religious, the beguines, offered a more independent and less structured form of explicit religious commitment to apostolic activity. "Both forms accepted and appealed to all classes of people. Both types of religious life were quite compatible with the growing urban culture of the day, and both provided an approved form of religious life without enclosure."[56] In this climate, the Sisters of the Common Life and the Brothers of the Common Life both emerged in the latter part of the fourteenth century. Behind them both was Geert Groote, a man of deep religious experience who, though influenced by Ruysbroeck, was neither mystical nor monastic. He dedicated his life to social work and church reform. At one point he gave his house to a group of women who formed themselves into sisters who lived in community, actively engaged in work in society on the basis of religious motivation, but took no monastic vows. They became The Sisters of the Common Life. The Brothers were founded a bit later by a disciple of Groote on the same basic principles. By the end of the fifteenth century both Brothers and Sisters of the Common Life were prominent in Belgium, Holland, and western Germany.[57] The spirituality of this movement as reflected in the *Imitation of Christ* will be analyzed in its turn.

Conciliarist Ecclesiology

The narrative of the first part of this chapter showed that conciliarism was a complex phenomenon in the historical life of the Western church. One may alternatively characterize it as a historical

---

55. Julian of Norwich, *Showings: Julian of Norwich*, trans. and intro. by Edmund Colledge and James Walsh (New York: Paulist Press, 1978).

56. Ranft, *Women and the Religious Life*, 85.

57. Oakley, *The Western Church*, 100–102.

movement, a set of ideas, or a doctrine. It had roots in Aristotelianism and the canonical tradition. As a historical movement it sought to resolve a profound political crisis of the schism within the Western church that left in its wake scandal and spiritual turmoil. It also served as a basis for a particular church polity or government. As a set of ideas or a doctrine, it had representatives across a spectrum of left, right, and center.[58] The aim in schematically laying out a generalized version of the ecclesiology of conciliarism is not advocacy but historical representation. But at the same time the movement generated important ecclesiological principles of lasting value and some of them will be retrieved at the end of the chapter.

One way of accomplishing the delicate task of presenting a complex movement in a brief space is to concentrate on representative texts of noted conciliarists. These include Henry of Langenstein, a theologian and vice chancellor at the University of Paris at the outset of the schism in 1378.[59] Pierre d'Ailly was active in academic circles as professor and chancellor of the University of Paris, in the church as confessor of the king and an archbishop, and in political affairs.[60] Jean Gerson was a gifted theologian, poet, humanist, and preacher who succeeded Pierre d'Ailly as chancellor of the University of Paris in 1395 and with him was active at Constance.[61] Dietrich of Niem was an official of the Roman curia and wrote after the Council of Pisa on the prospect of a council that might finally end the schism.[62] These texts span the time of the schism and represent the anguish and dialectical skill of theologians who were loyal to the church and

---

58. Oakley distinguishes three broad types of conciliarism within each of which there were variations. *Council Over Pope?* 61–74.

59. Henry of Langenstein, *A Letter on Behalf of a Council of Peace* (1381), in *Advocates of Reform: From Wyclif to Erasmus*, ed. Matthew Spinka (Philadelphia: The Westminster Press, 1953), 106–39. This work is cited in the text as Langenstein by paragraph number and page.

60. Pierre d'Ailly, *Useful Propositions*, in *Unity, Heresy and Reform, 1378–1460*, ed. C. M. D. Crowder (London: Edward Arnold, 1977), 52–54. Cited in the text by name, number of the proposition, and page.

61. John Gerson, *A Tractate on the Unity of the Church* (1409), in *Advocates of Reform*, 140–48. This work is cited in the text as Gerson by paragraph number and page.

62. Dietrich of Niem, *Ways of Uniting and Reforming the Church* (1410), in *Advocates of Reform*, 149–74. This work is cited in the text as Niem by page number.

the papacy and bent on saving the institution.[63] Despite the abstraction from intense political tensions and negotiations, despite an obvious oversimplification, and despite the differences among these theologians, their views are represented here in a unified analytical framework.

The issues. Of the many issues underlying the conciliarist movement, two broad problems dominated the imagination of theologians, clergy, and all those people who were aware of the situation. The one was the polity of the church, or the nature of its organizational structure; the other was the question of reform.

The schism raised the question of the structure of the authority of the church in a new, forceful, political way. During and after the Gregorian reform, the position of the papacy in the church was defended against *Imperium*, the secular order of authority, or the world. The prerogatives of the papacy concerned the whole church and were established especially over against and in relation to temporal life and authority. But with the schism the papacy itself was called into question, and it was reconsidered from within, or in relation to, the church itself. It is true that conciliarist theory flourished when the nature and function of the papacy existed in a situation of extreme crisis. If the schism had not occurred, it is doubtful that conciliarism would have gained so much momentum and prominence. But the critical situation helped to place in relief intrinsic elements and dimensions of the church sometimes overlooked or taken for granted, as well as the depth at which a solution had to be sought. The theologians who addressed the problems appealed to tradition and to ideas that carried precedent from before the crisis itself. It is difficult to imagine today, in a time when pluralism is taken as a matter of course, the depth of the scandal of a divided Western church, and the fact that the papacy, the juridical and symbolic unifying center of the church, was the agent of division. At the very start of the schism Langenstein wrote: "Already, however, by means of this schism, seeds of discord and ill will are being scattered abroad in the provinces and among the religious orders, the common people, the

---

63. To restore the papacy, "the unity of the church in one undoubted vicar of Christ," was a kind of mantra that Gerson repeated at the head of each paragraph of his essay on the unity of the church.

princes, the prelates, and the priests, which are in future times going to be continually bursting forth" (Langenstein, 2, 108).

The second issue was reform. In the background of the rise and the goals of conciliarism was a need and desire for reform in the church, not just in the papacy, but in the whole structure of life in the church, "in head and members." The Avignon papacy contributed to the increasing general awareness of abuses in the church, and the schism made these perceptions still more acute. A council in this situation represented to the imagination consensus and commonly accepted legislation, and thus appeared to be an instrument or ve-hicle of the needed reform. By the beginning of the second decade of the 1400s, the situation appeared desperate: "Today the unity of the head is lost, for three dare to call themselves pope. Today there is a division among the members, for obedience and submission is granted to every one of them. Today there is a disappearance, nay, a complete abandonment, of good moral practices, for simony, ava-rice, the sale of benefices, tyranny, and cruelty hold sway, approved as it were by wont amongst the ecclesiastics . . . " (Niem, 153). In this situation, conciliarist theory appears as foundational ecclesiology, an exploration of basic principles.

Three basic principles of conciliarism. One can understand the essence of conciliarism as a generalized system of ideas based upon three foundational principles: that the deepest level of the unity of the church was prior to and transcended its institutional unity; that the ultimate authority of the church lay in this communitarian di-mension of the whole; that the whole church as a body could elect and stand in judgment upon the pope.

The first principle operated more like a tacit supposition than an overt proposition. It begins with the conviction that the church is a unity, a theme seen from the very beginning in Ignatius, Cyprian, and Augustine. Dietrich of Niem cites Cyprian, "the church is one," and understands this unity as a vast congregation of people spiritu-ally united in Christ (Niem, 150). Without this fundamental idea and ideal as a strongly supposed value, there would not have been a crisis. This unity, however, had to be seen as transcending the ac-tual division, and adhering in a community prior to the institution of unity, the papacy. This corresponded to both the canonical and theological tradition which understood the church as a corporation, the unified body of Christ. It subsists as a society of people analogous to a single communion of people. "Although the Pope, inasmuch as he is the Vicar of Christ, can, in a certain way, be said to be the head of the Church, nevertheless the unity of the Church does not necessarily depend upon — or originate from — the unity of the Pope" (d'Ailly, 2, 52). In short, one views the church as a whole; universally it exists as the corporation of the faithful. The unity does not simply lie in the unity of an institutional structure but exists on a level prior to it. Institution is not excluded, certainly, or there would have been no impetus toward healing the schism. But the basis of the unity lies deeper than the structure, and the structure functions to reflect and preserve the communion.

The second principle says that the ultimate basis of or for authority in the church lies in the corporation as a whole, in the church as a living community. "From Christ, the head, his mystical body which is the Church, originally and immediately has its power and authority, so that in order to conserve its own unity, it rightly has the power of assembling itself or a general council representing it" (d'Ailly, 3, 52). This constitutes the premise of conciliarism: ultimate authority in the church lies in the *whole,* in the total assembly of the faithful united to Christ. Here rests the power to depose a pope. Here lies the authority to summon a council and solve the problem of two or three rival popes. A council would be the direct representative of the whole church. One can see the principles of Marsilius at work here: the weightier part of the legitimate legislator. Langenstein states the principle clearly when he says "that the Universal Church, of which a general council is representative, is superior to the college of cardinals and to every other particular grouping (*congregatio*) of the faithful and to every single person of whatever dignity, even to the holder of the highest dignity, or precedence, the lord pope, in matters that are to be described later. Therefore, recourse must be made to such a powerful council, as to the supreme authority, in the present matter affecting the whole church" (Langenstein, 13, 118). "Therefore, the authority of a general council is greater than that of the pope and the college of cardinals" (Langenstein, 13, 119).

The third principle simply draws out the consequence of the first two when taken together by stating explicitly the relation between the church as *congregatio fidelium* and the office of the papacy. The whole church as a body possesses the authority to elect the pope and to stand in judgment of the pope. Henry of Langenstein says that the power to elect a pope resides with the bishops as a group: "The power of appointing the pope resides primarily with the whole company of the bishops of the faithful" (Langenstein, 14, 123). It should revert to all the bishops when the cardinals are unable to act. Gerson adds that "the mystical body of the church, perfectly established by Christ, has, no less than any civil, mystical, or truly natural body, the right and the power to procure its own union," that is, not to wait upon a pope to convene a council (Gerson, 2, 141–42). In the words of Dietrich of Niem, "since the pope is a son and member of the Universal Church, as I have said, the Universal Church can bind him [and] resign his right to the papacy for him . . . " (Niem, 166).

Dietrich of Niem provided the clearest statement of these principles with his distinction between what he called the "universal church" and the "apostolic church" and his description of the way the two related to each other. The "universal church" is the whole assembly of Christians, the whole historical movement at any given time, the body of the faithful. The universal church "is made up of various members of Greeks, Latins, and barbarians who believe in Christ, of men and women, of peasants and nobles, of poor and rich, constituting one body, which is called Catholic. The head of this body, the Universal Church, is Christ alone. The others, such as the pope, the cardinals and prelates, the clerics, the kings and princes, and the common people, are the members, occupying their various positions" (Niem, 150–51). The pope is not the head of this church; Christ is; the pope is only the vicar of Christ. This church as a corporate whole is the subject of the power and authority of the church; these powers are still there if there were no pope on any given occasion.

The "apostolic church" is the governing structure, the hierarchy, within the universal church. The apostolic church "is included in the Catholic Church, and is made up of the pope, the cardinals, the bishops, the prelates, and the churchmen" (Niem, 151). These churchmen are those in orders or those holding office as distinct from the laity. They constitute the hierarchically ordered officers of ministry.[64] These and this structure, often called the Roman Church, is the instrument by which the church functions. "It embodies the instrumental and operative functions of the keys of the Universal Church and exercises its power of binding and loosing" (Niem, 151). It has less authority than the universal church, and functions on behalf of the universal church. The apostolic church, the hierarchy, "cannot have greater authority or power than that which is granted to it by the Universal Church. These two churches, therefore, differ as genus and species, since all of the Apostolic Church is Catholic, but not the other way around" (Niem, 152).

This functional view of the pope operates as a principle that is sometimes explicit, sometimes tacit. For example, relative to this crisis and whether the popes should resign: "The pope either received the papacy for his private advantage or for the common good. If [he received it] for the common good, then the common good demands his resignation" (Niem, 156). Dietrich holds that "the pope cannot ordain or decree anything in the Church beyond what is and has been granted to him in the first place by Christ himself and then by the Universal Church" (Niem, 170). The pope cannot exercise his authority except within the universal church and as a function of the universal church which grants this function (Niem, 171).[65]

The arguments of conciliarism. Conciliarism did not merely assert the primacy of community over office, or that the head of the church, the vicar of Christ, was subordinate to a council. This had to be argued, and the case was made philosophically, theologically, historically, and legally. The accumulated weight of the arguments made a significant impression.

The social philosophical arguments from natural law and the theological arguments from divine law often overlapped. The community had an intrinsic right to unity, and in the community itself was provided the basis of authority. Transferred to the church, this means

---

64. Spinka, *Advocates of Reform*, 151, n. 10.

65. This is asserted over against a view in which the pope, receiving authority from Christ, stands over the council. The difference between the frameworks of understanding here is considerable.

that "[t]he power of appointing the pope resides primarily with the whole company of the bishops of the faithful" (Langenstein, 14, 123). Actual papal authority is due to positive law, and this does not, and cannot, outweigh natural and divine right. No human law can deter a council; the common good demands it. If there is no head of the church, "the church, by divine as well as by natural law (which no positive law properly understood hinders), is able to assemble in a general council representing her in order to procure for herself one undoubted vicar" (Gerson, 2, 141; also d'Ailly, 4, 53; 7–8, 53). The right for holding a general council and establishing the unity of the church in one earthly head corresponds with immutable divine and natural law (Gerson, 10, 146).

Historical arguments too were forceful; the canonists' study of the traditions of laws mediated a remarkable historical consciousness. The history of the papacy shows that the way popes were appointed was human. Christ did not establish a method of appointing successors of Peter, and in fact popes have been appointed in at least six different ways. Therefore one finds no divine or divine positive law on how a pope should be designated (Langenstein, 7–10, 110–11; 14, 122).

The legal arguments too were important; an illegal solution would dig the hole deeper. Several general legal principles guided the thinking, all revolving around the common good. For example, it was argued that as local matters require local synods, so too "new and difficult cases which concern the whole world must be discussed by a general council. 'For what affects all must consistently be dealt with by all or by the representatives of all'" (Langenstein, 13, 117).[66] Conciliarists also had to contend with the provision that it had become the prerogative of the pope to summon a council. Generally it was argued that particular provisions of the law cannot stand against the common good and should be ignored if they conflict with it. "Therefore if laws and rights are made for the sake of the common good, the common good is a law greater than any right" (Niem 153–54).

---

66. This was a legal maxim from Roman law that was introduced into canon law by Innocent III. Spinka, *Advocates of Reform*, 117, n. 15.

One of the main legal arguments was from the principle of epieikeia. By definition law is general and deals with common relationships. Neither the law nor the lawgiver envision special cases, nor can law deal with every case. In a case not envisioned by the lawgiver, the law does not hold. Rather, one may even have to follow the opposite of what the law prescribes in order to achieve what the law actually envisaged. In other words, it may be that justice can be achieved only when the law is broken. Henry of Langenstein put it this way: "Thus it happens that certain people, ignorant of the law and unlearned in theology and moral philosophy, who wish that the common laws and positive decrees be observed in every instance according to the outward appearance or surface of the words, often act contrary to justice and the common good, and against the intention of the legislators. In doing this they are truly transgressing the dictates of reason for the sake of certain traditions of men, whose intention they do not take into account, and are also disdaining to listen to the just interpretation of the laws . . . " (Langenstein, 16, 131; also d'Ailly, 9, 54).[67]

On this basis the church appeals to secular rulers to help solve the problem. Call a council: "a general council must be summoned without the authority of the pope, to undertake matters for the common good of the whole company of the faithful" (Langenstein, 16, 130). This was not merely possible or permissible, according to Henry, but obligatory and indispensable. Dietrich maintained that "at the present time the convocation belongs to the emperor or the king of the Romans under pain of mortal sin and everlasting punishment. In his absence or when there is no emperor, I say that this belongs to the other secular kings and princes" (Niem, 169).

In sum, the pope is subordinated to the good of the whole church. He is not an absolute monarch; the office is not in service of itself. Rather the pope is elected and is a representative for the good of the whole and subordinate to the whole church. The pope cannot alter the will of councils which more closely represent the whole.

Conciliarist government of the church. Conciliarist theory flourished during the schism because, as Henry put it, "it is clearer than

---

67. The principle of epieikeia has its source in Aristotle's *Nichomachean Ethics* and was adopted by Thomas Aquinas who lays it out in his *Summa Theologiae*, II-II, q. 120, a.1.

the light of day that no other human way than that of a council has been found by which this schism can be completely settled..." (Langenstein, 13, 121). Few people at the Council of Constance were not conciliarists of some sort, because the theory opened up a solution to the problem. But conciliarism appears differently in the context of the ongoing government of the church, and some version of this was intended by the conciliar decree *Frequens,* which legislated councils every ten years after the takeoff period. In the minds of some, councils would become not only the theoretical but also the effective legislative and governing body of the whole church. And this would be true not only when they were in session, but also when they were expected or in preparation on a regular basis. Councils would exert a constant influence as people could appeal from the pope to a future council for a decision in a disputed matter.

The language of Dietrich, which shows the frustration that was common after Pisa but before Constance, takes on new meaning in the context of the government of the Western church. A council, he wrote, even one over which the pope does not preside, "is superior in authority, dignity, and function. The pope himself is bound to obey such a council in all things. Such a council can limit the power of the pope. To such a council, as it represents the Church Universal, the keys of binding and loosing were granted. Such a council can take away the papal rights. From such a council no one can appeal. Such a council can elect, deprive, and depose the pope. Such a council can set up new laws, and destroy old ones. The constitutions, statues, and regulations of such a council are immutable and cannot be set aside by any person inferior to the council" (Niem, 160). A council should never concede to a pope the ability to interpret or alter the statutes of a general council (Niem, 166). "A holy general council which represents the Universal Church cannot concede to any private individual, by whatever dignity he may be adorned, even to the pope himself, the authority and power of granting dispensations from, or changing and interpreting in any other way, the statutes of a holy council.... The Universal Church, as has been said, is a power superior to the pope. Thus it follows that this great power of the Universal Church cannot be communicated to an inferior by a council since he is not legally competent to possess it..." (Niem, 167).

In sum, conciliarism succeeded in providing the principles and authorizing the structures for restoring the papacy. But it failed as a blueprint for governing the church, and with this failure the lines of many of its healthy ecclesiological principles were erased.

Nicholas of Cusa

In his early career Nicholas of Cusa represents a reprise of conciliarist theory after Constance and during the Council of Basel. He was born in 1401 in the village of Cues on the Mosel between Trèves and Koblenz. As a young cleric he studied at Heidelberg and in 1417 went to the University of Padua where he graduated as a Doctor in Canon Law in 1423. Thereafter he became the secretary of the Cardinal legate in Germany. Cusanus's public career began at the Council of Basel, which he attended officially as a canon lawyer representing an appeal to the council in a dispute over the archbishopric of Trèves; in 1433 he wrote the work *The Catholic Concordance* in which he defended a conciliarist ecclesiology. It established him as a significant figure at the council. By the end of 1433 "Nicholas had taken up an antipapal attitude in a most definite way."[68] Over the next couple of years, however, his attitude changed for a variety of reasons, and by 1436 Cusanus had shifted his allegiance away from a disorganized and increasingly antipapal council and toward the possibility of a more centralized papal leadership negotiating a union with the Greek Church. In 1437 he joined the group which abandoned Basel and became part of the mission approved by the pope to sail to Constantinople and escort the Patriarch, Emperor and other members of the party to the West. The rest of Nicholas's life as cardinal, legate, bishop, and diplomat, and the other extensive writings of this brilliant renaissance man, have less bearing on his ecclesiology, with a major exception mentioned further on. He died in 1464.

One can see the fruit of Cusanus's study of canon law in *The Catholic Concordance* as he marshals texts from the history of the

---

68. Henry Bett, *Nicholas of Cusa* (Merrick, N.Y.: Richwood Publishing, 1976, originally London: Methuen, 1932), 21. Bett provides an eighty page biography of Nicholas of Cusa. Yves Congar also gives a brief interpretation of Cusanus's ecclesiology in *L'Eglise: De saint Augustin à l'époque moderne* (Paris: Editions de Cerf, 1970), 330–35.

church and combines them with political philosophical reasoning.[69] "Concordance" suggests a synthesis of divergent views into a harmonious resolution: holding things together. The following account cannot do justice to the subtlety with which he accomplishes this, but it provides the logic of the argument and thus indicates the advance Cusanus makes on conciliarist theory. This interpretation follows Sigmund who finds in Cusanus a tensive harmony between conciliar supremacy and the divinely appointed primacy of the pope mediated by a theory of representation.

Conciliarism. Cusanus in this early period is clearly a conciliarist. He writes that "a universal council that represents the Catholic Church has power directly from Christ and is in every respect over both the pope and the Apostolic See" (CC, II.16.148).[70] The supremacy of councils in matters of faith also pertains to historical doctrines; popes cannot reverse conciliar doctrines with present-day decrees (CC, II.18.177). How do councils represent the faithful? Through the bishops. He uses Cyprian to say that the people are in the bishops, and the bishops represent the people and together the whole church (See CC, II.6.37.).

Hierarchy and papacy. The first eight chapters of *The Catholic Concordance* describe the hierarchical ordering of the church in parallel with the heavenly hierarchy. "The highest order consists of the bishop, priests, and deacons, all consecrated. The intermediate order is made up of the subdeacons, acolytes, and exorcists, who are mixed. The lowest are the readers, the porters, and the tonsured, who are not consecrated" (CC, I.7.41).[71] On the position of the pope,

---

69. Nicholas of Cusa, *The Catholic Concordance,* ed. and trans. Paul E. Sigmund (Cambridge: Cambridge University Press, 1991). This work is cited in the text as CC by book, chapter, and paragraph.

70. The pope is subject to the council in matters of faith. "Indeed in decisions on matters of faith which is why he possesses the primacy, he is subject to the council of the Catholic Church" (CC, I.15.61). Cusanus held that "the more certainly and truly that synod represents the church, the more its judgment tends toward infallibility rather than fallibility, and that this judgment is always better than the individual judgment of the Roman pontiff who represents the church in a very uncertain way [*confusissime*]" (CC, 18.158). This is said on the expressed assumption that such a synod includes the pope as its head; the point is that the larger body is naturally more representative.

71. Cusanus is dependent on Pseudo-Dionysius in his view of hierarchy; it represents an important framework of his understanding. In fact a double hierarchy defines the church: "There is a sacramental hierarchy (based on the power of orders) which

Cusanus says that, although all the bishops have the same powers, "Peter was set over the others so that there might be a unity of concordance" (CC, I.6.35). Thus he concludes "that the primacy in the church is established in its reality by Christ through the church for the purpose of church unity and is intended by God as a ministry for its service" (CC, II.34.264). "Hence just as Peter was prince of the apostles, the Roman pontiff is prince of the bishops since the bishops succeeded the apostles" (CC, I.15.61). "Just as he [the pope] is first in matters of faith and is judge of the faith" (CC, II.7.95), so it is that a council cannot define matters of faith without the pope (CC, II.2.74).

Consent, election, and representation. The key to how Cusanus holds together a divinely appointed papal ruler of the church and a superior council lies in the idea of representation which, in turn, is based on freedom, consent, and election. "For if by nature men are equal in power and equally free, the true properly ordered authority of one common ruler who is their equal in power cannot be naturally established except by the election and consent of the others and law is also established by consent" (CC, II.14.127; also II.14.331).[72] These ideas from natural law theory of election and consent are given political viability through representation. That is, he links representation and election: "the one who is to be over all should be chosen by all," and "no one should be set up over unwilling subjects" (CC, II.18.163). Cusanus says that "every ecclesiastical or spiritual rulership was established by Christ through the mediation of human consent. For legitimate superiors are those established by the consent of their subjects. We are obliged to obey them because of having given them our consent as established in authority by men from among men" (CC, II.34.262). Even Peter, "unless he had the

---

culminates in the rank of bishop, as in the earlier theories. But there is also a governmental or administrative hierarchy, and in this the pope is supreme." Paul E. Sigmund, *Nicholas of Cusa and Medieval Political Thought* (Cambridge, Mass.: Harvard University Press, 1963), 130. Cited hereafter as NC.

72. "On this point for one body to be established in a harmony of subjects and ruler, reason and natural and divine law all require that there be mutual consent in this spiritual marriage which is demonstrated by the election by all and the consent of the one elected, just as a spiritual marriage is rightly established by consent between Christ and his church." CC, II.18.164.

elective consent to their subordination from the representatives of all the others I would not believe that he was the leader or ruler or judge of all the others" (CC, II.34.262).

This idea of representation in its turn is converted into a series of ascending representative bodies, thus giving early church practice a kind of modern twist. Cusanus reasons that "any ruler represents his subjects in proportion to the generality of the representation, so that the pope represents the whole church in a vague way, and he represents his patriarchate in a more direct way, his clergy yet more certainly, and finally he represents his daily council, as it were, in a single body" (CC, II.18.163). In effect, he takes Dionysius's descending hierarchy and looks at it from the bottom up. He conceives of ascending councils and representation when he writes that "when a smaller council with general powers is to be created, it should be made up of the representatives of those subject to it or of those who have the right to participate in it. Therefore the same thing should be done in the case of the cardinals who represent the provinces subject to the Roman church in its daily council" (CC, II.24.202). The greater the representation, the greater the authority by the principle of the weightier part (ibid.).[73]

In this way, Cusanus believes that he has reconciled the tension between pope and council, between hierarchy and the community, within a certain harmony. The council is supreme over the pope; yet the pope has rulership, power to command and to legislate. How to understand the relationship? Cusanus opts for what he calls an intermediate position in which "the power of the Roman pontiff as to preeminence, priority, and rulership, is from God by way of man and the councils; namely, by means of elective consent" (CC,

---

73. In the system, laity would elect or consent to appointed priests; bishops would be elected by chapters representing priests; archbishops would be elected by bishops with consent of clergy; archbishops would elect cardinals representing church provinces, and they would elect the pope. Legislation at each level would be done by the appropriate body; there would be diocesan, provincial, and national councils as in earlier days. It is a visionary scheme based upon consent (Paul Sigmund, "Introduction," CC, xxvi). On the ascending system of elections: "Through a hierarchical system of councils the lower ranks would have a voice, although a limited one, in church government" (ibid., xxvii). "The council and the cardinals derive their legitimacy from those below rather than from those above them, and from the laity (in an indirect fashion) as well as from the clergy." Ibid., xxviii.

II.34.249). "And in my judgment the arguments on the one side that coercive rulership in the church comes only from God, and on the other side that it exists only by the election and consent of men and the church, are correctly harmonized in this intermediate position" (CC, II.34.264). "And although we insist that the pope is not the universal bishop but the first over the others, and we base the force of the holy councils not on the pope but on the consent of all, at the same time since we defend truth and maintain the rights of everyone, we rightly give honor to the pope" (CC, II.13.126).[74]

Cusanus also developed a theology of religions. Scandalized by the killing in the name of religion involved in the fall of Constantinople in 1453, he wrote the short work entitled *The Peace of Faith*.[75] His theology of religions is dialectical and revolves around a tension between the one and the many. On the one hand, transcendentally all religions are one and differ in their rites (PF, 6). Authentic worship of the one God underlies the diversity of rites (PF, 68). Because unity is behind all plurality, and all faiths are rooted in and quest for the same wisdom, they share this common logic of attachment to the one ground of reality and truth: "the same faith is presupposed everywhere" (PF, 10–11). On the other hand, the whole vision is christocentric and trinitarian. Cusanus's work is a dialogue involving the wise from all the religions. But his conception of ultimate reality is conceived and articulated from a Christian standpoint. Nevertheless it is an extraordinary vision for the time,

---

74. Did Cusanus alter his ecclesiology on becoming papalist? Sigmund indicates that much remained the same, but there were some pointed changes. "The pope is now more than simply an administrator established by the bishops and the church, as he sometimes appeared to be in *The Catholic Concordance*. He is the *caput* of the ecclesiastical corporation, which is the universal church" (Sigmund, NC, 238; also 243). This is of course a major change. But he still maintained that "the power to govern the church was given by Christ to both the pope and bishops," and that if the pope exceeds the limits of his authority, as for example in heresy, the church can withdraw from him. Sigmund, "Introduction," CC, xxxiii.

75. Nicholas of Cusa, *The Peace of Faith*, as presented by James E. Biechler and H. Lawrence Bond, trans., *Nicholas of Cusa on Interreligious Harmony* (Lewiston, N.Y.: Edwin Mellen Press, 1990). This is cited as PF by paragraph number. This work is situated, analyzed, interpreted, and related to the late twentieth-century discussion by Roger A. Johnson, "The Beginnings of a Modern Theology of Religions: Nicholas of Cusa (1401–1464)," Boston Theological Society, Internet at www.bostontheological.org/colloquium/bts/.

and its dialectical character gives the vision a potentiality beyond his statement.

Juan de Torquemada and Pius II: *Execrabilis*

We turn now to the most important ecclesiologist in the fifteenth century in terms of later influence: Johannes de Turrecremata, or as he is generally known, Torquemada.[76] Born in 1388 in Valladolid, he entered the Dominicans as a youth, and later, in 1417, he traveled as part of a Spanish delegation to the Council of Constance. After the council he studied theology at the University of Paris and returned to Spain in 1425. In 1431, as part of a team representing the Dominicans, he attended the Council of Basel where early on he spoke in a voice moderating the opposition between council and pope. But as the council grew more adversarial toward the papacy, Torquemada became more papalist, and Eugenius IV rewarded him with the office of Master of the Sacred Palace in 1434. In 1439, after Basel had deposed Eugenius, the pope counterattacked by denying the authority of Constance's *Haec Sancta;* Torquemada supported him in a public debate and in December was made a cardinal. On the death of Eugenius IV Torquemada found the time to write and composed his *Summa de Ecclesia* between 1449 and 1553, his master work in ecclesiology, and "the most comprehensive medieval synthesis of ecclesiological doctrines acceptable to Rome" (JT, 19). Torquemada continued to write and be engaged in the intellectual and political affairs of the church right up to his death at 80 in 1468 (JT, 1–30).

From a Thomist and papalist perspective Torquemada in his *Summa* considers first the nature of the church, then in Books II and III its governmental structure of pope and council, with a fourth given to schism and heresy. Descriptively he defines the church as "the totality of the faithful who assemble on the basis of worship of the one true God and the confession of one faith."[77] He then shows

---

76. A brief account of Torquemada's ecclesiology can be found in Congar, *L'Eglise,* 340–44. See also Erwin Iserloh, "Theology in the Age of Transition," *Handbook,* 585–94, for a brief sketch of his life and thought. In the account that follows I rely on Thomas M. Izbicki, *Protector of the Faith: Cardinal Johannes de Turrecremata and the Defense of the Institutional Church* (Washington, D.C.: Catholic University of American Press, 1981). This work is cited in the text as JT by page number.

77. Congar, *L'Eglise,* 340.

analytically that Christ is the principle efficient cause of the church, working instrumentally through the sacraments; the formal cause that unites people into a church is the union of each one with Christ in faith; the final cause is eschatological salvation, participation in the glory of the living God. The organization of the following account follows Izbicki who draws as well from Torquemada's other writings and emphasizes five elements that distinguish this ecclesiology.

The church as institution. Although Torquemada used the phrase *congregatio fidelium* to define the church, he understood and stressed the visible institutional church, "the sacramental and juridical body dedicated to the salvation of souls" (JT, 51). His understanding of the church was essentially monarchical (JT, 50). In the wake of his experience of the conciliarism at Basel, he intended to negate every idea that the subject of the power to govern the church lay in the whole church as a corporation. In contrast to that he held that supreme authority rested squarely in the papacy (JT, 48–49).

The papacy. Against conciliarism and the assaults of the Hussites only a strong papal church could preserve its unity. "According to Turrecremata, pope and Roman Church had supreme power of ecclesiastical government by Christ's own mandate" (JT, 77). Christ founded a papal monarchy. "In fact, after Christ the pope was the second founder of the church. As Christ was the rock on which the church rested, so Peter was the cornerstone of the edifice" (JT, 83). On the one hand he wrote that "the pope holds the place of Christ in the church" (JT, 84 quoting Torquemada). On the other hand he assigned such powers to the pope that papal acts were the acts of the church as such (JT, 84). So, for example, the pope was infallible, although such powers were assigned to the office and not the person (JT, 77). At the same time Torquemada recognized that the pope was not absolute in the sense of there being no limits to his power. To protect the church against papal abuse, he held that heretical teaching or flagrant immorality would amount to a self-deposition of the pope (JT, 87–94).

Hierarchy. Torquemada thought of the clergy as the "more worthy side of the ecclesiastical body" (JT, 53). This conception is fleshed out in a conception of a hierarchy united under the pope which Izbicki characterizes in this way: "By virtue of the plenitude of power, the pope was head of the visible church, commanding obedience from the other bishops even to the point of intervening in their work of ecclesiastical government. Bishops were papal agents who received a share of jurisdiction *in partem sollicitudinis* [as a share in the pope's plenitude of power]. Even the power of orders, in which bishops were the pope's equals, was affected by the plenitude of power, which regulated pastoral ministry. Bishops, metropolitans, primates, and patriarchs were all part of a hierarchy of jurisdiction whose summit was the papacy. Jurisdiction was diffused through this hierarchy via confirmation of elections, made directly or through intermediaries. Each grade of the hierarchy was supposed to supervise the conduct of members in the lower grades, correcting or removing unworthy prelates. Unjust sentences could be appealed all the way to the pope, the font of all jurisdiction. Since the lesser clergy received their share of jurisdiction from the bishops, the pope could grant local exemptions from episcopal authority, making monks and friars directly subject to Rome. The important principle to be safeguarded in granting of exemptions was that of obedience to the Vicar of Christ" (JT, 59–60).

The extent to which this vision depends upon Pseudo-Dionysius is not clear. Some say that this conception of hierarchy represents the very kernel of Torquemada's ecclesiology, and it is drawn from Dionysius. But Izbicki plays down this dependence. According to him, although Dionysius was frequently cited, the language had become a commonplace and was not decisive: Torquemada was more Aristotelian and Thomistic than Platonic and Dionysian (JT, 72–74).

The general council. After his experience at Basel, Torquemada questioned the validity of *Haec Sancta* and, with papal encouragement, he developed the interpretation of it "as the act of one obedience of the Schism," i.e., that of John XXIII, and thus not a decree of the whole council (JT, 97).[78] He also attacked *Frequens*. At the same time he acknowledged a place for general councils. Torquemada

---

78. Paul de Vooght, "La Déviation de Turrecremata," *Les Pouvoirs de Concile et l'Autorité du Pape au Concile de Constance* (Paris: Editions du Cerf, 1965), 137–62, traces the evolution of Torquemada's thinking in the course of the Council of Basel and thereafter. Through a number of interventions at the council and afterward, and with a series of theological and canonical arguments, he gradually dismantled the authority of *Haec Sancta* in his own mind. On the one hand, Torquemada had a major influence

defined a universal council as "an assembly of the greater prelates of the church, specifically called by the authority of the Roman pontiff, to do something for a common purpose concerning the Christian religion, under the pope's presidency or with another [a legate] in his place" (JT, 100–101 citing Torquemada). The distinctiveness of Torquemada's view lies in the complete subordination of the council to the pope. "The chief elements he emphasized were the welfare of the church, the authorization given by the pope, and the presence of the greater prelates" (JT, 101). Since the church is essentially a monarchy, even if one held that a council represented the church, that would be a monarchy with a papal head. An assembly of prelates had their very authority from jurisdiction granted by the pope (JT, 102). Finally, only bishops had a right to participate: all others could assist only at the invitation of the pope (JT, 103).

Sacred and secular power. Both of these spheres of authority were autonomously justified, each promoted a distinct aspect of human existence, and each needed the other to complete itself. Such were the Thomistic foundations of his teaching (JT, 108–12). But given the unity of the two spheres in Christendom, Torquemada held that the two powers or authorities should be coordinated by a single directing force, and he naturally "assigned this role to the pope, head of the spiritual power" (JT, 113). In this he used the standard argument that the spiritual was the higher and directing power relative to the temporal. This did not give the pope the right to wield the temporal sword, but as a spiritual director of its use for spiritual ends it gave him considerable power.

Torquemada assigned to the papacy the judicial supremacy over Christendom: the pope is the chief judge in spiritual matters. "As chief judge, the pope could impose severe penalties on princes, particularly excommunication. . . . Although the pope did not create kingdoms or kings, he could . . . depose rulers guilty of heresy, tyranny, or incompetence. Moreover, he could release the subjects of erring princes from their oaths of allegiance" (JT, 115). All of this comes under the heading of spiritual responsibility for the good of all

---

in shaping the subsequent papalist rejection of the authority of *Haec Sancta*. On the other hand, De Vooght controverts each of his arguments.

Christians, and as such Izbicki calls it a theory of the indirect power of the pope or the church in temporal affairs (JT, 115–16). Relative to the influence of lay rulers on the church, Torquemada did allow for some influence on their part for the well-being of the church. This is conceded pragmatically and in only certain cases when the church seems to be at an impasse, for example, when emperors assisted in the summoning of a council (JT, 116–18).

Such was the ecclesiological legacy of Juan de Torquemada. It would have its most significant influence a century later when it was republished and informed the Catholic response to the Protestant Reformation.

In January of 1460, Pius II promulgated the bull *Execrabilis*, which attempted formally to put an end to conciliarism. It should be recalled that the second of the two major decrees of the Council of Constance, *Frequens*, legislated that councils should be held every ten years forever. "Thus, by a certain continuity, there will always be either a council in existence or one expected within a given time."[79] The bull *Execrabilis* was precisely aimed at those who "suppose that they can appeal from the pope . . . to a future council."[80] We have seen that earlier councils tried to address appeals to a higher authority which, when they became routine, disrupted the exercise of authority at whatever level they occurred. The point of *Execrabilis*, then, was to reestablish absolute papal authority. Thus Pius II decreed that "we condemn appeals of this kind, reject them as erroneous and abominable, declare them to be completely null and void." He also decreed that anyone violating this command or even assisting in such a process by that very fact "incurs excommunication from which he cannot be absolved except though the pope and at the time of death."[81]

---

79. *Frequens*, in Tanner, *Decrees*, 439.

80. Pius II, *Execrabilis*, in Heiko Oberman, *Forerunners of the Reformation* (New York: Holt, Rinehart and Winston, 1966), 238. "For . . . who would not consider it ridiculous to appeal to something which does not now exist anywhere nor does anyone know when it will exist?" Ibid.

81. Ibid., 238–39. But decrees such as *Execrabilis* were not necessarily accepted at face value, and many canonists continued to hold the superiority of a council to the pope into the sixteenth century. It would, therefore, be "a serious mistake to speak of a collapse of the conciliar idea." Karl August Fink, "Renaissance and Humanism," *Handbook*, 527. Moreover, it was generally acknowledged that the failure to implement

The developments in formal ecclesiology during this period were extraordinary. From it the focus now moves to matters more closely aligned with the Christian life.

Thomas à Kempis

While conciliarist theories buzzed in response to ecclesiastical crisis in high places, and ecclesiology gradually shifted back to reflect the centrality of the pope, the spirituality initiated by Geert Groote spread across northern Europe. Thomas à Kempis is credited by many with providing its classical written expression. Born in the Netherlands in 1380, a couple of years after the beginning of the Western schism, Thomas à Kempis led a simple life. He joined a monastery in 1399 where his older brother was prior, and he remained in the monastery until he died. He was ordained and acted as master of novices for a time. He copied manuscripts and also wrote works of devotion and sermons. The fame of this man lies almost exclusively in the attribution to him of authorship of *The Imitation of Christ*.[82] The composition may have consisted in collecting and assembling various writings of the time. The *Imitatio Christi* carries a twofold importance: it reflects and articulates the major themes of the spiritual movement in northern Europe already in progress, the *devotio moderna;* as all classics do, the *Imitatio* took on a life of its own and was reckoned until recently the most widely read piece of Christian literature after the bible. As such it became a major secondhand interpreter of what the Christian life is meant to be.

Many people today regard the *Imitatio* as quite boring, repetitive, and alien to postmodern Western culture. But that very distance enables an appreciation of its distinctiveness and implicitly the particularity of the church in the late Middle Ages. The analysis of the text which follows seeks to provide a summary of some major themes

---

Frequens, independently of the relation of pope and council, was "the real cause of the crisis in the church and of the secularization of the Curia." Ibid., 528.

82. Thomas à Kempis, *The Imitation of Christ*, ed. Edward J. Klein (New York: Harper and Brothers, 1941). The authorship is still debated. This English translation is chosen for its stately, classical character. Some of its propositions are immediately recognizable as corresponding to clichés in modern English, such as, "I'd rather feel compunction than know how to define it." The citations in the text are to book and chapter.

of the *Imitation*, with an eye to characterizing the *devotio moderna* which it represents. The aim, then, is to capture the character of this spirituality which was internalized by religious, priests, and laity: those dedicated to a monastic spirituality and those involved in the world.[83]

Some of the themes or qualities that mark this view of the Christian life can be singled out by a series of key words. One is *christocentrism:* this is a christocentric spirituality; Christian life is the following of Christ. The Christian loves Jesus above all things; he alone is worthy of absolute trust; all else will fail. "What may this world give thee but through the help of Jesus. To be without Jesus is a pain of hell, and to be with him is a pleasant paradise" (IC 2.8). *Affectivity:* its devotion to Christ is affective; it appeals to religious feeling and emotion, but this is quiet and not enthusiastic. Devotion is directed to the passion of Christ and to personal contact with him in the eucharist. "This is it that I pray for, this is it that I desire: that I may be wholly joined to thee, and that I may withdraw mine heart from things created, and through the Holy Communion and oft saying Mass, that I may savour and taste eternal things" (IC 4.13).

Discipline: affectivity is controlled by technique, by meditation and disciplined practice of virtue. A regular spirituality involves patterned behavior and self-reflection. "In the morning thou shalt take a good purpose for that day following, and at night thou shalt examine diligently how thou hast behaved thee, in work, in deed, and in thought" (IC 1.19). This spirituality is marked by *moralism and self-knowledge:* perfection consists in self-knowledge and the fulfillment of one's obligations, together with a careful practice of virtue. "The life of a good religious man should shine in all virtue and be inwardly as it appeareth outwardly" (ibid.). Spiritual persons take stock of themselves, are inwardly aware of themselves: "Where art thou when thou art not present to thyself" (IC 2.5)? One also finds a stress on *interiority and subjective intention:* goodness lies in the

---

83. For an analysis of the *devotio moderna,* including its embodiment in The Brothers of the Common Life and its written expression in the *Imitation of Christ,* see Erwin Iserloh, "The *Devotio Moderna,*" *Handbook,* 426–43. The *devotio moderna* was a northern movement; other spiritual writers and styles of spirituality typical of France, Spain, or Italy had their own vitality. But choosing a particular school allows closer analysis and helps keep the imagination tied to everyday Christian life.

goodness and purity of one's intentions, the underlying motives with which one performs ordinary actions. "Help me, my Lord Jesus, that I may persevere in good purpose and in thy holy service unto my death" (IC 1.19). "After our purpose and after our intent shall be our reward" (ibid.). The spiritual life is directed by a pure mind and a simple intent: a pure mind consists in love; a plain intent is singlemindedness in looking toward God (IC 2.4). The enemy here is multiplicity, changing attitudes and loyalties, inner division; the defense is focused and steadfast trust in and self-direction toward God (IC 3.33, 59).

Withdrawal and world-renunciation: there should be a certain withdrawal from the world, from the goings-on of society. Quiet and even solitude are necessary for the spiritual life. To be attached to God is to be detached from worldly things. "Thou shalt much profit in grace if thou keep from all temporal cares, and it shall hinder thee greatly if thou set price on any temporal thing" (IC 2.5). "As oft as I have been among worldly company I have departed with less fervour of spirit than I had when I came" (IC 1.20). But gatherings of spiritual people and spiritual conversation is praised (IC 1.10). The *Imitatio* proposes a basic *asceticism:* the ideals of self-control, self-abnegation, and humility ensure a freedom of the human mind and spirit by detachment from worldly goods, pleasures, and self-indulgence. Those who seek worldly goods or satisfactions "have no perfect liberty nor freedom of spirit, for all things shall perish that be not wrought by God" (IC 3.32). "I am but vanity and nought before thee, an unconstant man and feeble.... In thee shall I be glorified and in thee always shall I joy. And in myself I will glory in nothing but my infirmities" (IC 3.40).

The practice of *devotional reading* was encouraged; especially the reading of scripture is recommended, and through it direct contact with Christ in the New Testament. But this reading was not for gaining wisdom or learning. One should not read scripture with curiosity in order to learn high truths; "read meekly, simply, and faithfully, and never desire to have thereby the name of learned" (IC 1.5). There is thus a certain *anti-intellectualism* in the *Imitatio*, perhaps reacting against the arid intellectualism of theological speculation of the day and its lack of bearing on the problems of life. In any case, speculative knowledge, learning about Christianity, is minimized, and the work appears to disparage the intellectual life. "For high curious reasons make not a man holy nor righteous, but a good life maketh him beloved with God. I had rather feel compunction of heart for my sins than only to know the definition of compunction. If thou knewest all the Bible without the book, and the sayings of all philosophers by heart, what should it profit thee without grace and charity" (IC 1.1)?[84] *Hostility to humanism:* this spirituality seems to reject the humanistic resurgence of the period; it in no way acknowledged the advancement of human culture and knowledge; it was antithetical to the Italian Renaissance. "They that have great learning desire commonly to be seen and to be holden wise in the world" (IC 1.2). "The more knowledge thou hast, if thou live not thereafter, the more grievously shalt thou be judged for the misusing thereof" (ibid.). In the end, the highest and most profitable learning consists in despising the self (ibid.).

In sum, aside from the reading of the bible, and from the devotion to the eucharist, there seems to be little attention to the church in this spirituality. It reflects a "modern" monasticism, lived in the world but with detachment: it is not *of* the late medieval world but *in* it, while being dedicated to a certain individualistic withdrawal, simplicity, interiority, and personal ascesis, and affective clinging to Jesus Christ.[85]

Christian Self-Understanding

The term "self-understanding" in this heading provides an inexact designation for topics connected with faith-knowledge, both in the church at large and in the discipline of theology. As for the general level of education in the church, the majority of Christians were quite

---

84. Even those who study out of love of God "profit more in forsaking all things than in studying for high and subtle learning" (IC.3.43).

85. One should be careful not to overgeneralize the significance of many of these themes. This spirituality was not explicitly aimed against nominalist theology, not the promoter of humanism, not mystical, not antiecclesial, even though it was individualistic. See Oakley's review of a realistic and revisionist interpretation of this spirituality as it was lived by The Sisters and Brothers of the Common Life in *The Western Church*, 100–13.

ignorant of their faith, and catechisms spread during this period to at least address the situation. These two centuries also contained decisive trends in theology that must at least be acknowledged. And the new wave of learning, the humanism of the Renaissance, also had a significant bearing on the Protestant Reformation which followed.

In a religion in which right doctrine mattered, it is fair to ask what the people knew and how they knew it. In fact the majority of people in the Middle Ages were illiterate and not formally educated.[86] Ordinary people learned their faith in the family, via popular custom, through sermons, and on the basis of the stories depicted in the stone and in the windows of the cathedrals.[87] In 1281 in England the archbishop of Canterbury ordered that every parish priest should "explain to the people simply and clearly the fourteen articles of the Creed, the Ten Commandments, the twofold precept of love of God and love of neighbor, the seven works of mercy, the seven deadly sins with their consequences, the seven cardinal virtues, and the seven sacraments of grace."[88] In 1357, also in England, the basic content of instruction was set in Latin and translated with expanded explanations into English verse with the title *The Lay Folks' Catechism*, consisting in 576 lines. The catechism was in fact written primarily for the clergy who did the teaching. As it was geared to oral instruction to be committed to memory, it relied heavily on numbers. Priests were to teach and preach the six things: the fourteen points of the creed, the ten commandments, the seven sacraments, the seven works of mercy, the seven virtues, and the seven deadly sins.[89]

---

86. The proportions here are relative, for there was a growth of literacy in Europe. At the highest level of society the universities had done their work. There were lawyers, notaries, judges, and other autonomous professionals; among townspeople the "spreading literacy" of merchants and bureaucrats increased the general level of self-consciousness and critical acumen. Lynch, *The Medieval Church*, 319.

87. The church in the Middle Ages did not have an institution for catechizing children, not even preparatory to confession and communion. It was the responsibility of the family to teach children the Our Father, the Hail Mary, the ten commandments. Only some children, those who attended school, would receive some religious training. Iserloh, "The Inner Life of the Church," *Handbook*, 578–80.

88. Berard L. Marthaler, *The Catechism Yesterday and Today: An Evolution of a Genre* (Collegeville, Minn.: The Liturgical Press, 1995), 12.

89. Marthaler, *The Catechism*, 12–13; see Thos. Frederick Simmons and Henry Edward Nolloth, eds., *The Lay Folks' Catechism or the English and Latin Version of*

Among his many works, Jean Gerson taught catechism and wrote catechetical works, the most widely read of which was entitled *Opus Tripertitum*. Written in 1395, the three parts of the catechism contained: first, a summary of basic Christian beliefs (creation, the trinity, the goal of life, original sin, incarnation, and redemption, and the ten commandments); second, the sacrament of confession and how to confess; third, preparation for a happy death. The audience of the catechism is also instructive. He addressed it to four distinct groups: "simple or illiterate priests who hear confessions; unlearned people who are unable to participate regularly in church instruction; children and youth in need of basic instruction; and individuals who visit hospitals and show concern for the sick."[90] Gerson also composed an *ABC des simples gens* which was no more than a list of things that Christians should know and could be enumerated as in the ten commandments, the seven sacraments, etc. The list was to be memorized.

At the other end of the spectrum of Christian knowledge stood the theologians and the discipline of theology taught in the universities. Perhaps two generalizations would be accepted by all historians, not without qualifications, but still with some relevance. Theology in the late Middle Ages reflects an experience of the absolute transcendence of God.[91] This is reflected in several areas: in the apophaticism of Meister Eckhart and Nicholas of Cusa; in nominalist epistemology that distrusted the ability of the mind to grasp the essence of things and move from there to all encompassing conclusions; in the firm distinction between what one could know about God through reason and the revelation which God actually provided humankind; and even more pointedly in the distinction between God's absolute power (*potentia absoluta*) and God's ordered power (*potentia ordinata*). This last distinction tells much: God is absolute, sovereign, and purely transcendent freedom, unbound by anything but contradiction itself. What one can experience or know of God in this world

Archbishop Thoresby's Instruction for the People, Early English Tract Society, Original Series 118 (London: Kegan Paul, Trench, Trübner, 1901).

90. Marthaler, *The Catechism,* 14.

91. Heiko Oberman, *The Harvest of Medieval Theology* (Cambridge, Mass.: Harvard University Press, 1963), 56–57, 88.

at best is a particular, limited or ordered manifestation and not the transcending reality itself of God. Distinctions like these emerge out of experience. They preserve God's mysterious integrity from naive, reductionist pictures or conclusions drawn directly from the harsh reality of life. Only some kind of distinctions such as these, for example, could have helped relieve the senselessness of the devastation wrought in Europe by the plague.

But, second, granted the limits of reason to encompass the absolute, and granted the sphere of God's self-revelation in the Christian economy, late medieval theology reveled in the power of the human mind to speculate, make distinctions, and argue logically to conclusions. The nominalists, by narrowing the field of revelation proper to what God had actually taught, opened up whole areas of the "untaught" to speculation and logical inference, to what God could have done had God exercised unrestricted freedom.[92] In any case, theological analysis and rhetoric became strongly logical and deductive, and its arguments stretched into esoteric problems divorced from the real faith life of the community.

Against such a background, the theological dimensions of the Renaissance appear as a sharp alternative. By definition this movement involved looking back, reawakening the past, and retrieving it for the present. It looked to the ancient biblical and patristic texts and found a positive theology that appealed much more directly to the Christian life. Indeed, the humanists defined Christianity itself as a reasonable way of life, and this contrasted with the scholastic view in two ways. As a way of life, Christianity was not primarily a set of doctrines or truths to be defined; moral virtue was intrinsic to the religious reality itself on the personal and social levels. Its reasonableness, therefore, did not lie in philosophical distinction or speculation, but in a positive historical reason that drew the tradition forward historically from the past. No one embodied these impulses better than Erasmus.

Erasmus

Erasmus was born in Rotterdam in 1466. He received his early education in a school in the tradition of The Brothers of the Common

---

92. Ibid., 51.

Life. These educators embodied the *devotio moderna,* and this affected Erasmus. At university age, he joined the Canons Regular of St. Augustine, was ordained, and received permission to live outside the monastery. He studied theology at the University of Paris and thoroughly disliked it. In 1499 he traveled to England where his friendship with Thomas More and other humanists confirmed him in his vocation: Erasmus became the quintessential humanist. He edited classical texts of the Fathers and the New Testament; he wrote on education, on classical wisdom, on politics; he wrote satire, theology, and treatises on the Christian life. He enjoyed fame in his own day, lived all over Europe at various times, and stirred controversy throughout his lifetime. He died in 1536.

The significance of Erasmus lies in the scope and influence of his writings. One sees in Erasmus how some themes from Franciscan spirituality and certain virtues reflected in *The Imitation of Christ* developed further at the beginning of the sixteenth century, and how they could provide critical contrast in a period ripe for reform. Erasmus used the ideals of simplicity and humility as a backdrop to unmask the pretensions of every aspect of the institutional life of the church and of society as well. Often considered an immediate precursor of the Reformation, Erasmus never joined the movement of Luther. This multifaceted man is frequently judged from one perspective or another in a partisan way. Two works of Erasmus, the most popular during his lifetime, shed light on the church at the end of the Middle Ages. The *Enchiridion,* Erasmus's essay on the Christian life, illustrates how he shifted the spirituality of the *Imitation* in the direction of engagement in the world and society.[93] It represents the influence of the Renaissance on Christian life in Europe. *In Praise of Folly* walks down all the paths of late medieval life: Grammarians, Poets, Rhetoricians, Scholars, Lawyers, Logicians, Scientists, Theologians, Religious, Monks, Preachers, Kings, Nobles, Bishops, Cardinals, Popes and Priests, and holds them all up to scorn.[94] But

---

93. Erasmus, *The Enchiridion (Handbook of the Christian Soldier),* in *Advocates of Reform,* ed. Matthew Spinka (Philadelphia: Westminster Press, 1953). References in the text are to this edition by page number.

94. Erasmus, *In Praise of Folly,* in *The Essential Erasmus,* ed. John P. Dolan (New York: New American Library, A Mentor Book, 1964). References in the text are to this edition by page number.

this text is more than merely amusing satire; the criterion of judgment lies in the Christian values found in the *Enchiridion:* this is Christian social critique.

Enchiridion. Life is a perpetual warfare; one is constantly under attack from the flesh, the devil, and the world. One has to be vigilant and have a strategy for life to withstand the attacks and attain victory (Enchiridion, 296). Erasmus proposes in the *Enchiridion* some general rules or maxims or principles which can guide the Christian life in the world. The application of these rules will enable one "to emerge from the errors of this world as if from a sort of inextricable labyrinth, and reach the pure light of spiritual life" (Enchiridion, 321). They address three main evils or human debilities: blindness, passions of the flesh, and weakness or infirmity. "Blindness obstructs judgment. The flesh corrupts the will. Infirmity shatters constancy" (Enchiridion, 322). These rules, however, are less prescriptions that can be literally followed and more moral maxims urging basic attitudes, steeling convictions, and encouraging decisiveness. For example, the first rule, against the evil of ignorance, presses the Christian to internalize the truth of Christ and scripture as God's own truth (Enchiridion, 322–23). The second rule speaks of decisiveness, the need to act now, to cut through the bonds that hold back commitment, to recognize that the decision to lead a Christ-centered life is an urgent either / or decision. "[L]et not the affection of loved ones hold you back, let not the allurements of the world recall you, let not domestic cares delay you. The shackles of worldly business are to be cut through, whenever they cannot be disentangled" (Enchiridion, 323).

Erasmus's fourth rule may be compared with the *devotio moderna* and the spirituality of the *Imitation of Christ.* It counsels "that you set before you Christ as the only goal of your whole life, to whom alone you dedicate all zeal, all efforts, all leisure and business" (Enchiridion, 328). "Christ" refers to the person and all that he taught. One should "gaze toward Christ alone, your sole and highest good, so that you may love nothing, be in awe of nothing, seek after nothing, other than Christ himself, or for Christ's sake. Hate nothing, tremble at nothing, flee nothing, other than wickedness, or for the sake of wickedness" (Enchiridion, 328). Once Christ occupies the place as end or goal, things of this world may be conceived as means, or intermediate objects that "either help or hinder those going toward Christ" (Enchiridion, 329). Such are, first of all, knowledge, and then "health, gifts of nature, eloquence, beauty, strength, rank, favor, authority, prosperity, reputation, birth, friends, family possessions" (329). As means, however, they are not all equal and must be evaluated in the light of Christ. "From this end the usefulness or unusefulness of all means is to be measured." (329)

This rule illustrates the position of Erasmus relative to the tradition of the *Imitatio*. Erasmus too counsels against the lures and temptations of the world. "If you are in the world, you are not in Christ... if you identify the world with ambition, delights, desire, lust — indeed, if you are a dweller in the world in this sense of the word, you are not a Christian" (Enchiridion, 324–25). He also accepts the maxim: "It is better to be less wise and to love more than to be wiser and not love" (Enchiridion, 329). But he has transformed the logic of a pure intention with distinction, nuance, and realism. Rank, station, learning, and even money are to be used spiritually by the Christian soldier for spiritual ends. "You love letters. Rightly, if for Christ's sake." "Suppose money comes your way: if it in no wise hinders you from a good mind, use it... " (Enchiridion, 329). In this case, and more generally, Erasmus stands within the tradition of the *Imitation* in many respects, while at the same time he has utterly transformed it in the direction of engagement as opposed to withdrawal. God's gifts of creation should be used for the attainment of God's values in the world.

In Praise of Folly. This work of Erasmus put into prose, and thus into conversation around Europe, thoughts that were entertaining and critical. His goal is to relativize, ridicule, and correct. He relativized by adopting the perspective of detached distance; Folly looks down from above upon those devoted to her. His caricature of his characters completely undermines their pretensions: "Everywhere they throng in so many forms of folly and fabrication each day that a thousand Democrituses would not be sufficient for laughing at them" (Folly, 136).

Erasmus did not limit himself to ecclesiastical types; he spanned the professions of the day. But ecclesiastics receive a good deal of attention. He described the silly and filthy habits of the monks and their absurd preaching; the self-indulgent lives of bishops; how far from their predecessors, the apostles, the cardinals had fallen; the huge extravagance of the papal court; the worldly activities of the priests (Folly, 148–60). In all of this the measure is the gospel, the message of Jesus, simplicity, humility, moderation, in short, the spirituality he imbibed from the Brothers of the Common Life. Once again, the latent critical power of the gospel finds new literary expression.

It would be singularly unacademic to describe the state of theology at the end of the fifteenth century by adopting Erasmus's caricature of it; what cannot be satirized? Yet Erasmus himself was a student of theology at the University of Paris; and whether or not his descriptions were meant to be fair, he makes the point of a theology dealing with questions that do not relate to the life of the people. "Could God the Father have taken upon Himself the likeness of a woman, a devil, an ass, a gourd, or a piece of flint? Then how would that gourd have preached, performed miracles, or been crucified?" Theologians also examined ethical issues: "it is better to want the earth to perish, body, boots, and breeches (as the saying goes), than to tell a single lie, however inconsequential." The methods of approach to these questions were variously directed by "the Realists, Nominalists, Thomists, Albertists, Occamists, and Scotists." They analyzed thoroughly by means of "the formal, material, efficient, and final causes." The theologians "insist that their own conclusions, subscribed to by a few students, are more valid than Solon's laws and preferred before a pope's decrees.... And they announce these conclusions as if they were oracles" (Folly, 143–47).

Erasmus fits remarkably well in the line of Francis, Wyclif, and à Kempis: an erudite portrayal of a practical Christianity, a Christian life of virtue and moderation and control. It focuses on Christ and a life patterned on evangelical virtues. It is of course not antiintellectual, since Erasmus was a scholar, and it urges engagement rather than withdrawal from the world. But it is antispeculative and dogmatic, against the intellectualism of the theology of the time. Inevitably Erasmus is compared with his contemporary Luther, and in this contrast the spiritual life in Erasmus appears moralistic: he recommends a life of virtue and simple Christian charity. *In Praise of Folly* brings these themes to bear on European society. In response to the question "What should be the character of Christian society?" the norm was Christ and "the works of mercy and charity." There can be no separation between Christ, Christian values, and life in the world. Without some such relativization and critical appraisal of what was in place, there could not have been a Reformation.

DESCRIPTION OF THE CHURCH IN THE LATE MEDIEVAL PERIOD

The late medieval church was not a bridge between, on the one side, the church of the High Middle Ages come to fruition with Innocent III and Lateran IV and flourishing during the thirteenth century, and, on the other side, the church of the early modern period, the sixteenth-century Protestant Reformation, and the breakup of Christendom. The church in the fourteenth and fifteenth centuries was a church in its own right which underwent a considerable amount of development. If the period after the Gregorian reform was one of institutional consolidation, impulses toward regionalization if not fragmentation were at work in the late medieval church. In a way, the title of this section itself falsifies the reality. One should not think that this church functioned as one large tightly knit institution. Regional churches were certainly bound together administratively through the center. But communications did not foster a common European horizon and corporate consciousness among ordinary people, and in some respects the center appeared alienating during this period. The whole church was a conglomerate of city, town, and rural churches which were more self-consciously taking on regional distinctiveness.

The following description of the church begins with a characterization of the environment in which it existed. From there the synthesis takes up the church to which the historical narrative and various texts bear witness according to the now familiar framework.

Environment

A description of a typical city at the beginning of this period will set the imagination. Liège may be considered such a large town at the beginning of the period we have been considering.[95] It "boasted, besides its cathedral, seven collegiate churches, twenty-six parish churches, two Benedictine monasteries — St. James and St. Laurence — an Augustinian house of St. Giles, the Praemonstratensian community at Mont-Cornillon, and a Cistercian house, Val-St. Lambert."[96] Over three hundred monks and clerics studied in the seven schools in the town and surrounding abbeys. In general the town was marked by a vibrant religiosity among both religious and "lay people who wished to undertake some communal aspects of religious life. . . ."[97] The church of Europe was made up of many churches such as this, some larger, others smaller. But one should also not forget the church in castle towns and rural areas, where lords or knights ruled by decree, and life was often elemental and violent. For example, after his election as pope at Constance, it took Martin V two years gradually to negotiate a safe route back to Rome.

The world of these towns and cities, the world of secular affairs "outside" the church and well beyond its control, always has a decisive influence on the church. In Christendom, when church and world are so united, not without distinctions, no other factor has a stronger influence on church evolution, for the social-political world is wholly "inside" the church. A simple list of some major developments in the history of Europe will help define the church in this period.

Geopolitically, the frontiers of Europe shifted and this impinged on the church on a macro-level, the church as a whole. Crusades and the desire to mount crusades continued into the late Middle Ages and then waned; but after Constance a crusade was launched against the Hussites. In 1453 Constantinople fell to the Turks, ending the status of that city as the capital of Eastern Christianity since its founding by Constantine. The loss of this Christian center intensified the threat of Islam along the boundaries of the Western church. At the end of

---

95. The number of cities expanded greatly during the late Middle Ages. Germany alone, by the end of the fifteenth century, contained three thousand designated cities. But twenty-eight hundred of them had a population of less than one thousand people. Iserloh, "The Inner Life of the Church," *Handbook*, 566. The distinction between "city" and "town" is not clearly drawn here.

96. Rubin, *Corpus Christi*, 164.

97. Ibid., 166.

the fifteenth century the search for a new route to India led to the discovery of the Americas and a sudden expansion of the Western imagination.

On the level of ideas, difficult though it be to measure the degree of their influence, the interest in the natural and human world that allowed Aristotle's philosophy to flourish should not be minimized. The pervasiveness of some fundamental assumptions that were continuous from Aquinas through Marsilius and Ockham and throughout the discussion of the premises of conciliarism indicate a way of thinking in tension with complete reliance on revealed doctrines and conceiving things "from above." The celebration of the human, the focusing on human potential and creativity represented in renaissance humanism, coexisted in tension with a sense of human sinfulness and suffering and the utter transcendence of God.

The autonomy of nature and the integrity of natural phenomena find expression in a sense of the Creator endowing natural entities and even societies with their own laws and rights. This strengthened the assumptions of the divine rights of kings and secular rulers. Generally, the late Middle Ages witnessed a gradual emergence of nations. Philip IV's ability not to coexist in parallel with Boniface VIII and his successor but to dominate them provides a good example of the complement of ideology and social-political development. Another example of the growing sense of nations is seen in the voting by nations at Constance and Basel. The resurgence of the papacy in the fifteenth century was due in part to a general antipathy among monarchical rulers to democratic ideas; against democratic movements monarchs made common cause. Interest in nature, Aristotelian language, law, bureaucracy, and administration added up to more and more autonomous nation states.[98]

The theory of the papacy entered a new phase in the late Middle Ages. From the Gregorian reform onward into the early fourteenth century the tension between pope and secular ruler provided the dominant context for understanding papal power. Theologians and canonists also reflected on the theological and juridical status of the

---

98. Tierney, *Crisis*, 97–98.

office within the church itself, but these issues were not problematic. Suddenly, with the schism in 1378, the very status of the papacy within the church was thrown into question and subjected to intense analysis and discussion. The shift of the context and problematic for understanding the papacy, from confrontation with *imperium* to its internal logic within the church itself, mediated a development in the institution itself.

Finally, in 1456 Gütenberg published a printed edition of the bible. The invention of the printing press is often considered a watershed in Western history: it represented the steady growth of communication and education during the later Middle Ages and stimulated a quantum leap in social communication across Europe.

Structures or Government of the Church

From one point of view one could argue that there were no major or innovative changes in the structures of the Western church in the Middle Ages after the Gregorian reform. The offices of ministry remained in place but grew in terms of administrative and legal complexity.[99] Yet the structured ministries themselves changed from within in terms of meaning and efficacy. The following description takes note of papacy as an office, bishops, and parish priests.

The history of the papacy over these two centuries appears quite astonishing when charted through its landmark events. The fact that the king of France could bully an otherwise strong pope was symptomatic. This was followed by the Avignon papacy, a major schism, the short-lived dominance of conciliarism at Basel, the reassertion of papal power, and then the renaissance papacy that is generally remembered for its corruption or worldliness. The Avignon papacy, with its extensive system of taxation and its very location within the French sphere of influence generated antipapal feeling.[100] On the eve of schism no unified theory of church authority and government commanded the field.[101] Although the schism itself did not disrupt the personal or local life of ordinary Christians in the parishes, it caused considerable scandal and fragmented religious orders that

---

99. Cooke, *Ministry,* 114.
100. Knowles, *The Middle Ages,* 407.
101. Tierney, *Foundations,* 218.

spanned the different regional loyalties.[102] The schism also resulted in an increasing secular control and a gradual loss of papal power over local national churches.[103] After Constance, Nicholas of Cusa's moderate, conciliarist synthesis proposed that a truly ecumenical council representing the five patriarchates was superior to the pope in authority. But the papal monarchy reasserted itself in the second half of the fifteenth century in a style that was scandalous and remained divided from the East.

An analysis of the papacy across these two centuries may yield the impression that the absolute power of the papacy over the church was no different at the beginning of the sixteenth century than it was in the thirteenth century. But the intervening history had changed everything; the hold of the papacy on the whole church was far from absolute; its symbolic power, religious authority, and theological cogency had been sharply weakened. "The pope was still the head of the universal church, but in most places local rulers had severely limited his exercise of power."[104] Many reasons explain why conciliarism, especially conciliar government, could not have worked and popes regained their status.[105] But one also has to ask why the Protestant Reformation broke free. At the end of the fifteenth century at least three distinct understandings of the authority of the pope and his headship of the church were abroad. The first was juridical: the pope enjoyed administrative power and authority over the whole church. The second was theological: the pope served as source and ground of the spiritual integrity and life of the church. These two were combined in Torquemada. But there was also a third view, the remnant of conciliarism, which combined the juridical, the theological, and the symbolic: the pope exercised the ministry of unity on the basis

---

102. Knowles, *The Middle Ages*, 425.

103. Ibid., 426. Lynch, *The Medieval Church*, 319–20, 322. The increasing nationalism of the churches meant a certain decline of *Latinitas* and a beginning of the fragmentation of the unified culture of Christendom (Knowles, *The Middle Ages*, 456). More and more during this period popes negotiated with local rulers and developed concordats that regulated practical issues of church government according to the specific demands of the local situation (Thompson, *The Western Church*, 222–24). This was part of the tactics by which Eugenius IV outflanked the Council of Basel. Lynch, *The Medieval Church*, 334.

104. Lynch, *The Medieval Church*, 335.

105. See Knowles, *The Middle Ages*, 424–25 for a list of reasons.

of and in service of the whole body of the faithful. If and when he failed to represent that unity with integrity, he essentially lost his affective, symbolic, and religious authority.

This period shows no major development in office of bishop: bishops directly oversaw cult, penitential discipline, and administration of church properties. The bishop was also responsible for the needy of his diocese and looked after the general economic, social, military, moral, and intellectual fabric of society. The resources of the diocese were administered through a variety of systems and, generally, chancery offices gradually assumed more importance during this period.[106]

Complaints about priests indicate that the office of the priest and the conduct of nonpriestly clerics needed reform. Conciliar deliberations at Vienne included a concern for the lifestyle of nonordained clerics; it was also a concern at Constance. Wyclif complained about the lack of celibacy among the clergy generally. As a group the clergy were not highly educated and simple primers were meant for clergy and laity alike. The element of financial gain was closely associated with clerical life and priesthood. The system of benefices attached to positions that could be held by individuals or corporations such as monasteries who did not in fact perform the ministries seems to have been widespread. Both Lateran IV and Wyclif addressed the practice.[107] Indeed, Wyclif's writings express "almost all the popular charges against the Catholic Church of the later Middle Ages. . . ."[108] All this does not mean that model priests and clerics were totally lacking. But all agreed on the need for reform.

More positively, however, an idea of what the priest actually did in his parish in the fourteenth century England can be gleaned from a work entitled *Instructions for Parish Priests*.[109] The work turns first

---

106. Cooke, *Ministry*, 364–65.
107. Cooke, *Ministry*, 363.
108. Knowles, *The Middle Ages*, 452.
109. John Myrc, *Instructions for Parish Priests*, ed. Edward Peacock (London: Kegan Paul, Trench, Trübner, 1868, revised 1902). This book is an English translation of a Latin work that was quite common and standard in the late Middle Ages all over Europe. This translation dates from the first half of the fifteenth century and was composed in 1,934 verses in rhyming couplets by Myrc who was a Canon Regular at a monastery in Lilleshall, Shropshire, England. The book is a practical, how-to manual giving "directions how priests with little book-learning or experience were to teach the

and immediately to the person of the *priest* himself: if he is ignorant, he will lead his flock into sin; he should therefore read this book carefully. And if he does not live a virtuous life, his preaching and teaching will have no effect. The priest should dress like a cleric and avoid the worldly pursuits of the town. *Birth* occasions many matters of attention: the role of midwives, baptism in case of crisis, the duties of godparents, the degrees of spiritual relationship that are set up with this role. *Marriage* too elicits basic instruction on betrothals, irregular marriages, and the sexual duties of husband and wife. Matters surrounding the *church* as a building prompt reflections on it as God's house, proper decorum in the churchyard, and how to behave in church. It also takes up tithes. The manual instructs the priest on the *eucharist* and what he should communicate to the people. It gives precise instructions on how the sanctuary, altar cloths, vessels, the bread and wine, should be cared for; people should be instructed on the real presence, how to receive communion, the benefits of seeing the host. Basic *teaching* that has to be passed on is covered: the Our Father, Hail Mary, the Creed, the fourteen articles drawn from it, the seven sacraments with explicit attention to baptism, confirmation, confession and penance, eucharist, and extreme unction. By far the greatest attention is given to *confession*, especially how to lead a person through a thorough examination of conscience, and how to assign the proper penance calibrated to venial sins and to mortal sins. Detailed *moral instruction* is carried along in the preparations for confession.

This picture of a rural or town parish is extraordinary in its analogy with such parishes all over Europe in the fourteenth century and even throughout the world today. Few if any members of ordinary rural Catholic parishes any place in the world would fail to recognize the elementary structure, the topics, the practices. These are presented here in a rudimentary, unsophisticated form, rhymed to

---

faith to their flocks." As Myrc put it, he intended the vernacular translation for those who "haue no bokes of here owne" (Myrc, *Instructions*, 59). The work does not contain anything out of the ordinary but provides a general picture of the duties and concerns of the parish priest in the villages and towns at this time. I present this picture by the topics treated in the work.

facilitate memorization, but apart from that in unadorned simplicity. Yet the essentials described here correlate with the metaphysical theology of Aquinas, the legal representation of the canonists, and the formal ecclesiology of thinkers like Nicholas of Cusa and Juan de Torquemada.

Members of the Church: Active Laity

The members of the church were all the people in the cities, towns, and rural areas, with the exception of Jews. They were not a widely lettered laity for these societies did not provide a general literary training. The early catechisms indicate a low level of reflective or theological understanding of the faith; one would expect various kinds of superstition associated with folk religion. But it does not follow that the church was made up of a passive laity merely consuming clerical mediation of word and sacrament. Membership in the church was highly participatory in town and city as religion spilled over into a social life structured by feasts and processions. The fraternities or confraternities that began to multiply in the fourteenth century were agencies of lay religious activity focused in a variety of ways. Women too were active in the church. Catherine of Siena stood high above the horizon, of course, but the beguines were only momentarily suppressed at Vienne, and other associations of the laity ran parallel to them. Lay people had an articulated spirituality in the *devotio moderna* in the north of Europe. The *Imitation of Christ* incorporated heavy doses of a monastic spirituality and a spirituality of canonical religious life. But it also provided religious principles for lay people living in society that would warn them against being corrupted by the values of the world.

Goals or Mission

The goals or mission of the church did not change substantially in the late Middle Ages. Torquemada stated the goal of the church with scholastic clarity: the purpose of the church was to lead people to final salvation and everlasting glory. The goal, mission, and self-understanding of the church coalesced in its role of mediator of salvation from God in Jesus Christ. All that it did participated in this most general mission of sanctifying life in this world as it moved toward the next. The catechisms did not formulate an apologetic understanding of the church; the church's existence was taken for granted as priests drummed home creed, sacraments, commandments and other aspects of the moral life.

Activities of the Church

The activities of the church in the late Middle Ages are generically identical with preceding centuries; as the sanctifier of society the church administered the sacraments; the shifts were not sharp but simply reflected different times and situations. Another way of characterizing the activity of the church, however, would be in terms of the Christian life on the personal, parochial, and diocesan levels. The focus falls on the towns rather than the rural villages.

The late Middle Ages produced a remarkably reflective understanding of how to live the Christian life. At first sight, the differences between the spirituality of Erasmus and the *Imitatio Christi* seem more obvious than any similarity or one to one correspondence.[110] But certain general qualities are important for marking the spiritual ideals of the whole period. This spirituality was simple, uncluttered, moralistic, humble. Erasmus took these qualities, gave them an erudite, literary form, and applied them squarely to life in the world of his day. Indeed, across these centuries one sees the deep, abiding influence of the spiritual values reflected in Francis. These included a retrieval of a certain image of the earthly Jesus, and an appropriation of his life to meet the demands of Christian life of the time. This Jesus and this spirituality provided values for life and also for fierce criticism of the hypocrisy of the world. Wyclif and Erasmus both represent a turn to the New Testament as a place where Christ could be directly experienced, thus providing a source for a self-conscious or reflective Christian life. This complements by counterpoint a strongly sacramental mediation of grace. It also points to a longing for the "pure form" of Christian origins, a turning toward a more direct and experiential access to Christ in the

---

110. John O'Malley, "Introduction," *Collected Works of Erasmus*, vol. 66, *Spiritualia* (Toronto: University of Toronto Press, 1988), xli–xliii.

New Testament, thus bypassing in some measure the mediation of the institutional church.[111]

Beyond the level of personal Christian life one should consider the corporate life of the parish in the towns and cities. The parish is the most fundamental institutional form of the church and it was structured around worship, especially eucharistic assembly. But this parish life overflowed into society generally, and its integration into public life is perhaps the most defining aspect of medieval Christianity or Christendom. The confraternities in some ways constituted new subgroups, either under the parish structure or cutting across parish boundaries. They channeled religious energy in focused ways into society both for self-help and for altruistic or apostolic ends. When one attends to the various lay movements dedicated to apostolic activity, whether in education or hospitals or orphanages, one has to consider the parish life in the cities and towns of the late Middle Ages as dynamic and active.

Relation of the Church to World, Society

The church continued to have a symbiotic relationship to secular society: there was one religion, with the exception of the Jews, and this monopoly gave the church power in society at large. In various degrees in different locales the church shared secular power in society. On the one hand, secular rulers never stopped having considerable influence on the appointment of bishops after the investiture controversy and through the late Middle Ages. On the other hand, where bishops enjoyed temporal rule, they did not surrender it voluntarily to secular or lay rulers. The two spheres remained mixed under a variety of settlements. But the period showed a certain diminishment of the secular power of the papacy over Europe and the growth of the influence of secular rulers over the church in various regions.

Another aspect of the relationship of the church to the world is found in the renaissance papacy. The church in Rome especially was a patron of the arts, and the last half of the fifteenth century marks the beginning of the building of the Vatican that stands to-

---

111. Knowles, *The Middle Ages*, 464–66.

day. The two great projects were the Vatican library and the Basilica of St. Peter. In endorsing the new humanism, with its celebration of human achievement, the physical, the literary, and the artistic, the church at the center seemed to counter the ideas that the world was a deceptive and transitory dwelling place.[112] The other side of this embrace of humanism was the worldly life of several popes of this period. Rather than set a high tone for the rest of the church, Rome gave scandal when measured by the spiritual ideals outlined earlier.

Two aspects of church life at the end of the fifteenth century existed in a striking tension with each other: one was the revival of piety, spirituality, and sheer religious fervor; the other was widespread criticism if not disillusionment with the institutional church. The teaching of the popes was accepted, but they were criticized for their taxes and worldliness. Popular piety through the cult of saints, relics, pilgrimages, and local devotion flourished, as did dissatisfaction with priests because of their wealth, privileges, and moral failings. Thus "intense piety was often accompanied by anticlericalism...."[113]

Another aspect of the church's relation to the world is theological in character, but filled with relevance for the spirituality of everyday life. A thematic tendency toward Pelagianism marked the theology and the spirituality of the late Middle Ages. The following maxim catches the resonances of this theology: God will not withhold grace to those who do all in their power.[114] One can perceive a hint of it in the moralistic character of the spiritual life. This becomes more significant in the host of religious practices dedicated to shoring up merit before God and God's judgment. All of this would have scarcely been noticed were it not for the explicit reaction against it by Luther and the reintroduction of a strong anti-Pelagian spirituality.

Despite these turns and tensions in the church across these two centuries, one thing remained universal and constant: the desire for the reform of the church in head and members.

---

112. Ibid., 429.
113. Lynch, *The Medieval Church*, 338.
114. Oberman, *Harvest*, 175–77, 184.

PRINCIPLES FOR
A HISTORICAL ECCLESIOLOGY

All historical study of the church displays the tension between sameness and difference. The church never ceases to change; human communities are always changing; but they always bear their past with them. The church of the late Middle Ages bears the same general structure of the medieval church after the Gregorian reform. But it also underwent profound and significant changes, especially in the self-understanding of itself as an institutional whole. Most of the significant principles for understanding the church as such are taken from the conciliarist movement. The power, but not the coherence, of conciliarist thought was drawn mainly from the profound crisis in which the European church found itself: the schism of popes and territorial papal loyalties. This crisis was precisely not a normal situation. But the very abnormality of the situation allows one to recognize aspects of the church that are less apparent but still at work in more serene times.

The Functional Relation between Community and Institution

The principle of the functional relationship between community and institution was explained earlier; it was operative in the origin of the church; and one could trace it in an analysis of the church through each century of its existence. But the conciliarist episode in the church's life provides a lucid formulation of the principle. Dietrich of Niem caught it neatly with his distinction between the universal and the apostolic church. The "universal church" refers to the whole Christian community, all the men and women who are bound together in a common faith in God mediated through Jesus Christ. The "apostolic church" refers to the offices of ministry, the pope, cardinals, bishops, prelates, and other church people who hold the offices of ministry and thus authority. The point of the distinction is to relativize the structures of ministry to the body of the faithful.[115]

---

115. The distinction was operative in Ockham, and Ryan speaks of two ways of viewing the church: "One way sees the church principally as the congregation or community of the faithful and thus in terms of its members, whose association in faith is

Whether or not the ministers are conceived as being delegated by the community, sociologically and ontologically, that is, in terms of the genesis of the community, these offices are constituted by the community or a representative segment of it. The very essence of conciliarism, according to Tierney, was to locate the ultimate authority of the church in the whole, in the whole assembly of the faithful. "The whole Christian community was superior to any prelate, however exalted; the pope was to be a servant of the church rather than its master."[116]

The anomalous situation of the church allowed this principle to appear in a way that Boniface VIII could not have seen. He was a product of the Gregorian reform and a successor of Innocent III. The pope was the symbolic and juridical head of the Western church, which was the soul of Europe, so that to be cut off from Peter seemed to entail being cut off from the very channel of grace itself. But the Western schism set up a situation of pluralism. Everyone knew there was only one true pope; but no one knew for sure which one it was. It was thus simply impossible for one to claim that grace and salvation depended upon one's loyalty to the true or real pope. Practically speaking most people, that is, those adhering to the "other so-called popes," were not saved by adherence to the "true" pope. Thus the principle of Boniface VIII negated itself because the true pope was not known or did not exist; salvation had to have been mediated through the church as community. And this would be the case more generally whenever the juridically pluralistic character of the church was recognized.

Tension Between Unifying Structure and Pluralism

This tension is operative in the Western church when it is regarded as a whole or unity with an organized structure. It is a principle regard-

---

the principal reality of the church. The other view sees the church principally as the ensemble of the means of salvation — the 'deposit' of faith, the sacraments, ecclesiastical office — and thus a supra-personal institution" (Ryan, *The Nature, Structure and Function of the Church in William of Ockham*, 55). The two can be harmonious, but when the needs of one or other are not met, there will be conflict.

116. Tierney, *Foundations*, 3–6, text cited at p. 6.

ing the church as a large organization that will become particularly applicable after the sixteenth-century Reformation, but which can already be discerned at work in the late Middle Ages in several respects. One is the movement within the church toward regionalization and the loss of some control over churches at the periphery by the central authority of pope and curia. A second factor is ideological and consists in shifts of meaning. For example, there was a shift of meaning in the understanding of the church as the "body of Christ." This had a thoroughly theological sense in Thomas Aquinas; by the fifteenth century it had a strongly political and sociological meaning.[117] A third factor is also ideological and lies in alternative theories of church unity at work in the late Middle Ages. Tierney outlines them clearly: one said the unity of the church was secured by "a rigorous subordination of all members to a single head. . . . " This was the doctrine of papal sovereignty. The second applied to single churches and gradually to the whole church in the fourteenth century. In this theory, "the corporate association of the members of a church [was] the true principle of ecclesiastical unity," and members could exercise this authority in the absence of an effective head.[118] Looking at the church's development in this period in the light of these factors suggests a principle that is at once obvious and significant, especially when it is not observed. The more a large institution becomes diversified and pluralistic, the more flexible will the institutional administration have to become in order to preserve its unity. One can see this actually happening across these two centuries; reversing the movement launched by the Gregorian reform, Rome gradually ceded more control of the regional churches to local leadership. But instead of putting more weight on the theological bonds of unity, institutional and administrative unity was stressed in the new papalist ecclesiologies. The doctrine of papal sovereignty alone as the bond of unity would not be able to accommodate the demands for pluralism that erupted in the sixteenth century.

---

117. Oakley, *The Western Church*, 162–63. Neither should be understood in an exclusive sense, that is, without remainder. It is a question of emphasis.

118. Tierney, *Foundations of the Conciliar Theory*, 240.

The Existential Historical Character of Institutions

Another principle, drawn from a tension that has already been developed, finds a starkly clear instantiation during the schism and the conciliarist crisis. We have seen the polarity between subjectivity and objectivity in institution and sacrament, the tension between the objective character of the office and the existential historical manner in which a human individual fills it, exercises the authority that comes with it, and all of this in a specific historical situation. There are few sociological principles that are more obvious. But there is an inherent tendency either to forget the necessary tension or bipolarity of these two dimensions, or to assert either side without attention to the other. Objective authority can be lost or negated in a concrete situation; and charismatic authority can fail without institutional support.

What can be a more dramatic illustration of this principle than a papacy that caused division in the church? Petrine ministry is precisely a social symbolic ministry of the unity of the church. In the Western church, this became bolstered by various levels and degrees of juridical authority. Suddenly, by a fluke of history, the office itself became undone relative to its very purpose, and required an almost forty year period of intense reflection, negotiation, and political action to reconstitute itself. But the point that has to be made forcefully, for it underlies finally the historical character of the church, is that the papacy during this period was the very cause of the division, and thus historically and existentially negated its own objective function. "Objective" institutions in the end are not objective at all but historical.

The same principle was at work in the Council of Pisa. That council should have worked. Everyone thought it would work. It seemed to be canonically correct. And it would have worked, if people had adhered to the one newly elected pope. By contrast, the Council of Constance did work. It saved the papacy because, before electing the new pope, it first secured the deposition and resignation of two claimants and the promise of those loyal to the third that they would withdraw their obedience. In sociological terms, the objective character of the church's institutions ultimately rests on the corporate experience and consent of the body. In sum, the objective and subjective holiness and authority of institutions must be kept in tensive relation to each other.

The Basis of Church Unity Is Prior to Institution

This principle appears to be self-evident when one considers the gradual genesis or emergence of the church from the initial band of Jewish disciples of Jesus. It is interesting to encounter it again in the course of the history of the church as a structural principle. In the conciliarist period, this principle is implicit in the two principles just discussed, but it may be helpful to make it explicit.

This principle carries special relevance in a situation where a certain institutional pluralism obtains in the church. This is exactly what happened with the schism. In the wake of the Gregorian reform, "the other [Western] churches stood, in relation to the Roman Church, in a position of hierarchical subordination, dependent on it for their authority, for their very life. . . ."[119] The Roman Church with its bishop, the pope, was the head, and other churches were members, adding up to the universal church. The local churches were conceived as extensions of the center. This gradually changed in the late Middle Ages: generally through isolation from each other, secondly through nationalism, then through the breakup of the Western church into distinct and separate papal loyalties, and finally but more radically in the sixteenth century with the Protestant Reformation. In each case with increasing necessity, if the church was really one, then it had to be understood the way Dietrich of Niem defined the universal church: the whole assembly of believers. In short, the definition of the church in the Middle Ages, the *congregatio fidelium*, was gradually actualizing itself as a social-ontological definition. In other words, unifying structure was weakening so that the unity of the church had to be found more in its common faith in God as revealed in Jesus Christ.

---

119. Ibid., 242.

Conciliarist Theory without Conciliarist Government

It is most important that conciliarism be conceived as a movement of thought and conciliarist theory remain open. In fact there were all sorts of different theories or degrees of conciliarism.[120] Theoretically, one could have conciliarist theory of the church without conciliarist government. It is essential that this point be made: one does not have to resolve the question of the legal validity of the decree *Haec Sancta* in order to make this point. A conciliarist theory could say that authority was mediated to the pope through the church as community, so that the whole church is the source and ground of the pope's authority, even as the pope is genuinely the head of the church. Such was the ecclesiology of Cusanus. When for whatever reason there is no pope, the church as a whole still possesses this authority. There need not be a theoretical antithesis between whole church and its head, nor therefore between the whole church represented in council and its head. Only in exceptional circumstances does the church as a whole or in council exercise authority without the pope, as in the schism, or when there is no pope and a council is summoned. This is said with reference to the Western church in the late Middle Ages. After the Protestant Reformation, when pluralism of church polity becomes generalized, conciliarist principles themselves would have to be expanded to become inclusive.

Dialectical Relationship between Relation to God and to World, between Ideals and Actuality

The church is ontologically constituted and always exists by a twofold relationship, to God and to the world or history or society. These two relationships often related to each other in a tensive way. Its relationship to God through Jesus and the Spirit makes the church a medium or symbol mediating God's being present to the world; at the same time it is a finite community in the world as a part

---

120. According to Tierney, most respected canonists in the fourteenth century held that the church was a corporation, with the attendant principle that authority rested in all the members of the church as a body, and who conferred it on the head as a limited and conditional right to act on their behalf. They *also* held that all power was concentrated in the head of the church by a direct act of divine will. The result was that there was no consistent theory of papal monarchy in canon law. *Foundations*, 244.

of the world. Herein lies an inevitable tension between the ideals the church is called to actualize, and the lesser reality it actually is. Sometimes the actuality can contradict the idea or ideal, as when the papacy causes division or gives scandal by its worldly life, or when the clergy as a group appears grasping and venal and self-serving, and this is supported by custom and system. Erasmus based his *In Praise of Folly* on this tension: its fundamental structure is ironical; what is is the very opposite of what should be. What can be said positively about this structure is that the negativity always generates a positive reaction. In this broad instance this took the form of an intense corporate desire for reform. This desire for reform and the intense religious spirituality that supported it constituted the bridge between the late Middle Ages and the new era of the Western church which opened up in the sixteenth century.

Index

ecclesiology (*continued*)
  from above, 6, 9n12, 17–18, 18–25, 35, 62
  from below (historical), 4–14, 17–18, 26–56, 56–65, 89–110, 118–19, 132
  historical, 1–14, 17–66
  method of historical, 1–14, 19, 26–35, 44–50, 60–62, 69–71
  object of, 35–44
  and part-whole dialectic, 41–43, 51, 56, 58–59, 133–34, 262–64
  Pauline, 77–79, 83, 86, 95, 116–18
  principles for historical, 125–39, 191–97, 256–64, 337–44, 417–23
  sources of, 48–52
  and theological language, 39, 46–47, 60, 61
  See also church
Eckhart, Meister, 358, 374, 400
ecumenical movement, Protestant, 27, 31, 40–41, 43
ecumenism, 1, 8–9, 29–30, 42n28, 58
Edict of Milan, 201
egalitarianism, 117–18
ekklesia, 82, 97, 155
elders. *See* presbyters
emperors and church, 168–69, 180–82, 202, 213–14, 217, 220, 239, 244. *See also* two powers, doctrine of
Enchiridion (Erasmus), 402, 403–4
environment and organizational structure, 129–30
Ephesus, Council of, 212
epieikeia, principle of, 383
episcopalism, 106–7, 170–71, 173, 177, 182–86, 192, 229, 287, 290
eschatology, 80, 98, 99, 187–88, 235–36, 413–14
ethics, 101–2, 154–55, 158, 165, 253–55, 332–33
Erasmus, 401–6, 414, 423
Eriugena, John Scotus, 301
eucharist (Lord's Supper)
  development of in fourth century, 250
  in early Christianity, 52–53, 72, 87, 96, 97–100, 101–2, 119–21, 155
  in late Middle Ages, 370–73
  as meal, 98–99
  in Middle Ages, 273, 317, 331–32
  in post-Constantinian church, 248–50
  in pre-Constantinian church, 153, 156–59, 162–63, 165, 174, 187–88
  as sacrifice, 158, 163, 331
  in Thomas Aquinas's ecclesiology, 317
Eugenius III (pope), 306–7
Eugenius IV (pope), 356–57, 390, 410n103

Eusebius of Caesaria, 147, 149, 151, 201–2, 220–22, 224
excommunication, 294, 295, 341, 393
Execrabilis (Pius II), 358, 394
experience
  as ecclesiological source, 32–33, 51–52, 59–60
  religious, 373–75
  and social construction of reality, 89–90
Evans, Robert, 261

feudal system, 270–71, 276, 297, 311, 324, 334–36
feminism, 32–33
Filioque, 289, 290
Fink, Karl August, 350n11, 356n24
Fiorenza, Francis Schüssler, 111
Florence, Council of, 357
forgiveness of sin, 98–99, 157, 174, 195, 283
Foundations in Ecclesiology (Komonchak), 3
Francis of Assisi, Saint, 290, 311–14, 347, 414
Franciscans, 282, 298–99, 311–14, 325, 332, 347, 361
  Spiritual, 349
  spirituality of, 311–14, 361, 367, 402, 414
fraternities, medieval. *See* confraternities
freedom, religious, 341
Frend, W. C. H., 148, 205n13, 218
Frequens (Council of Constance), 355, 356, 384, 392, 394
Friars Minor, Order of. *See* Franciscans
functionality, principle of, 63–65, 171n63, 177, 193–96, 365–66, 381, 417–18

Galilean Christianity, 73, 107
Gaudium et Spes (Vatican II document), 31
Gelasius (pope), 213–14, 278n18, 334n110, 340
Gerson, Jean, 376, 377n63, 380, 400
Gewirth, Alan, 362
Gilbertines, 326
globalization, 1, 28–29, 40–41, 58
gnosis, Christian, 159
gnosticism, 87, 149
God as Spirit. *See* Holy Spirit
governance, church, 105–7, 121–23
grace, universal availability of, 30–31
Grant, Robert, 182n76
Greek Church. *See* Eastern Christianity
Greek philosophy, 101, 110, 144, 149, 258. *See also* Aristotelian thought; Platonism